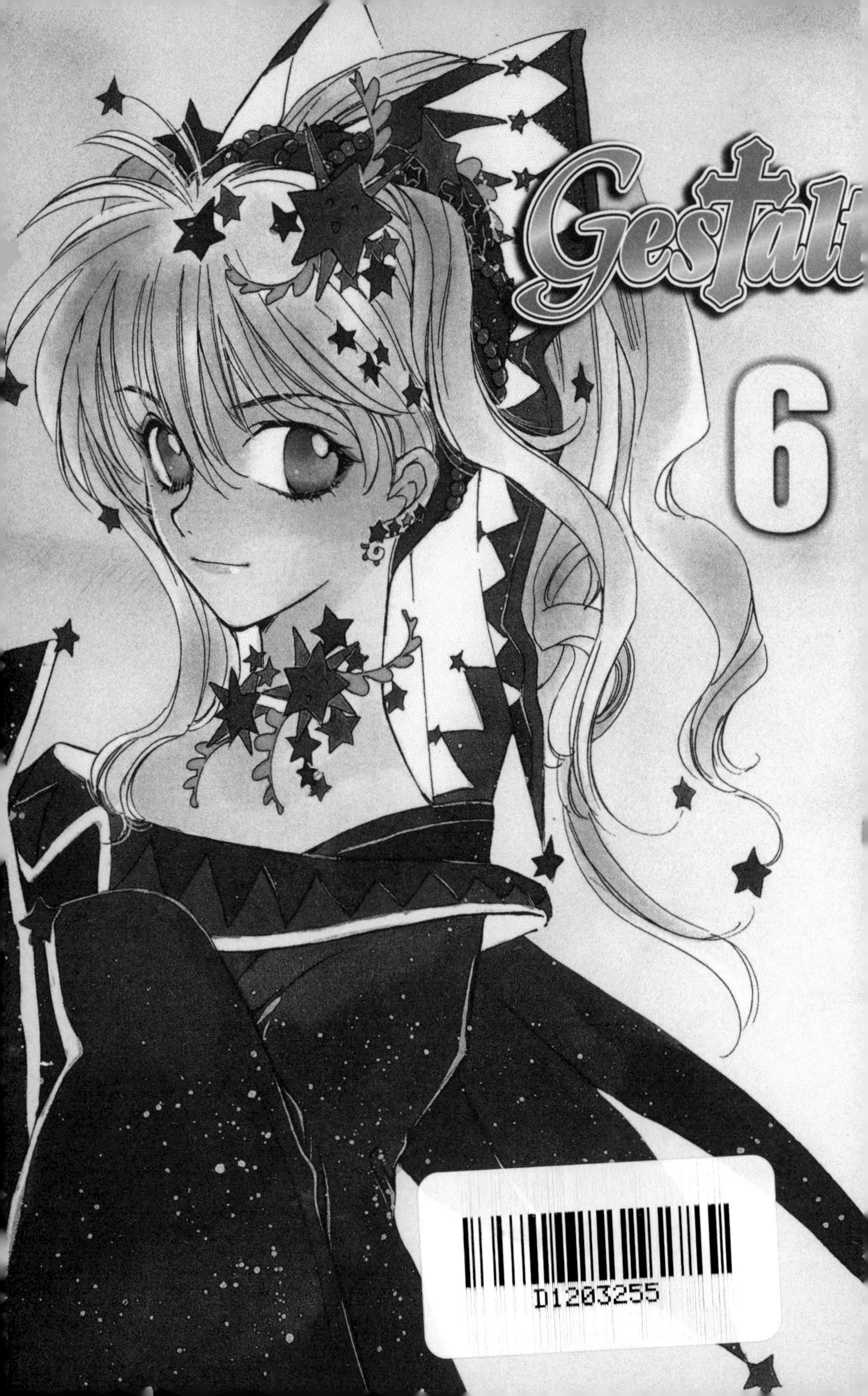
Gestalt
6

CONTENTS

6

Legend of the Great Beast

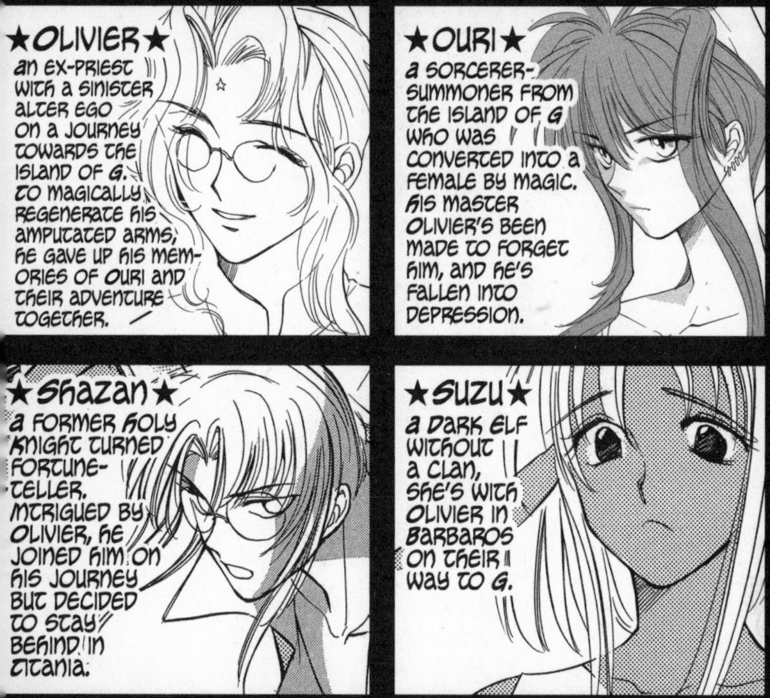
★OLIVIER★
an EX-PRIEST WITH a SINISTER ALTER EGO ON a JOURNEY TOWARDS THE ISLAND OF G. TO MAGICALLY REGENERATE HIS AMPUTATED ARMS, HE GAVE UP HIS MEMORIES OF OURI and THEIR ADVENTURE TOGETHER.
★OURI★
a SORCERER-SUMMONER FROM THE ISLAND OF G WHO WAS CONVERTED INTO a FEMALE BY MAGIC. HIS MASTER OLIVIER'S BEEN MADE TO FORGET HIM, AND HE'S FALLEN INTO DEPRESSION.
★SHAZAN★
a FORMER HOLY KNIGHT TURNED FORTUNE-TELLER. INTRIGUED BY OLIVIER, HE JOINED HIM ON HIS JOURNEY BUT DECIDED TO STAY BEHIND IN TITANIA.
★SUZU★
a DARK ELF WITHOUT a CLAN, SHE'S WITH OLIVIER IN BARBAROS ON THEIR WAY TO G.

CHARACTERS

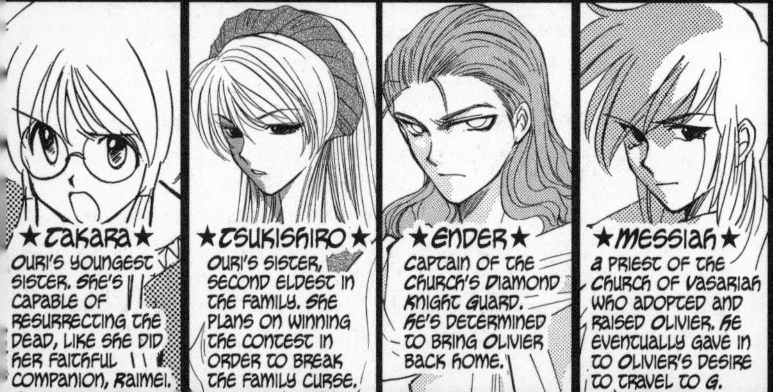
★TAKARA★
OURI'S YOUNGEST SISTER. SHE'S CAPABLE OF RESURRECTING THE DEAD, LIKE SHE DID HER FAITHFUL COMPANION, RAIMEI.
★TSUKISHIRO★
OURI'S SISTER, SECOND ELDEST IN THE FAMILY. SHE PLANS ON WINNING THE CONTEST IN ORDER TO BREAK THE FAMILY CURSE.
★ENDER★
CAPTAIN OF THE CHURCH'S DIAMOND KNIGHT GUARD. HE'S DETERMINED TO BRING OLIVIER BACK HOME.
★MESSIAH★
a PRIEST OF THE CHURCH OF VASARIAH WHO ADOPTED AND RAISED OLIVIER. HE EVENTUALLY GAVE IN TO OLIVIER'S DESIRE TO TRAVEL TO G.

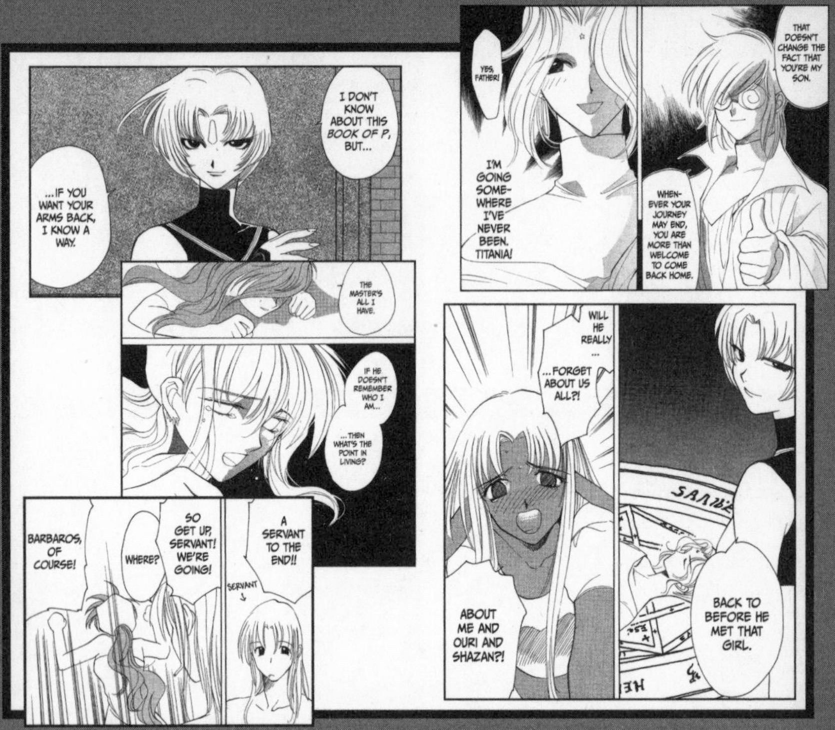
THAT DOESN'T CHANGE THE FACT THAT YOU'RE MY SON.
WHENEVER YOUR JOURNEY MAY END, YOU ARE MORE THAN WELCOME TO COME BACK HOME.
YES, FATHER!
I'M GOING SOMEWHERE I'VE NEVER BEEN. TITANIA!
I DON'T KNOW ABOUT THIS BOOK OF P, BUT...
...IF YOU WANT YOUR ARMS BACK, I KNOW A WAY.
BACK TO BEFORE HE MET THAT GIRL.
WILL HE REALLY ...
...FORGET ABOUT US ALL?!
ABOUT ME AND OURI AND SHAZAN?!
THE MASTER'S ALL I HAVE.
IF HE DOESN'T REMEMBER WHO I AM...
...THEN WHAT'S THE POINT IN LIVING?
A SERVANT TO THE END!!
SERVANT
SO GET UP, SERVANT! WE'RE GOING!
WHERE?
BARBAROS, OF COURSE!

Olivier was a priest of the Church of Vasariah until the day he fled the order to pursue the forbidden island of G. On his journey, he rescues Ouri, a slave girl with a secret identity. She's actually a man, a powerful sorcerer who's been transformed into a woman as part of a savage combat game against "her" siblings. Ouri quickly becomes smitten with Olivier and puts the game on hold to accompany him on his journey. The two are soon joined by Suzu and Shazan as they all make their way to G.
On their way, they seek to regain Olivier's lost arms by visiting Messiah. However, the enraged priest tries to force Olivier to end his journey and stay at home with him! He finally gives in after seeing how serious Ouri is about Olivier.
In Titania, they perform a ceremony to restore Olivier's lost arms. However, the ritual has its cost. Olivier loses every memory of Ouri and is transported back to where they first met in Barbaros.
Now forgotten, Ouri spends day after day in a slump until Shazan snaps him out of it and they resolve to go see Olivier.

THE STORY SO FAR

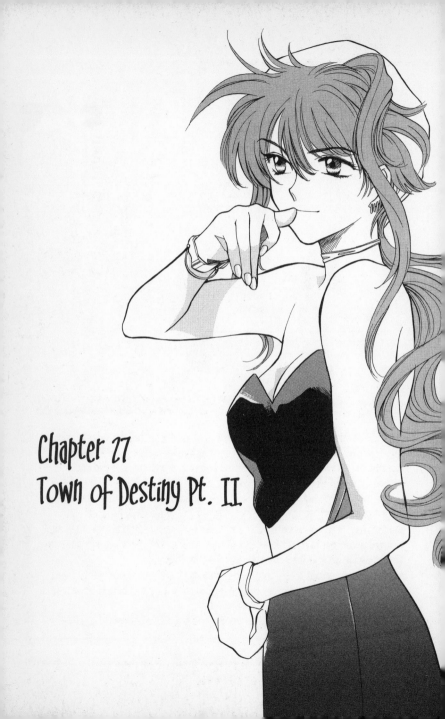

Chapter 27
Town of Destiny Pt. II.

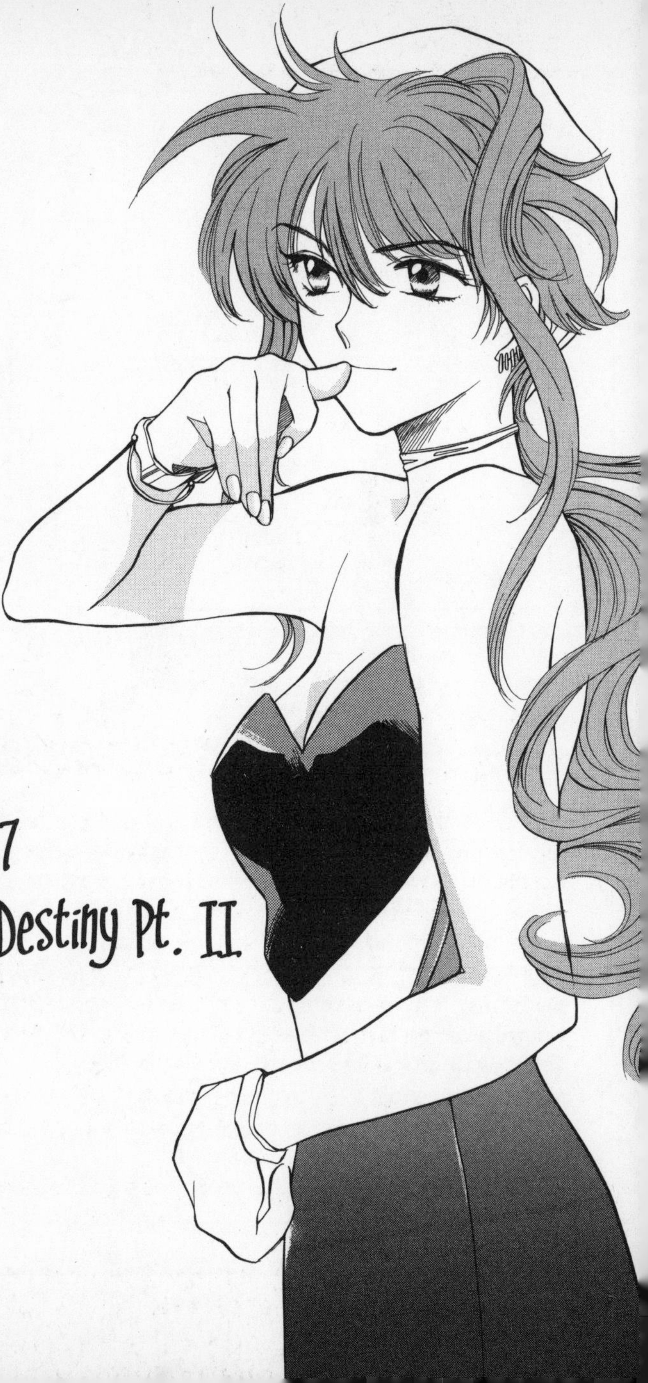

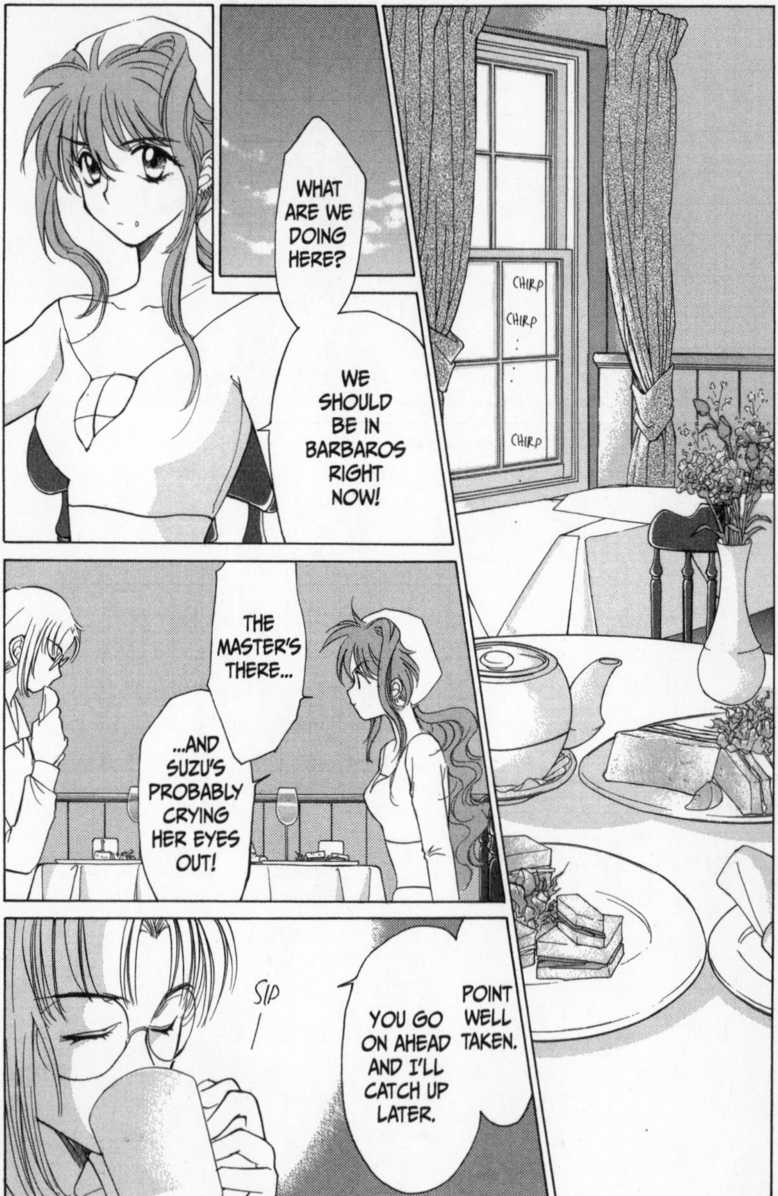
CHIRP
CHIRP
CHIRP
WHAT ARE WE DOING HERE?
WE SHOULD BE IN BARBAROS RIGHT NOW!
THE MASTER'S THERE...
...AND SUZU'S PROBABLY CRYING HER EYES OUT!
POINT WELL TAKEN.
YOU GO ON AHEAD AND I'LL CATCH UP LATER.
SIP

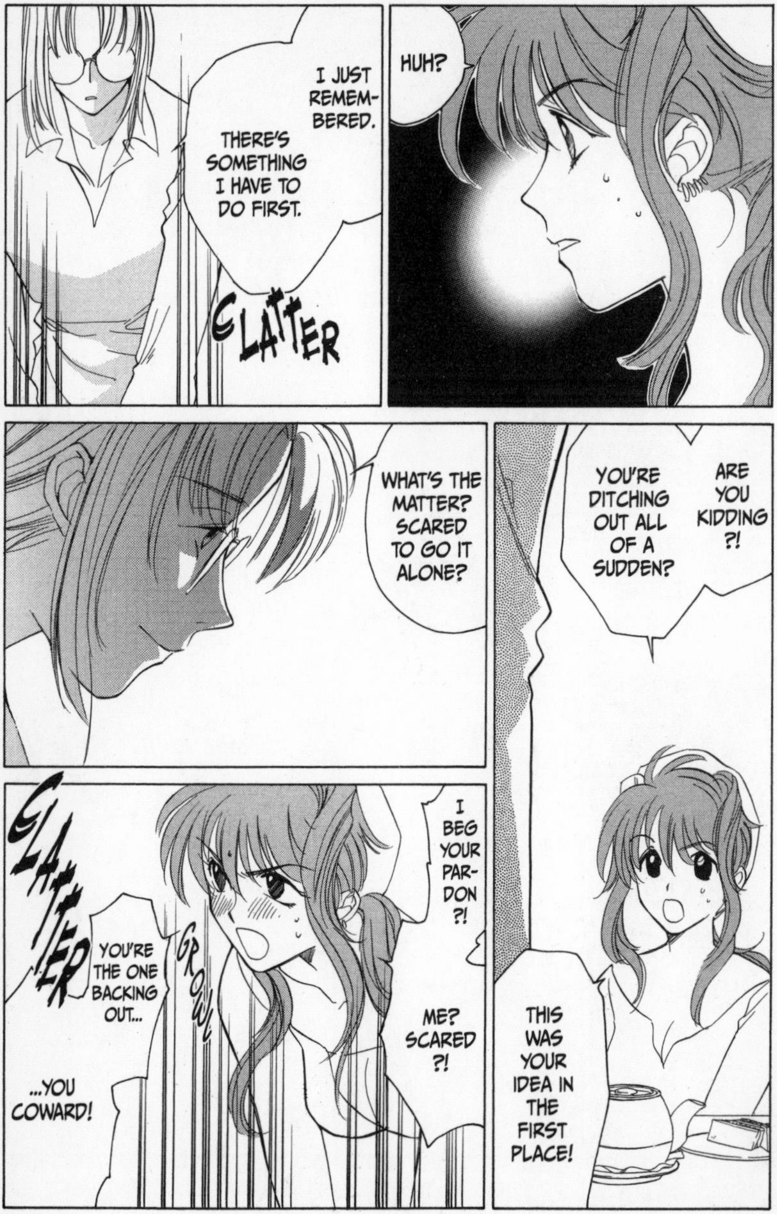
HUH?
I JUST REMEMBERED.
THERE'S SOMETHING I HAVE TO DO FIRST.
CLATTER
ARE YOU KIDDING?!
YOU'RE DITCHING OUT ALL OF A SUDDEN?
THIS WAS YOUR IDEA IN THE FIRST PLACE!
WHAT'S THE MATTER? SCARED TO GO IT ALONE?
I BEG YOUR PARDON?!
ME? SCARED?!
GROWL
YOU'RE THE ONE BACKING OUT...
CLATTER
...YOU COWARD!

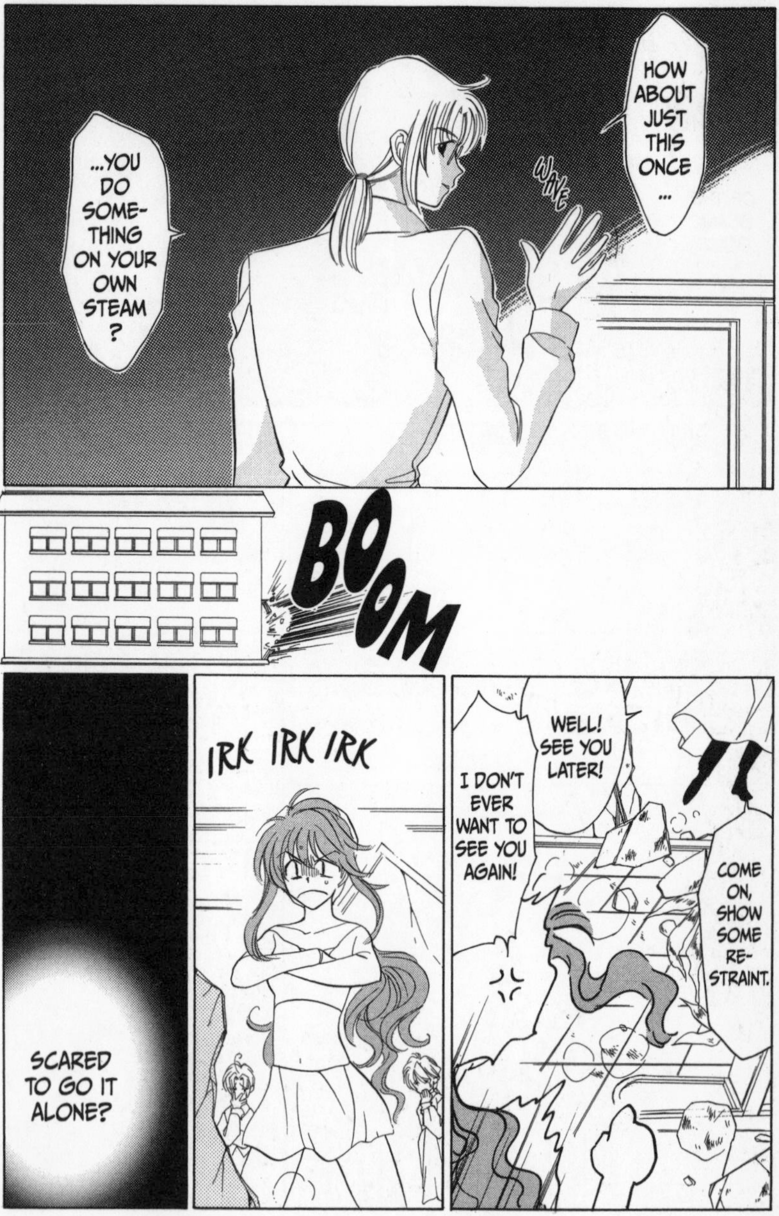
HOW ABOUT JUST THIS ONCE ...
WAVE
...YOU DO SOME-THING ON YOUR OWN STEAM ?
BOOM
WELL! SEE YOU LATER!
I DON'T EVER WANT TO SEE YOU AGAIN!
COME ON, SHOW SOME RE-STRAINT.
IRK IRK IRK
SCARED TO GO IT ALONE?

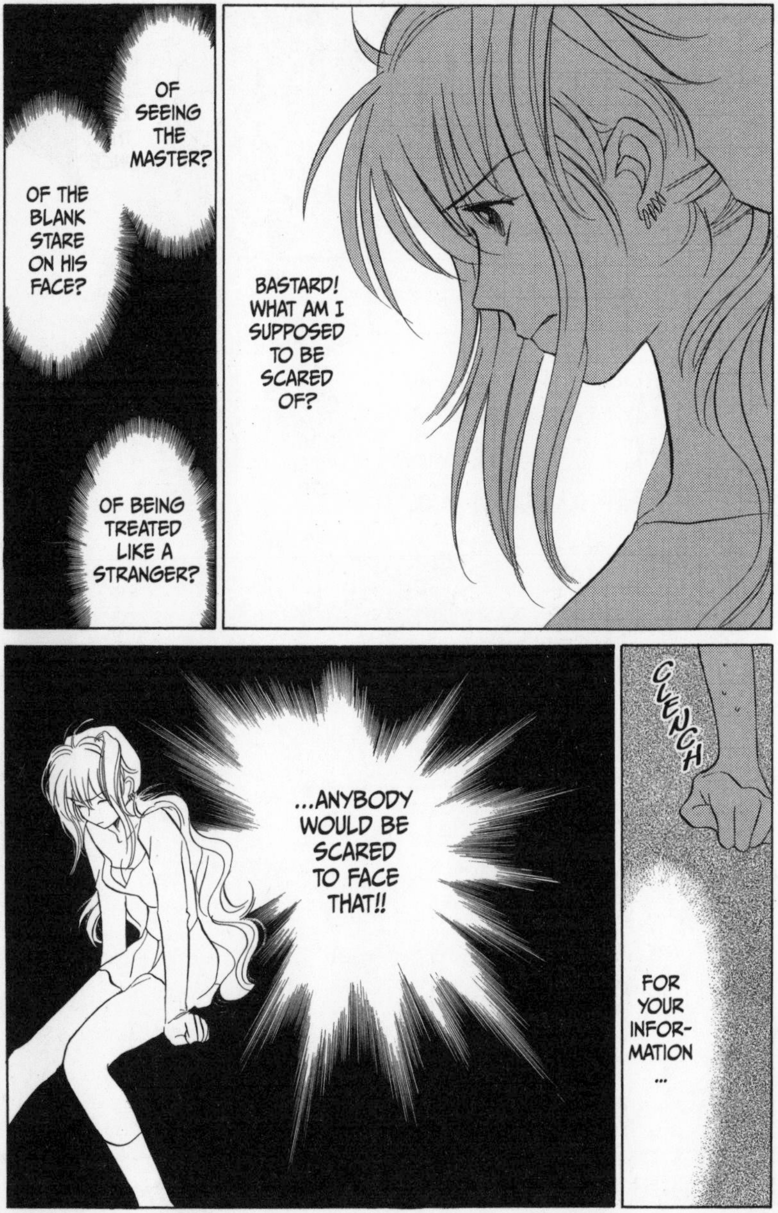
BASTARD! WHAT AM I SUPPOSED TO BE SCARED OF?
OF SEEING THE MASTER?
OF THE BLANK STARE ON HIS FACE?
OF BEING TREATED LIKE A STRANGER?
CLENCH
FOR YOUR INFORMATION...
...ANYBODY WOULD BE SCARED TO FACE THAT!!

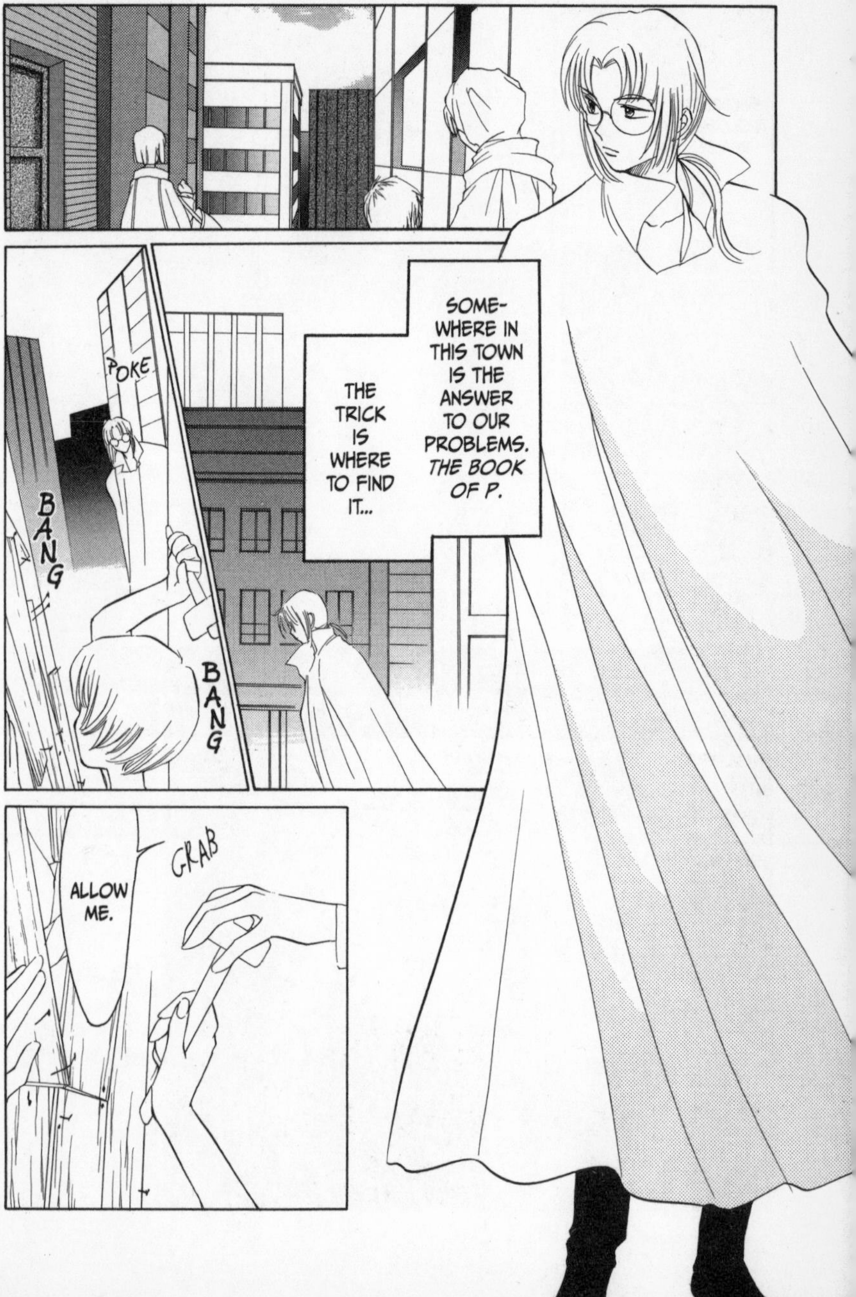
SOME-WHERE IN THIS TOWN IS THE ANSWER TO OUR PROBLEMS. *THE BOOK OF P.*
THE TRICK IS WHERE TO FIND IT...
POKE
BANG
BANG
GRAB
ALLOW ME.

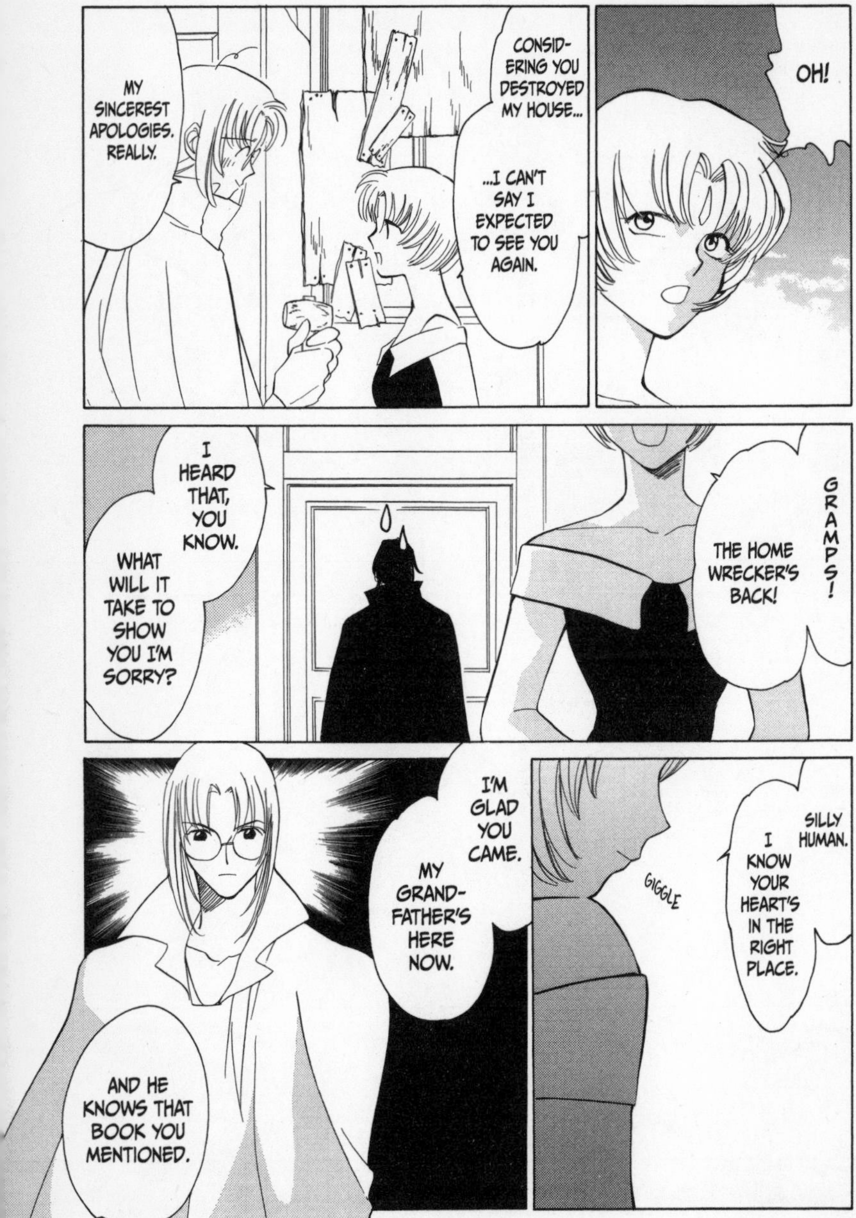
OH!
CONSID-ERING YOU DESTROYED MY HOUSE...
...I CAN'T SAY I EXPECTED TO SEE YOU AGAIN.
MY SINCEREST APOLOGIES. REALLY.
GRAMPS!
THE HOME WRECKER'S BACK!
I HEARD THAT, YOU KNOW.
WHAT WILL IT TAKE TO SHOW YOU I'M SORRY?
SILLY HUMAN.
I KNOW YOUR HEART'S IN THE RIGHT PLACE.
GIGGLE
I'M GLAD YOU CAME.
MY GRAND-FATHER'S HERE NOW.
AND HE KNOWS THAT BOOK YOU MENTIONED.

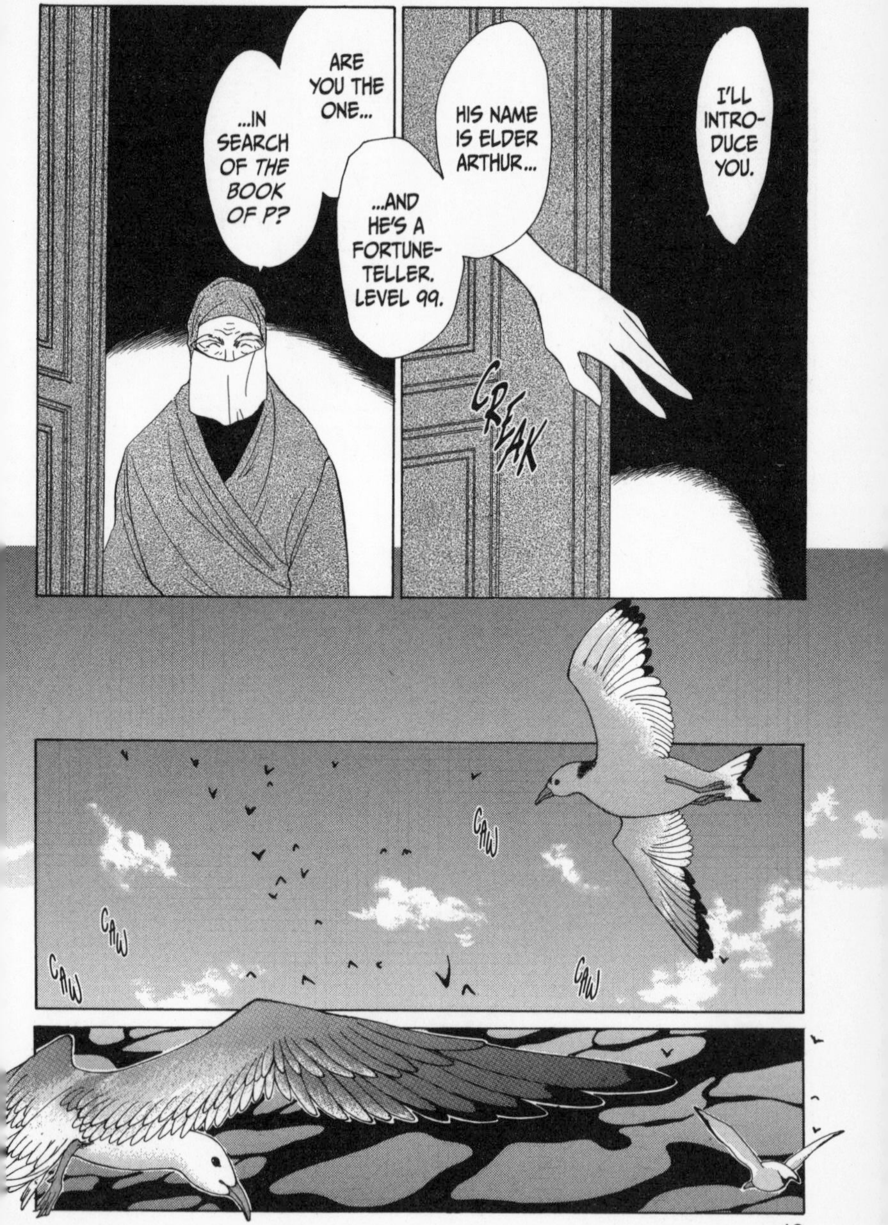
I'LL INTRODUCE YOU.
HIS NAME IS ELDER ARTHUR...
...AND HE'S A FORTUNE-TELLER. LEVEL 99.
CREAK
ARE YOU THE ONE...
...IN SEARCH OF THE BOOK OF P?
CAW
CAW
CAW
CAW

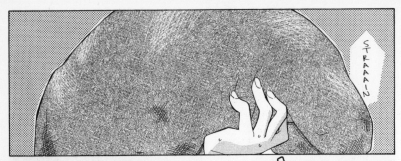

STRAAAAIN
SPLAT
GYAAAAH!
FATHER OLIVIER!!
I KNEW THIS JOB WAS TOO MUCH FOR YOU!
YOU'VE GOT TO TAKE IT EASY!
S...
SORRY. I JUST CAN'T GET THE HANG OF IT...
WHAT'S WRONG, NEWBIE?
ONE LITTLE SACK'S TOO MUCH FOR YOU?
HAHAHA!
UUURGH!
QUIET!
SO WHAT IF HE'S NOT A MEATHEAD LIKE YOU?!
TOUCH

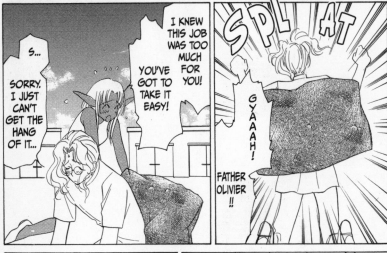

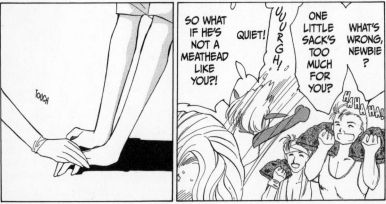

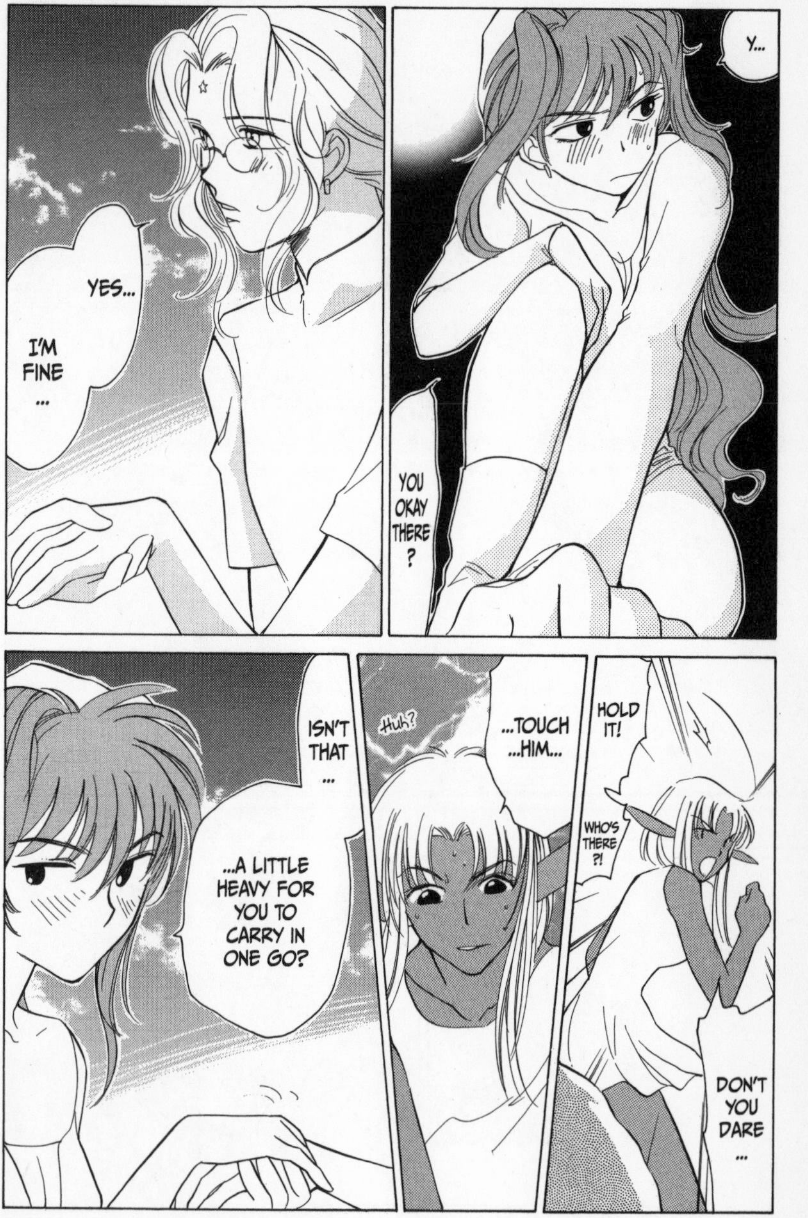
Y...
YOU OKAY THERE?
YES...
I'M FINE...
HOLD IT!
WHO'S THERE?!
DON'T YOU DARE...
...TOUCH ...HIM...
Huh?
ISN'T THAT...
...A LITTLE HEAVY FOR YOU TO CARRY IN ONE GO?

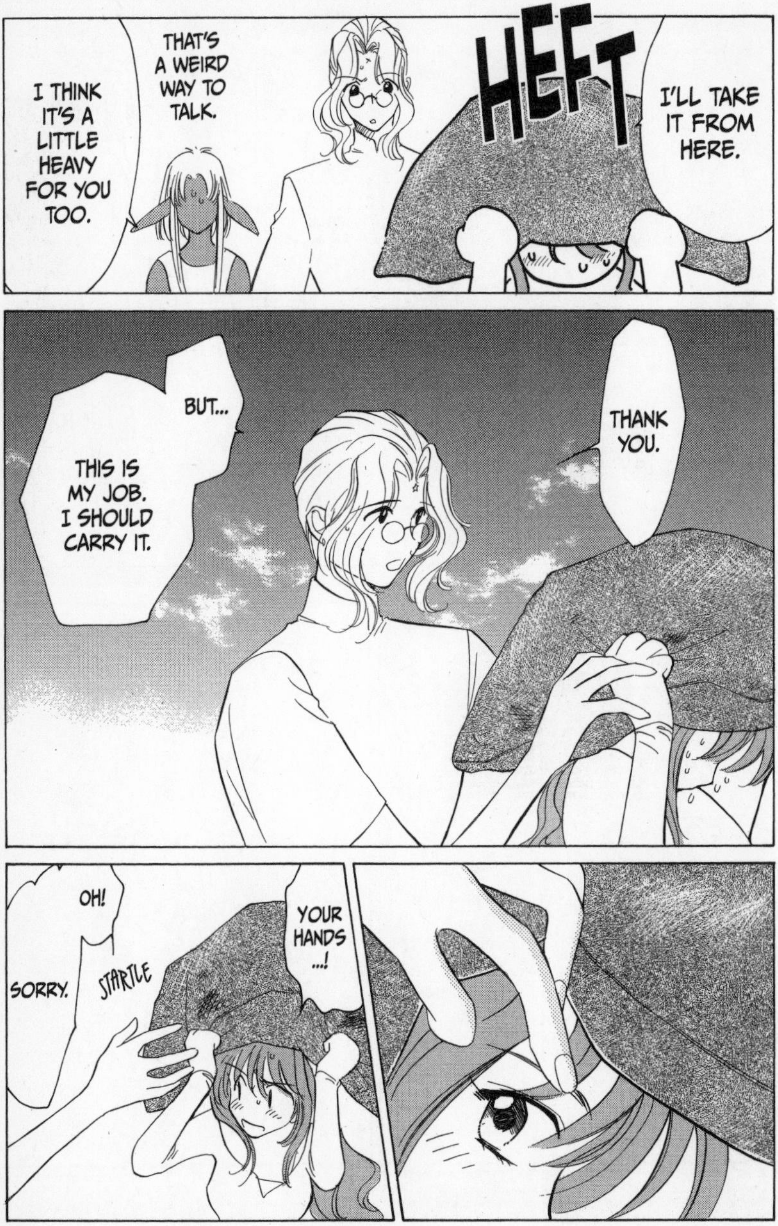
HEFT
I'LL TAKE IT FROM HERE.
THAT'S A WEIRD WAY TO TALK.
I THINK IT'S A LITTLE HEAVY FOR YOU TOO.
THANK YOU.
BUT...
THIS IS MY JOB. I SHOULD CARRY IT.
YOUR HANDS ...!
OH!
STARTLE
SORRY.

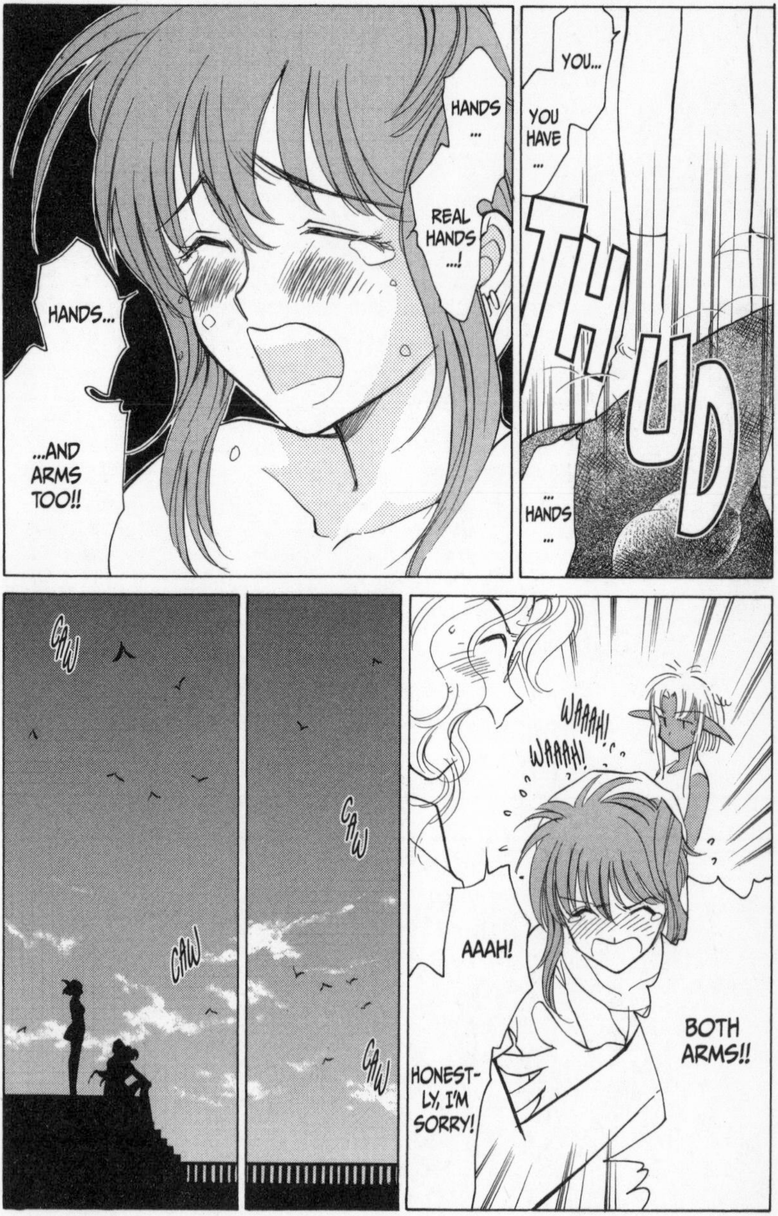
YOU...
YOU HAVE ...
THUD
... HANDS ...
HANDS ...
REAL HANDS ...!
HANDS...
...AND ARMS TOO!!
WAAAH!
WAAAH!
AAAH!
BOTH ARMS!!
HONEST-LY, I'M SORRY!
CAW
CAW
CAW
CAW

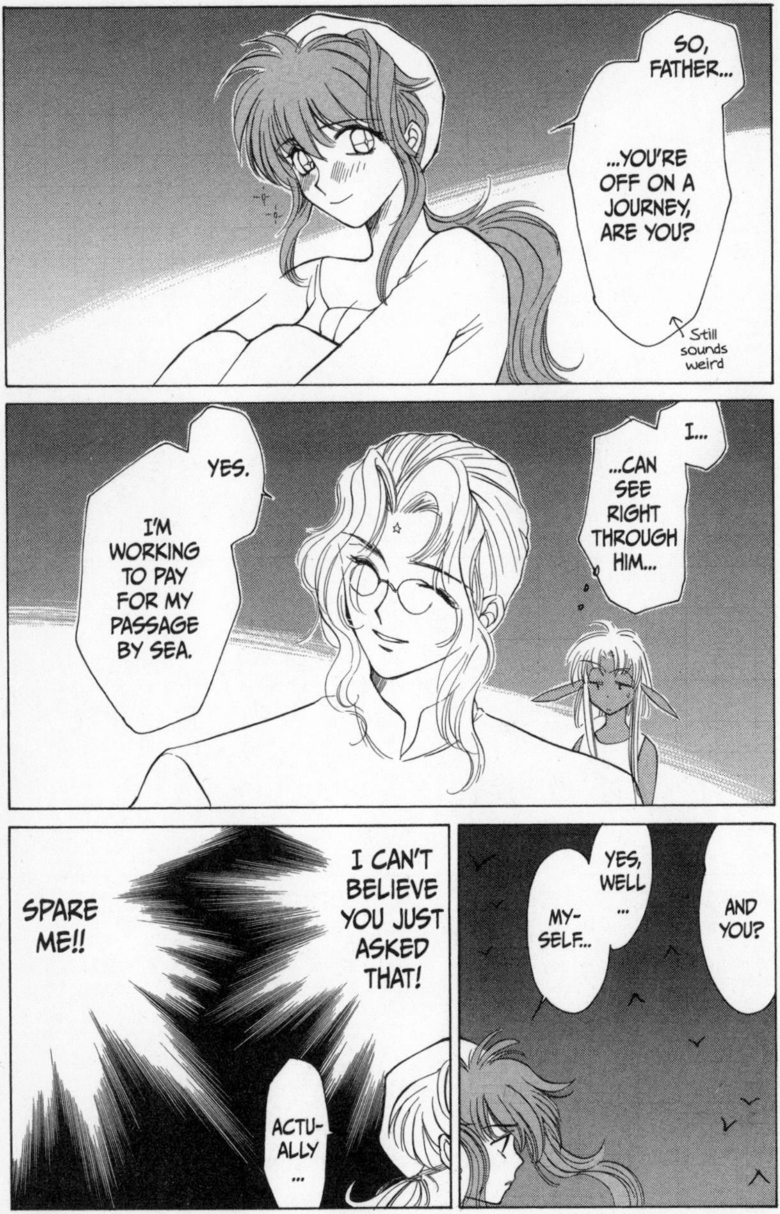
SO, FATHER...
...YOU'RE OFF ON A JOURNEY, ARE YOU?
Still sounds weird
I...
...CAN SEE RIGHT THROUGH HIM...
YES.
I'M WORKING TO PAY FOR MY PASSAGE BY SEA.
AND YOU?
YES, WELL ...
MY-SELF...
I CAN'T BELIEVE YOU JUST ASKED THAT!
SPARE ME!!
ACTU-ALLY ...

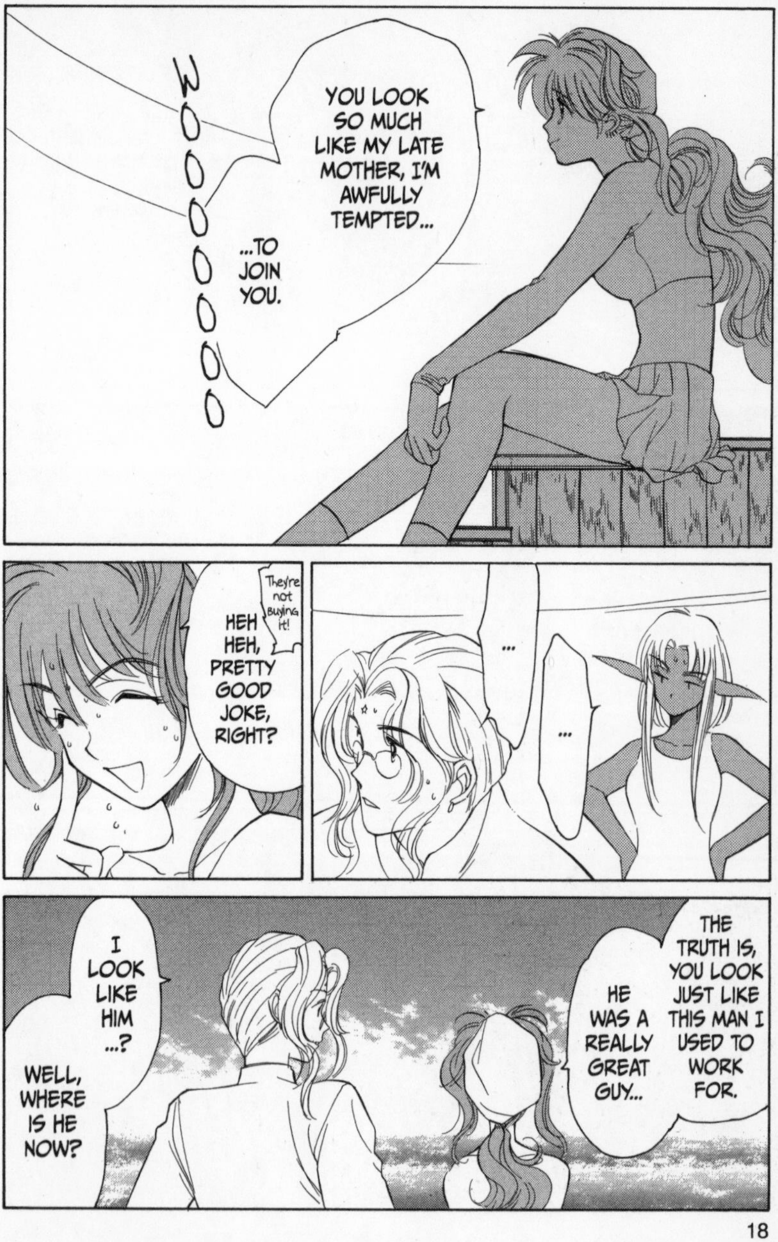
YOU LOOK SO MUCH LIKE MY LATE MOTHER, I'M AWFULLY TEMPTED...
...TO JOIN YOU.
WOOOOOOOO
...
...
HEH HEH, PRETTY GOOD JOKE, RIGHT?
They're not buying it!
THE TRUTH IS, YOU LOOK JUST LIKE THIS MAN I USED TO WORK FOR.
HE WAS A REALLY GREAT GUY...
I LOOK LIKE HIM ...?
WELL, WHERE IS HE NOW?

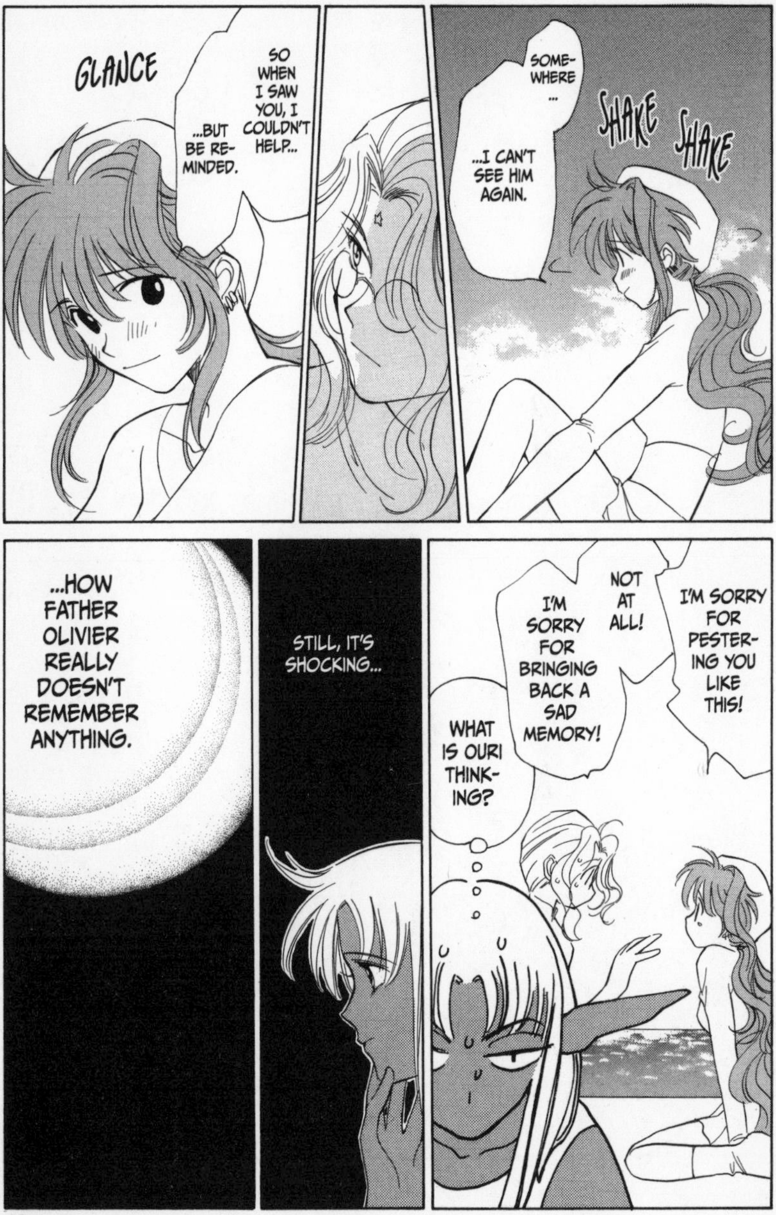
SOME-WHERE...
...I CAN'T SEE HIM AGAIN.
SHAKE SHAKE
SO WHEN I SAW YOU, I COULDN'T HELP...
...BUT BE RE-MINDED.
GLANCE
I'M SORRY FOR PESTER-ING YOU LIKE THIS!
NOT AT ALL!
I'M SORRY FOR BRINGING BACK A SAD MEMORY!
WHAT IS OURI THINK-ING?
STILL, IT'S SHOCKING...
...HOW FATHER OLIVIER REALLY DOESN'T REMEMBER ANYTHING.

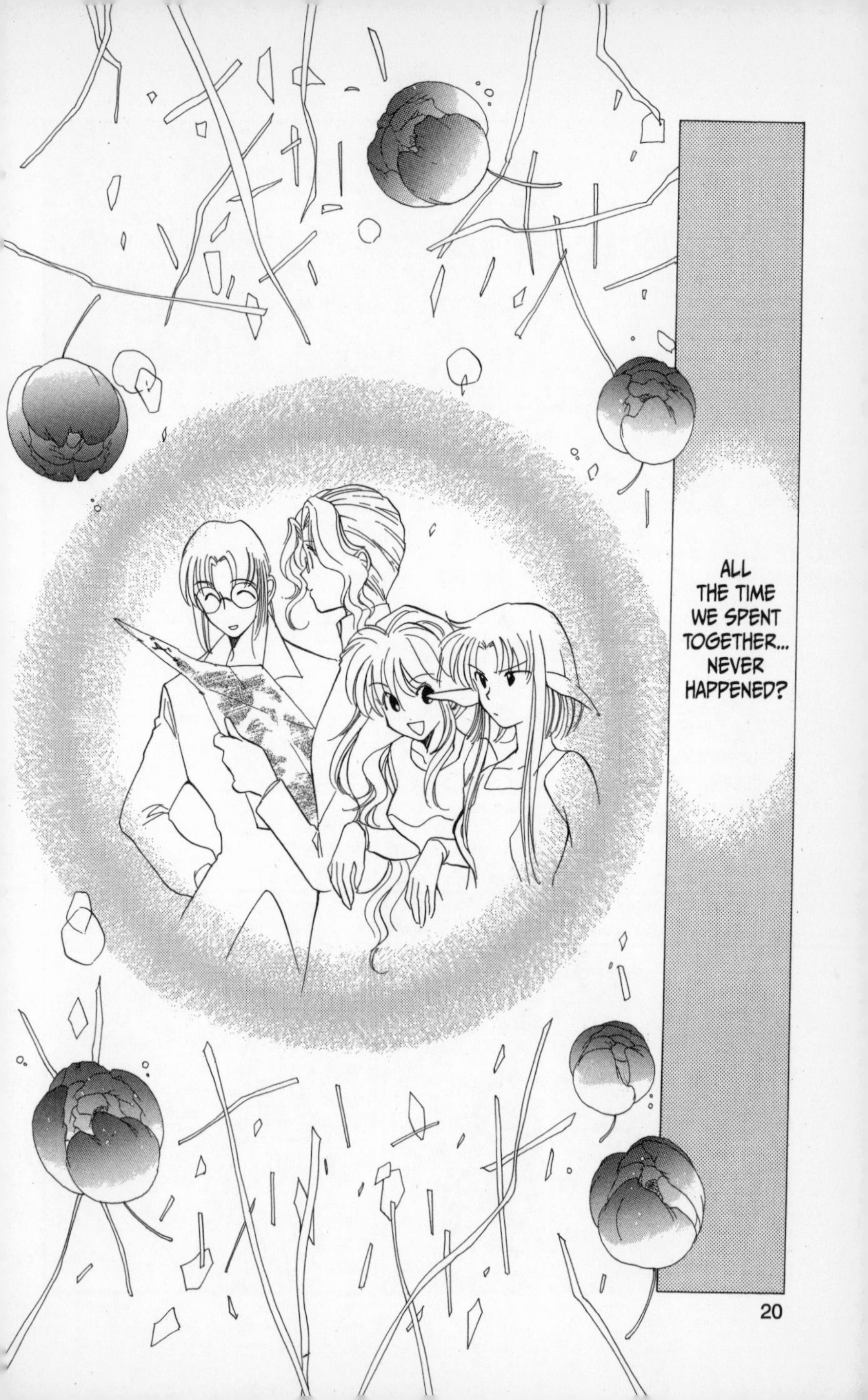
ALL THE TIME WE SPENT TOGETHER... NEVER HAPPENED?

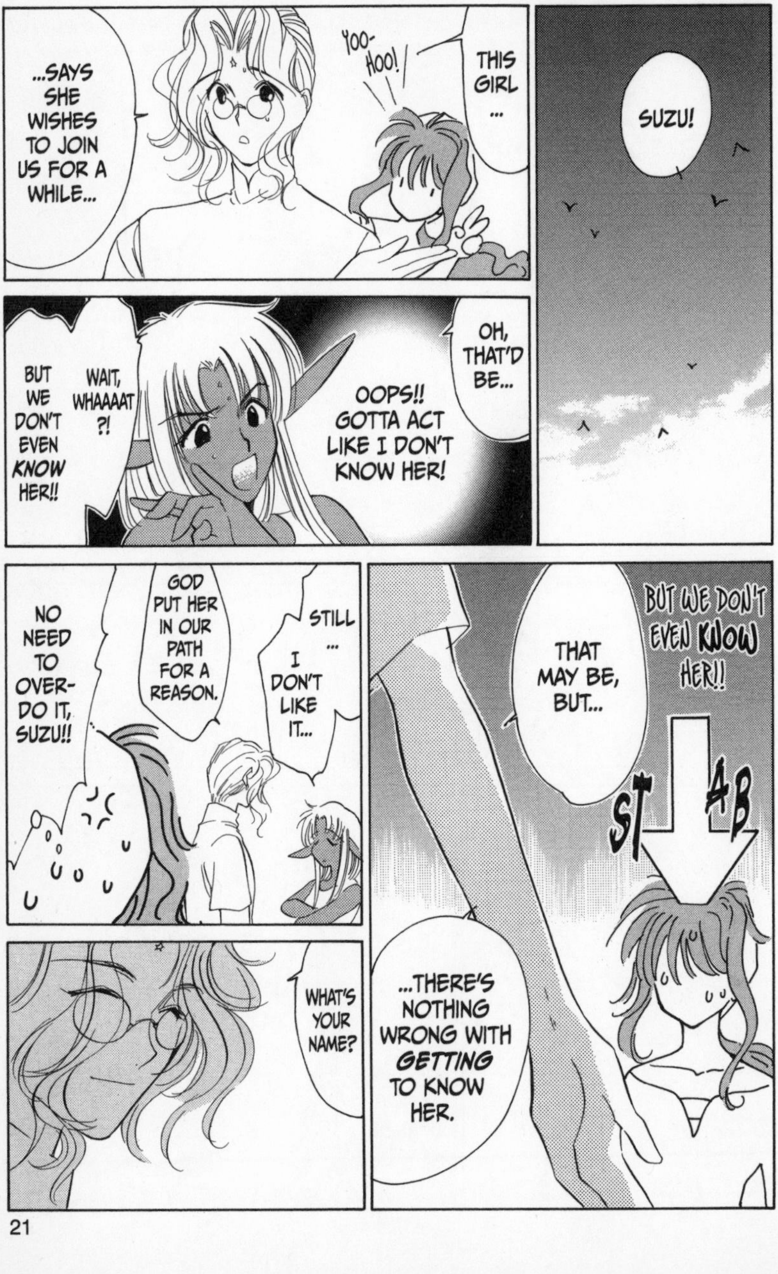
SUZU!
THIS GIRL ...
YOO-HOO!
...SAYS SHE WISHES TO JOIN US FOR A WHILE...
OH, THAT'D BE...
OOPS!! GOTTA ACT LIKE I DON'T KNOW HER!
WAIT, WHAAAAT ?!
BUT WE DON'T EVEN *KNOW* HER!!
BUT WE DON'T EVEN **KNOW** HER!!
THAT MAY BE, BUT...
STAB
...THERE'S NOTHING WRONG WITH ***GETTING*** TO KNOW HER.
STILL ... I DON'T LIKE IT...
GOD PUT HER IN OUR PATH FOR A REASON.
NO NEED TO OVER-DO IT, SUZU!!
WHAT'S YOUR NAME?

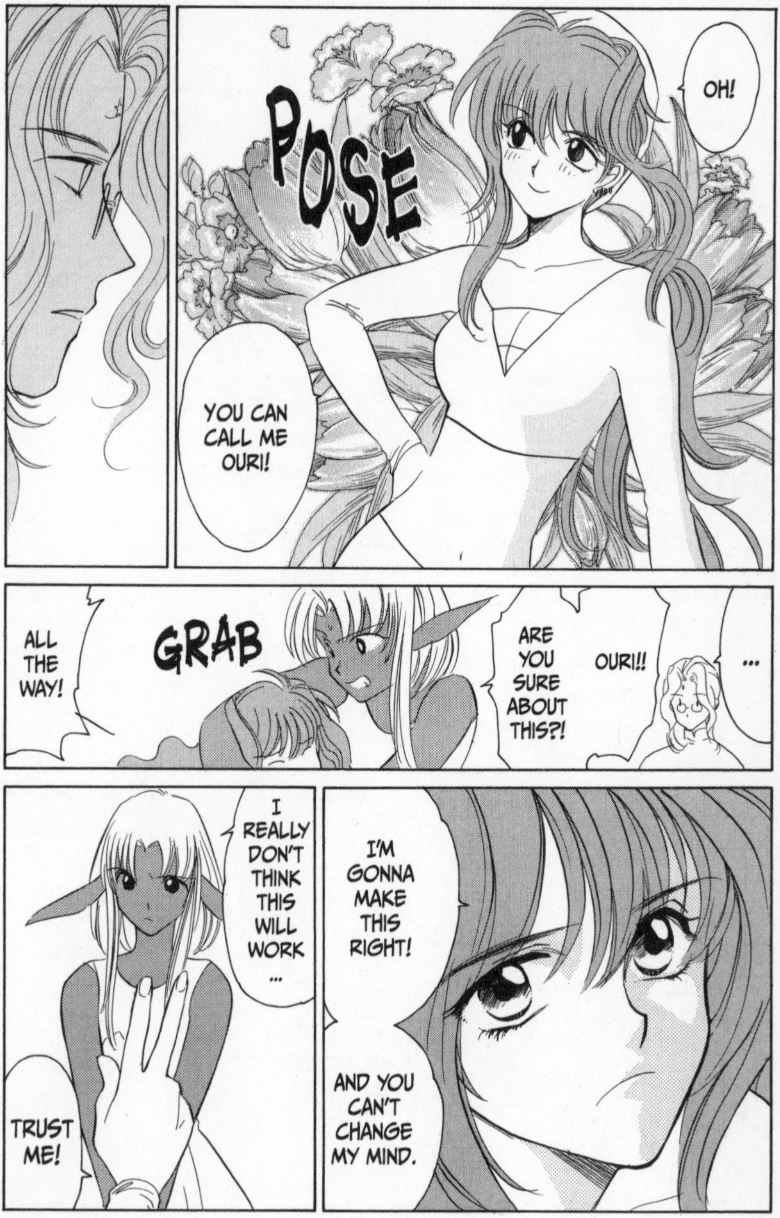
OH!
POSE
YOU CAN CALL ME OURI!
...
OURI!!
ARE YOU SURE ABOUT THIS?!
GRAB
ALL THE WAY!
I'M GONNA MAKE THIS RIGHT!
AND YOU CAN'T CHANGE MY MIND.
I REALLY DON'T THINK THIS WILL WORK ...
TRUST ME!

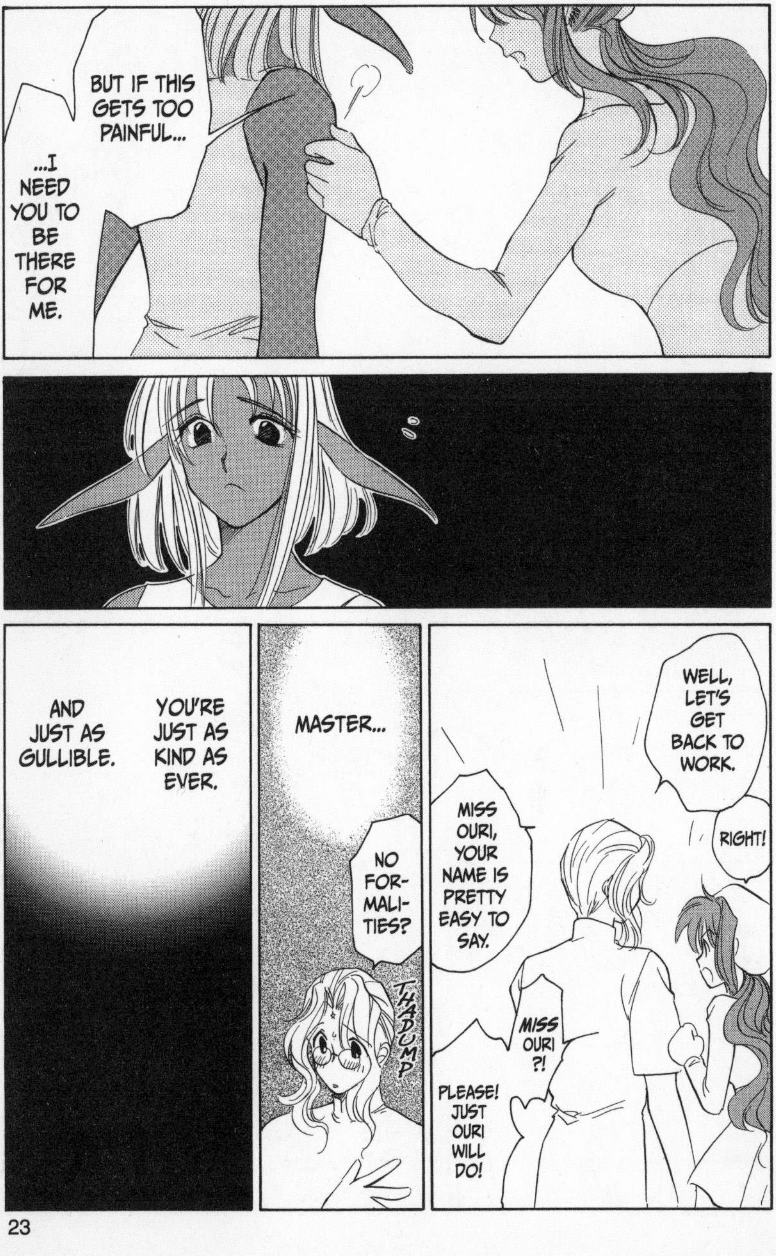
BUT IF THIS GETS TOO PAINFUL...
...I NEED YOU TO BE THERE FOR ME.
WELL, LET'S GET BACK TO WORK.
RIGHT!
MISS OURI, YOUR NAME IS PRETTY EASY TO SAY.
MISS OURI ?!
PLEASE! JUST OURI WILL DO!
MASTER...
NO FOR-MALI-TIES?
THADUMP
YOU'RE JUST AS KIND AS EVER.
AND JUST AS GULLIBLE.

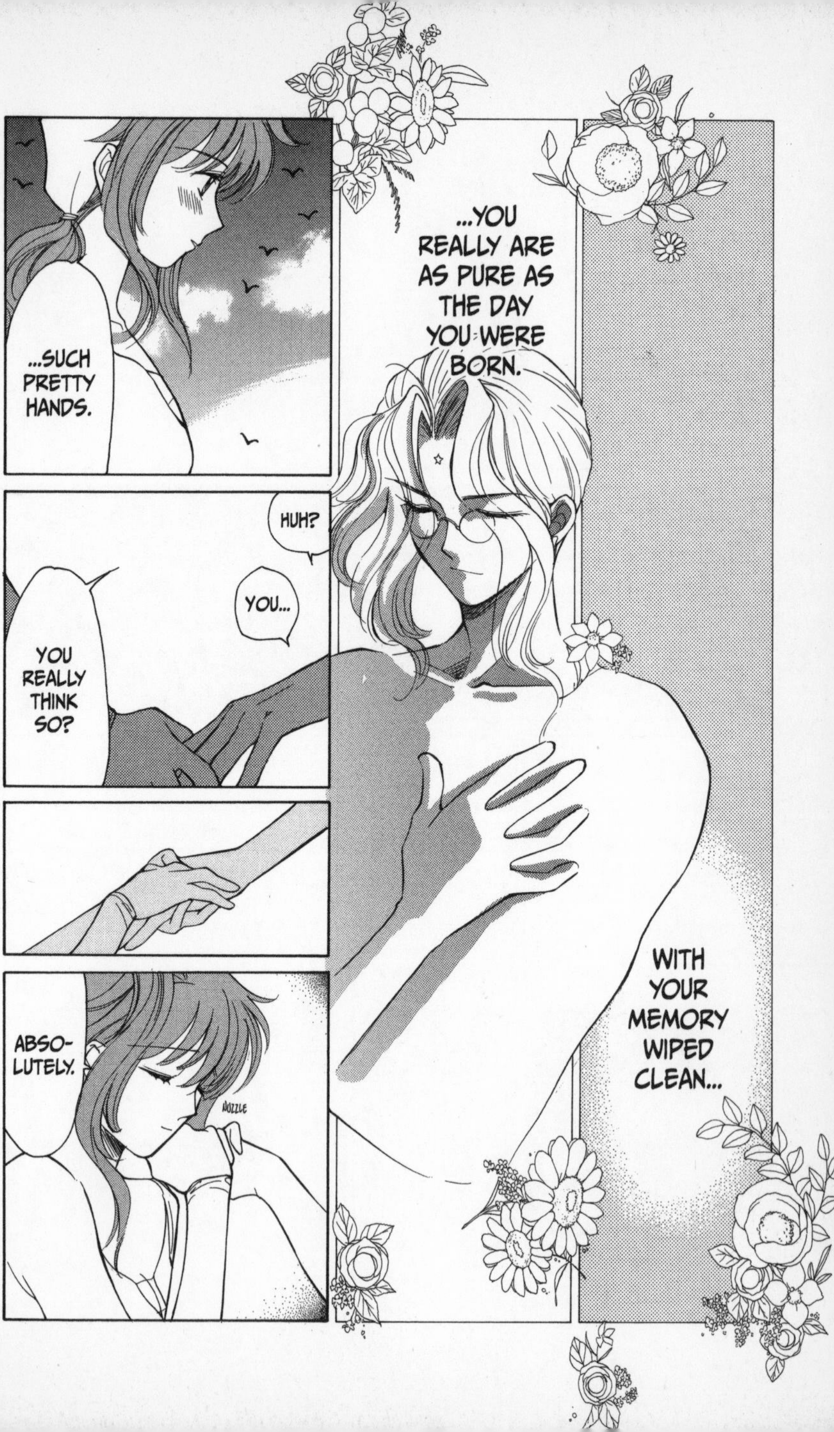
...YOU REALLY ARE AS PURE AS THE DAY YOU WERE BORN.
WITH YOUR MEMORY WIPED CLEAN...
...SUCH PRETTY HANDS.
HUH?
YOU...
YOU REALLY THINK SO?
ABSO-LUTELY.
NUZZLE

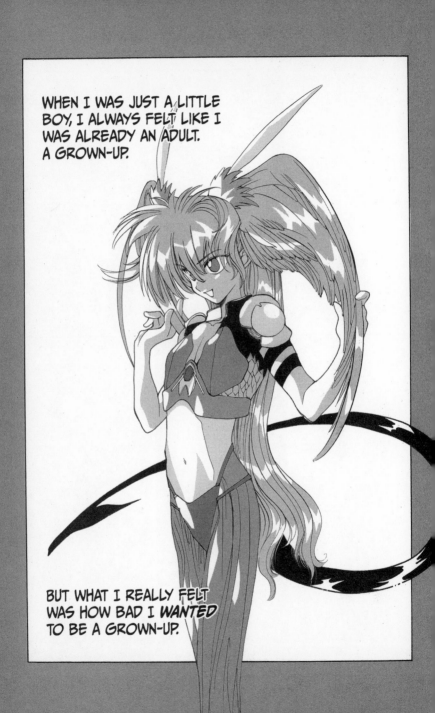

WHEN I WAS JUST A LITTLE
BOY, I ALWAYS FELT LIKE I
WAS ALREADY AN ADULT.
A GROWN-UP.

BUT WHAT I REALLY FELT
WAS HOW BAD I *WANTED*
TO BE A GROWN-UP.

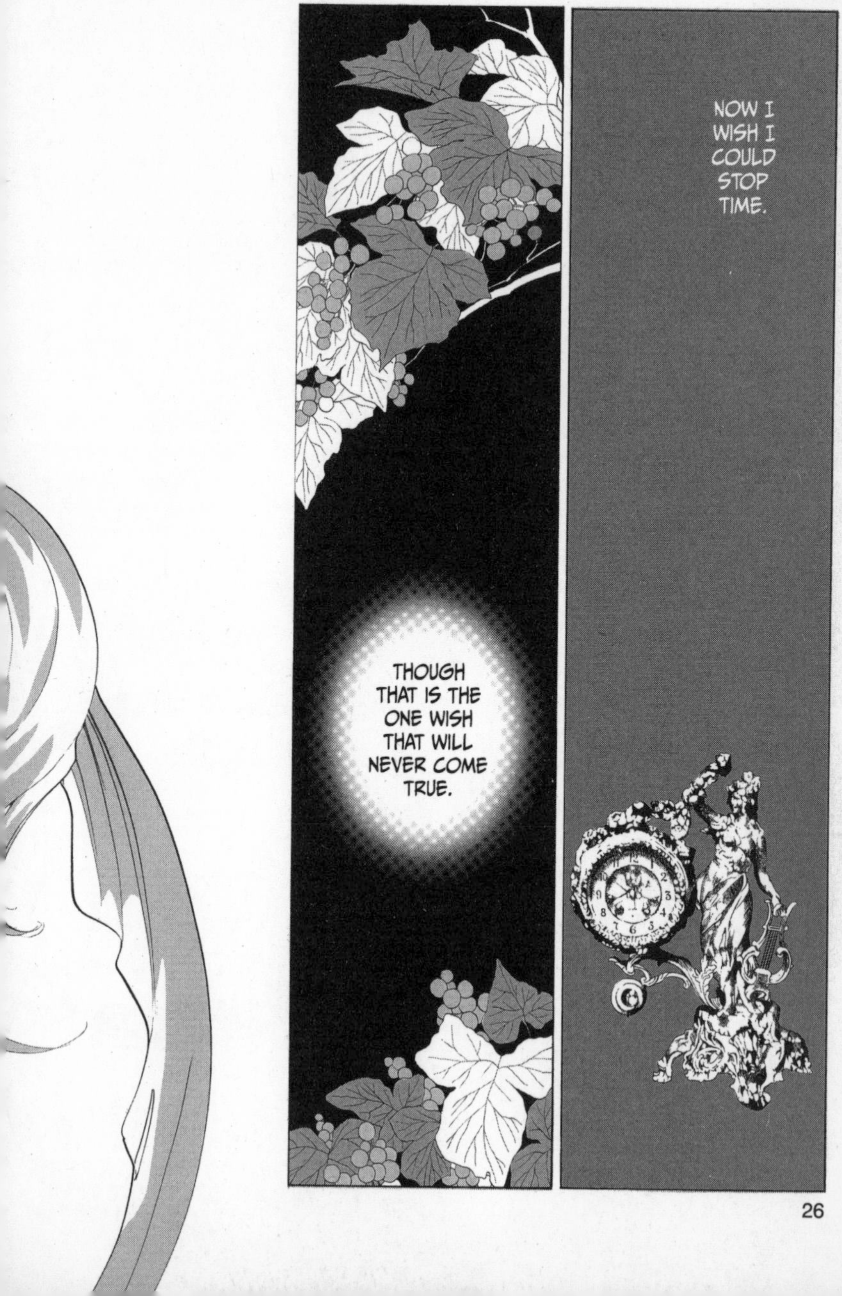
NOW I WISH I COULD STOP TIME.
THOUGH THAT IS THE ONE WISH THAT WILL NEVER COME TRUE.

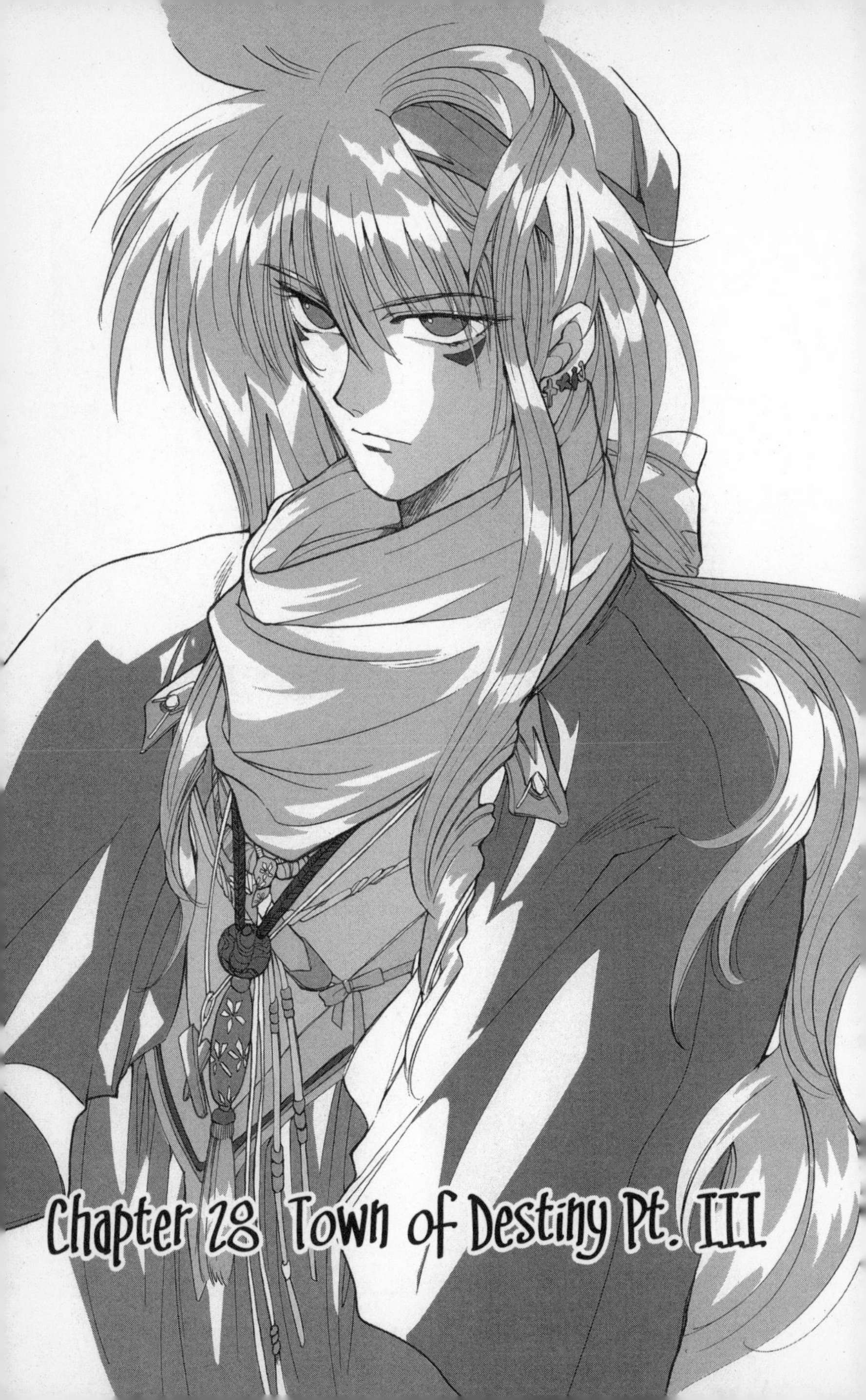

Chapter 28 Town of Destiny Pt. III

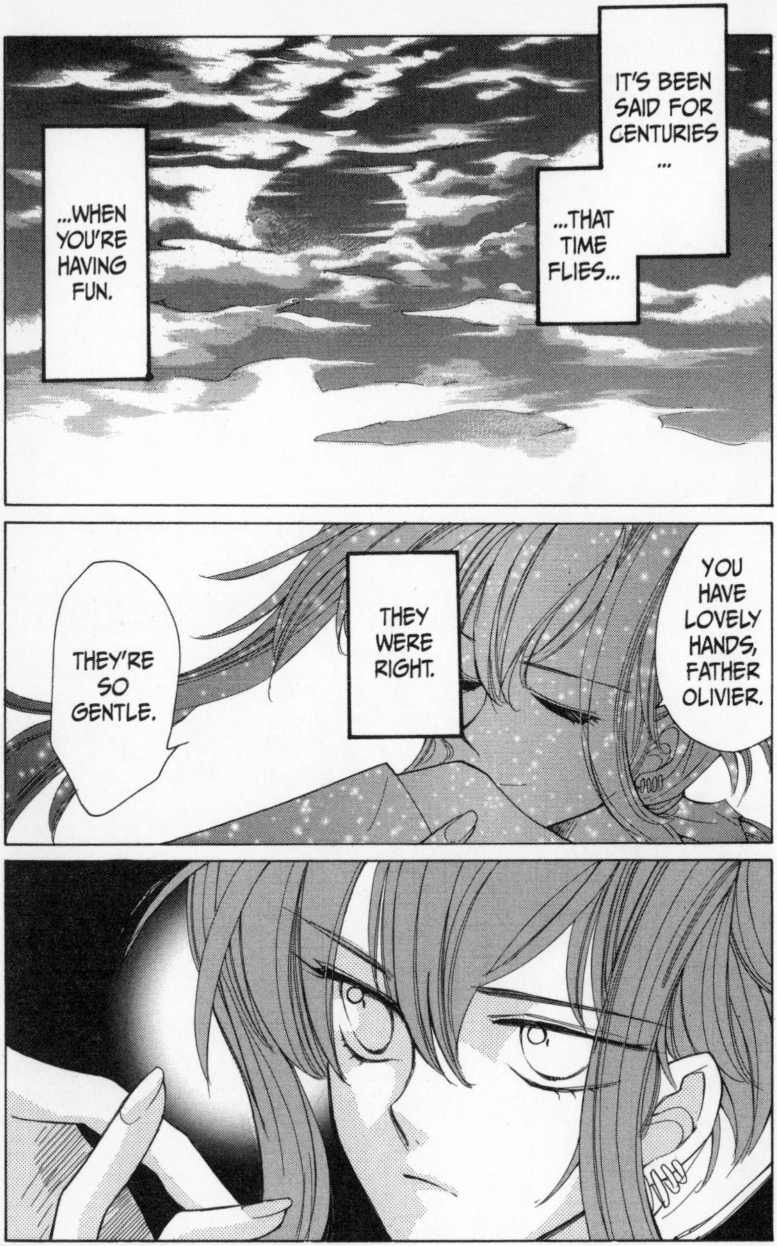
IT'S BEEN SAID FOR CENTURIES ...
...THAT TIME FLIES...
...WHEN YOU'RE HAVING FUN.
YOU HAVE LOVELY HANDS, FATHER OLIVIER.
THEY WERE RIGHT.
THEY'RE SO GENTLE.

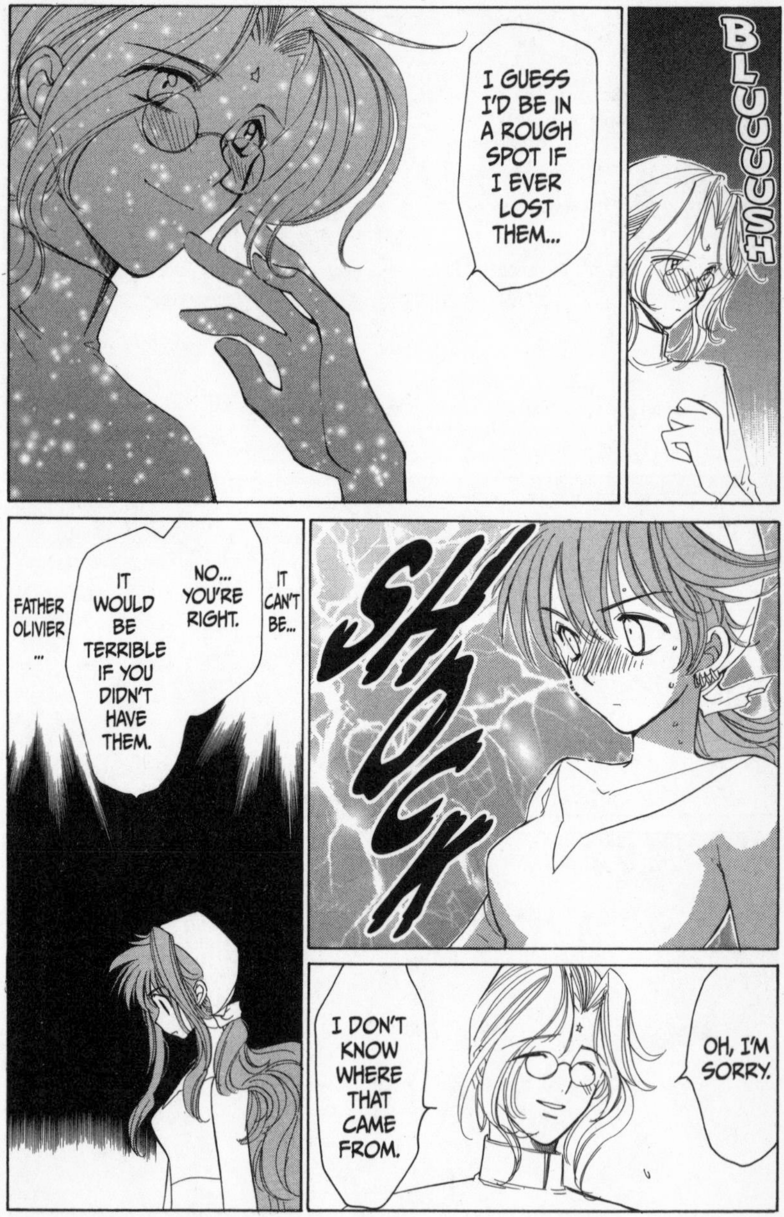
BLUUUUSH
I GUESS I'D BE IN A ROUGH SPOT IF I EVER LOST THEM...
SHOCK
OH, I'M SORRY.
I DON'T KNOW WHERE THAT CAME FROM.
IT CAN'T BE...
NO... YOU'RE RIGHT.
IT WOULD BE TERRIBLE IF YOU DIDN'T HAVE THEM.
FATHER OLIVIER ...

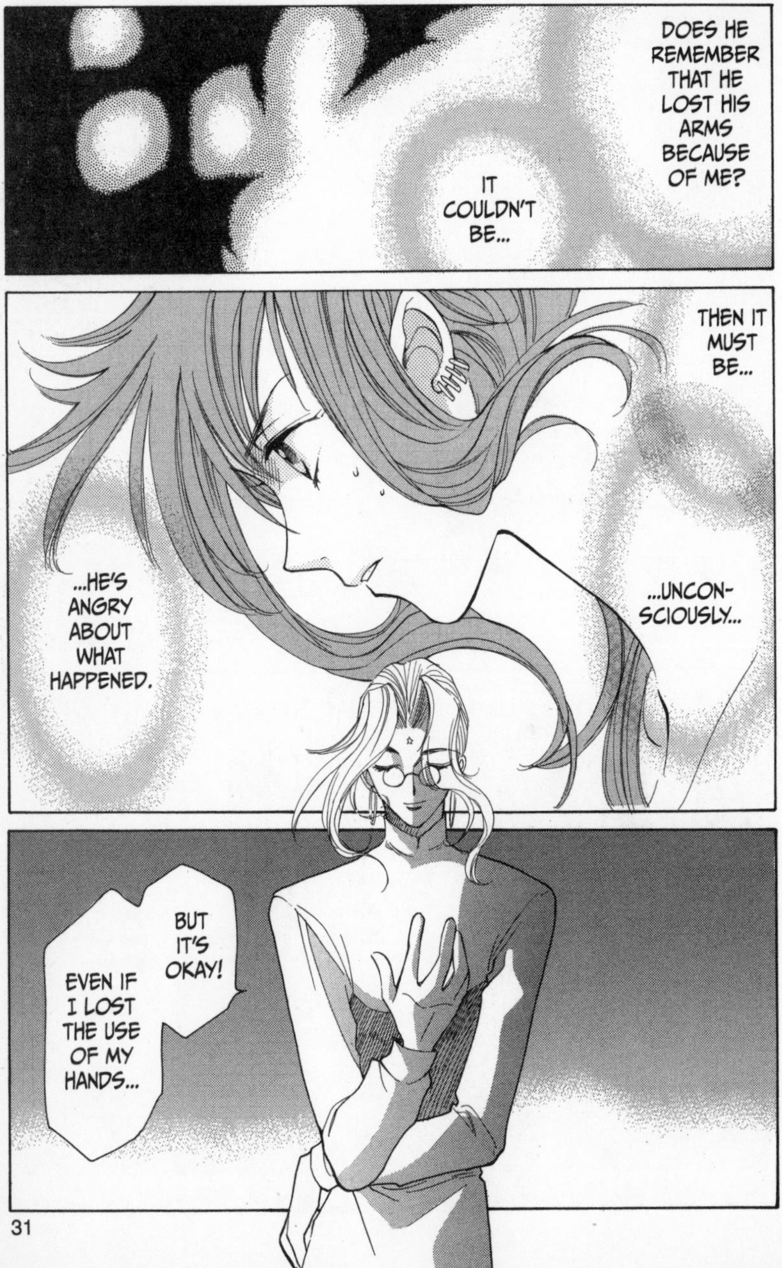
DOES HE REMEMBER THAT HE LOST HIS ARMS BECAUSE OF ME?
IT COULDN'T BE...
THEN IT MUST BE...
...UNCON-SCIOUSLY...
...HE'S ANGRY ABOUT WHAT HAPPENED.
BUT IT'S OKAY!
EVEN IF I LOST THE USE OF MY HANDS...

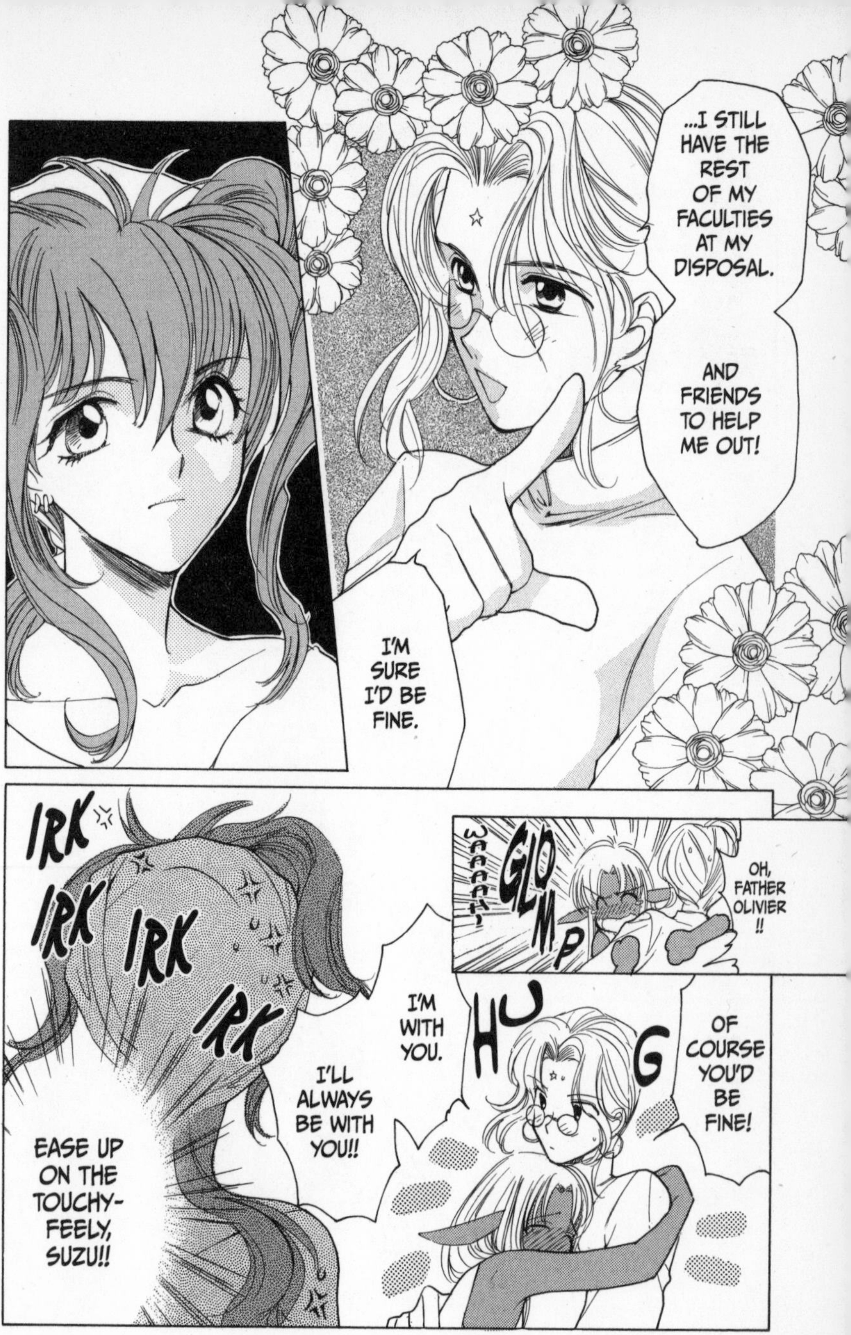
...I STILL HAVE THE REST OF MY FACULTIES AT MY DISPOSAL.
AND FRIENDS TO HELP ME OUT!
I'M SURE I'D BE FINE.
OH, FATHER OLIVIER !!
WAAAAAH!
GLOMP
OF COURSE YOU'D BE FINE!
HUG
I'M WITH YOU.
I'LL ALWAYS BE WITH YOU!!
IRK
IRK
IRK
IRK
EASE UP ON THE TOUCHY-FEELY, SUZU!!

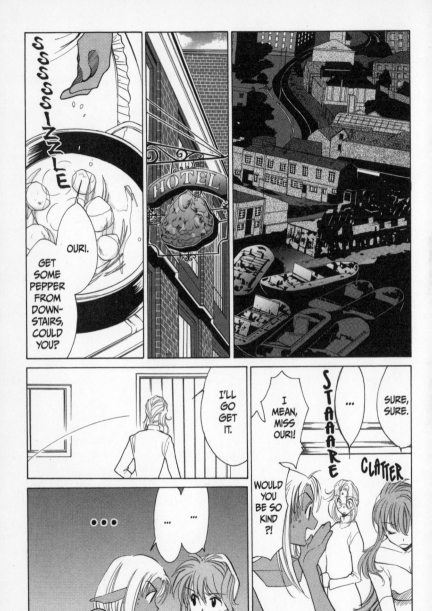

SSSSSIZZLE

OURI.

GET SOME PEPPER FROM DOWN-STAIRS, COULD YOU?

HOTEL

I'LL GO GET IT.

I MEAN, MISS OURI!

...

SURE, SURE.

WOULD YOU BE SO KIND?!

STAAARE

CLATTER

...   ...

33

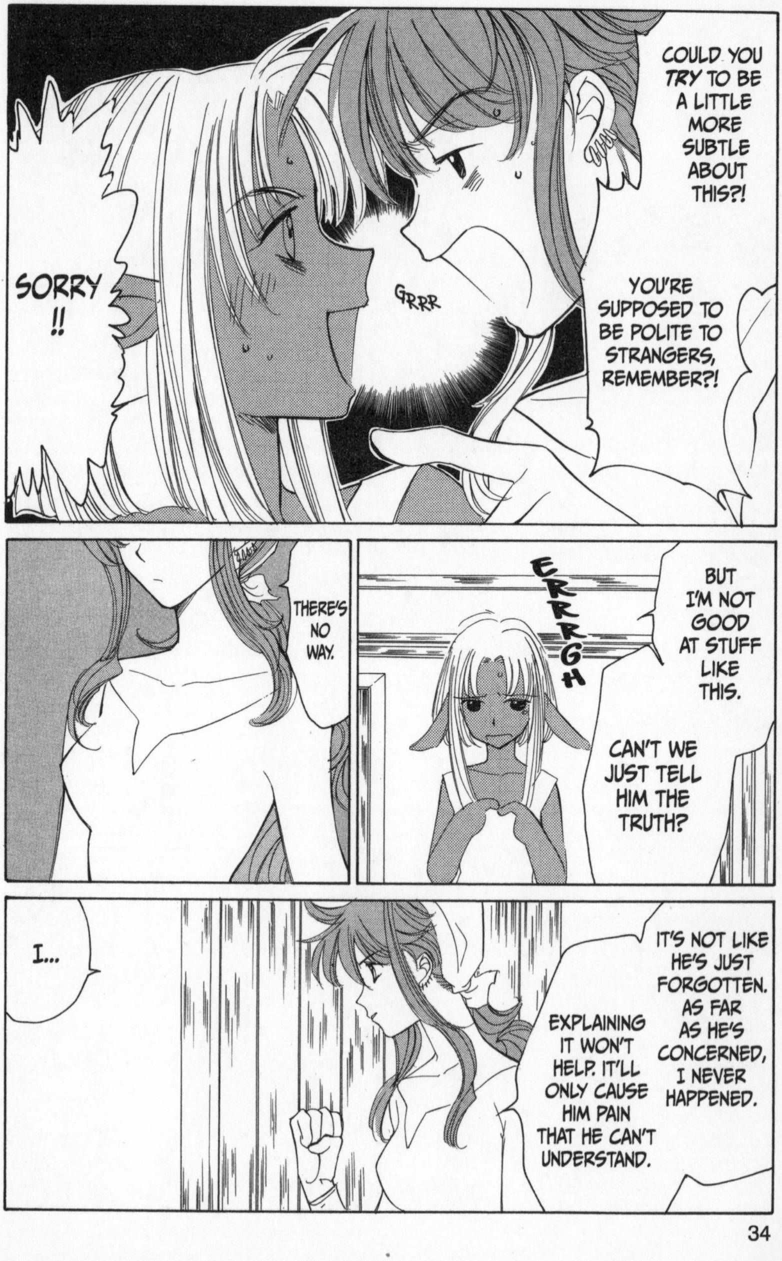
COULD YOU TRY TO BE A LITTLE MORE SUBTLE ABOUT THIS?!
YOU'RE SUPPOSED TO BE POLITE TO STRANGERS, REMEMBER?!
GRRR
SORRY !!
ERRRGH
BUT I'M NOT GOOD AT STUFF LIKE THIS.
CAN'T WE JUST TELL HIM THE TRUTH?
THERE'S NO WAY.
IT'S NOT LIKE HE'S JUST FORGOTTEN. AS FAR AS HE'S CONCERNED, I NEVER HAPPENED.
EXPLAINING IT WON'T HELP. IT'LL ONLY CAUSE HIM PAIN THAT HE CAN'T UNDERSTAND.
I...

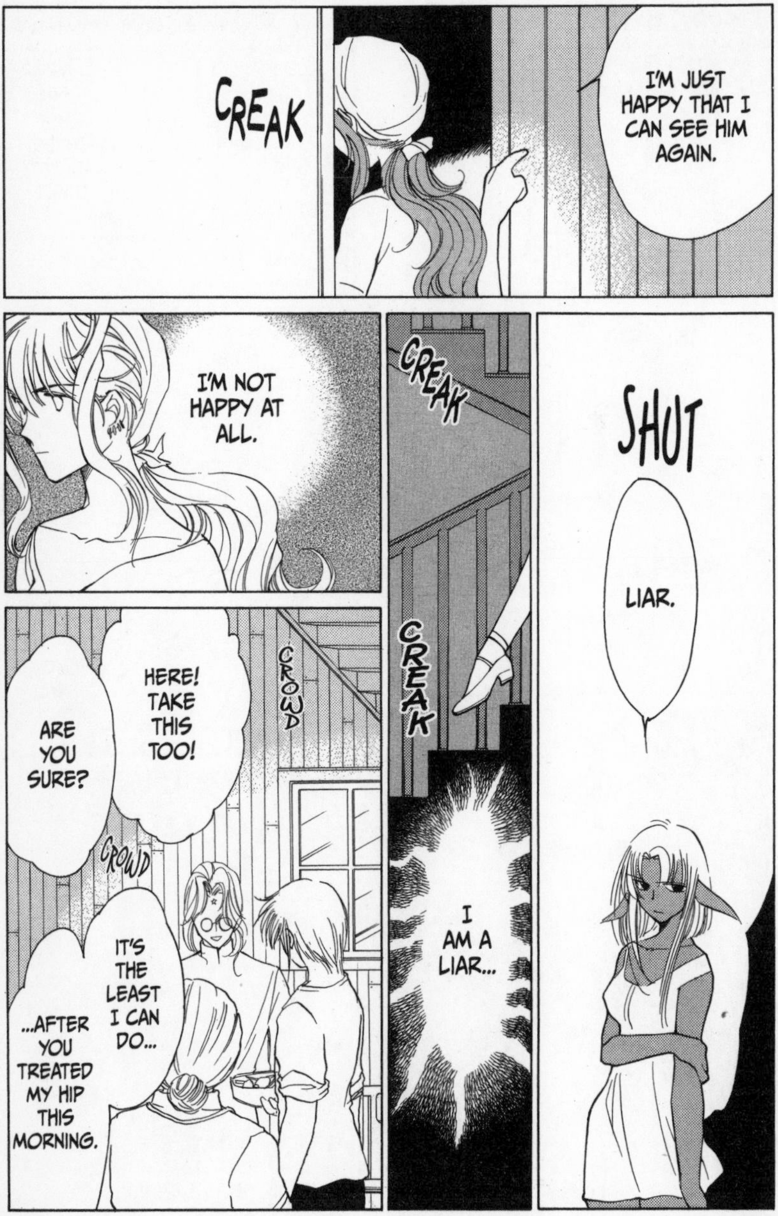
I'M JUST HAPPY THAT I CAN SEE HIM AGAIN.
CREAK
SHUT
LIAR.
CREAK
CREAK
I AM A LIAR...
I'M NOT HAPPY AT ALL.
CROWD
HERE! TAKE THIS TOO!
ARE YOU SURE?
CROWD
IT'S THE LEAST I CAN DO...
...AFTER YOU TREATED MY HIP THIS MORNING.

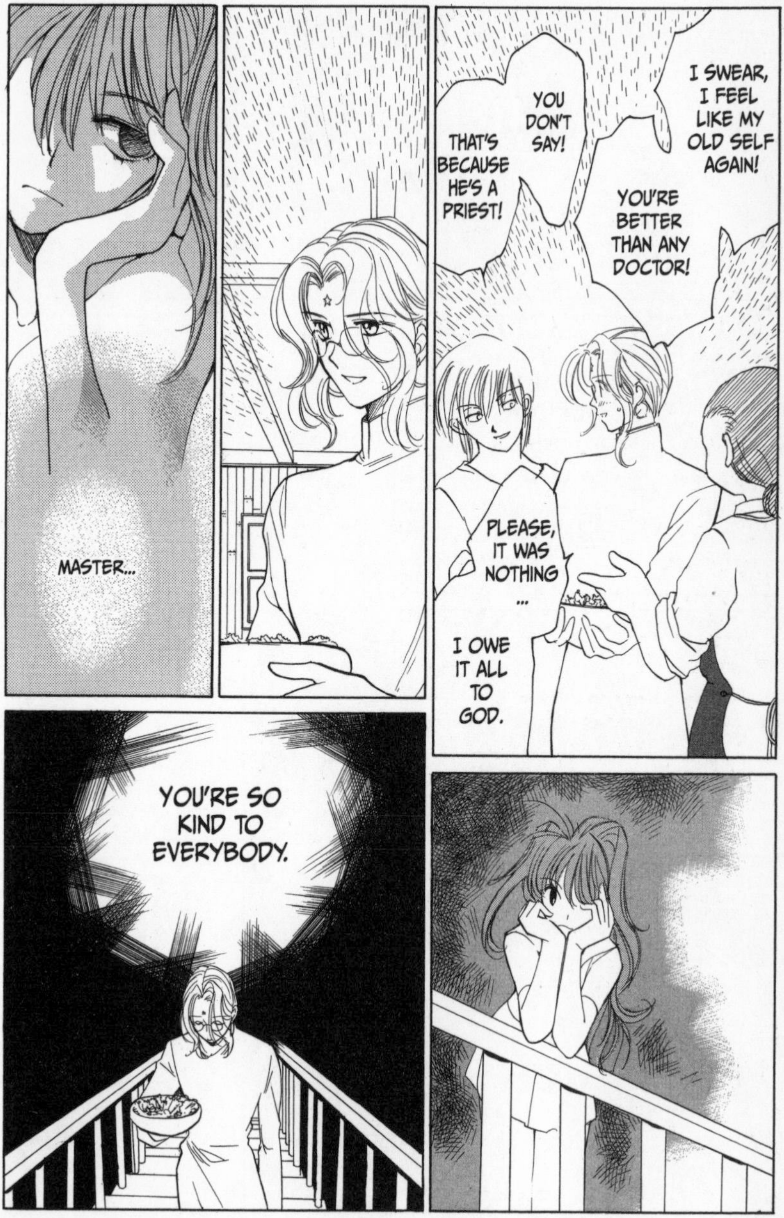
I SWEAR, I FEEL LIKE MY OLD SELF AGAIN!
YOU'RE BETTER THAN ANY DOCTOR!
YOU DON'T SAY!
THAT'S BECAUSE HE'S A PRIEST!
PLEASE, IT WAS NOTHING ...
I OWE IT ALL TO GOD.
MASTER...
YOU'RE SO KIND TO EVERYBODY.

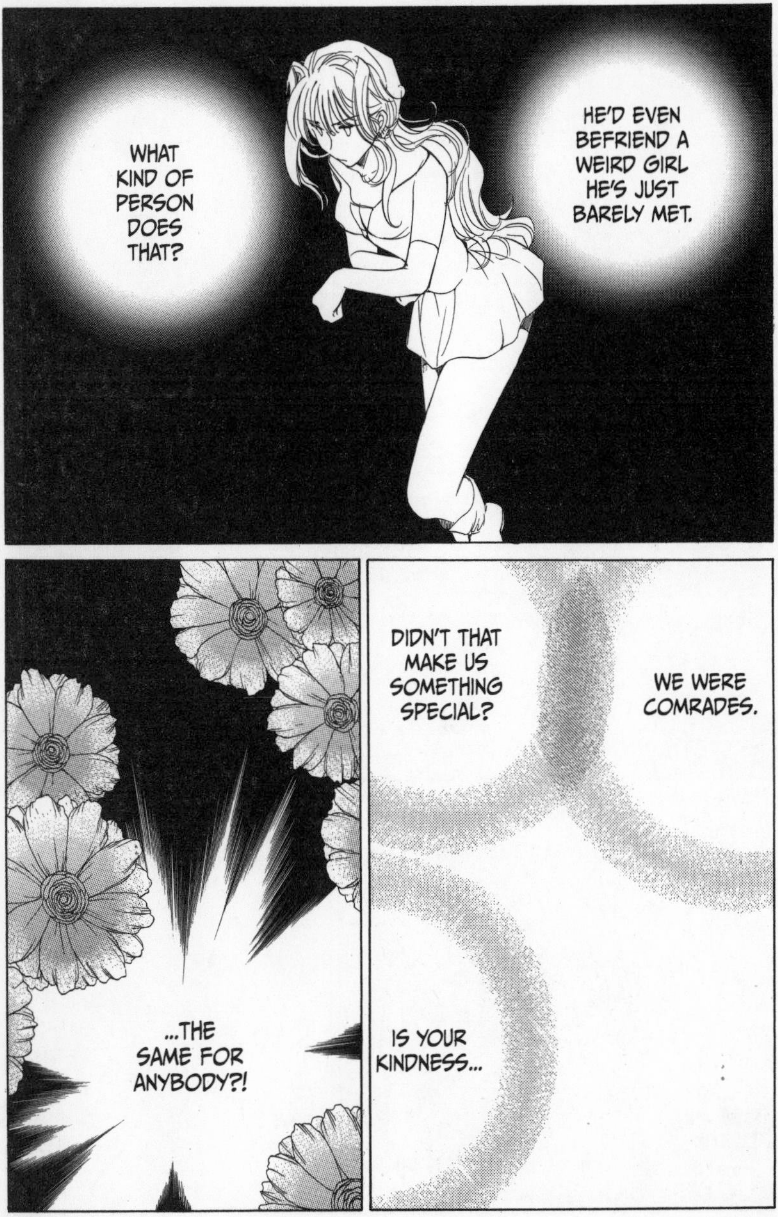
HE'D EVEN BEFRIEND A WEIRD GIRL HE'S JUST BARELY MET.
WHAT KIND OF PERSON DOES THAT?
WE WERE COMRADES.
DIDN'T THAT MAKE US SOMETHING SPECIAL?
IS YOUR KINDNESS...
...THE SAME FOR ANYBODY?!

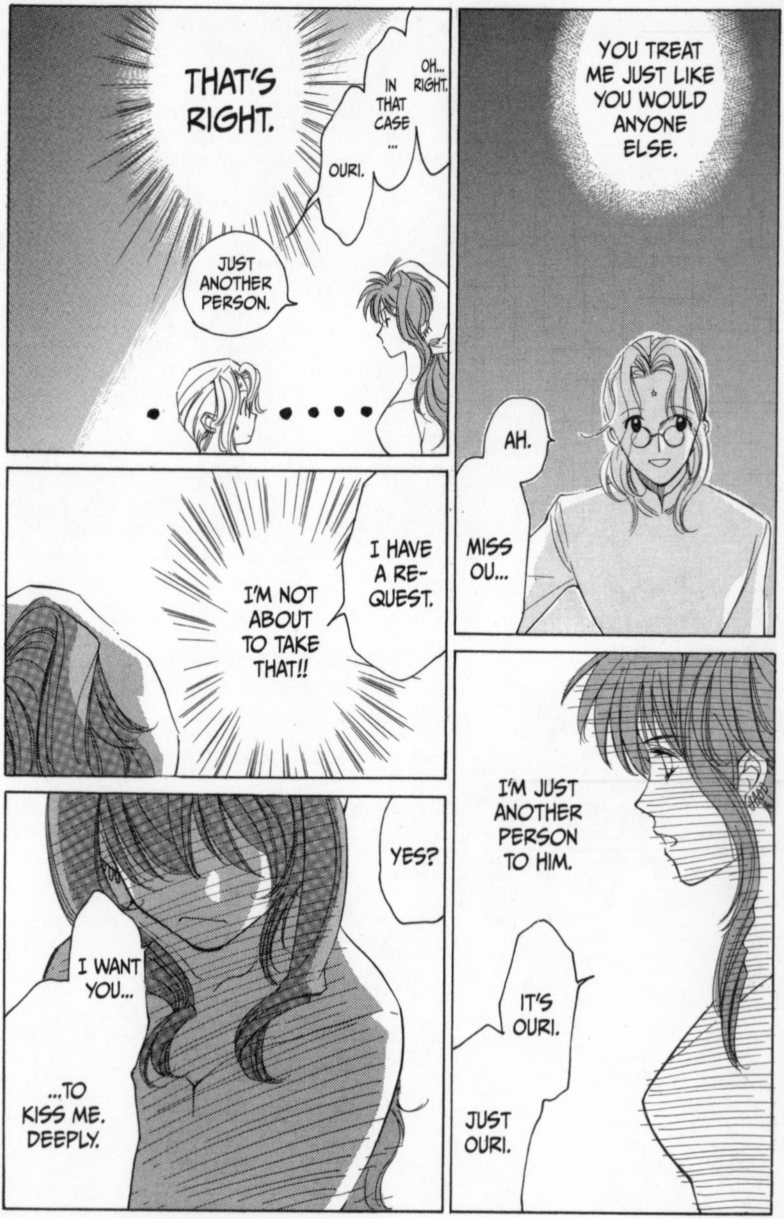

YOU TREAT ME JUST LIKE YOU WOULD ANYONE ELSE.
AH.
MISS OU...
I'M JUST ANOTHER PERSON TO HIM.
IT'S OURI.
JUST OURI.
OH... RIGHT.
IN THAT CASE ...
OURI.
JUST ANOTHER PERSON.
THAT'S RIGHT.
• ....
I HAVE A RE-QUEST.
I'M NOT ABOUT TO TAKE THAT!!
YES?
I WANT YOU...
...TO KISS ME. DEEPLY.

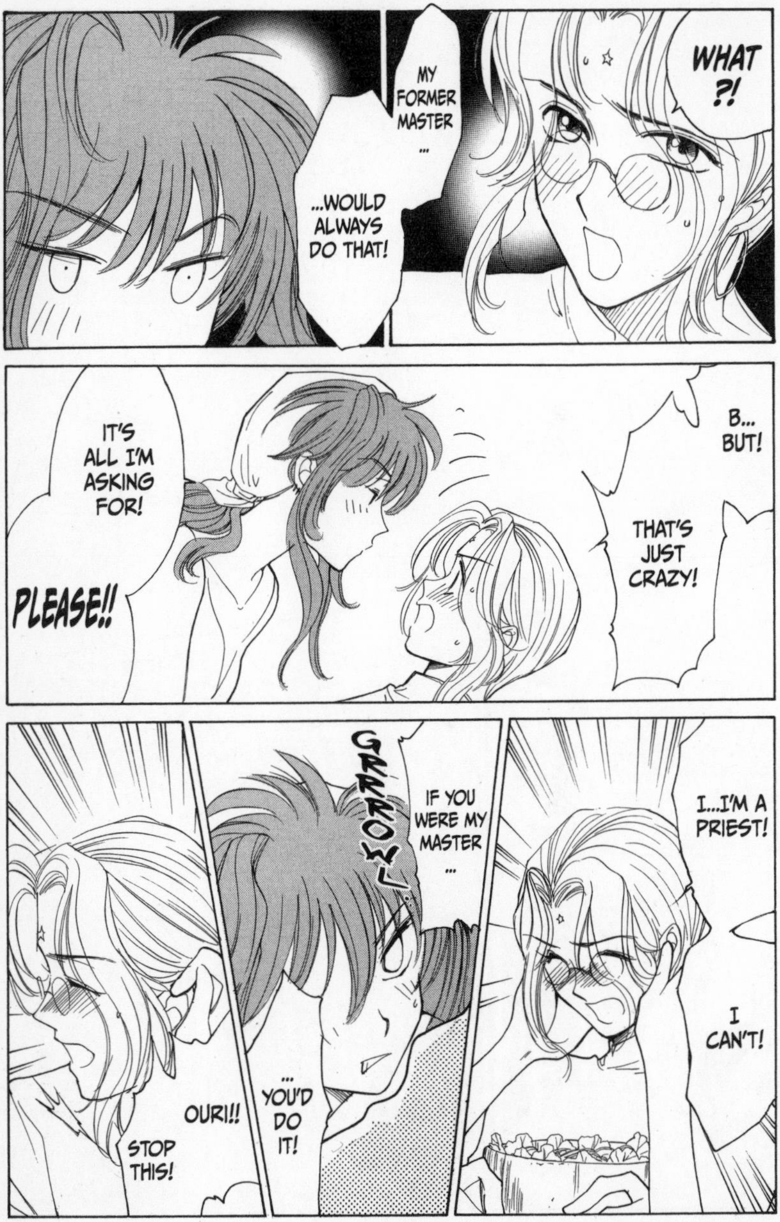
WHAT ?!
MY FORMER MASTER ...
...WOULD ALWAYS DO THAT!
B... BUT!
THAT'S JUST CRAZY!
IT'S ALL I'M ASKING FOR!
PLEASE!!
I...I'M A PRIEST!
I CAN'T!
GRRROWL
IF YOU WERE MY MASTER ...
... YOU'D DO IT!
OURI!!
STOP THIS!

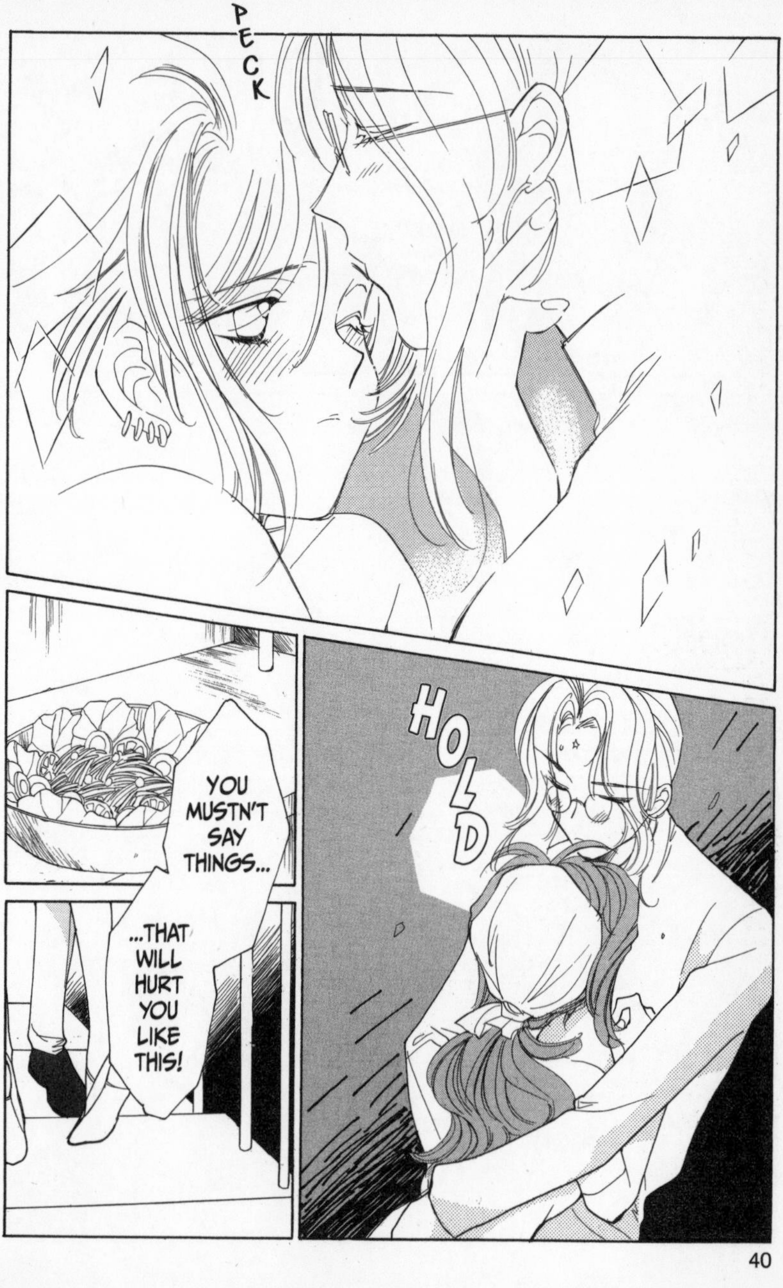
PECK
HOLD
YOU MUSTN'T SAY THINGS...
...THAT WILL HURT YOU LIKE THIS!

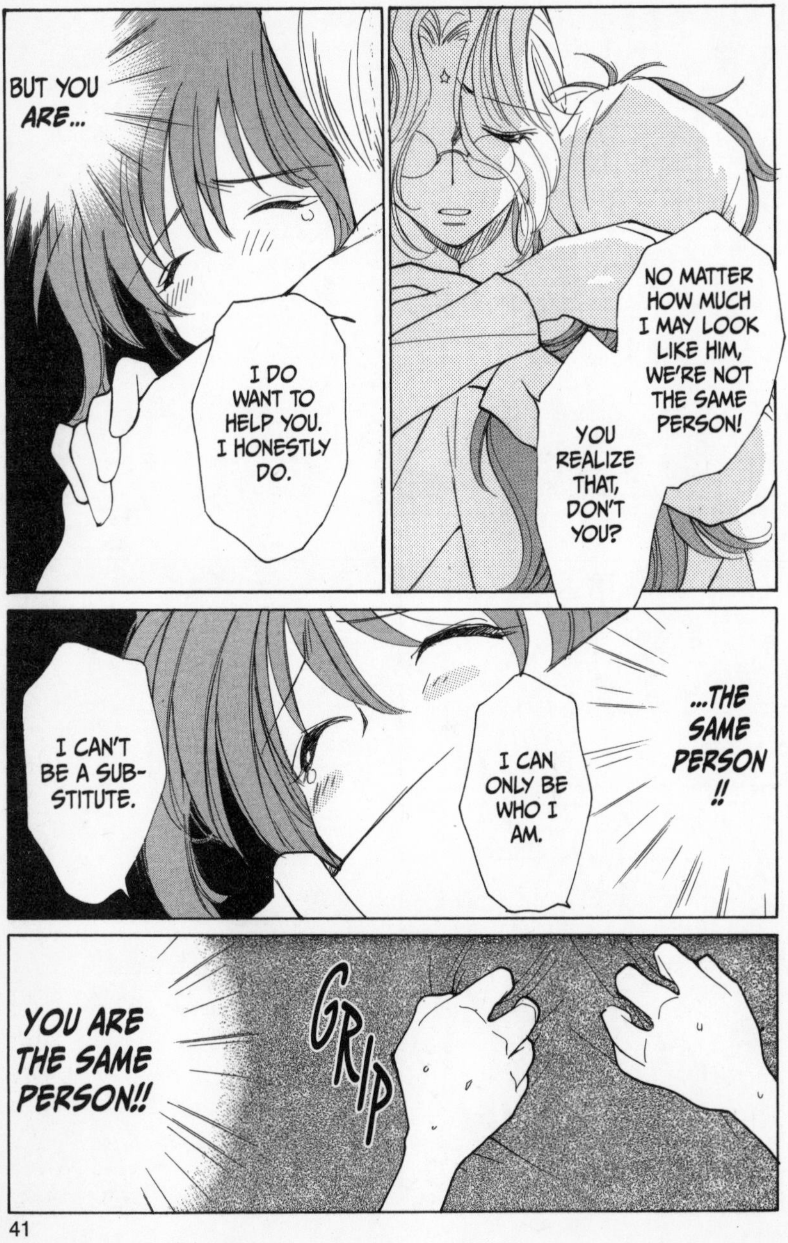
NO MATTER HOW MUCH I MAY LOOK LIKE HIM, WE'RE NOT THE SAME PERSON!
YOU REALIZE THAT, DON'T YOU?
I DO WANT TO HELP YOU. I HONESTLY DO.
BUT YOU ARE...
...THE SAME PERSON!!
I CAN ONLY BE WHO I AM.
I CAN'T BE A SUB-STITUTE.
GRIP
YOU ARE THE SAME PERSON!!

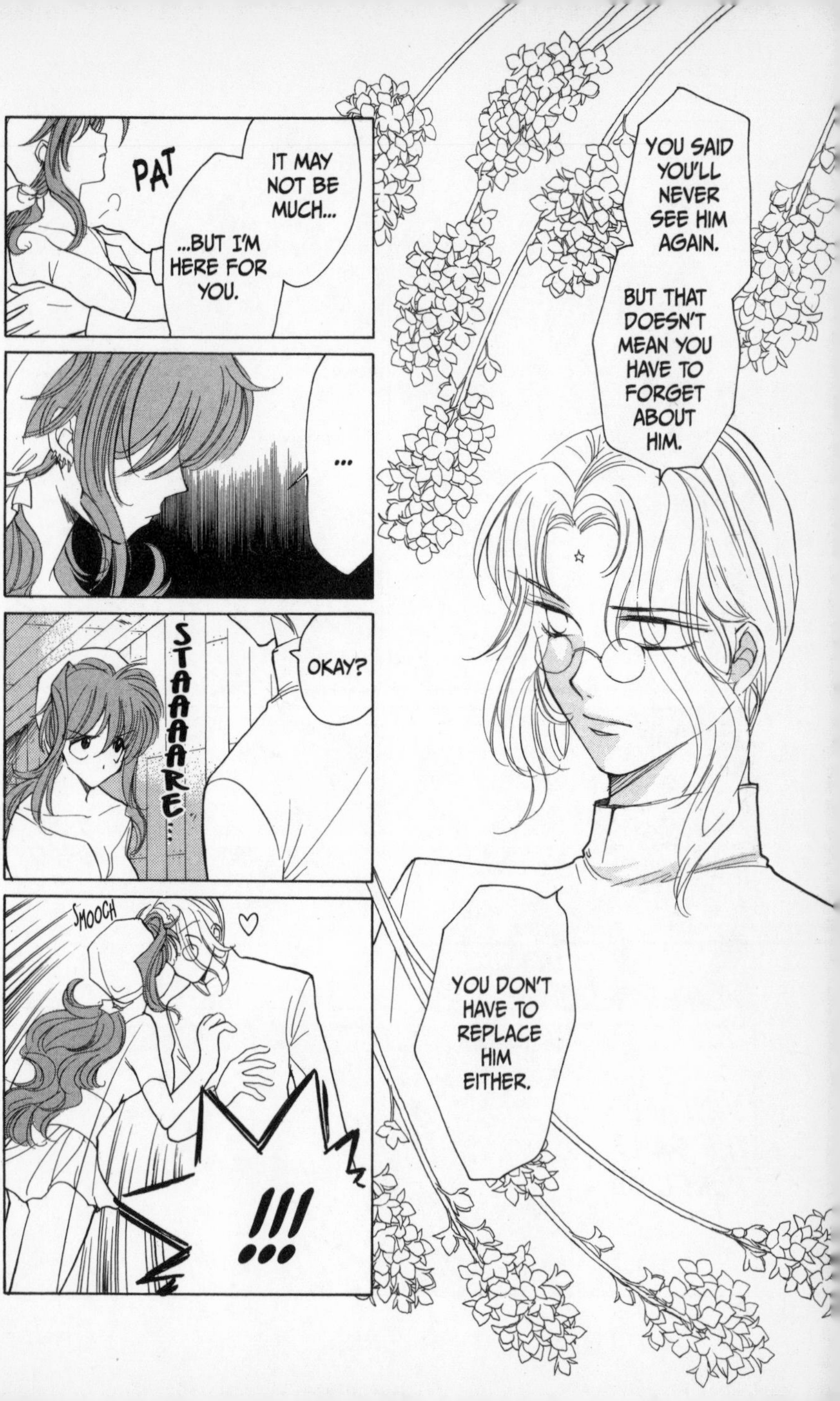
YOU SAID YOU'LL NEVER SEE HIM AGAIN.
BUT THAT DOESN'T MEAN YOU HAVE TO FORGET ABOUT HIM.
YOU DON'T HAVE TO REPLACE HIM EITHER.
IT MAY NOT BE MUCH...
...BUT I'M HERE FOR YOU.
PAT
...
OKAY?
STAAAAARE...
SMOOCH
!!!...

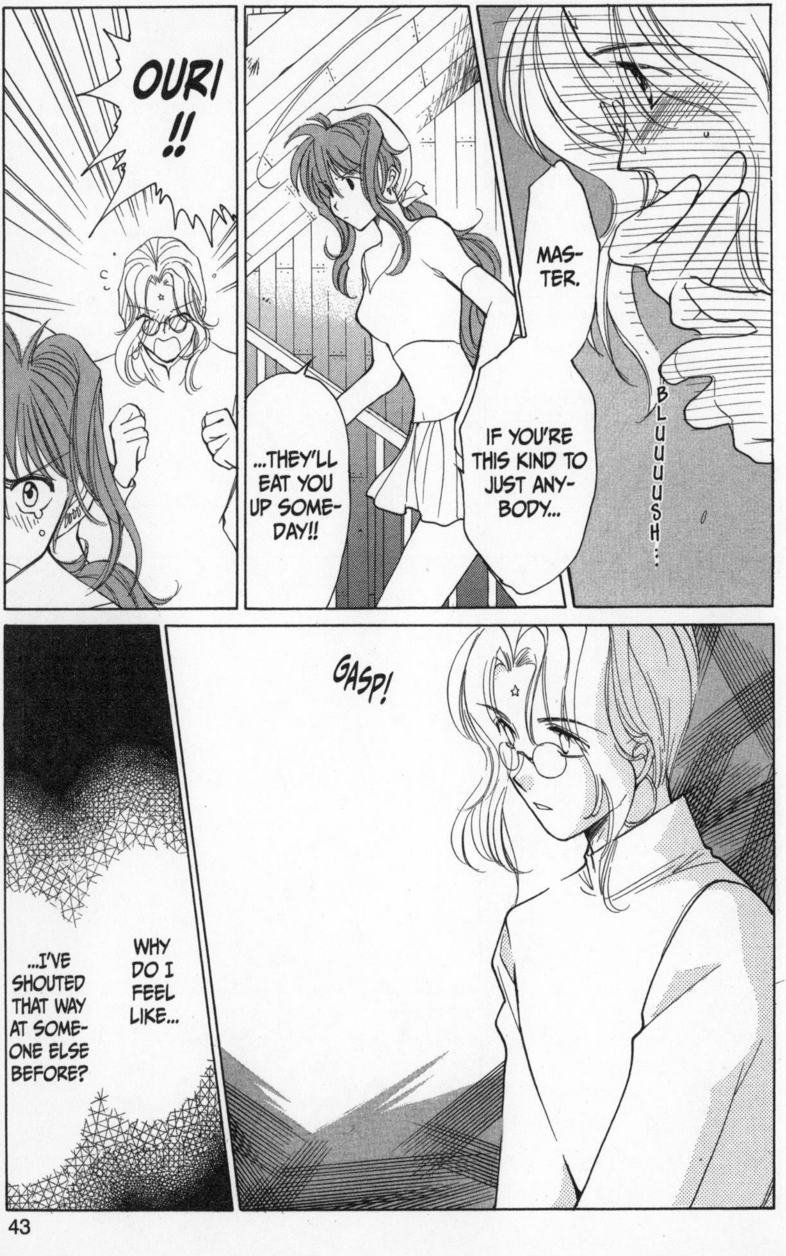
MASTER.
IF YOU'RE THIS KIND TO JUST ANYBODY...
BLUUUUSH...
...THEY'LL EAT YOU UP SOMEDAY!!
OURI !!
GASP!
WHY DO I FEEL LIKE...
...I'VE SHOUTED THAT WAY AT SOMEONE ELSE BEFORE?

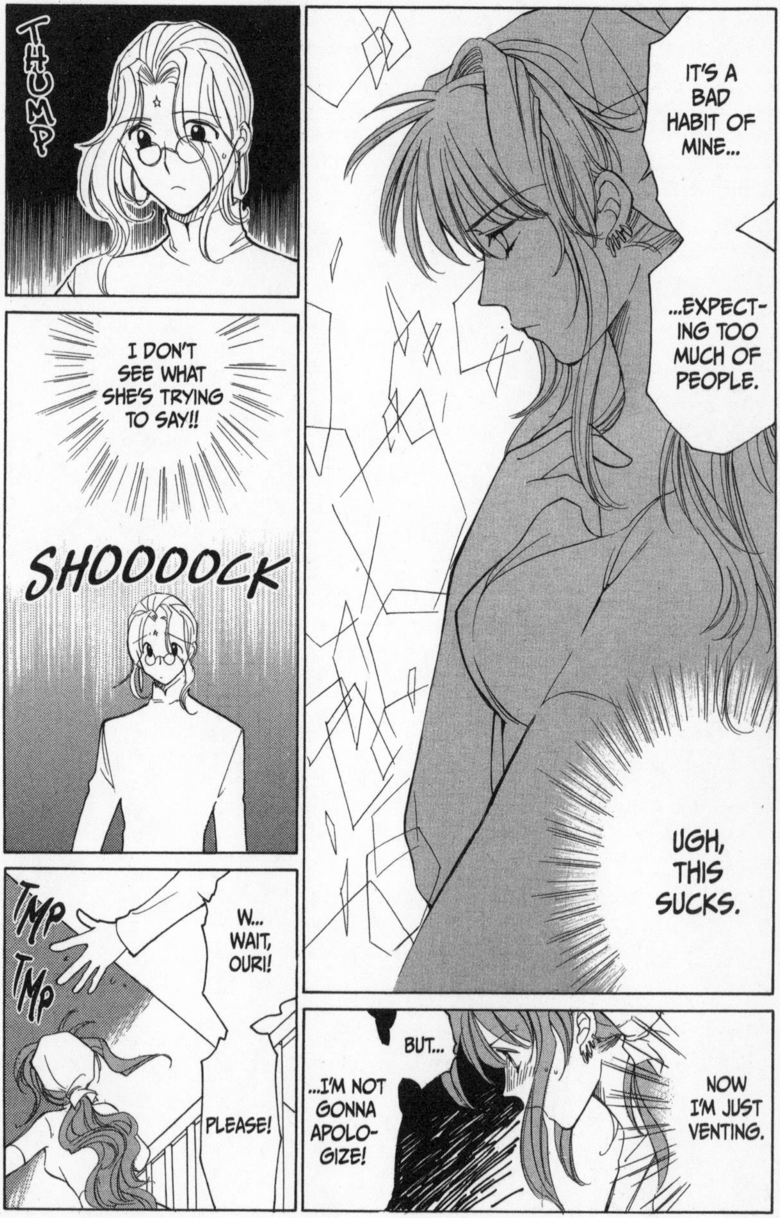
IT'S A BAD HABIT OF MINE...
...EXPECTING TOO MUCH OF PEOPLE.
UGH, THIS SUCKS.
THUMP
I DON'T SEE WHAT SHE'S TRYING TO SAY!!
SHOOOOCK
NOW I'M JUST VENTING.
BUT...
...I'M NOT GONNA APOLOGIZE!
TMP TMP
W... WAIT, OURI!
PLEASE!

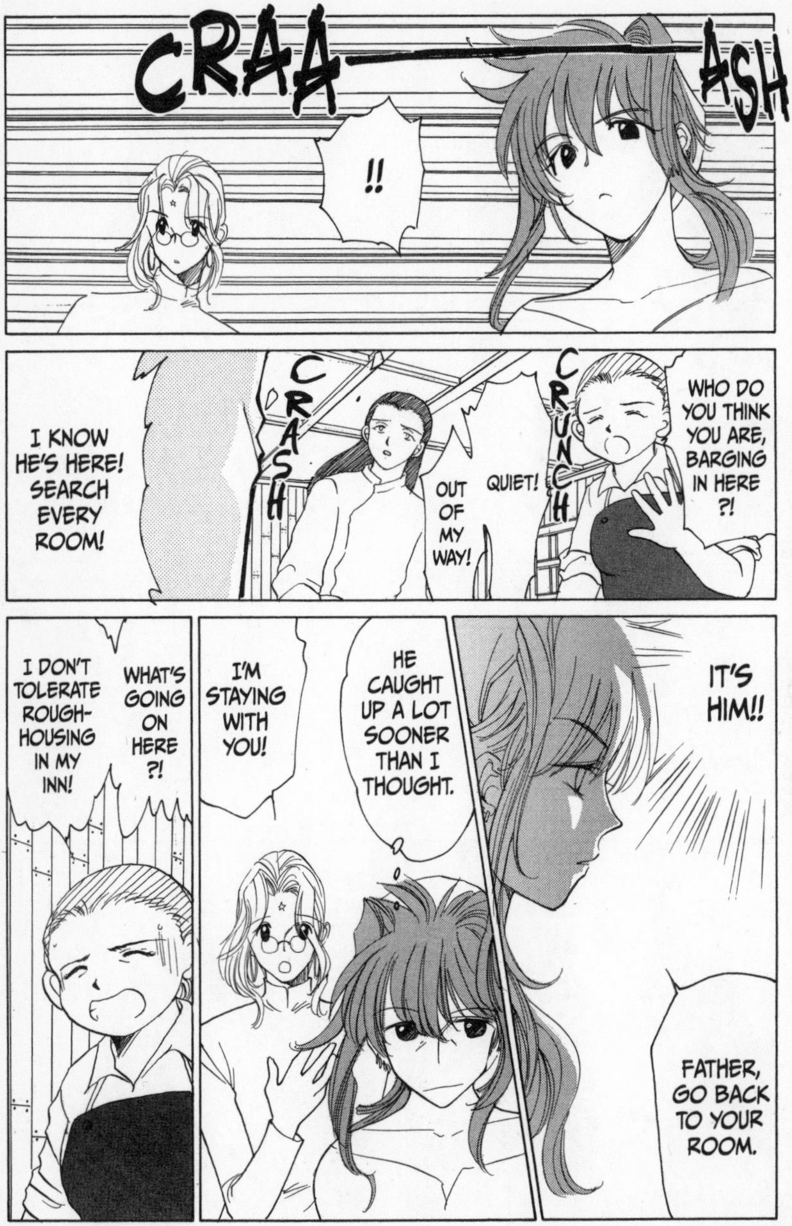
CRAA———ASH
!!
WHO DO YOU THINK YOU ARE, BARGING IN HERE ?!
CRUNCH
QUIET!
OUT OF MY WAY!
CRASH
I KNOW HE'S HERE! SEARCH EVERY ROOM!
IT'S HIM!!
FATHER, GO BACK TO YOUR ROOM.
HE CAUGHT UP A LOT SOONER THAN I THOUGHT.
I'M STAYING WITH YOU!
WHAT'S GOING ON HERE ?!
I DON'T TOLERATE ROUGH-HOUSING IN MY INN!

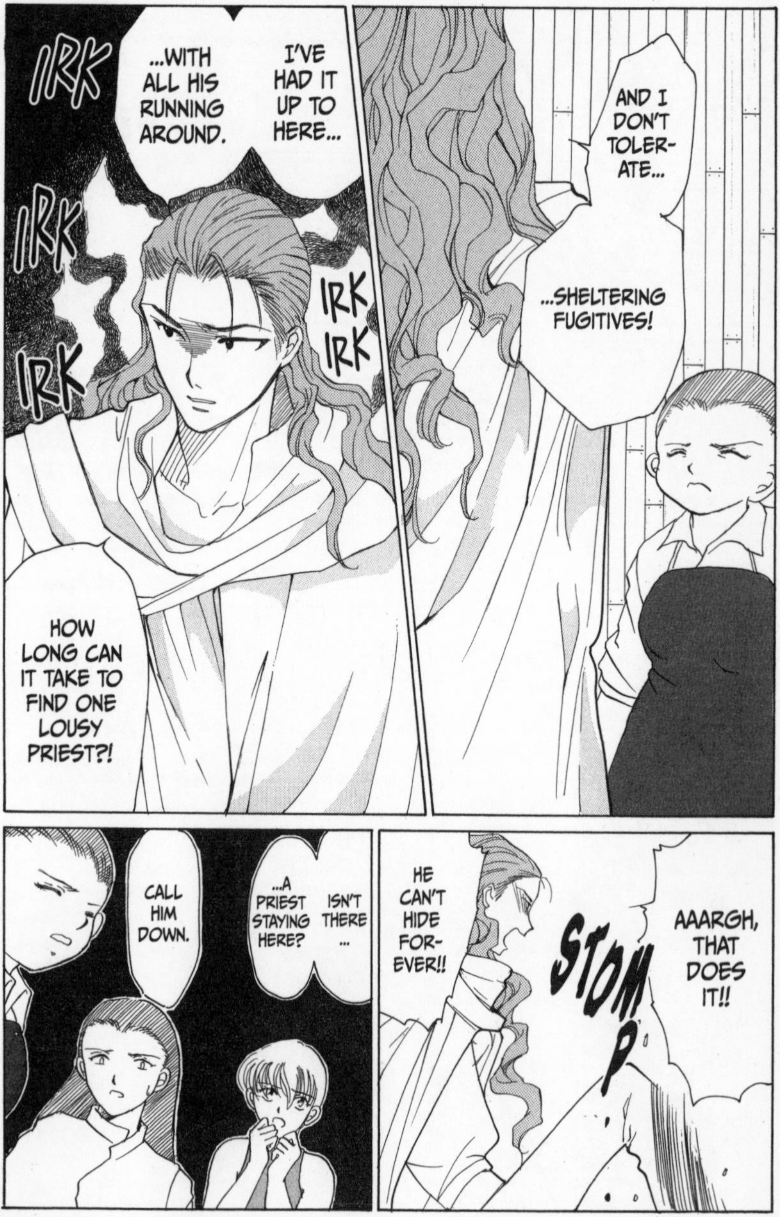
AND I DON'T TOLER-ATE...
...SHELTERING FUGITIVES!
I'VE HAD IT UP TO HERE...
...WITH ALL HIS RUNNING AROUND.
IRK
IRK
IRK
IRK IRK
HOW LONG CAN IT TAKE TO FIND ONE LOUSY PRIEST?!
AAARGH, THAT DOES IT!!
STOMP
HE CAN'T HIDE FOR-EVER!!
ISN'T THERE ...
...A PRIEST STAYING HERE?
CALL HIM DOWN.

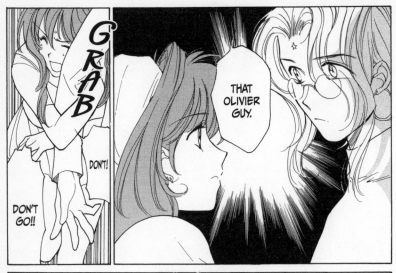

THAT OLIVIER GUY.
GRAB
DON'T!
DON'T GO!!
I'M THE ONE HE WANTS. IF I TURN MYSELF IN, HE'LL LEAVE THESE PEOPLE ALONE.
SQUEEEEZE
NO NO NO NO NO!
WE SHOULD TAKE THE BACK DOOR!
WHY?
HE'LL DO TERRIBLE THINGS TO YOU!
AND I DON'T THINK I HAVE WHAT IT TAKES TO FACE HIM RIGHT NOW!
I'm too vulnerable!
SOMETIMES IT'S BETTER TO FIGHT ANOTHER DAY!

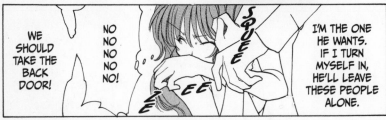

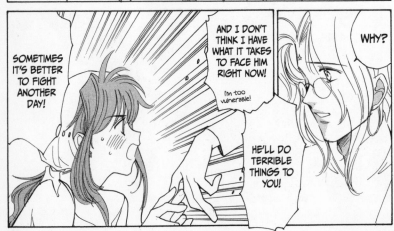

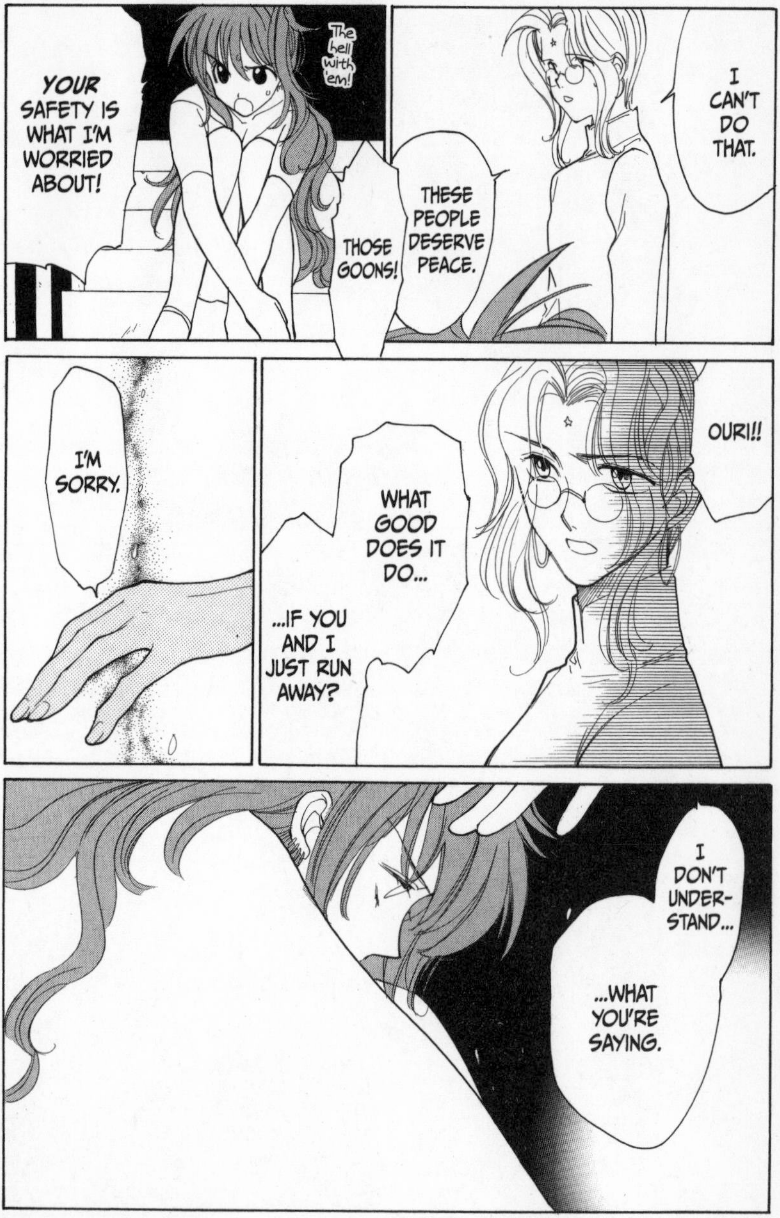
I CAN'T DO THAT.
THESE PEOPLE DESERVE PEACE.
THOSE GOONS!
The hell with 'em!
YOUR SAFETY IS WHAT I'M WORRIED ABOUT!
OURI!!
WHAT GOOD DOES IT DO...
...IF YOU AND I JUST RUN AWAY?
I'M SORRY.
I DON'T UNDER-STAND...
...WHAT YOU'RE SAYING.

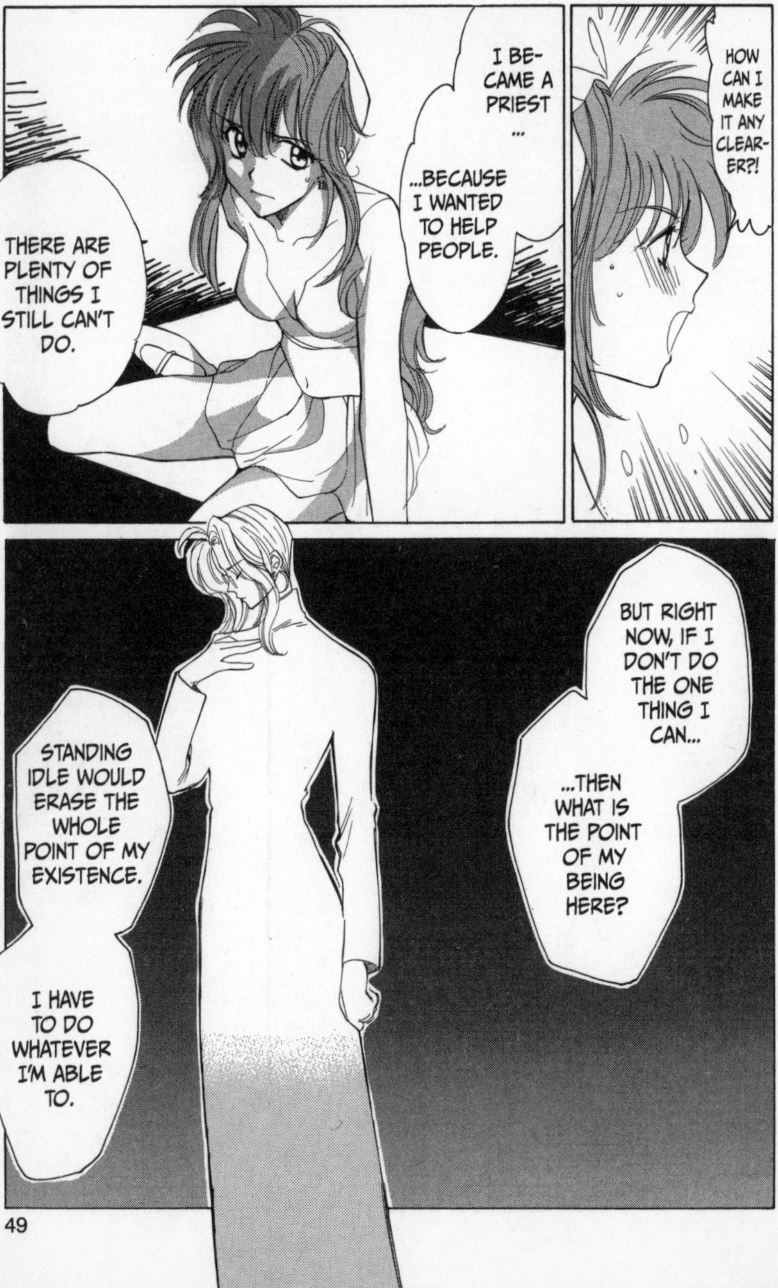
HOW CAN I MAKE IT ANY CLEARER?!
I BECAME A PRIEST ...
...BECAUSE I WANTED TO HELP PEOPLE.
THERE ARE PLENTY OF THINGS I STILL CAN'T DO.
BUT RIGHT NOW, IF I DON'T DO THE ONE THING I CAN...
...THEN WHAT IS THE POINT OF MY BEING HERE?
STANDING IDLE WOULD ERASE THE WHOLE POINT OF MY EXISTENCE.
I HAVE TO DO WHATEVER I'M ABLE TO.

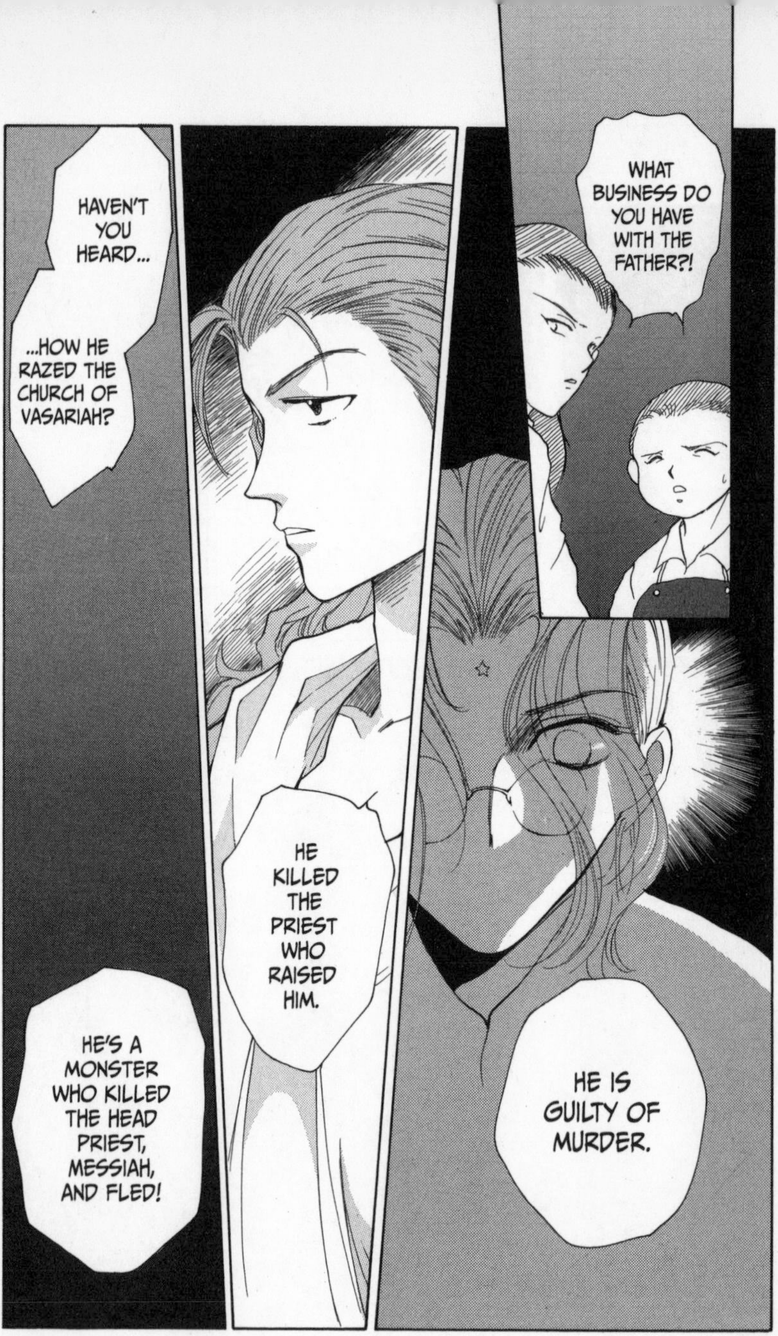
WHAT BUSINESS DO YOU HAVE WITH THE FATHER?!
HE IS GUILTY OF MURDER.
HE KILLED THE PRIEST WHO RAISED HIM.
HAVEN'T YOU HEARD...
...HOW HE RAZED THE CHURCH OF VASARIAH?
HE'S A MONSTER WHO KILLED THE HEAD PRIEST, MESSIAH, AND FLED!

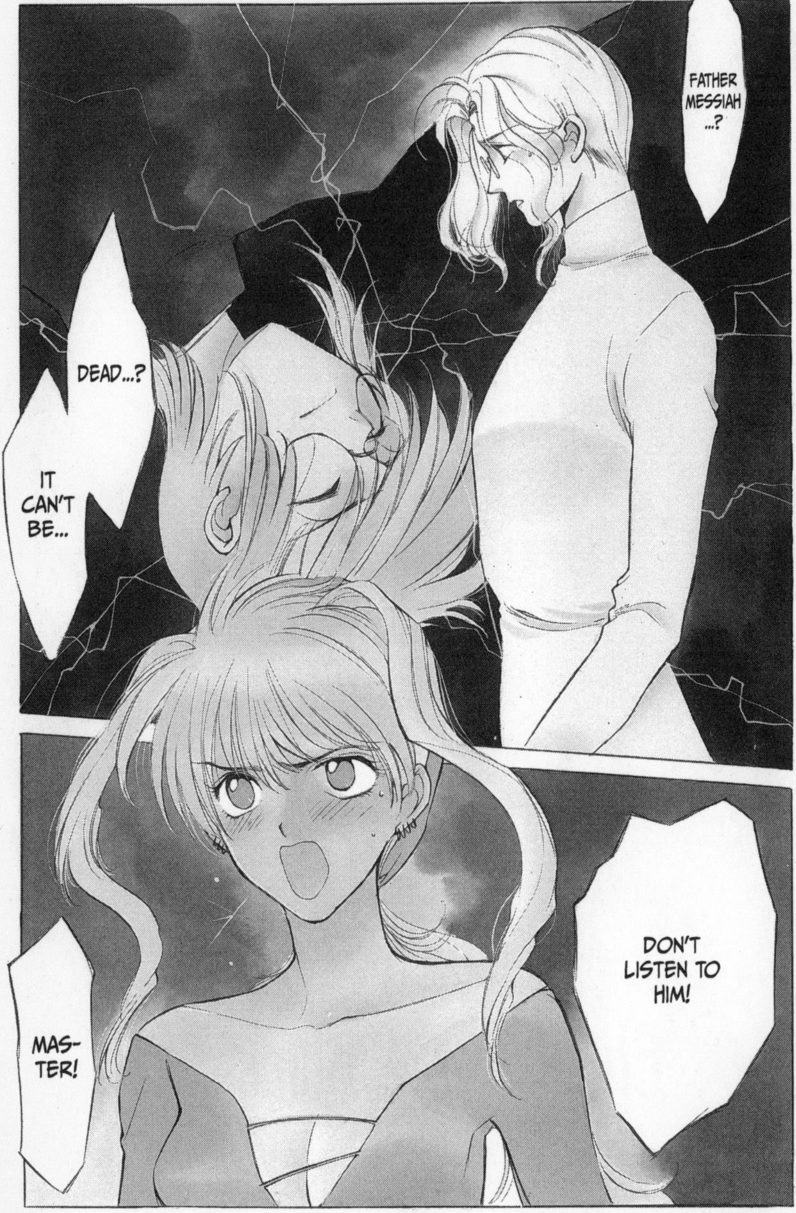
FATHER MESSIAH ...?
DEAD...?
IT CAN'T BE...
DON'T LISTEN TO HIM!
MAS-TER!

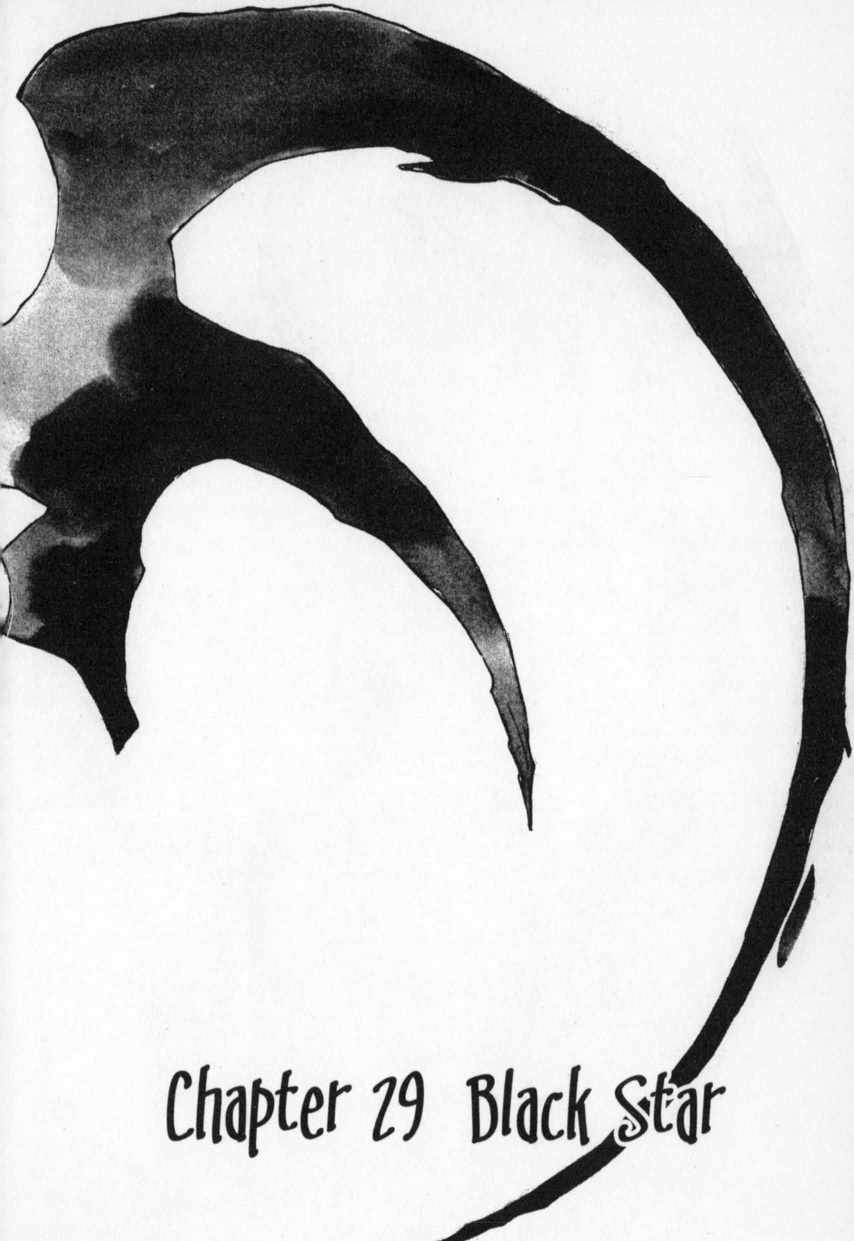

Chapter 29 Black Star

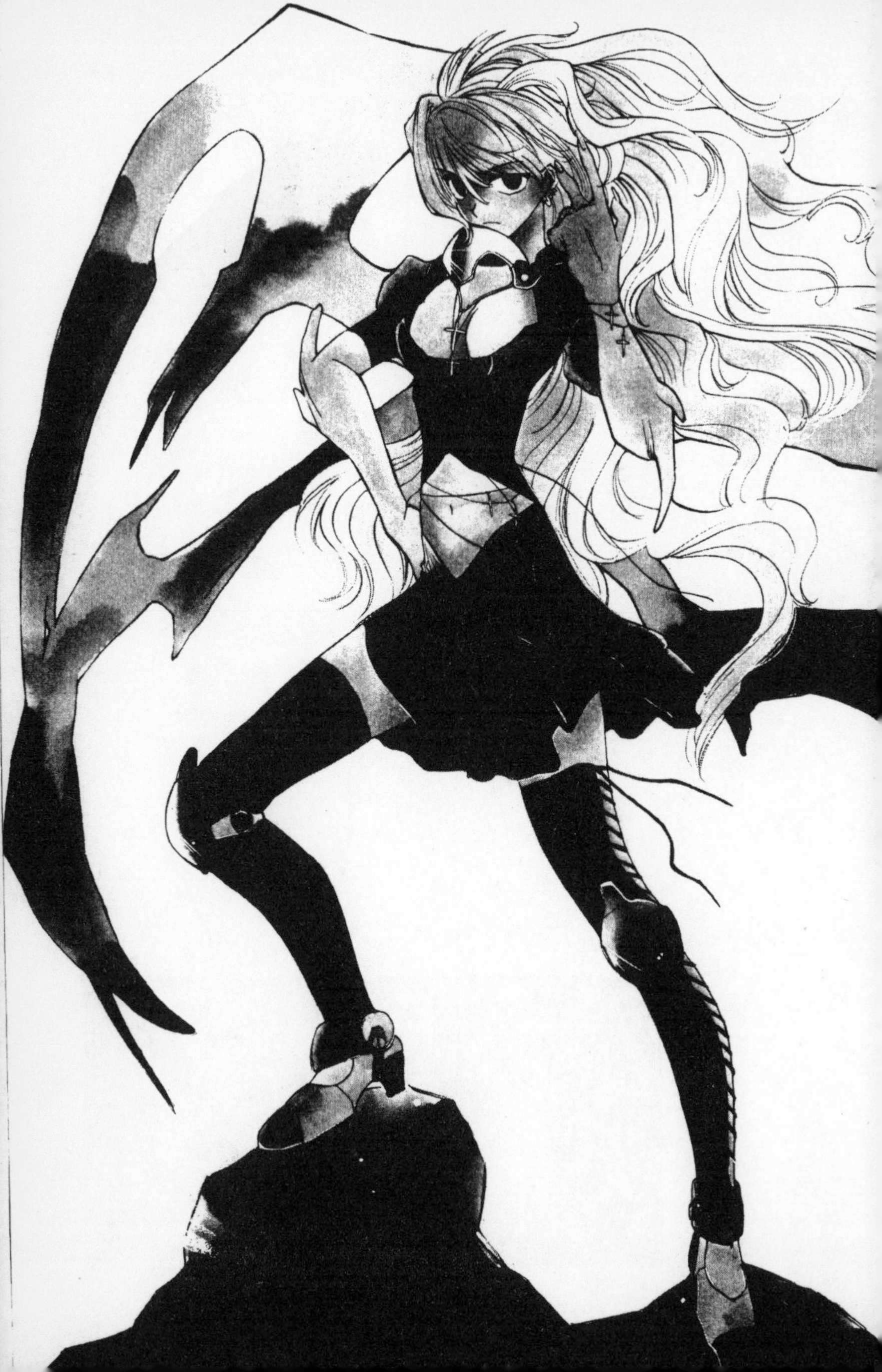

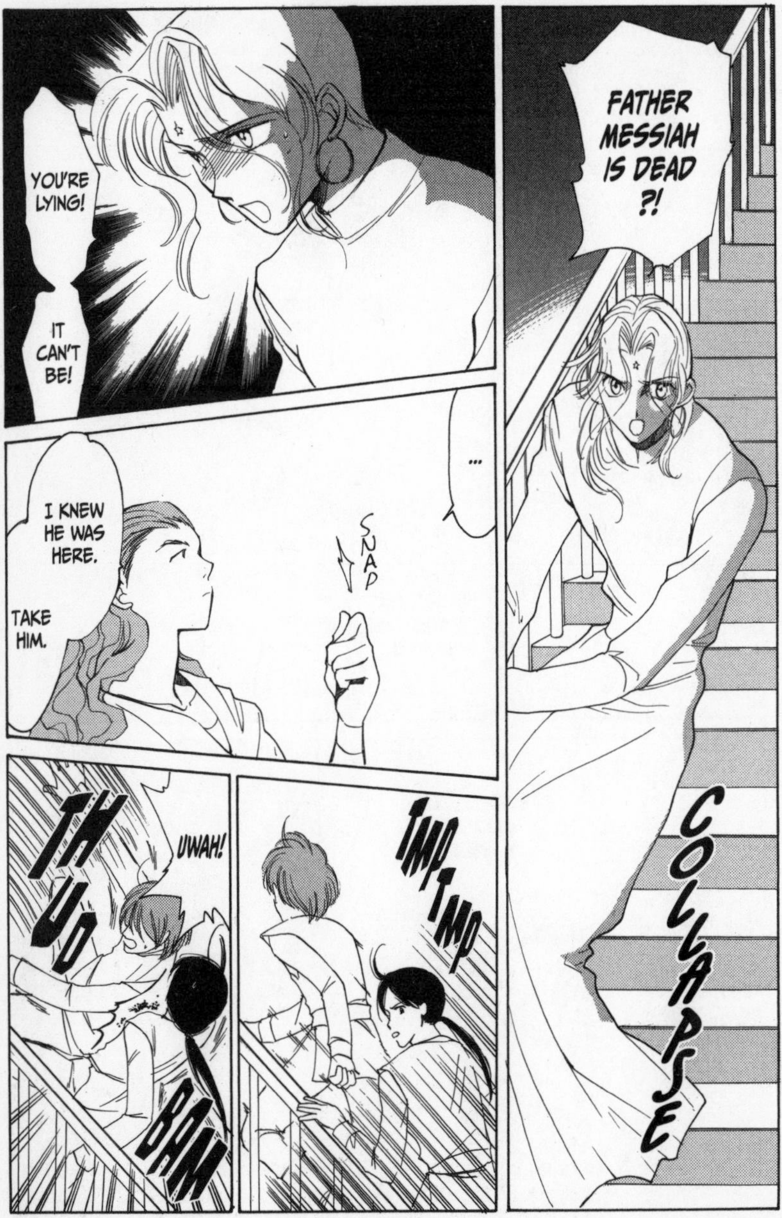
FATHER MESSIAH IS DEAD ?!
COLLAPSE
YOU'RE LYING!
IT CAN'T BE!
...
SNAP
I KNEW HE WAS HERE.
TAKE HIM.
TMP TMP TMP
UWAH!
THUD
BAM

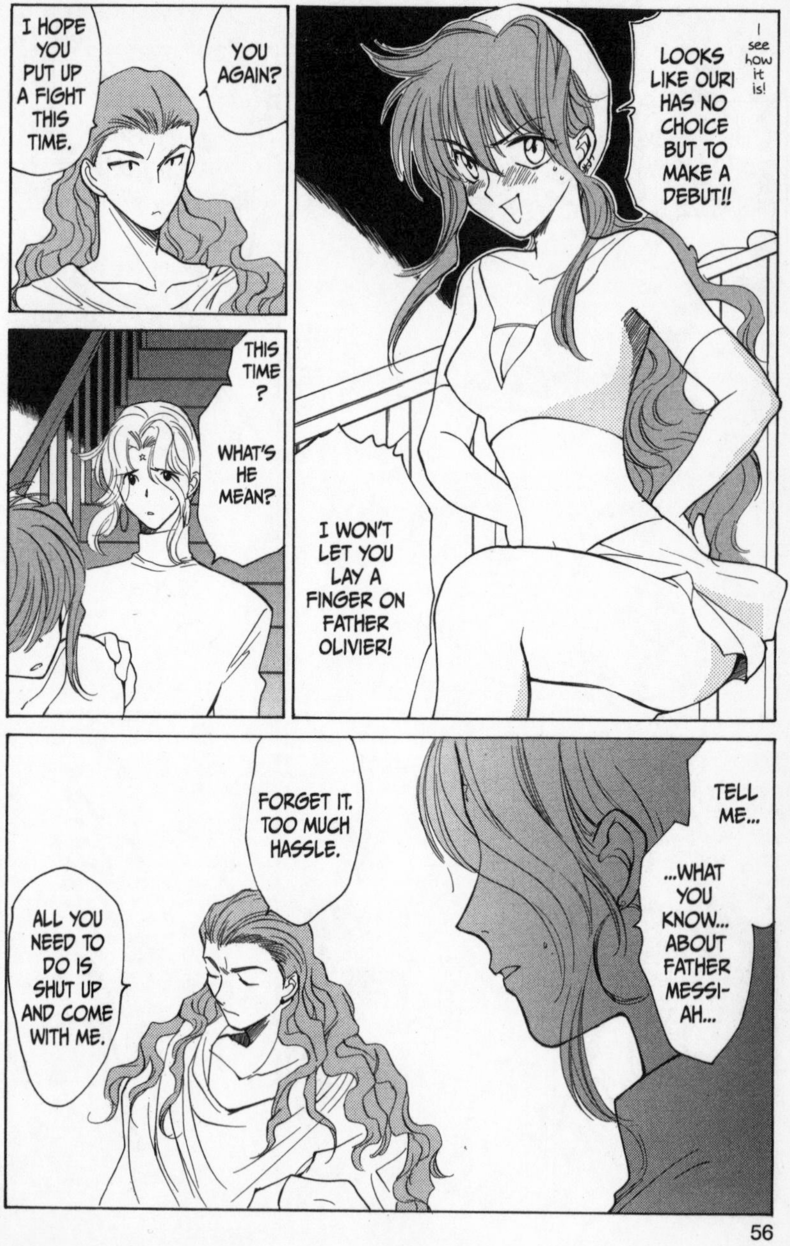
LOOKS LIKE OURI HAS NO CHOICE BUT TO MAKE A DEBUT!!
I see how it is!
I WON'T LET YOU LAY A FINGER ON FATHER OLIVIER!
YOU AGAIN?
I HOPE YOU PUT UP A FIGHT THIS TIME.
THIS TIME?
WHAT'S HE MEAN?
TELL ME...
...WHAT YOU KNOW... ABOUT FATHER MESSI-AH...
FORGET IT. TOO MUCH HASSLE.
ALL YOU NEED TO DO IS SHUT UP AND COME WITH ME.

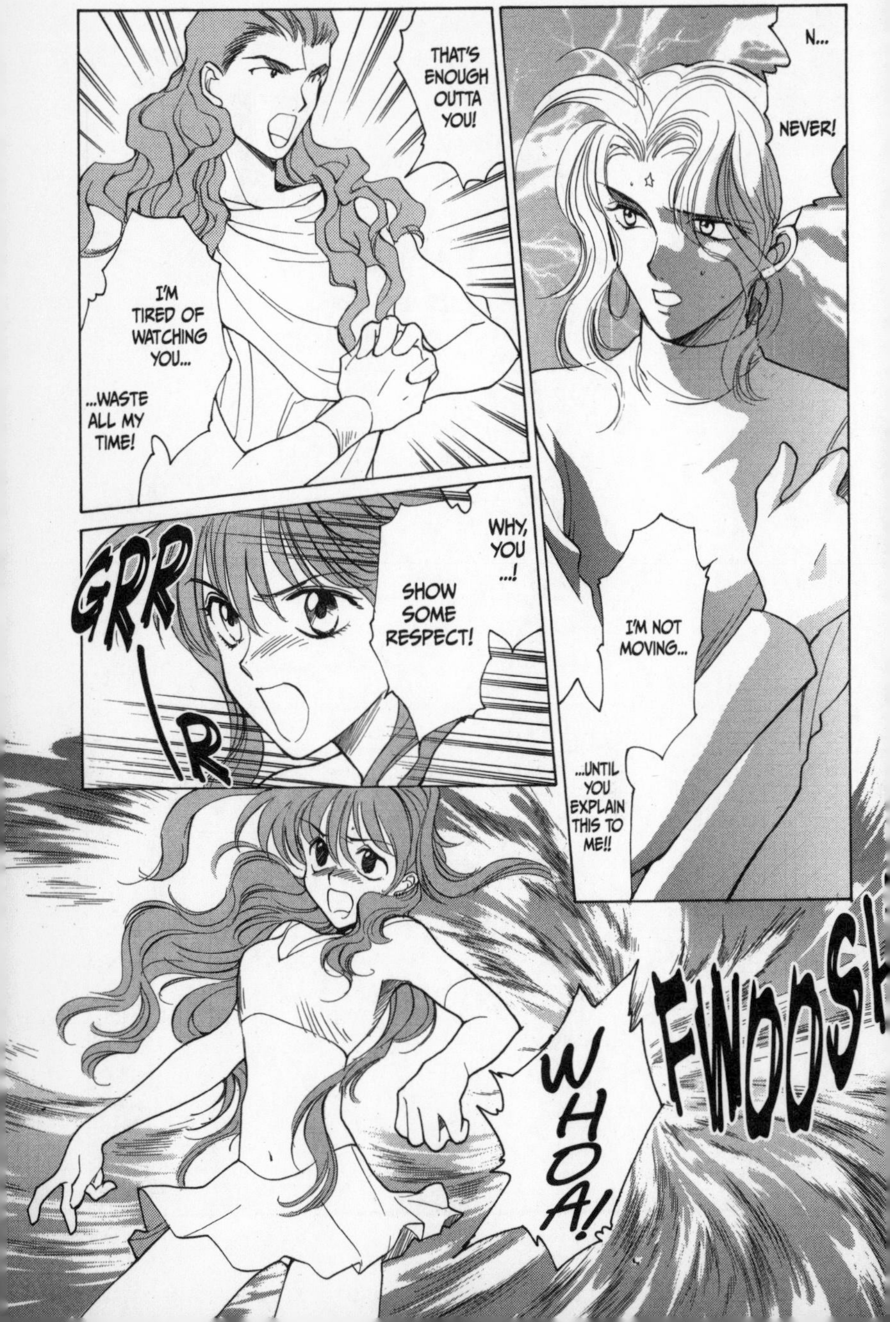
N...
NEVER!
I'M NOT MOVING...
...UNTIL YOU EXPLAIN THIS TO ME!!
THAT'S ENOUGH OUTTA YOU!
I'M TIRED OF WATCHING YOU...
...WASTE ALL MY TIME!
WHY, YOU ...!
SHOW SOME RESPECT!
GRRR
FWOOSH
WHOA!

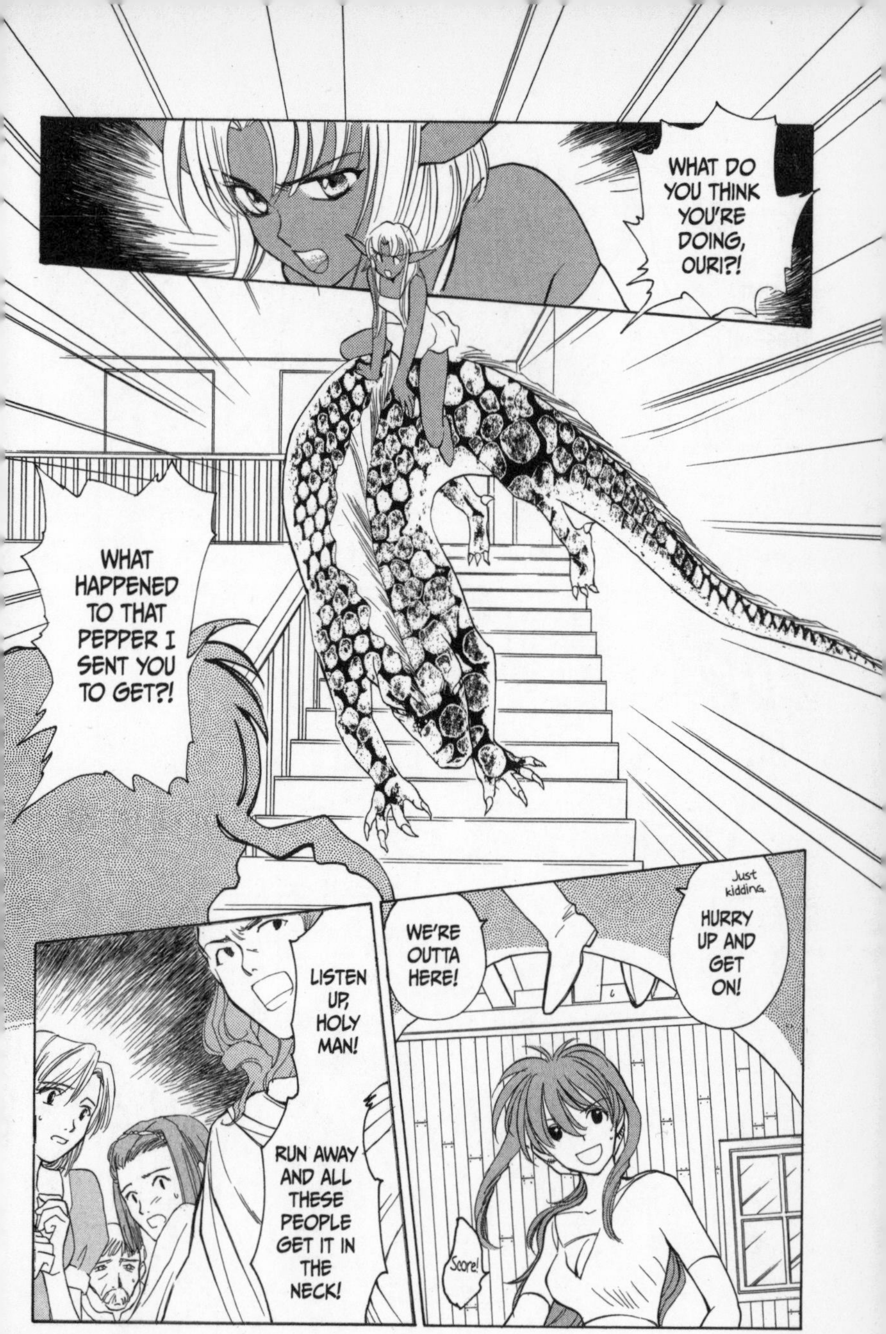
WHAT DO YOU THINK YOU'RE DOING, OURI?!
WHAT HAPPENED TO THAT PEPPER I SENT YOU TO GET?!
Just kidding.
HURRY UP AND GET ON!
WE'RE OUTTA HERE!
Score!
LISTEN UP, HOLY MAN!
RUN AWAY AND ALL THESE PEOPLE GET IT IN THE NECK!

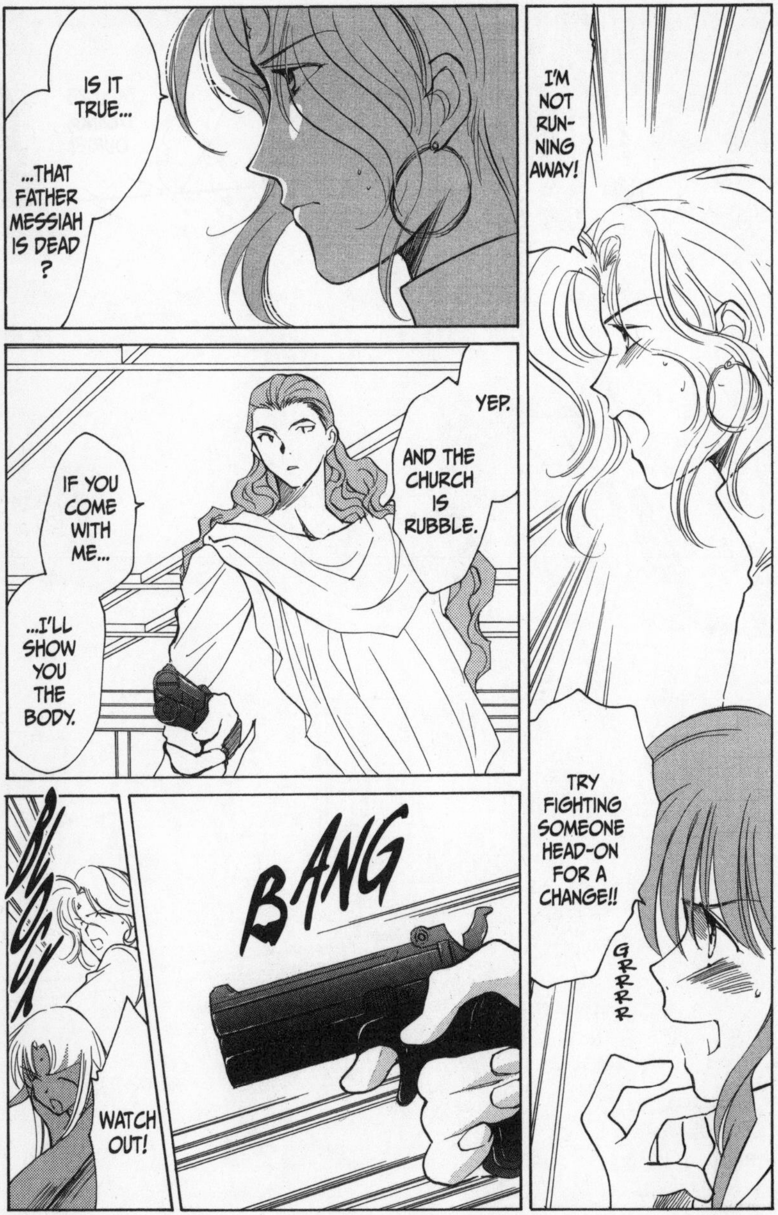
I'M NOT RUNNING AWAY!
IS IT TRUE...
...THAT FATHER MESSIAH IS DEAD?
YEP.
AND THE CHURCH IS RUBBLE.
IF YOU COME WITH ME...
...I'LL SHOW YOU THE BODY.
TRY FIGHTING SOMEONE HEAD-ON FOR A CHANGE!!
GRRRR
BANG
WATCH OUT!

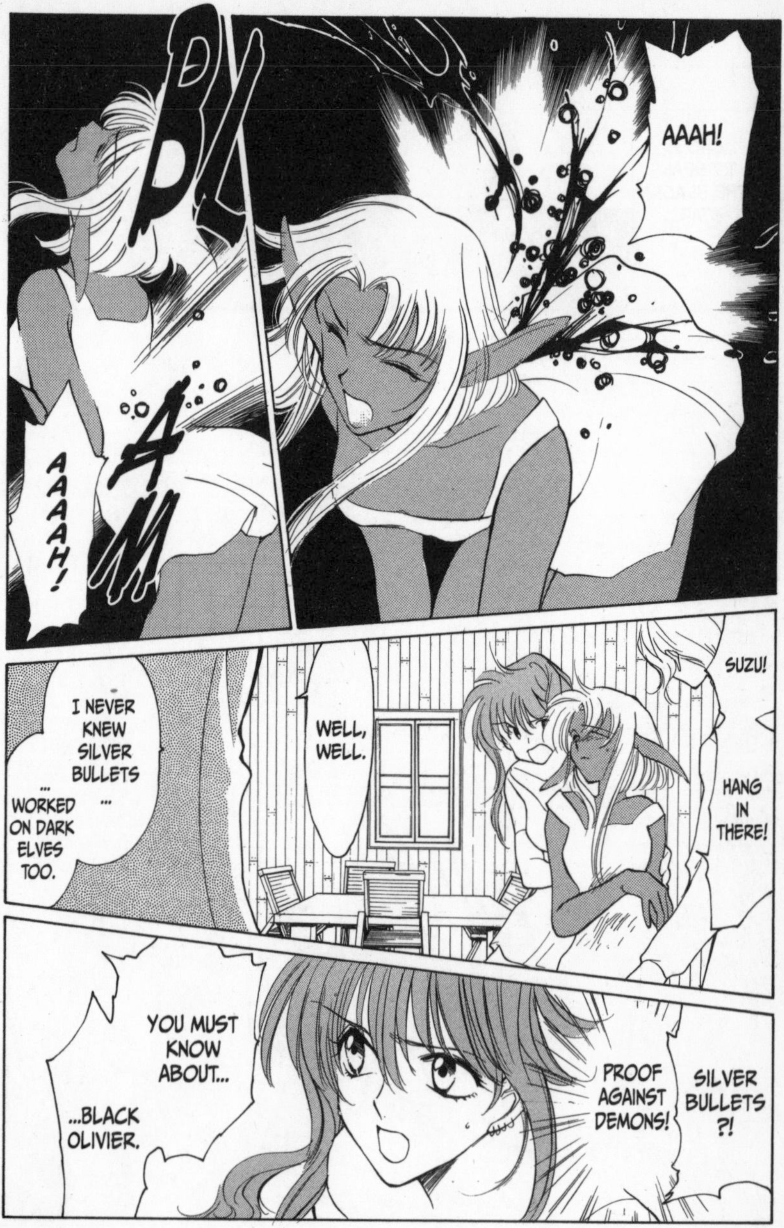
AAAH!
BAM
AAAAH!
SUZU!
HANG IN THERE!
WELL, WELL.
I NEVER KNEW SILVER BULLETS ...
... WORKED ON DARK ELVES TOO.
SILVER BULLETS ?!
PROOF AGAINST DEMONS!
YOU MUST KNOW ABOUT...
...BLACK OLIVIER.

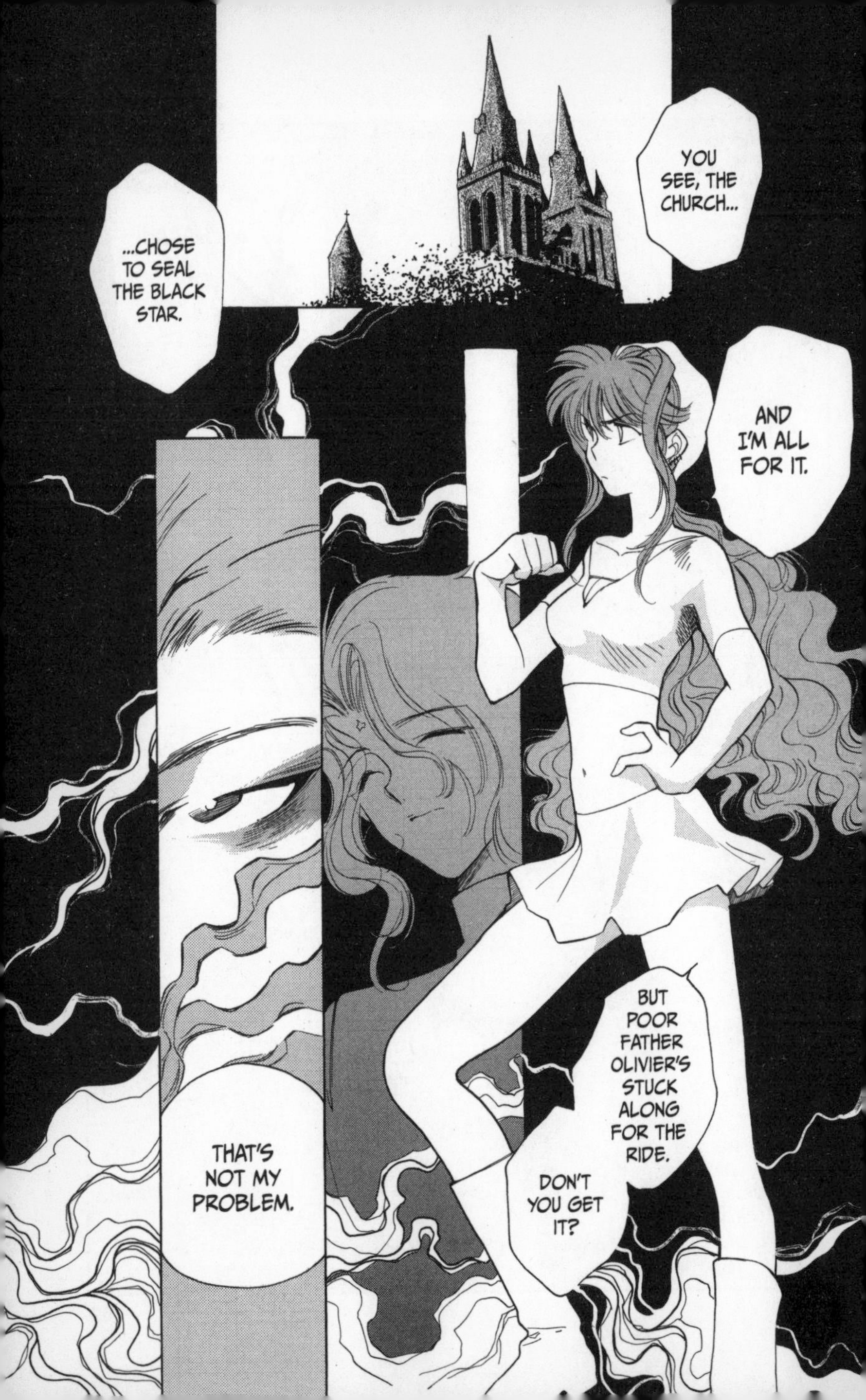
YOU SEE, THE CHURCH...
...CHOSE TO SEAL THE BLACK STAR.
AND I'M ALL FOR IT.
BUT POOR FATHER OLIVIER'S STUCK ALONG FOR THE RIDE.
DON'T YOU GET IT?
THAT'S NOT MY PROBLEM.

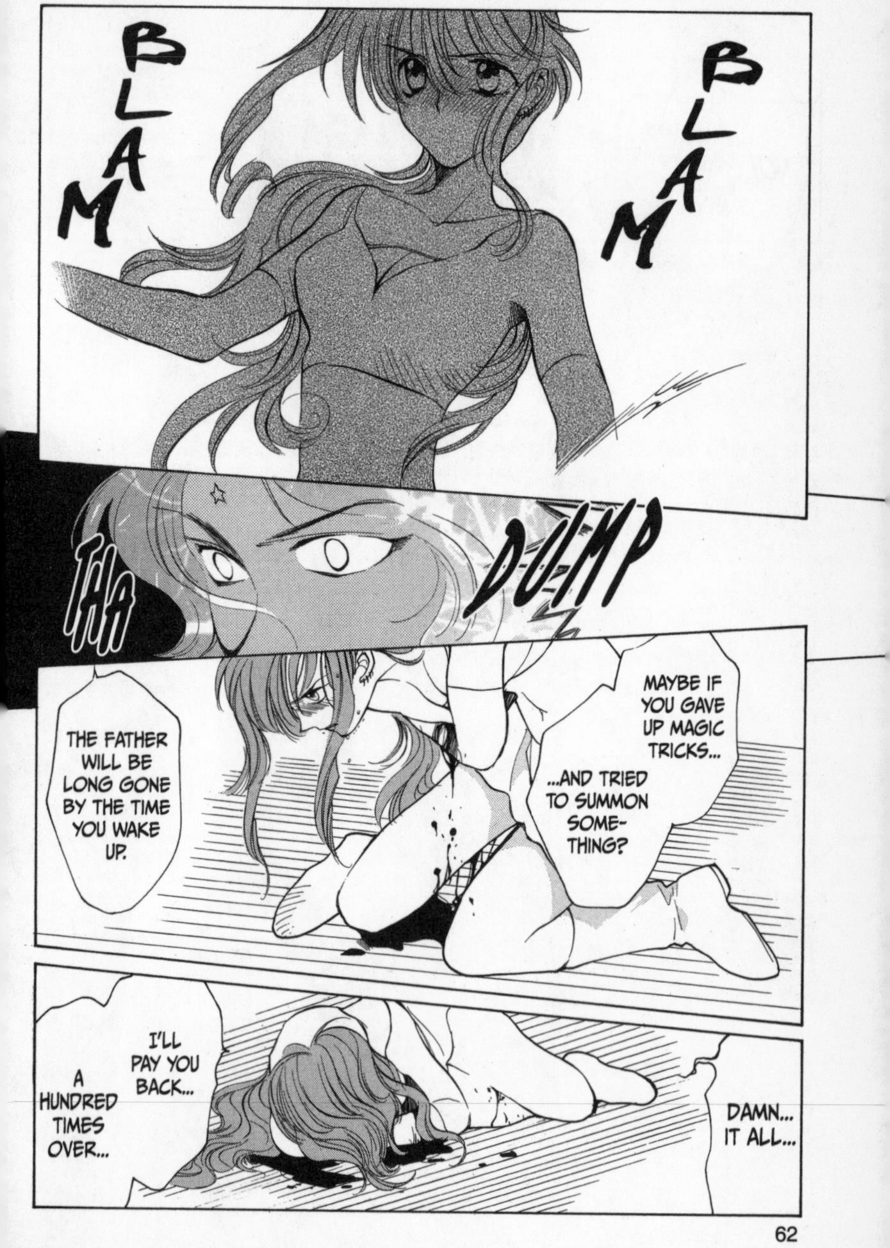
BLAM
BLAM
DUMP
THA
MAYBE IF YOU GAVE UP MAGIC TRICKS...
...AND TRIED TO SUMMON SOME-THING?
THE FATHER WILL BE LONG GONE BY THE TIME YOU WAKE UP.
DAMN... IT ALL...
I'LL PAY YOU BACK...
A HUNDRED TIMES OVER...

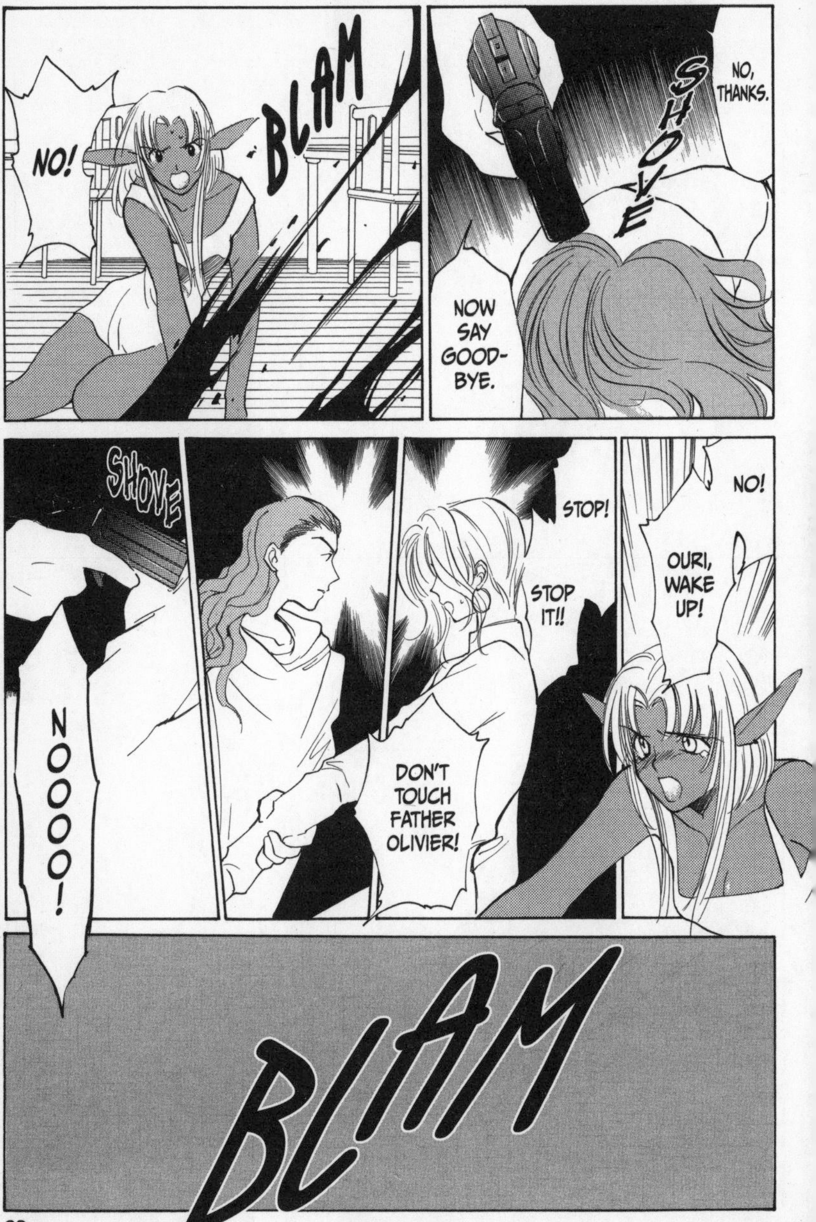
NO, THANKS.
SHOVE
NOW SAY GOOD-BYE.
BLAM
NO!
NO!
OURI, WAKE UP!
STOP!
STOP IT!!
DON'T TOUCH FATHER OLIVIER!
SHOVE
NOOOOO!
BLAM

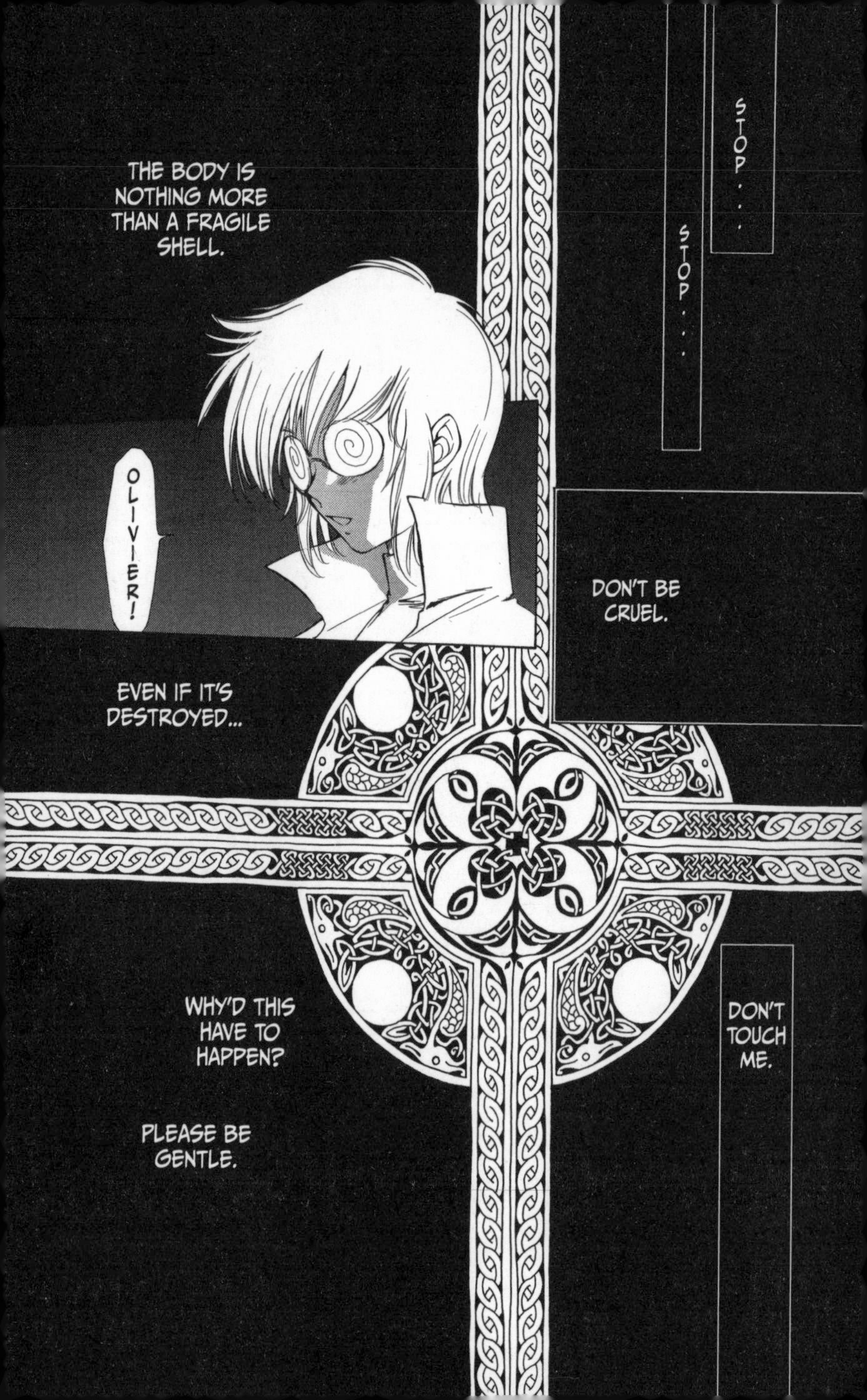
STOP . . .
STOP . . .
THE BODY IS NOTHING MORE THAN A FRAGILE SHELL.
OLIVIER!
DON'T BE CRUEL.
EVEN IF IT'S DESTROYED...
DON'T TOUCH ME.
WHY'D THIS HAVE TO HAPPEN?
PLEASE BE GENTLE.

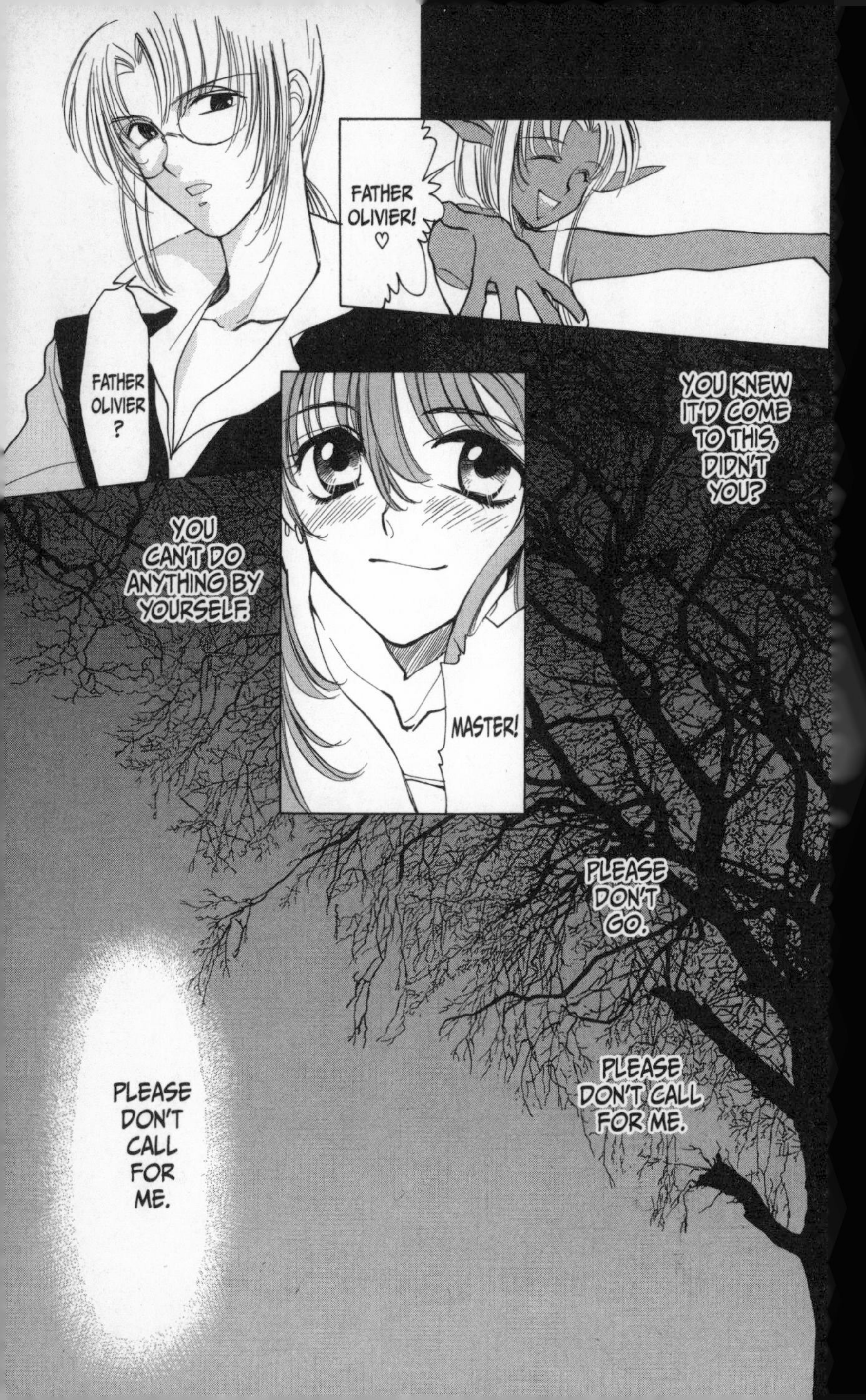
FATHER OLIVIER! ♡
FATHER OLIVIER?
YOU KNEW IT'D COME TO THIS, DIDN'T YOU?
MASTER!
YOU CAN'T DO ANYTHING BY YOURSELF.
PLEASE DON'T GO.
PLEASE DON'T CALL FOR ME.
PLEASE DON'T CALL FOR ME.

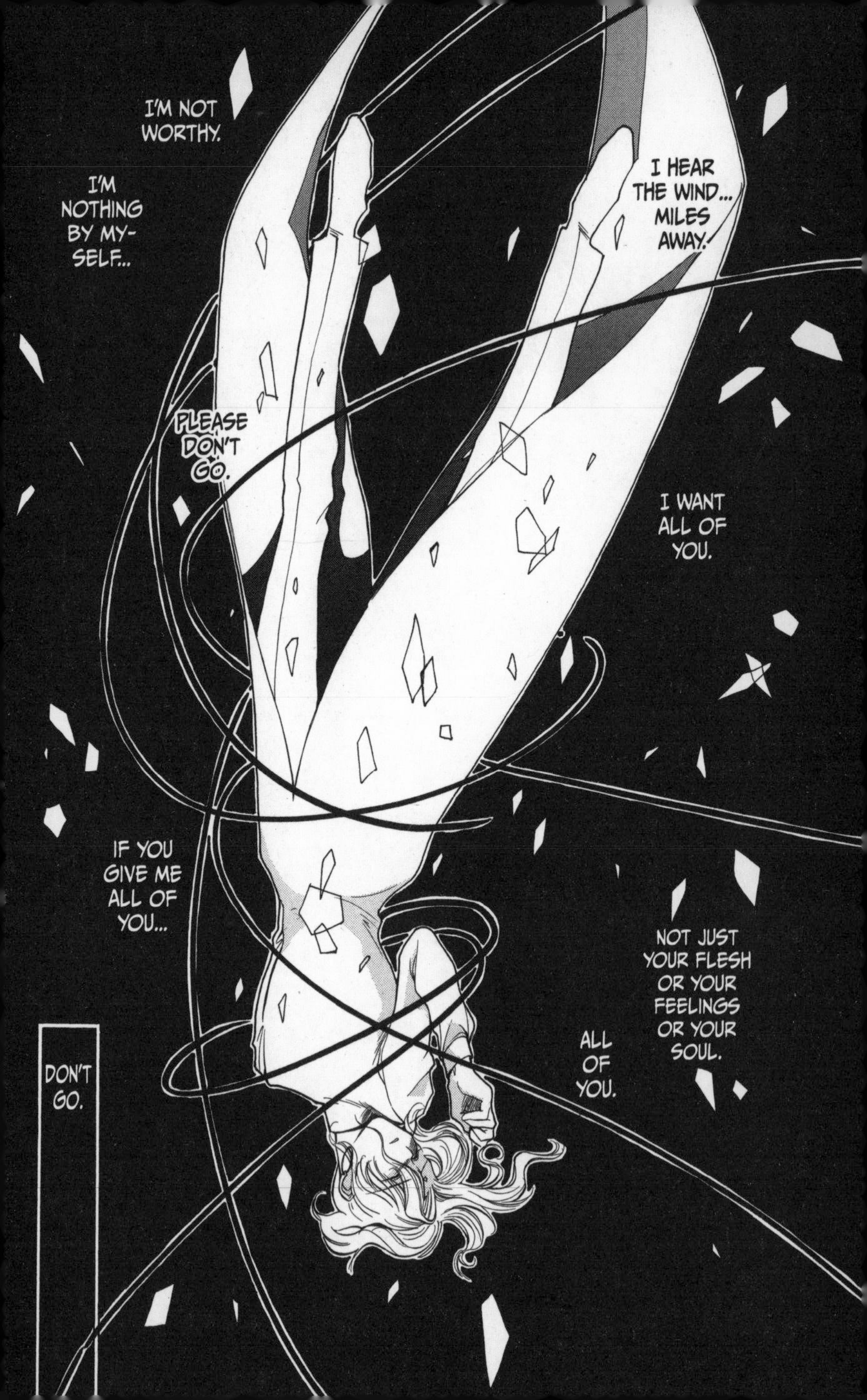
I HEAR THE WIND... MILES AWAY.
I'M NOT WORTHY.
I'M NOTHING BY MY-SELF...
PLEASE DON'T GO.
I WANT ALL OF YOU.
IF YOU GIVE ME ALL OF YOU...
NOT JUST YOUR FLESH OR YOUR FEELINGS OR YOUR SOUL.
ALL OF YOU.
DON'T GO.

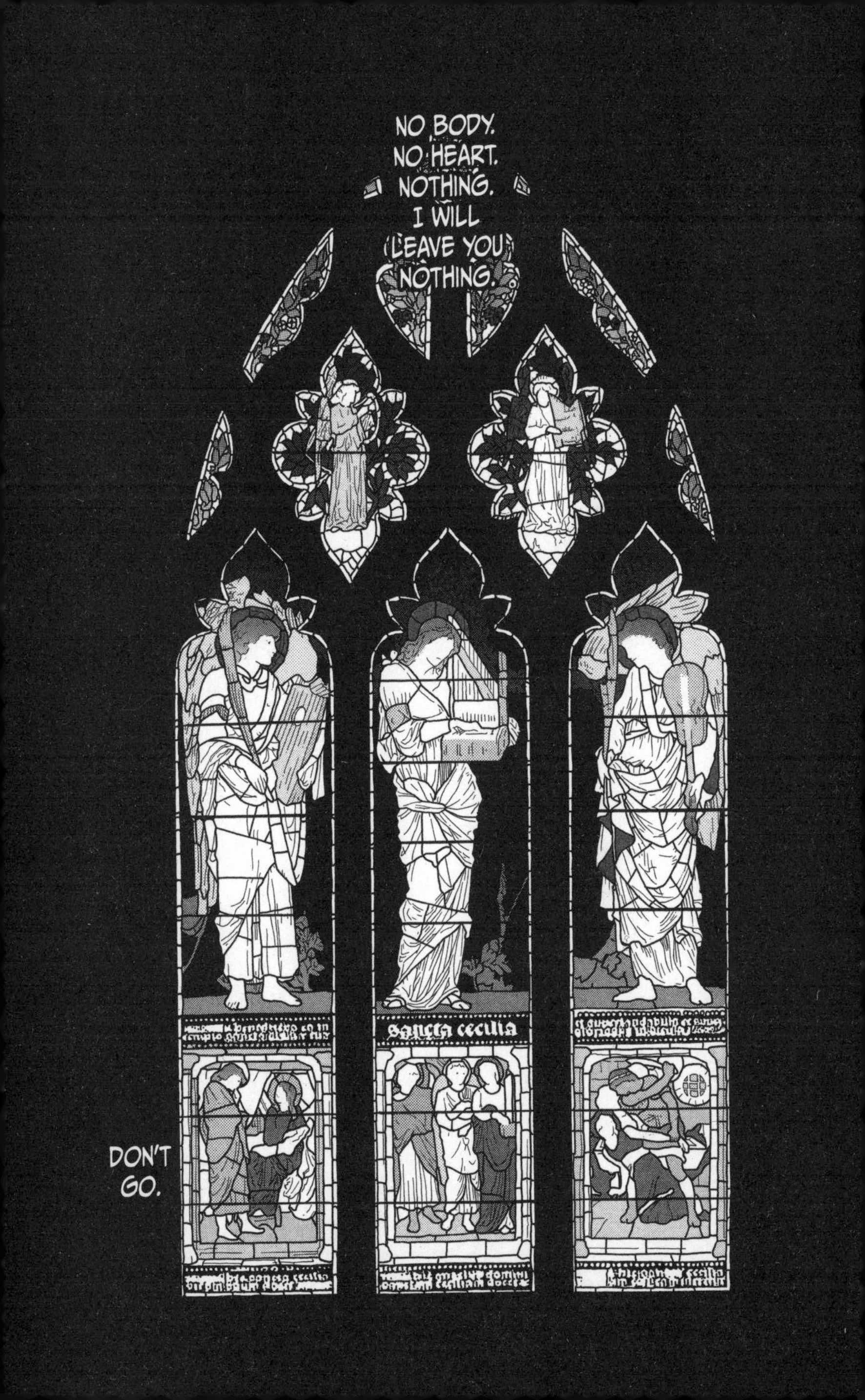
NO BODY. NO HEART. NOTHING. I WILL LEAVE YOU NOTHING.
sancta cecilia
DON'T GO.

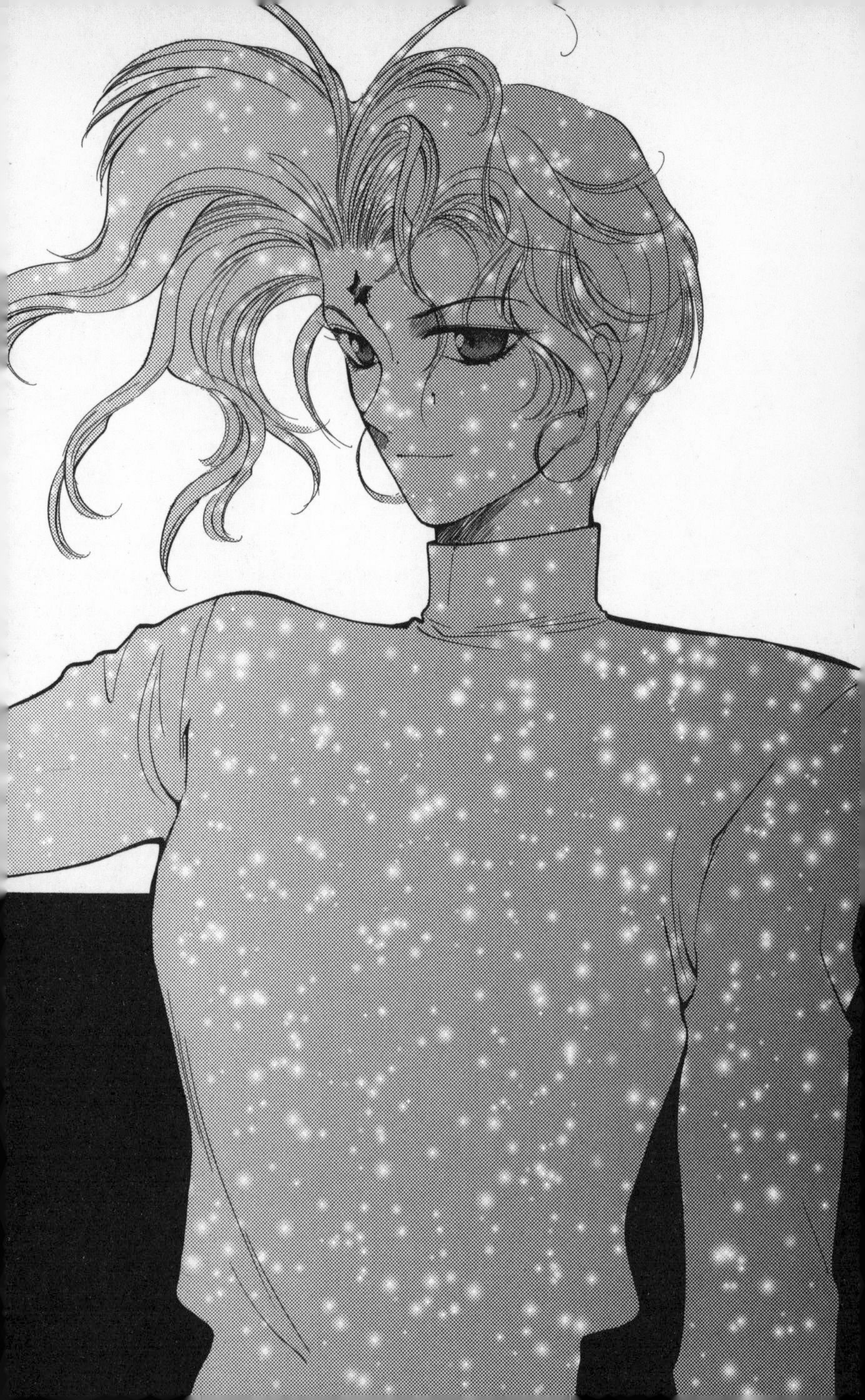

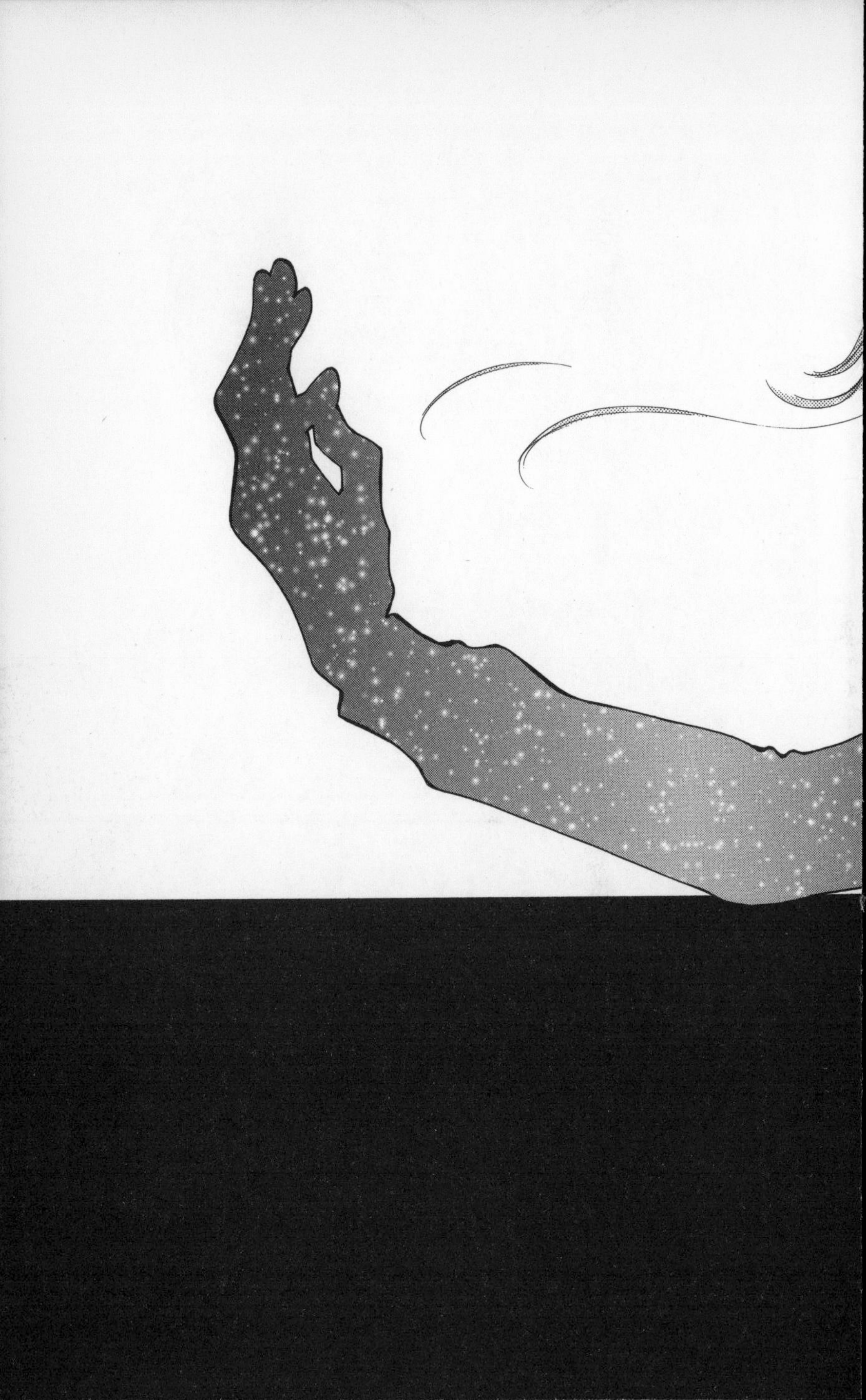

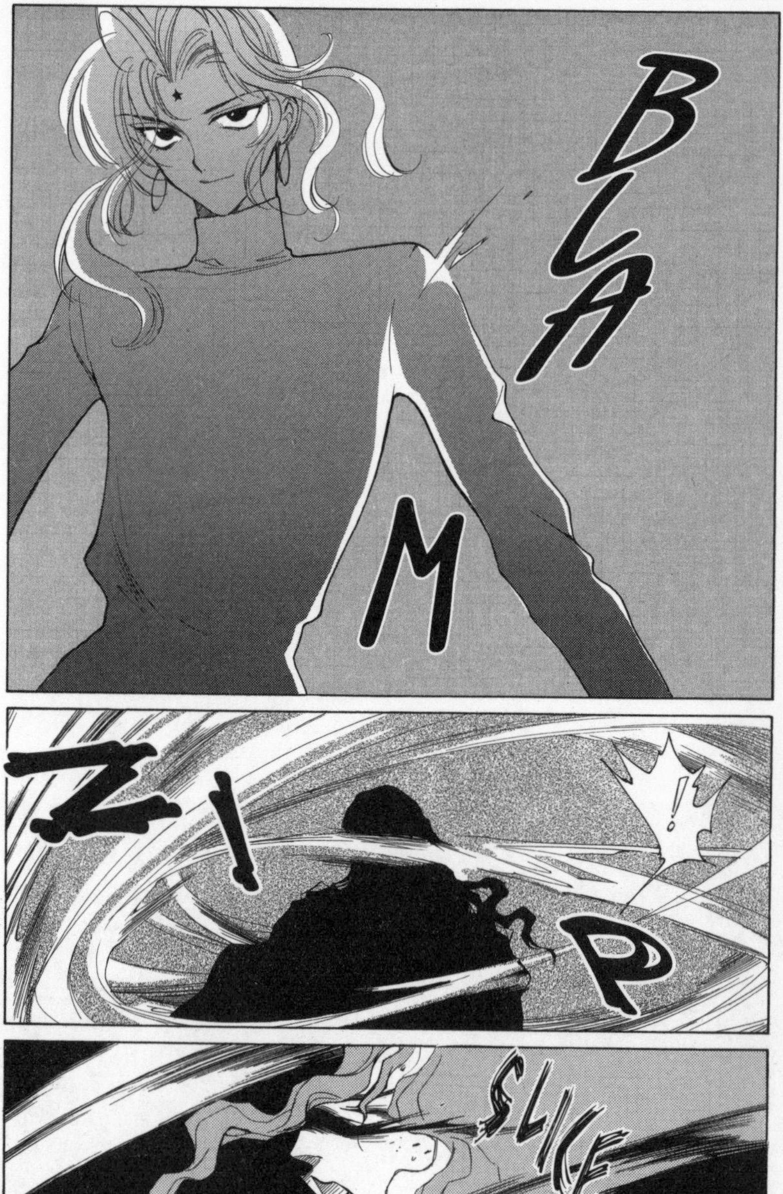
BLAM
ZIP
!
SLICE

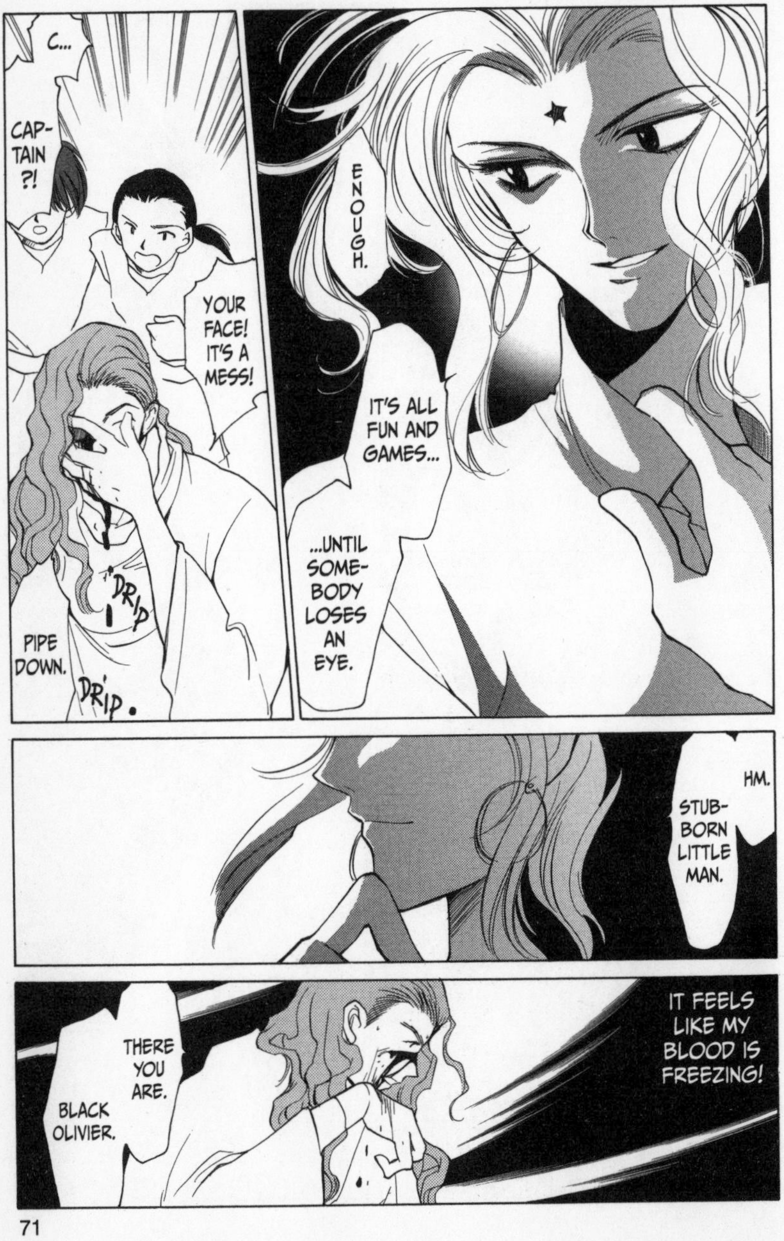
ENOUGH.
IT'S ALL FUN AND GAMES...
...UNTIL SOMEBODY LOSES AN EYE.
C...
CAPTAIN?!
YOUR FACE! IT'S A MESS!
DRIP
PIPE DOWN.
DRIP.
HM.
STUBBORN LITTLE MAN.
IT FEELS LIKE MY BLOOD IS FREEZING!
THERE YOU ARE.
BLACK OLIVIER.

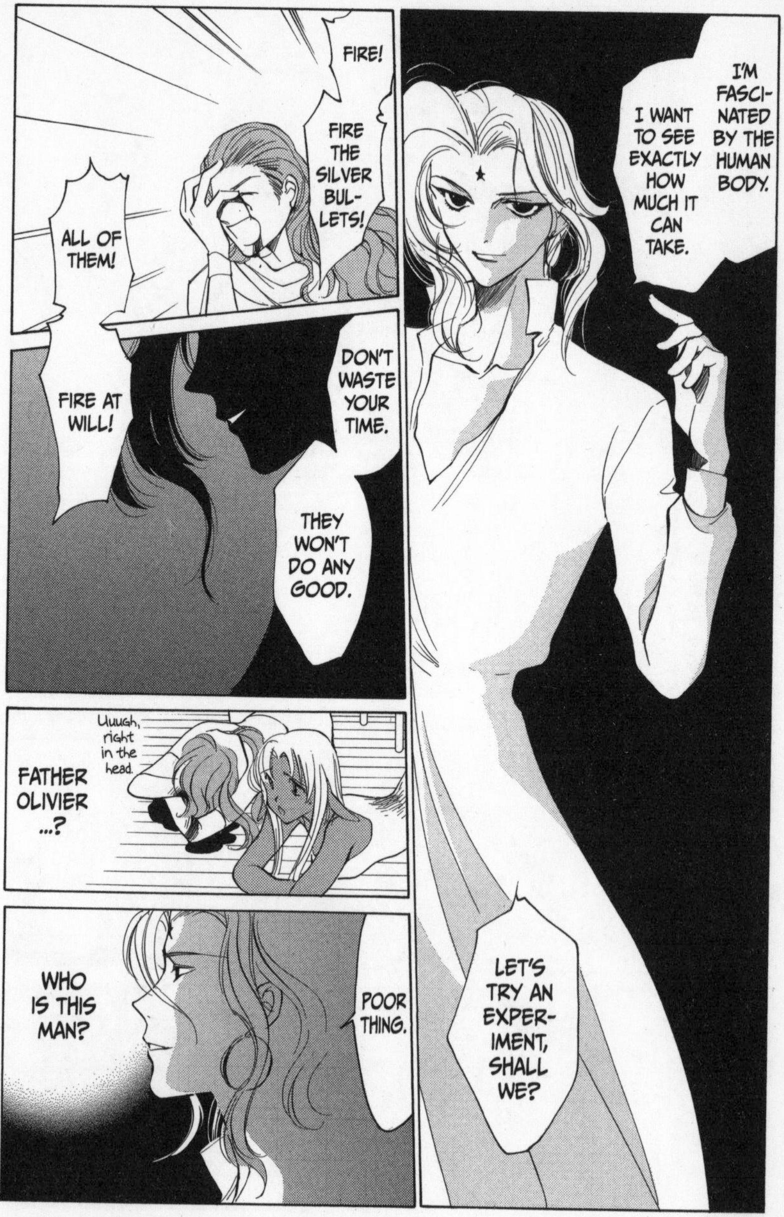
I'M FASCINATED BY THE HUMAN BODY.
I WANT TO SEE EXACTLY HOW MUCH IT CAN TAKE.
LET'S TRY AN EXPERIMENT, SHALL WE?
FIRE!
FIRE THE SILVER BULLETS!
ALL OF THEM!
DON'T WASTE YOUR TIME.
FIRE AT WILL!
THEY WON'T DO ANY GOOD.
Uuugh, right in the head.
FATHER OLIVIER ...?
POOR THING.
WHO IS THIS MAN?

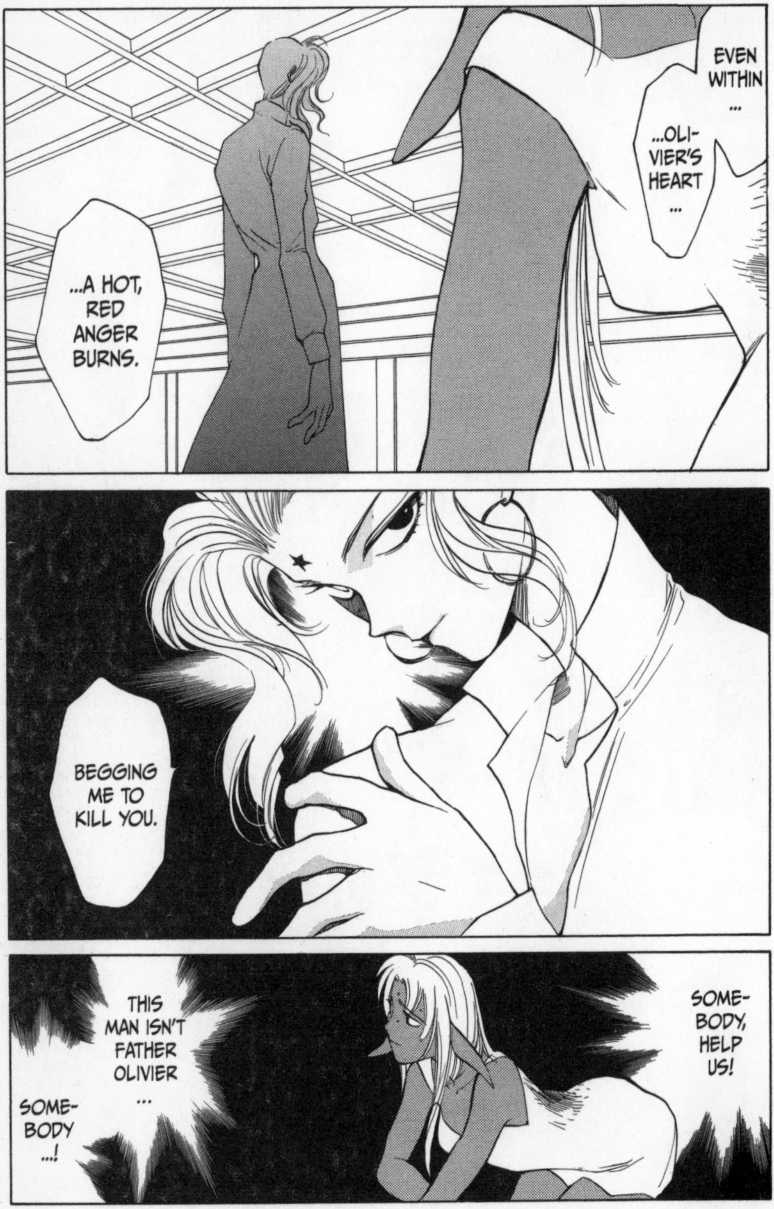
EVEN WITHIN ...
...OLI-VIER'S HEART ...
...A HOT, RED ANGER BURNS.
BEGGING ME TO KILL YOU.
SOME-BODY, HELP US!
THIS MAN ISN'T FATHER OLIVIER ...
SOME-BODY ...!

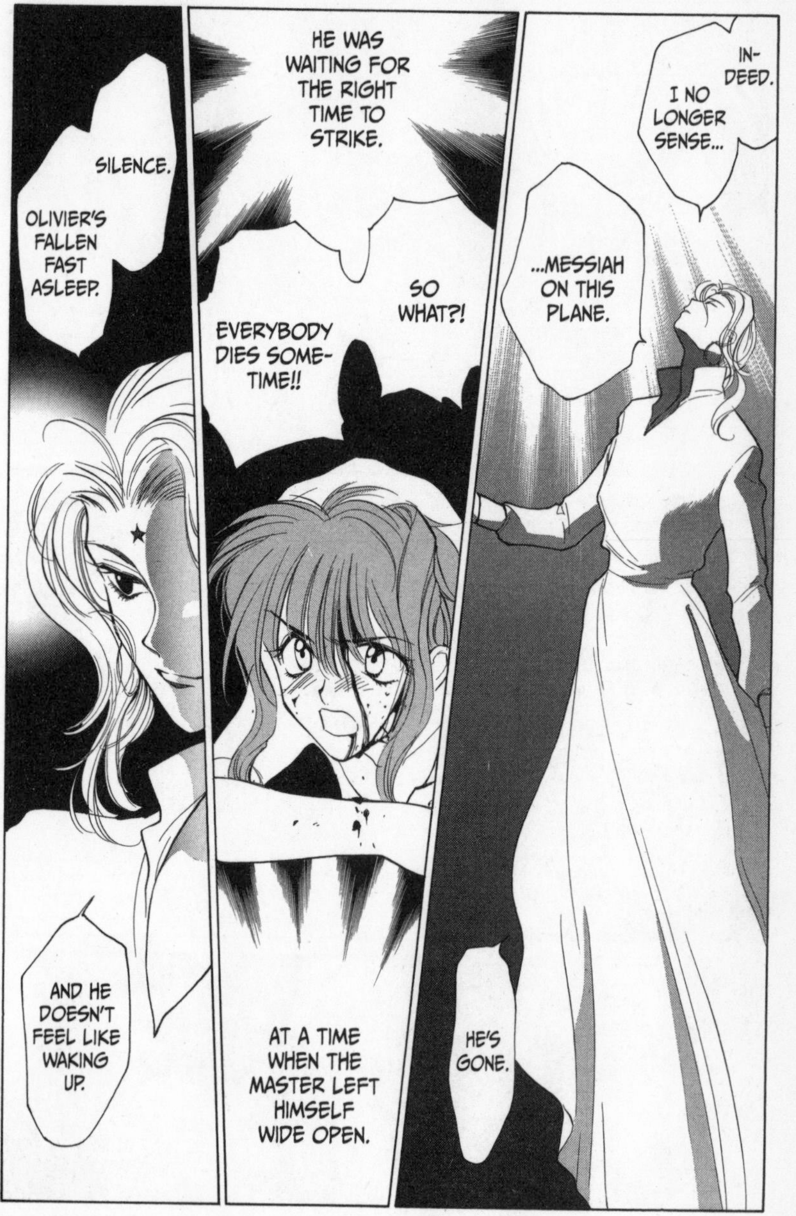
IN-DEED.
I NO LONGER SENSE...
...MESSIAH ON THIS PLANE.
HE'S GONE.
HE WAS WAITING FOR THE RIGHT TIME TO STRIKE.
SO WHAT?!
EVERYBODY DIES SOME-TIME!!
AT A TIME WHEN THE MASTER LEFT HIMSELF WIDE OPEN.
SILENCE.
OLIVIER'S FALLEN FAST ASLEEP.
AND HE DOESN'T FEEL LIKE WAKING UP.

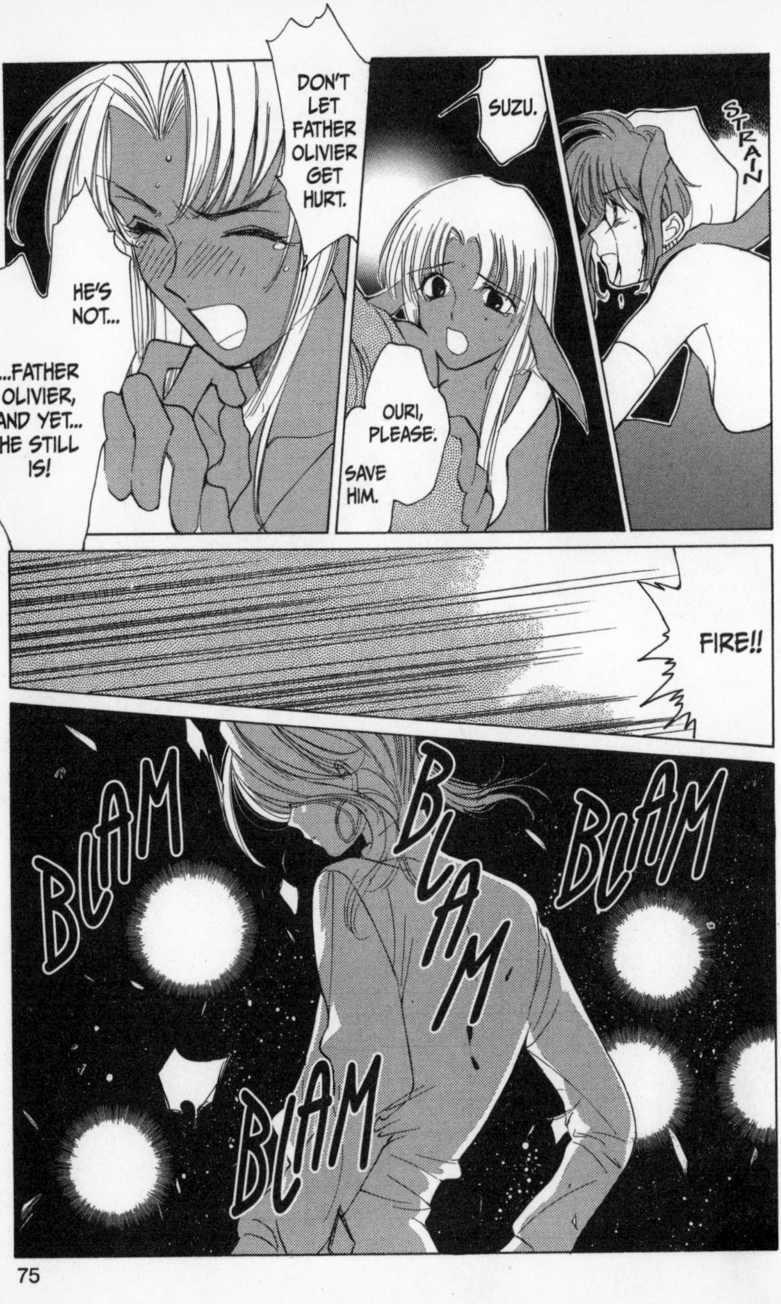
STRAIN
SUZU.
OURI, PLEASE.
SAVE HIM.
DON'T LET FATHER OLIVIER GET HURT.
HE'S NOT...
...FATHER OLIVIER, AND YET... HE STILL IS!
FIRE!!
BLAM
BLAM
BLAM
BLAM

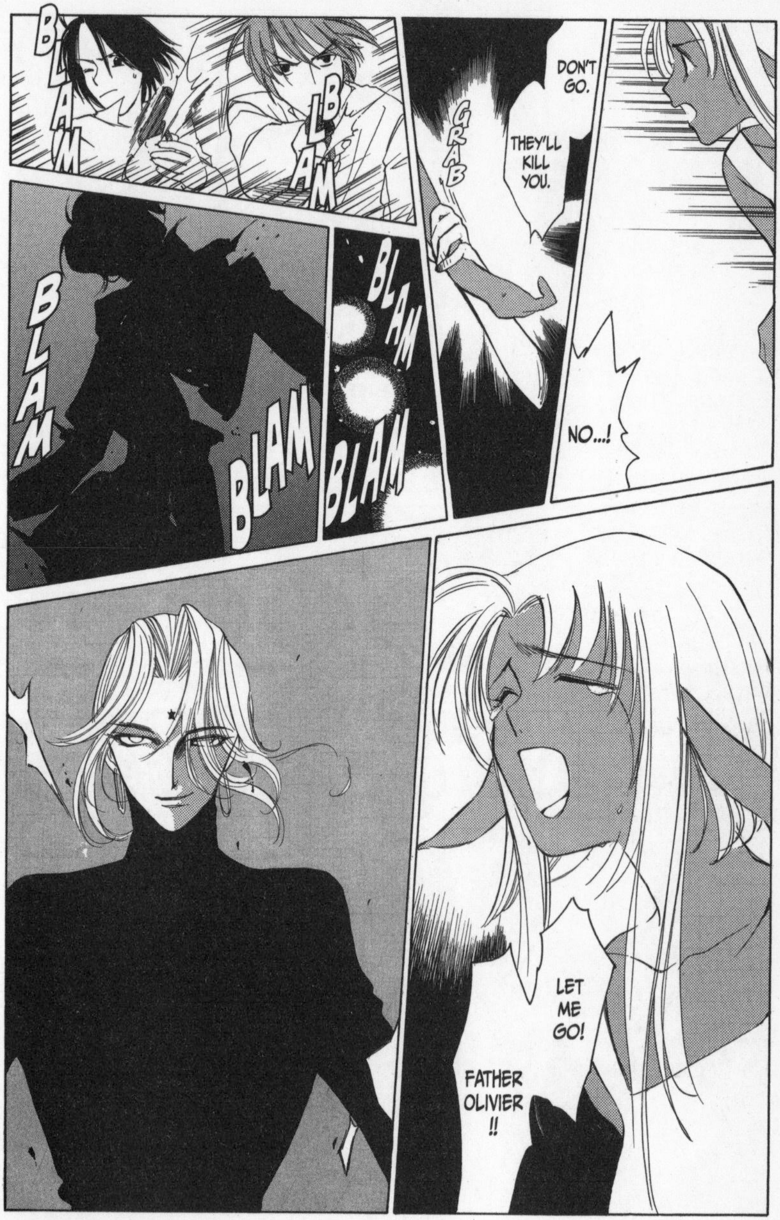
NO...!
DON'T GO.
GRAB
THEY'LL KILL YOU.
BLAM
BLAM
BLAM
BLAM
BLAM
BLAM
LET ME GO!
FATHER OLIVIER!!

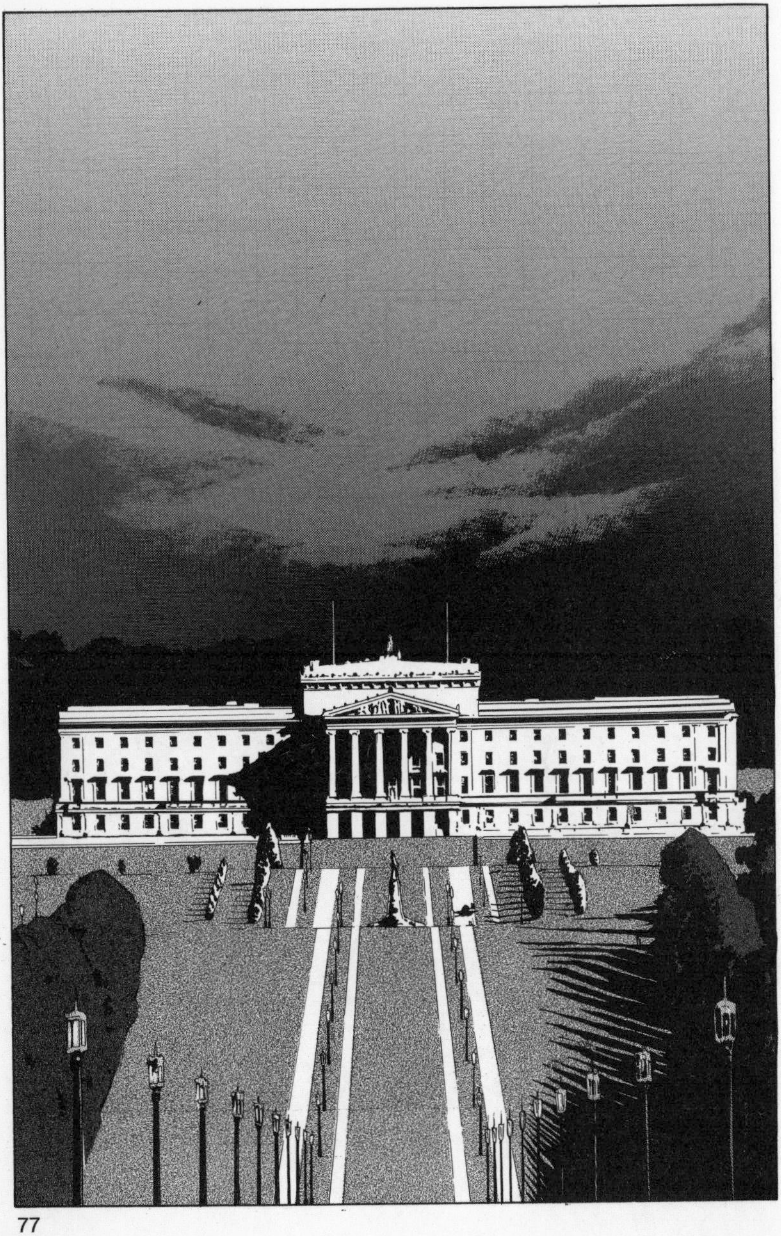

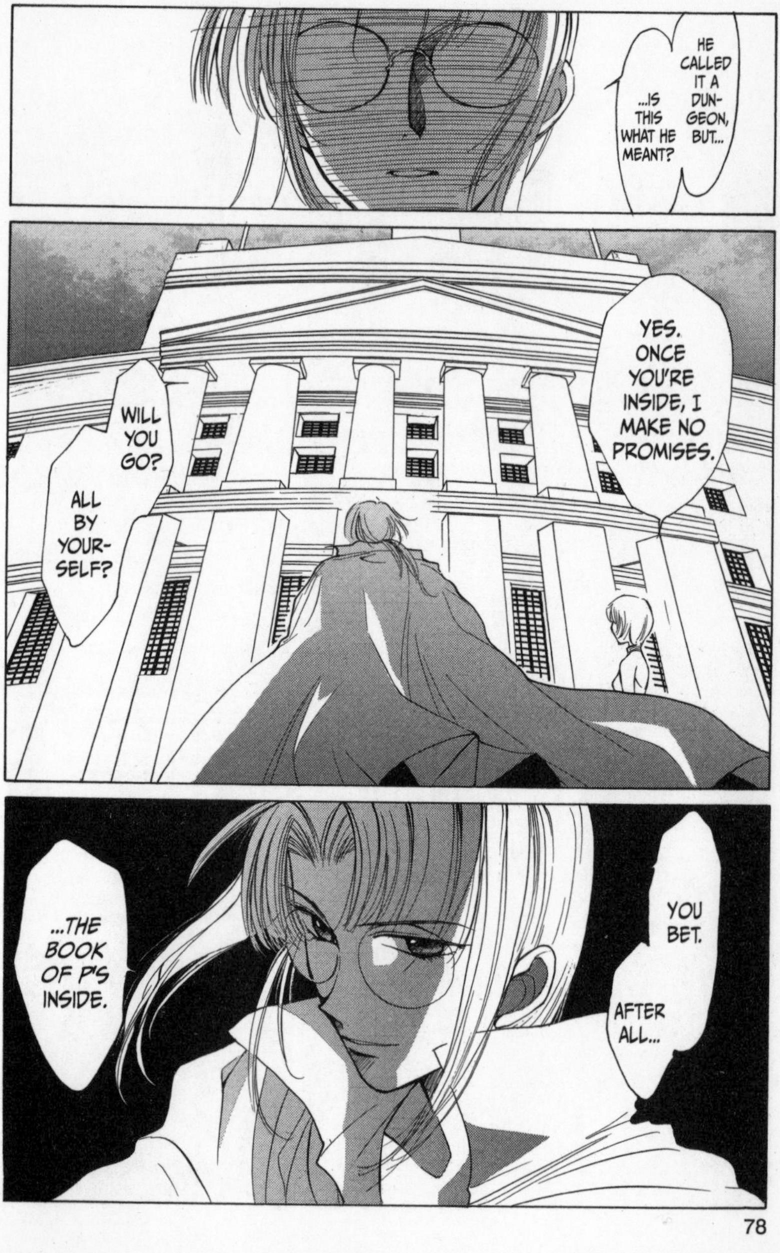
HE CALLED IT A DUN-GEON, BUT...
...IS THIS WHAT HE MEANT?
YES. ONCE YOU'RE INSIDE, I MAKE NO PROMISES.
WILL YOU GO?
ALL BY YOUR-SELF?
YOU BET.
AFTER ALL...
...THE BOOK OF P'S INSIDE.

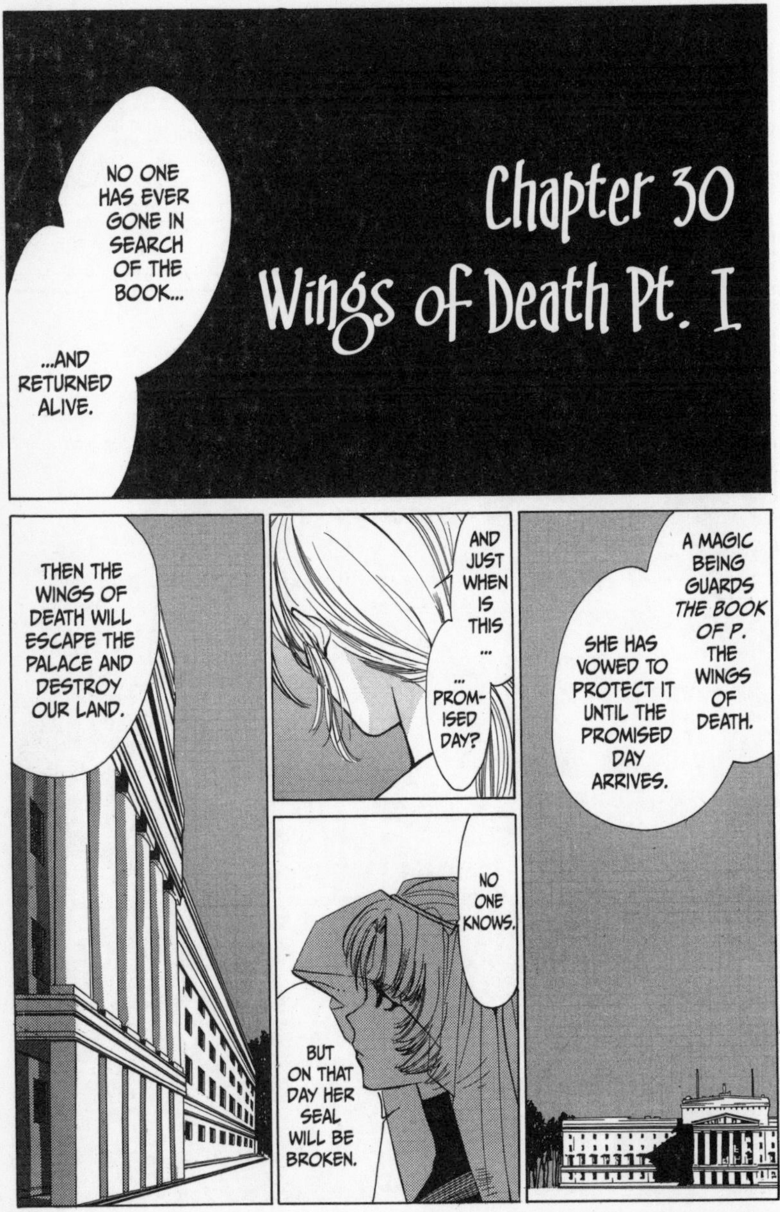
Chapter 30
Wings of Death Pt. I
NO ONE HAS EVER GONE IN SEARCH OF THE BOOK...
...AND RETURNED ALIVE.
A MAGIC BEING GUARDS *THE BOOK OF P.* THE WINGS OF DEATH.
SHE HAS VOWED TO PROTECT IT UNTIL THE PROMISED DAY ARRIVES.
AND JUST WHEN IS THIS ...
... PROMISED DAY?
NO ONE KNOWS.
BUT ON THAT DAY HER SEAL WILL BE BROKEN.
THEN THE WINGS OF DEATH WILL ESCAPE THE PALACE AND DESTROY OUR LAND.

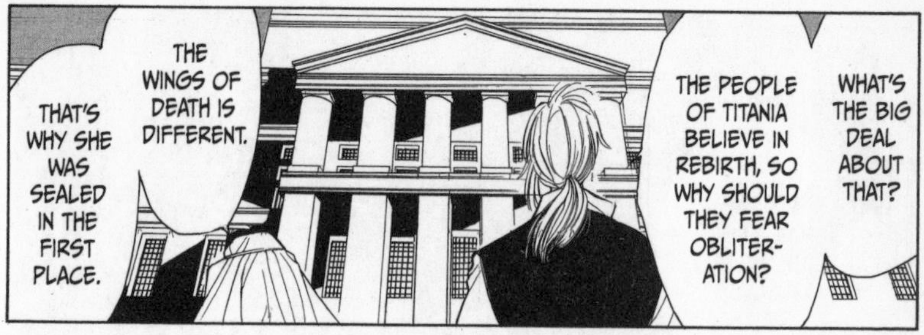
WHAT'S THE BIG DEAL ABOUT THAT?
THE PEOPLE OF TITANIA BELIEVE IN REBIRTH, SO WHY SHOULD THEY FEAR OBLITERATION?
THE WINGS OF DEATH IS DIFFERENT.
THAT'S WHY SHE WAS SEALED IN THE FIRST PLACE.

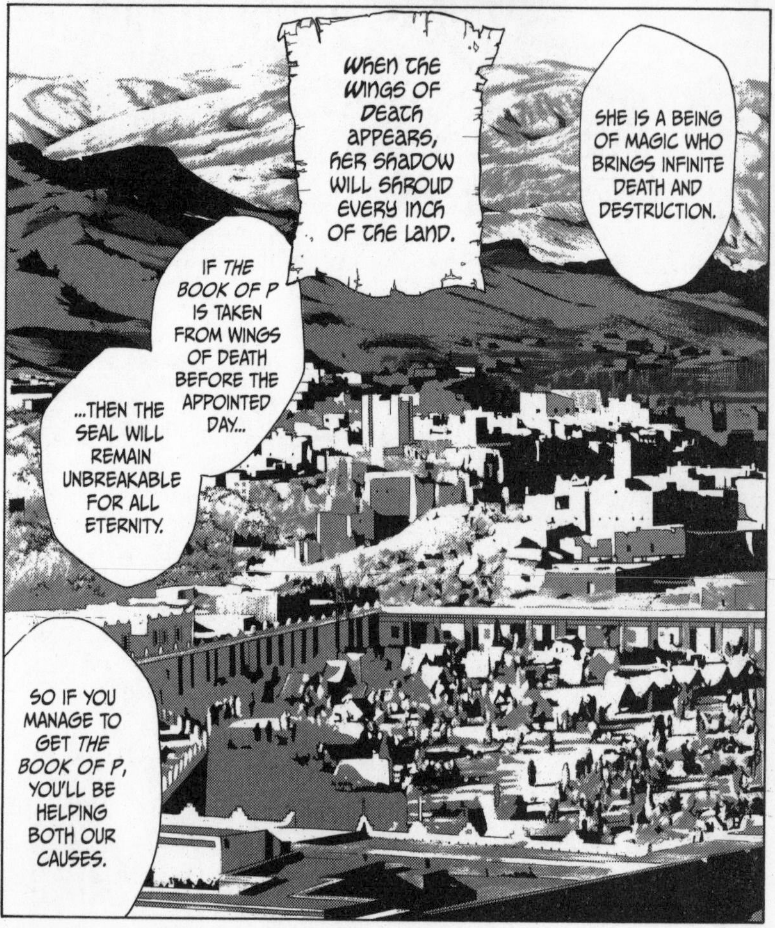
SHE IS A BEING OF MAGIC WHO BRINGS INFINITE DEATH AND DESTRUCTION.
WHEN THE WINGS OF DEATH APPEARS, HER SHADOW WILL SHROUD EVERY INCH OF THE LAND.
IF *THE BOOK OF P* IS TAKEN FROM WINGS OF DEATH BEFORE THE APPOINTED DAY...
...THEN THE SEAL WILL REMAIN UNBREAKABLE FOR ALL ETERNITY.
SO IF YOU MANAGE TO GET *THE BOOK OF P*, YOU'LL BE HELPING BOTH OUR CAUSES.

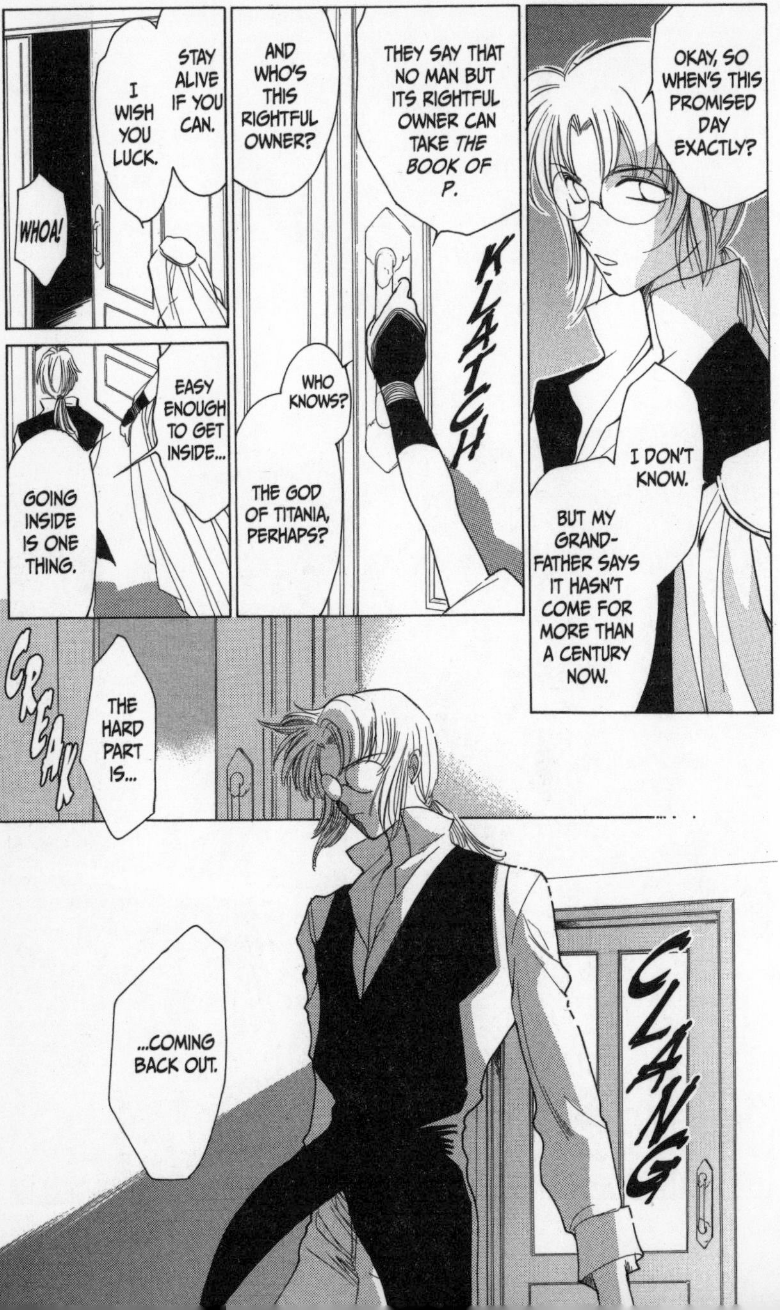
OKAY, SO WHEN'S THIS PROMISED DAY EXACTLY?
I DON'T KNOW.
BUT MY GRAND-FATHER SAYS IT HASN'T COME FOR MORE THAN A CENTURY NOW.
THEY SAY THAT NO MAN BUT ITS RIGHTFUL OWNER CAN TAKE *THE BOOK OF P.*
AND WHO'S THIS RIGHTFUL OWNER?
KLATCH
WHO KNOWS?
THE GOD OF TITANIA, PERHAPS?
STAY ALIVE IF YOU CAN.
I WISH YOU LUCK.
WHOA!
EASY ENOUGH TO GET INSIDE...
GOING INSIDE IS ONE THING.
CREAK
THE HARD PART IS...
...COMING BACK OUT.
CLANG

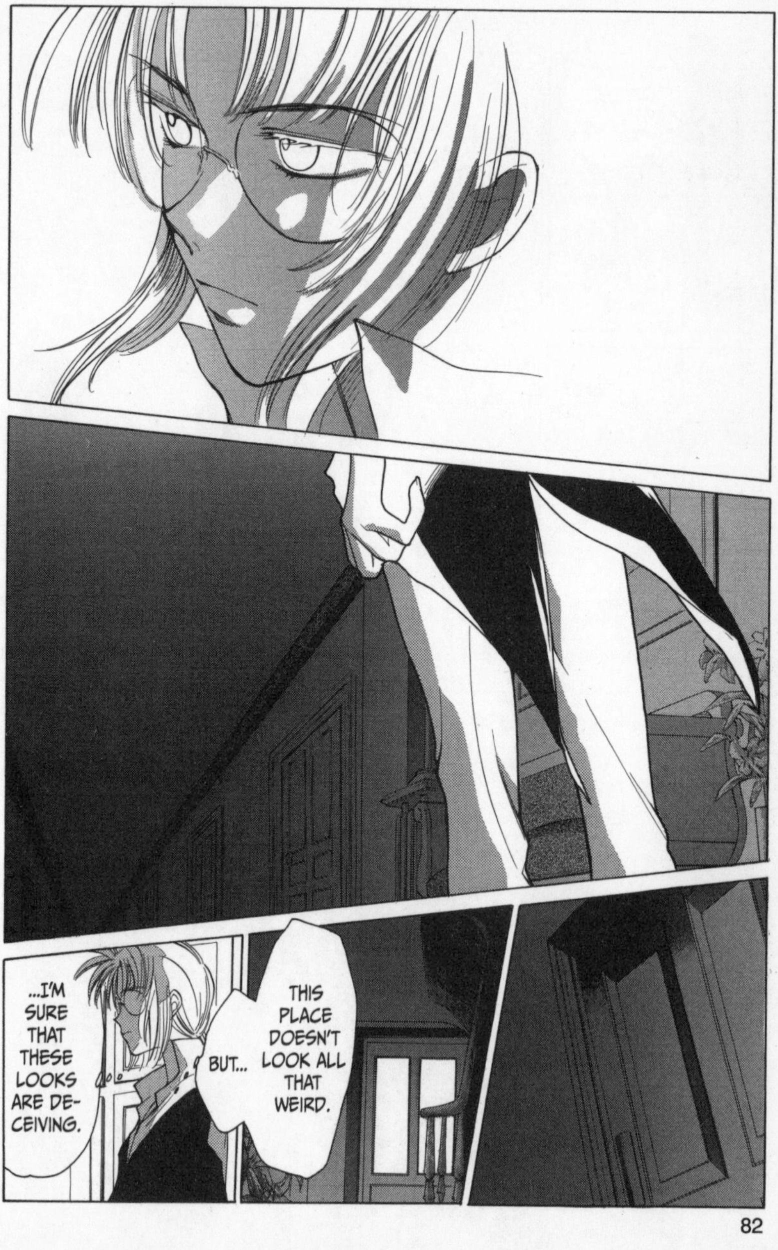
THIS PLACE DOESN'T LOOK ALL THAT WEIRD.
BUT...
...I'M SURE THAT THESE LOOKS ARE DE-CEIVING.

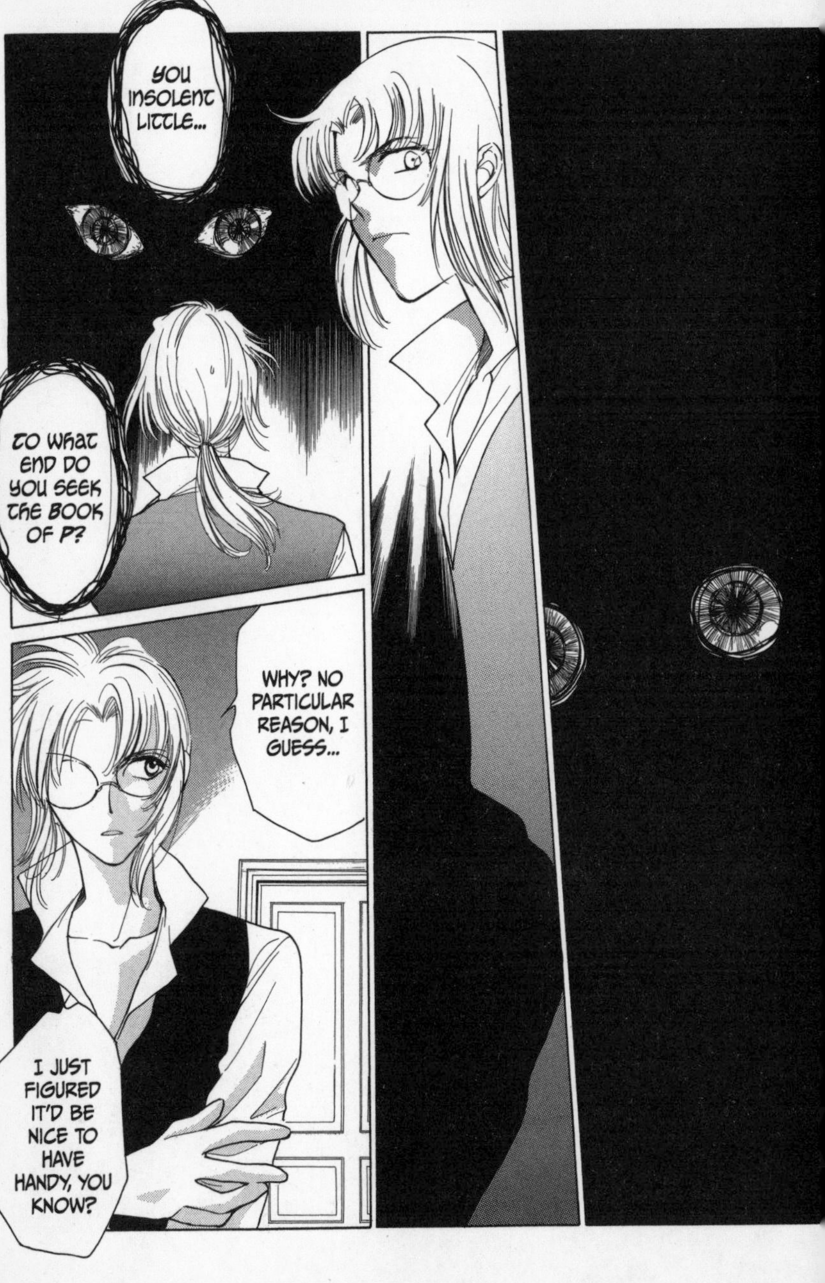
YOU INSOLENT LITTLE...
TO WHAT END DO YOU SEEK THE BOOK OF P?
WHY? NO PARTICULAR REASON, I GUESS...
I JUST FIGURED IT'D BE NICE TO HAVE HANDY, YOU KNOW?

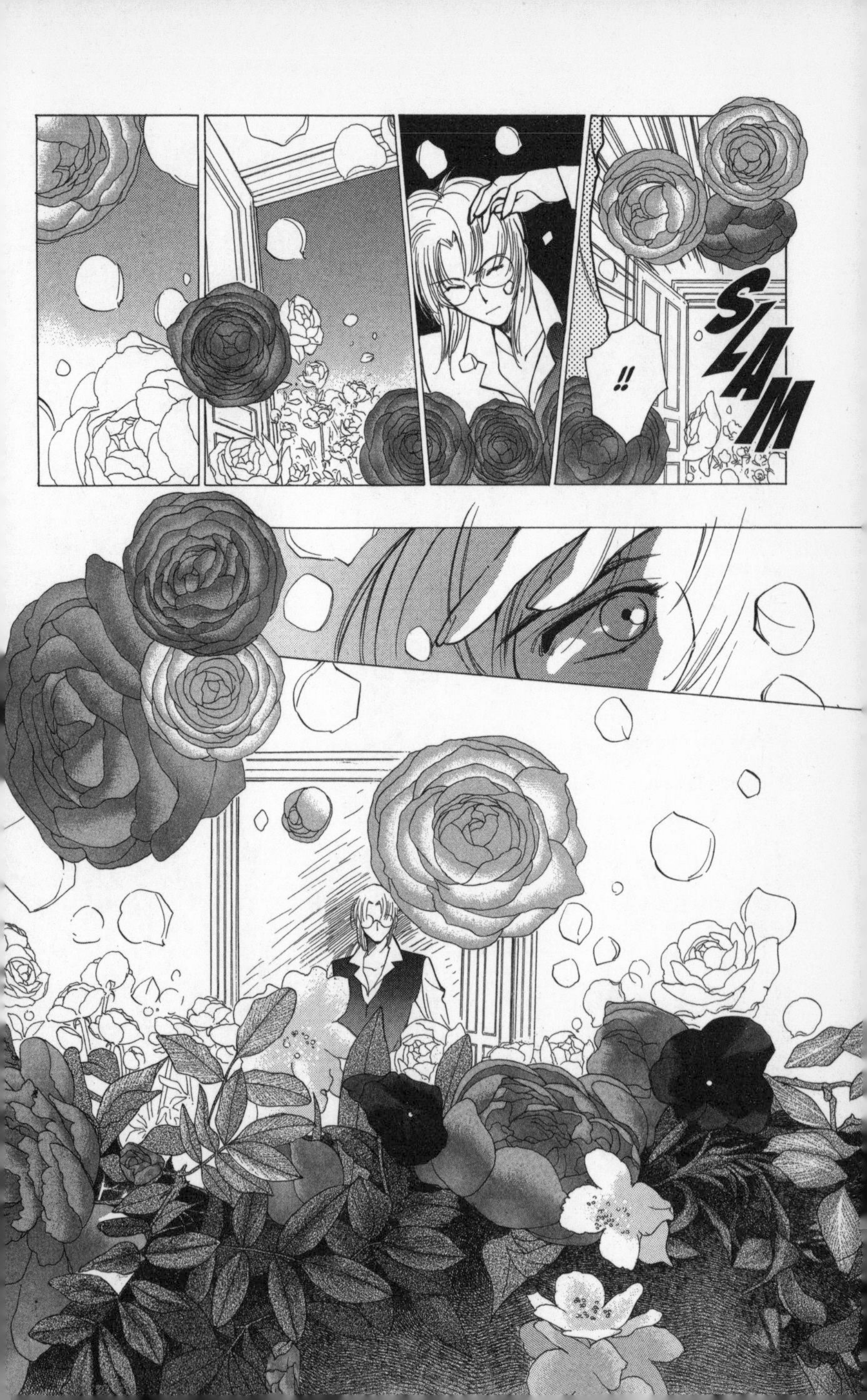
SLAM
!!

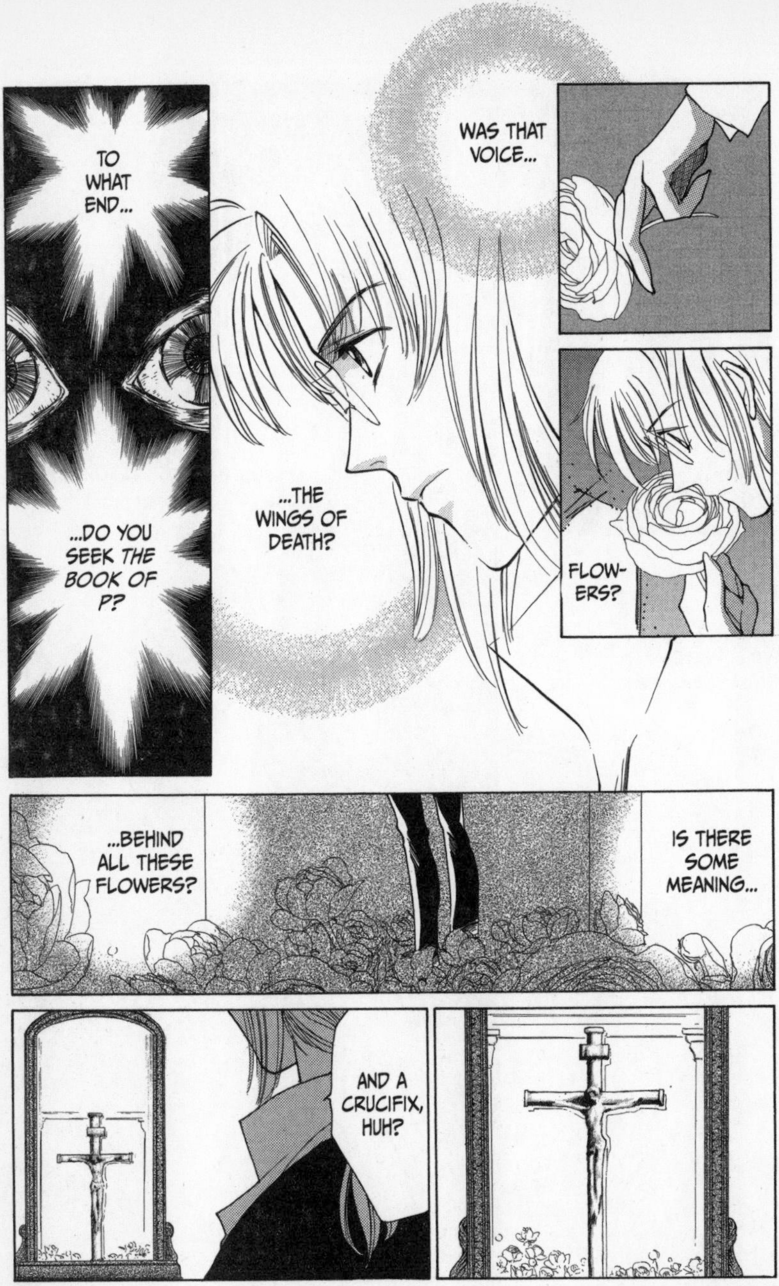
WAS THAT VOICE...
FLOWERS?
...THE WINGS OF DEATH?
TO WHAT END...
...DO YOU SEEK *THE BOOK OF P*?
IS THERE SOME MEANING...
...BEHIND ALL THESE FLOWERS?
AND A CRUCIFIX, HUH?

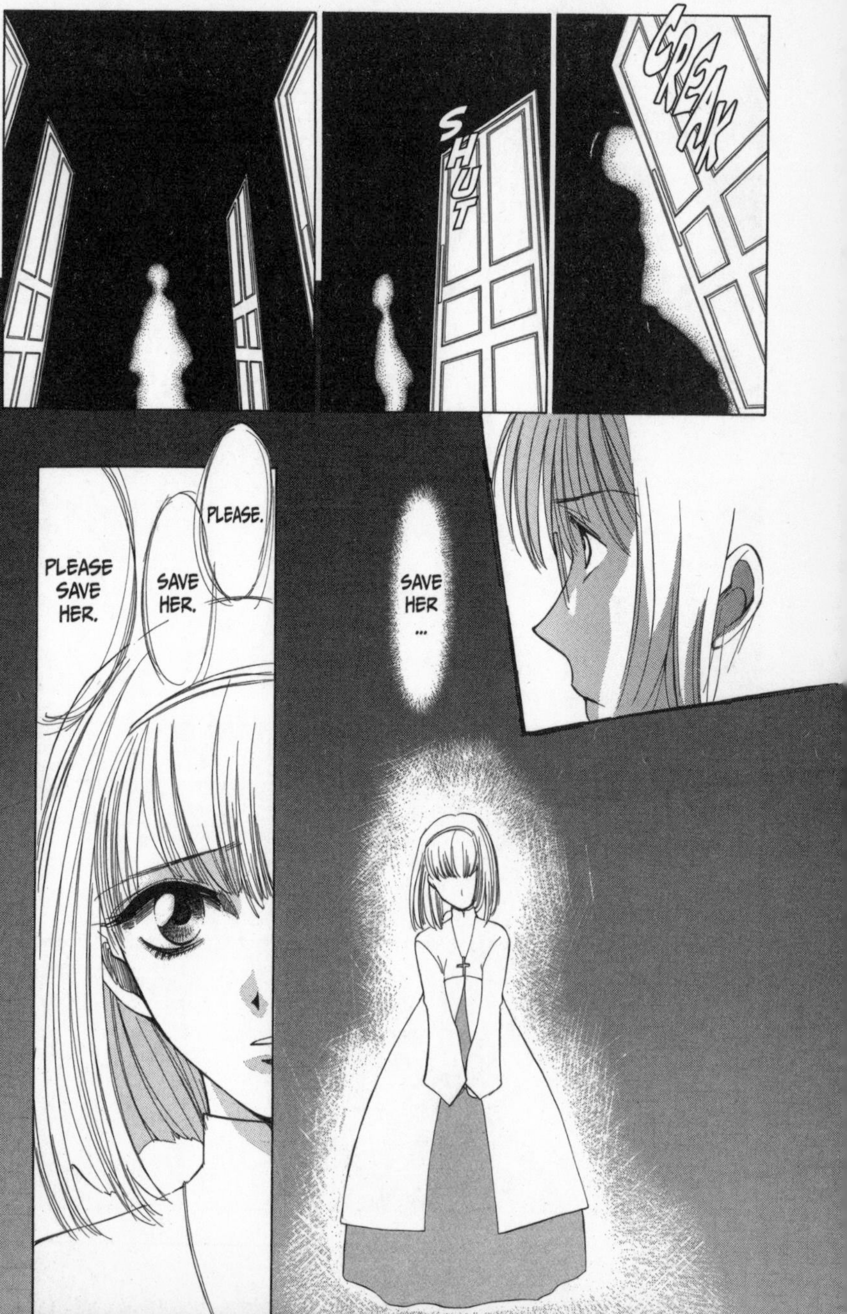
CREAK
SHUT
SAVE HER ...
PLEASE.
SAVE HER.
PLEASE SAVE HER.

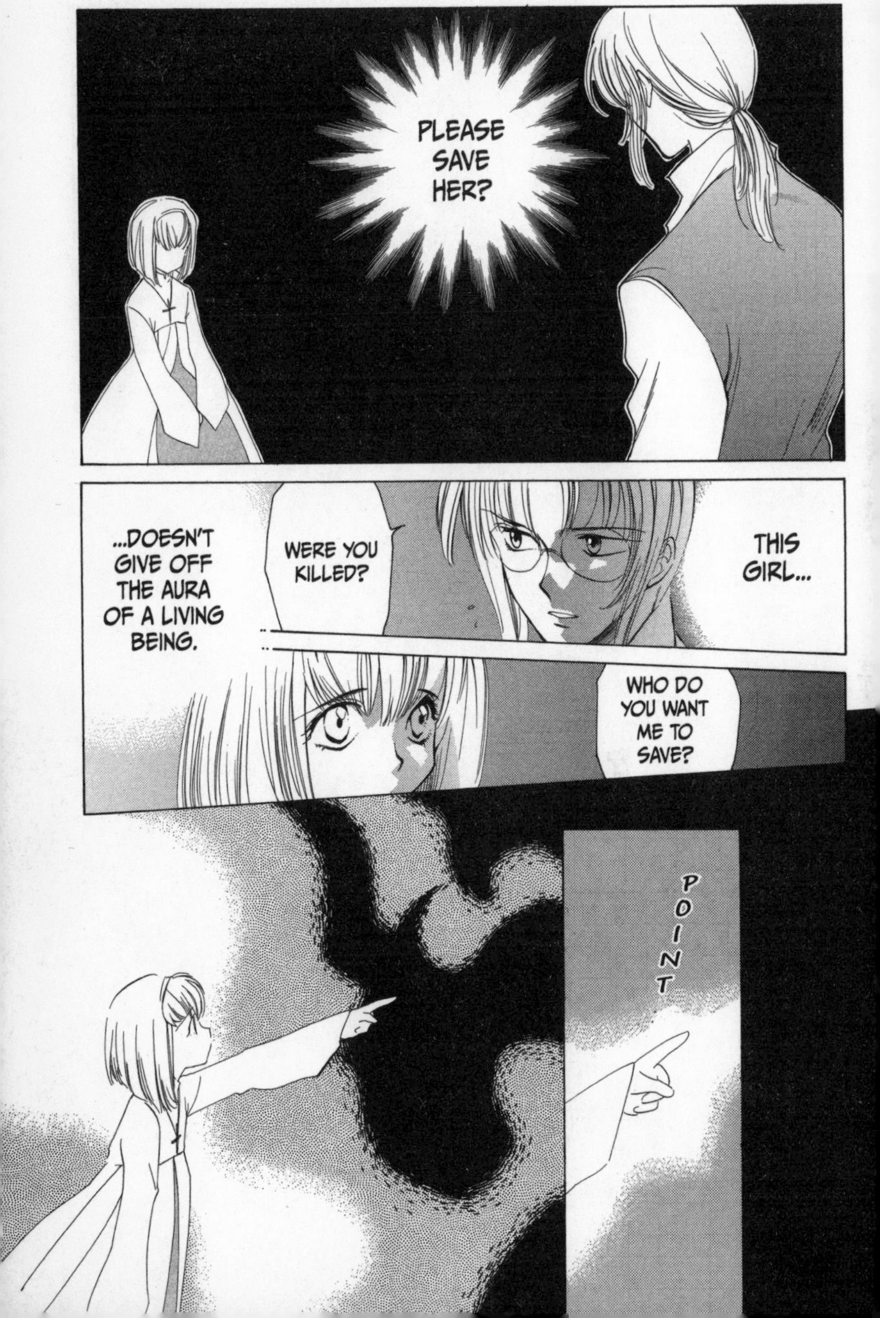
PLEASE SAVE HER?
THIS GIRL...
WERE YOU KILLED?
...DOESN'T GIVE OFF THE AURA OF A LIVING BEING.
WHO DO YOU WANT ME TO SAVE?
POINT

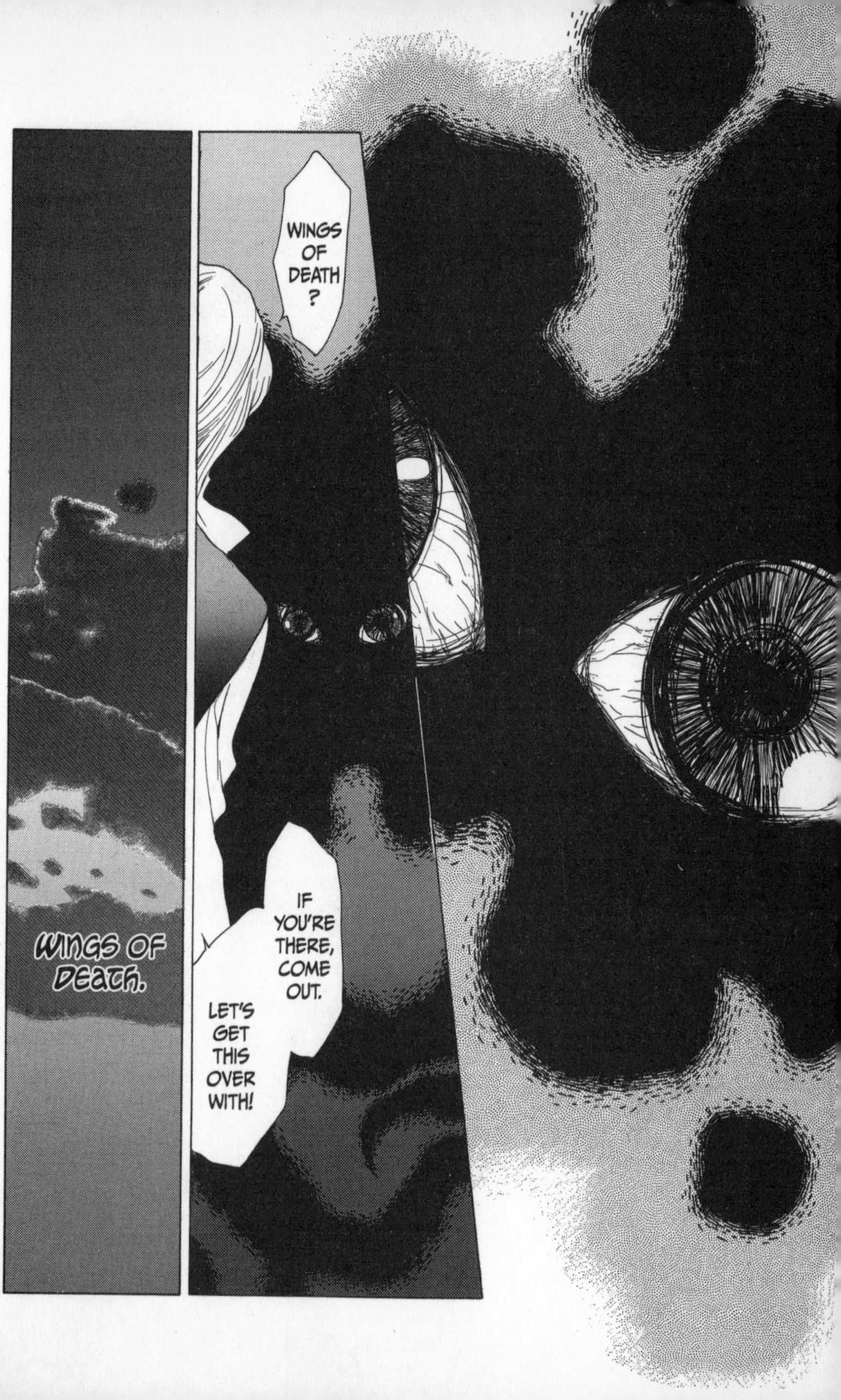
WINGS OF DEATH?
IF YOU'RE THERE, COME OUT.
LET'S GET THIS OVER WITH!
WINGS OF DEATH.

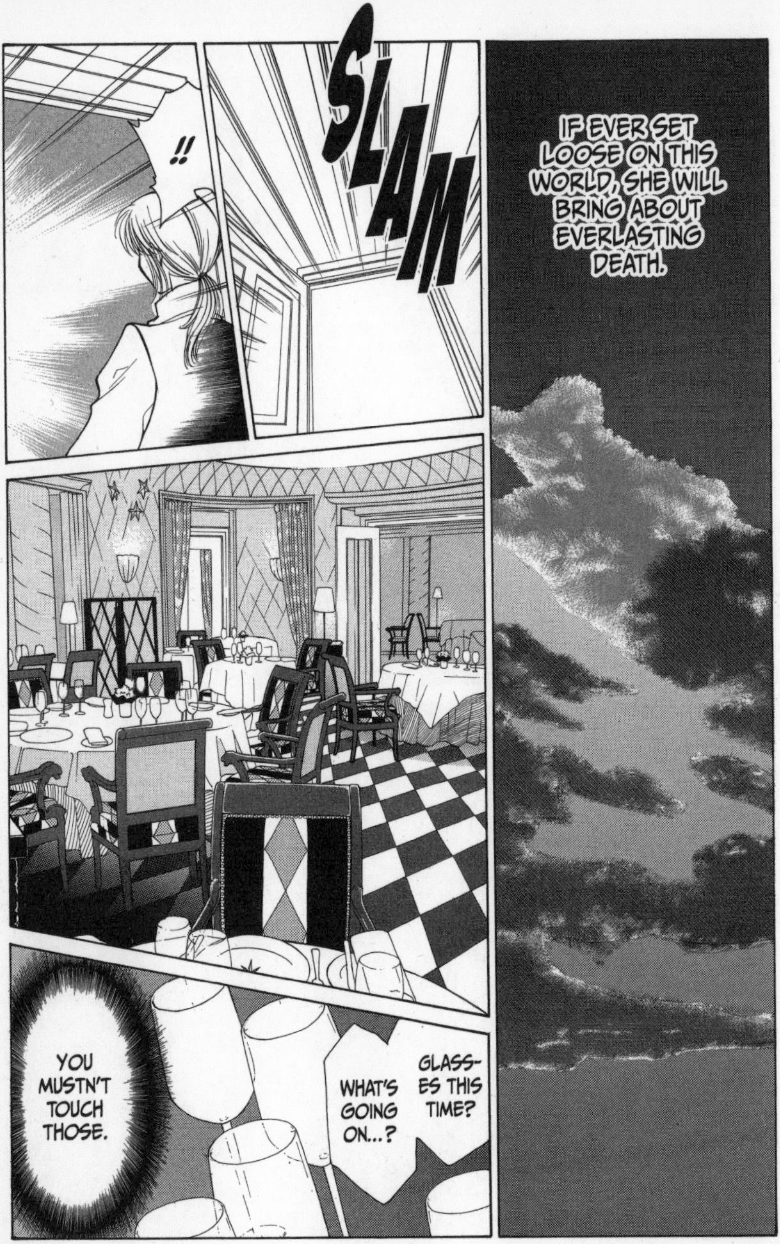
IF EVER SET LOOSE ON THIS WORLD, SHE WILL BRING ABOUT EVERLASTING DEATH.
SLAM
!!
GLASS-ES THIS TIME?
WHAT'S GOING ON...?
YOU MUSTN'T TOUCH THOSE.

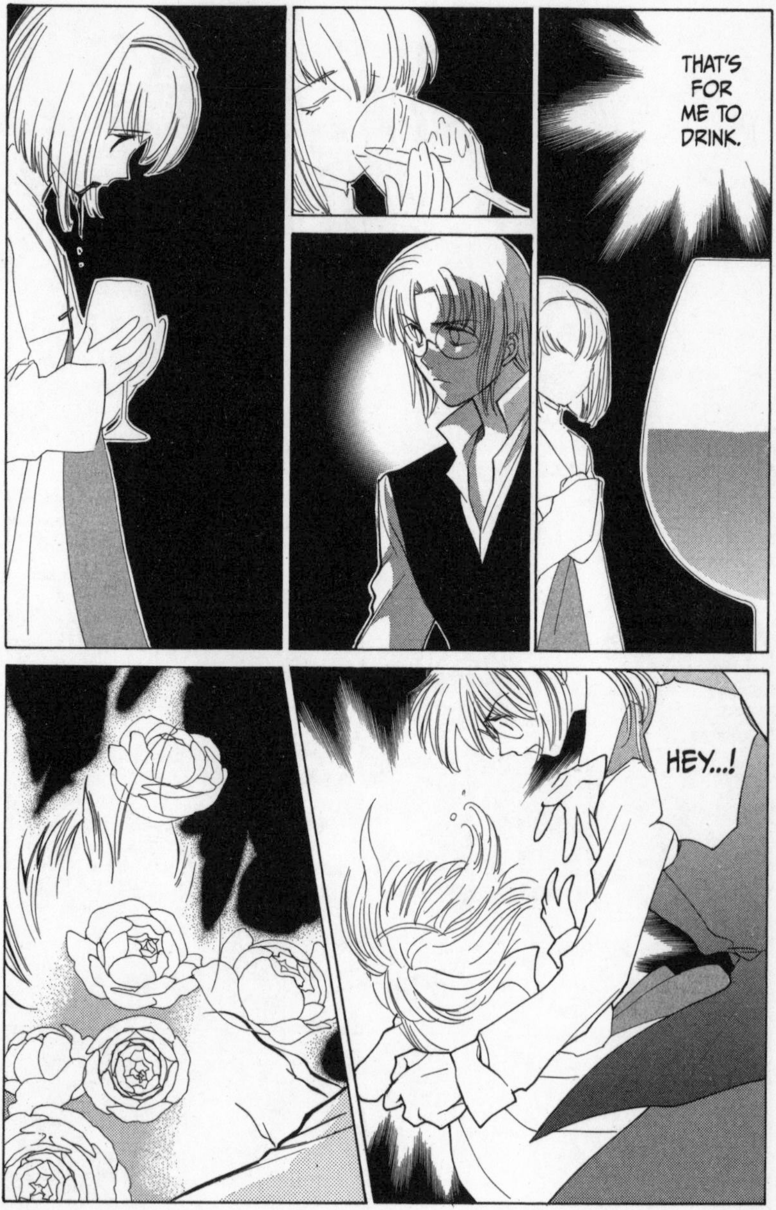
THAT'S FOR ME TO DRINK.
HEY...!

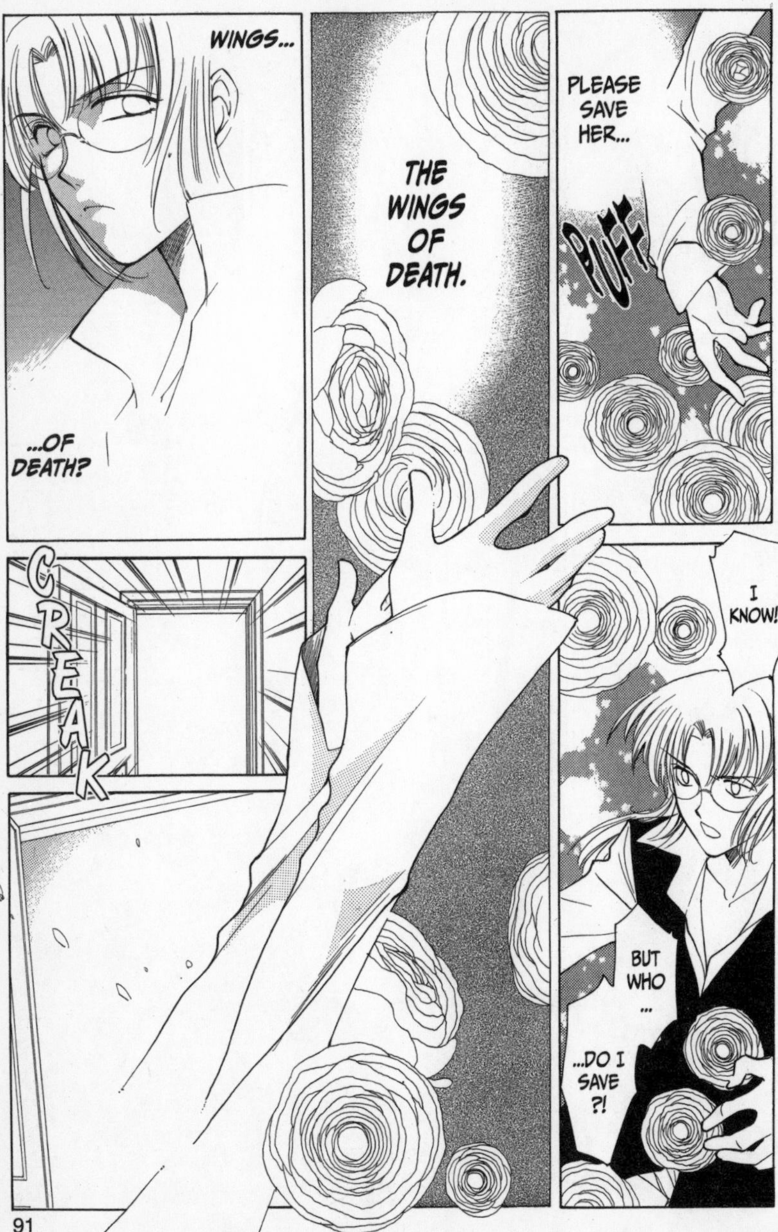
PLEASE SAVE HER...
PUFF
THE WINGS OF DEATH.
WINGS...
...OF DEATH?
I KNOW!
BUT WHO ...
...DO I SAVE ?!
CREAK

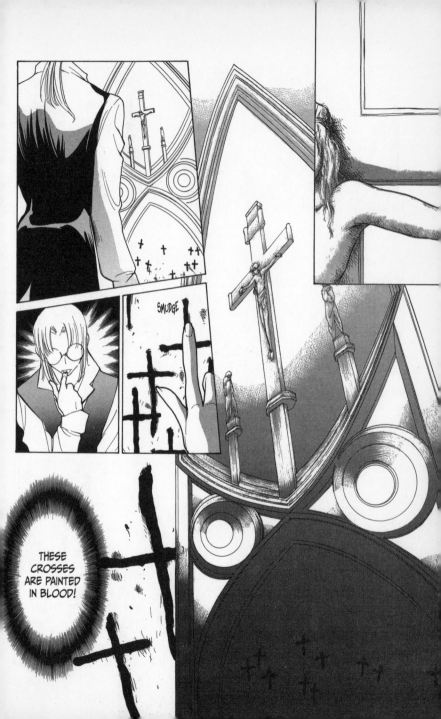

SMUDGE

THESE CROSSES ARE PAINTED IN BLOOD!

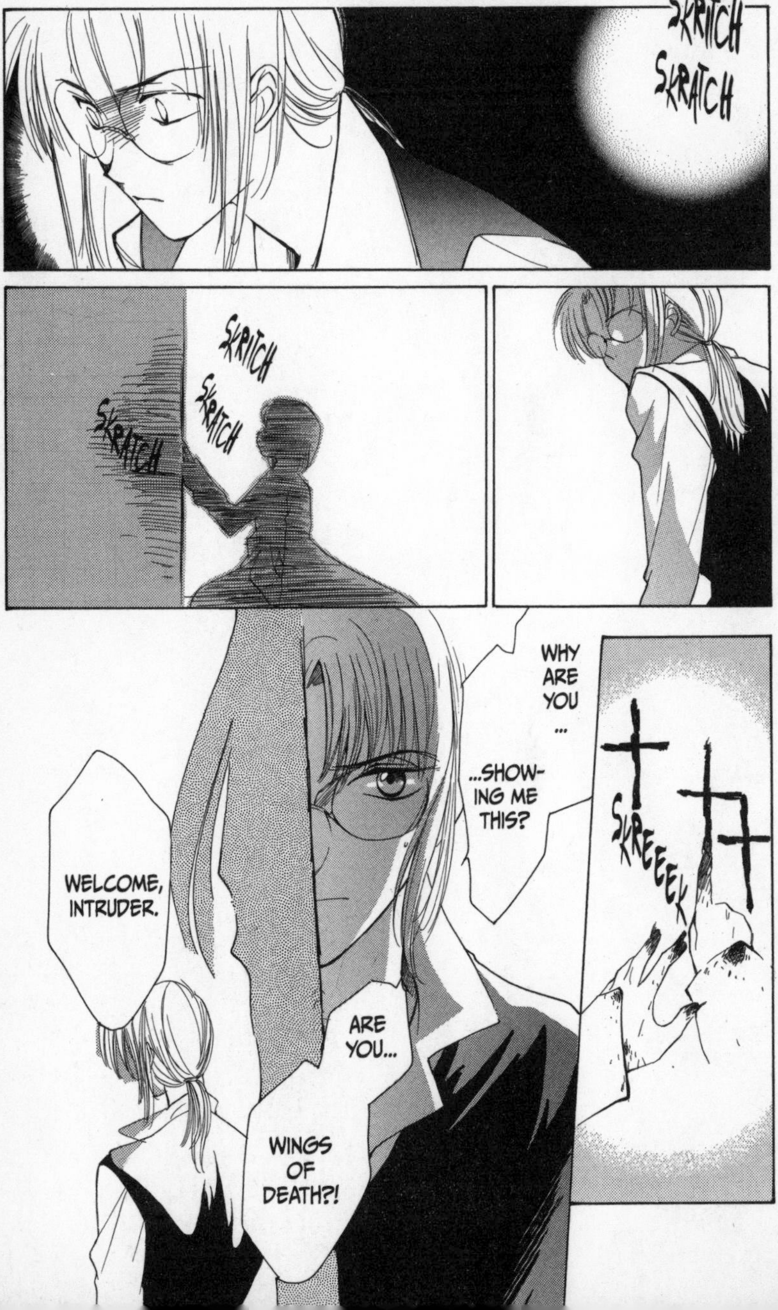
SKRITCH
SKRATCH
SKRITCH
SKRATCH
SKRATCH
SKREEEEK
WHY ARE YOU ...
...SHOW-ING ME THIS?
WELCOME, INTRUDER.
ARE YOU...
WINGS OF DEATH?!

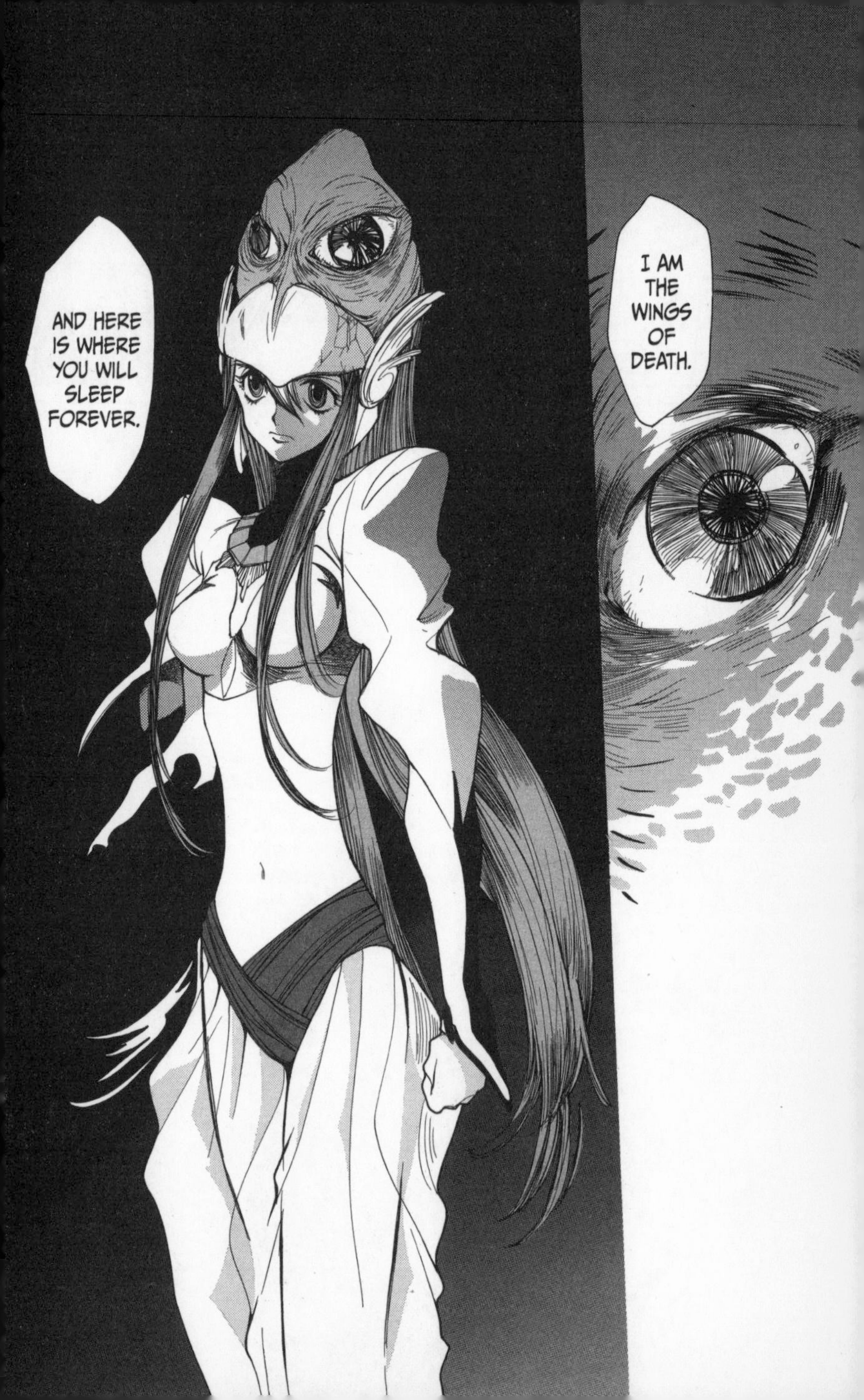
I AM THE WINGS OF DEATH.
AND HERE IS WHERE YOU WILL SLEEP FOREVER.

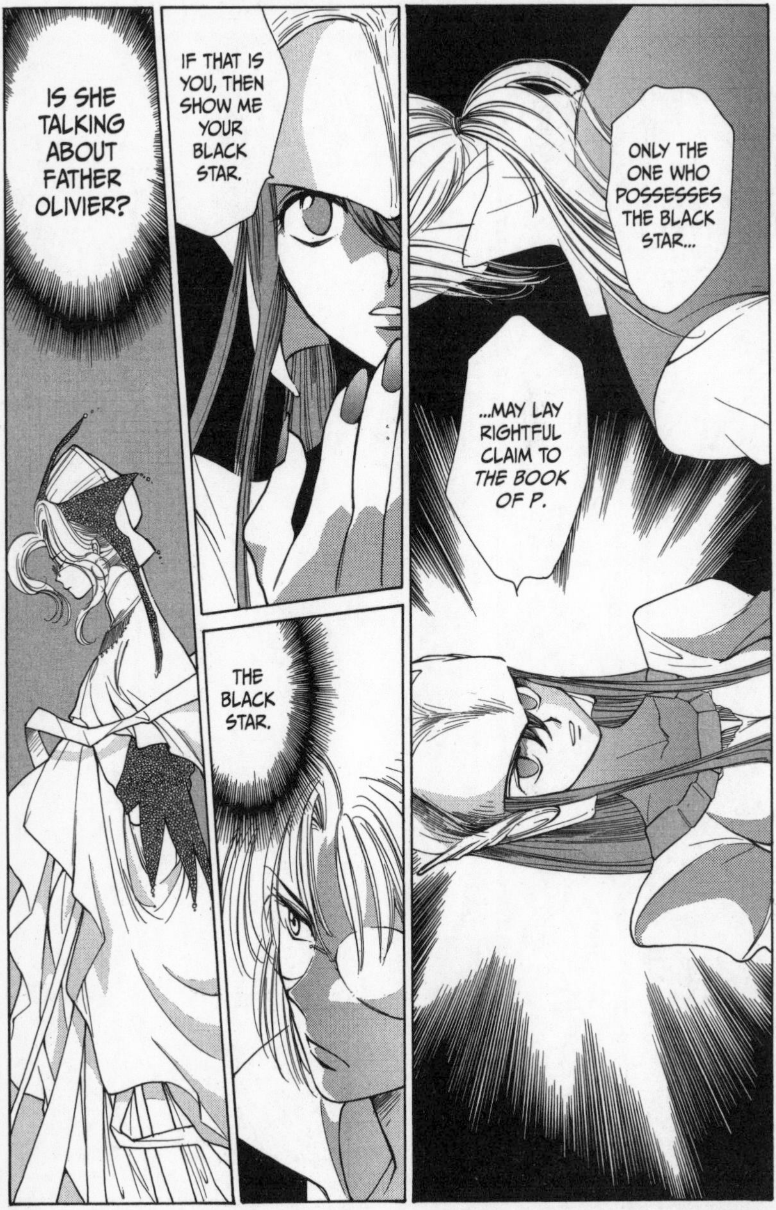
ONLY THE ONE WHO POSSESSES THE BLACK STAR...
...MAY LAY RIGHTFUL CLAIM TO *THE BOOK OF P*.
IF THAT IS YOU, THEN SHOW ME YOUR BLACK STAR.
THE BLACK STAR.
IS SHE TALKING ABOUT FATHER OLIVIER?

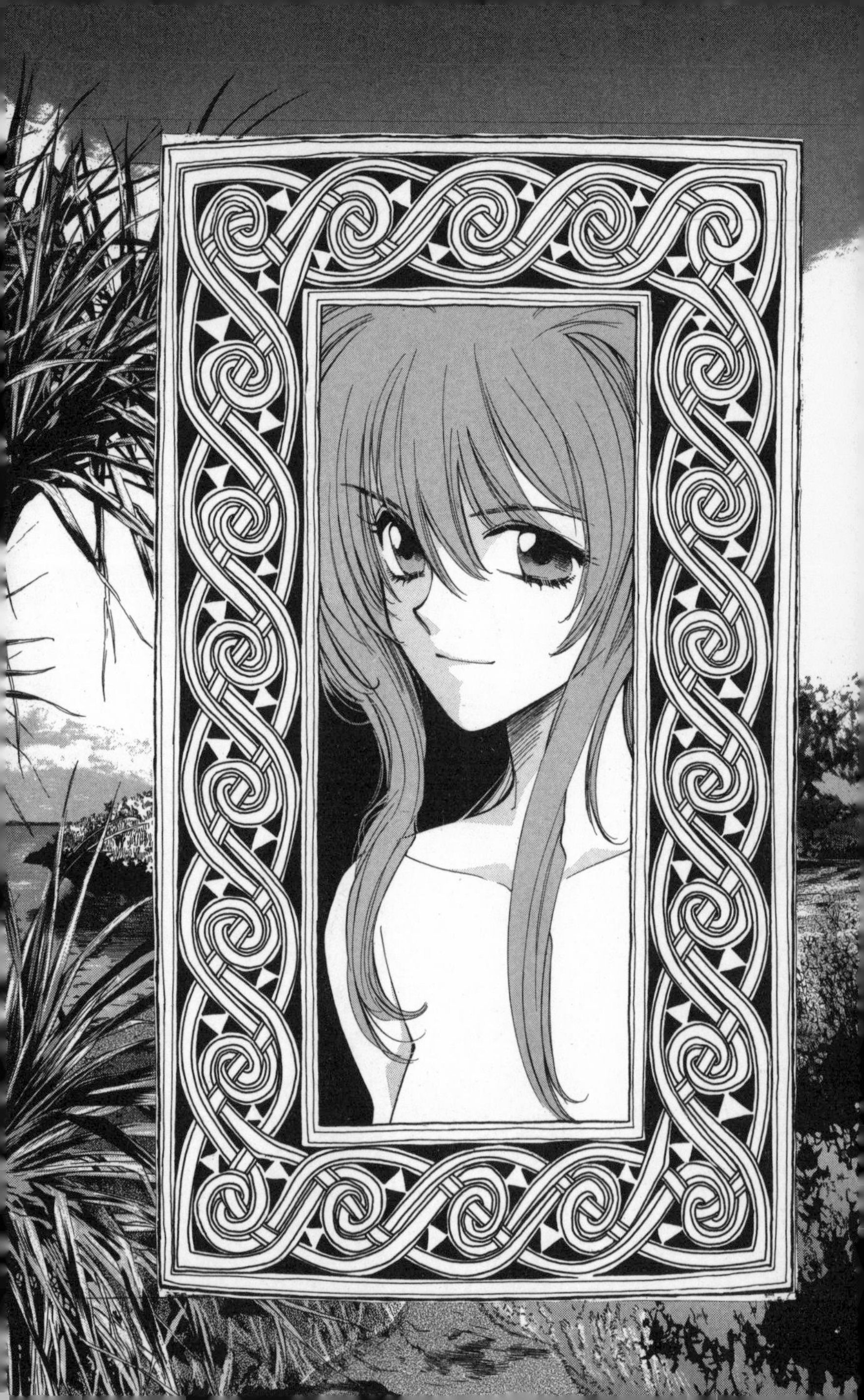

Chapter 31 Wings of Death Pt. II

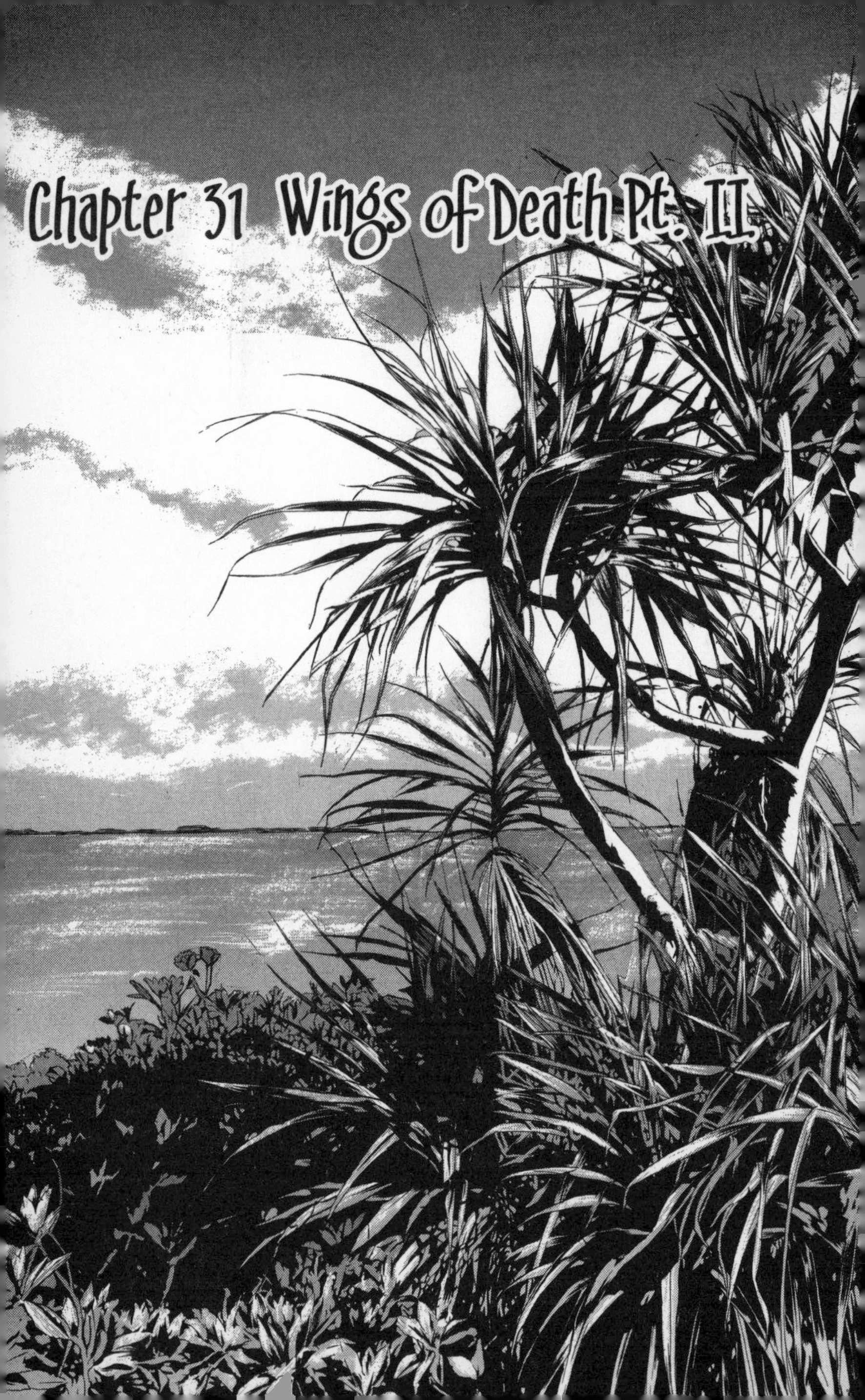

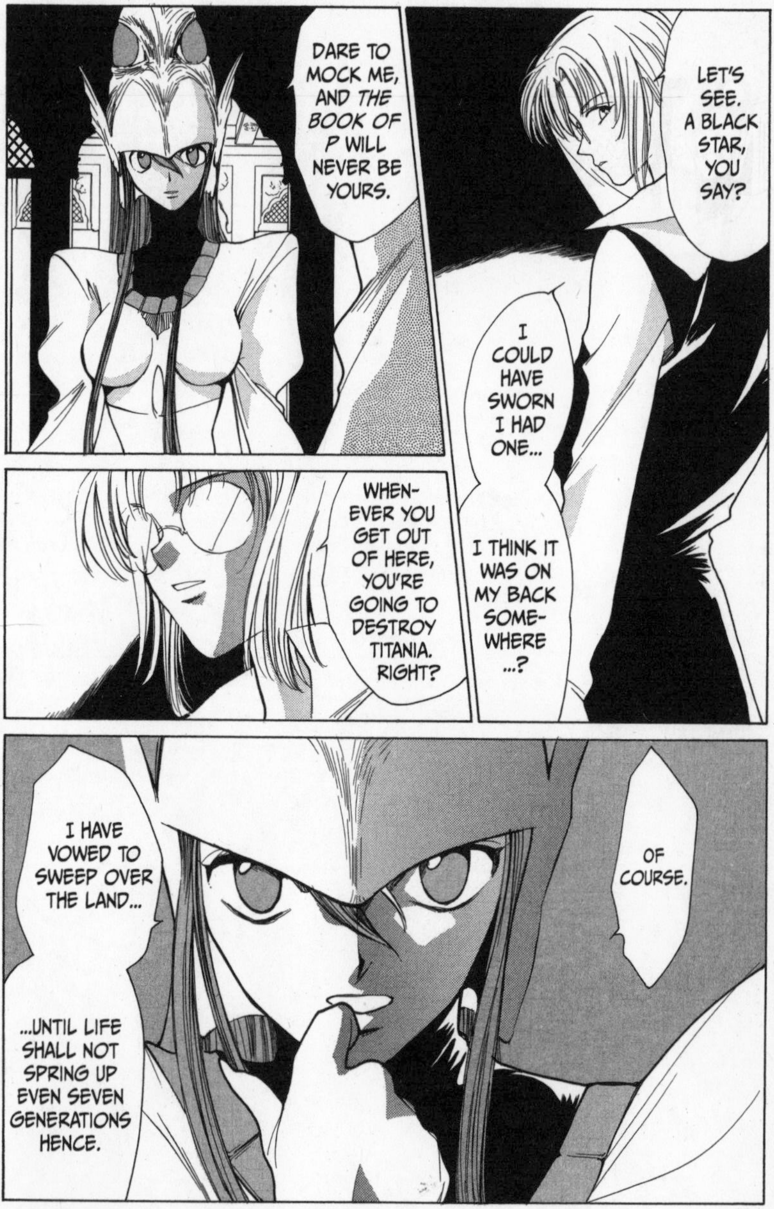
LET'S SEE. A BLACK STAR, YOU SAY?
I COULD HAVE SWORN I HAD ONE...
I THINK IT WAS ON MY BACK SOME-WHERE ...?
DARE TO MOCK ME, AND *THE BOOK OF P* WILL NEVER BE YOURS.
WHEN-EVER YOU GET OUT OF HERE, YOU'RE GOING TO DESTROY TITANIA. RIGHT?
OF COURSE.
I HAVE VOWED TO SWEEP OVER THE LAND...
...UNTIL LIFE SHALL NOT SPRING UP EVEN SEVEN GENERATIONS HENCE.

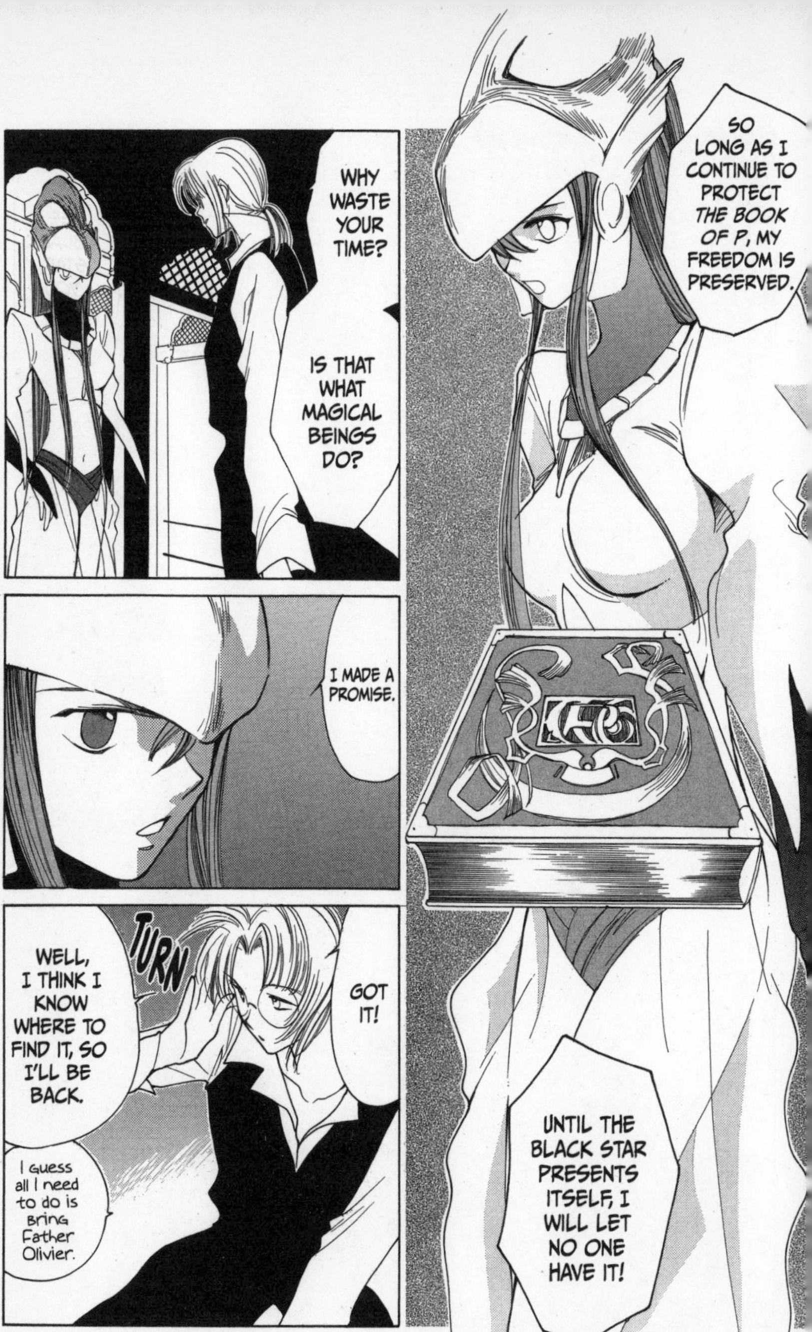
SO LONG AS I CONTINUE TO PROTECT *THE BOOK OF P*, MY FREEDOM IS PRESERVED.
UNTIL THE BLACK STAR PRESENTS ITSELF, I WILL LET NO ONE HAVE IT!
WHY WASTE YOUR TIME?
IS THAT WHAT MAGICAL BEINGS DO?
I MADE A PROMISE.
GOT IT!
TURN
WELL, I THINK I KNOW WHERE TO FIND IT, SO I'LL BE BACK.
I guess all I need to do is bring Father Olivier.

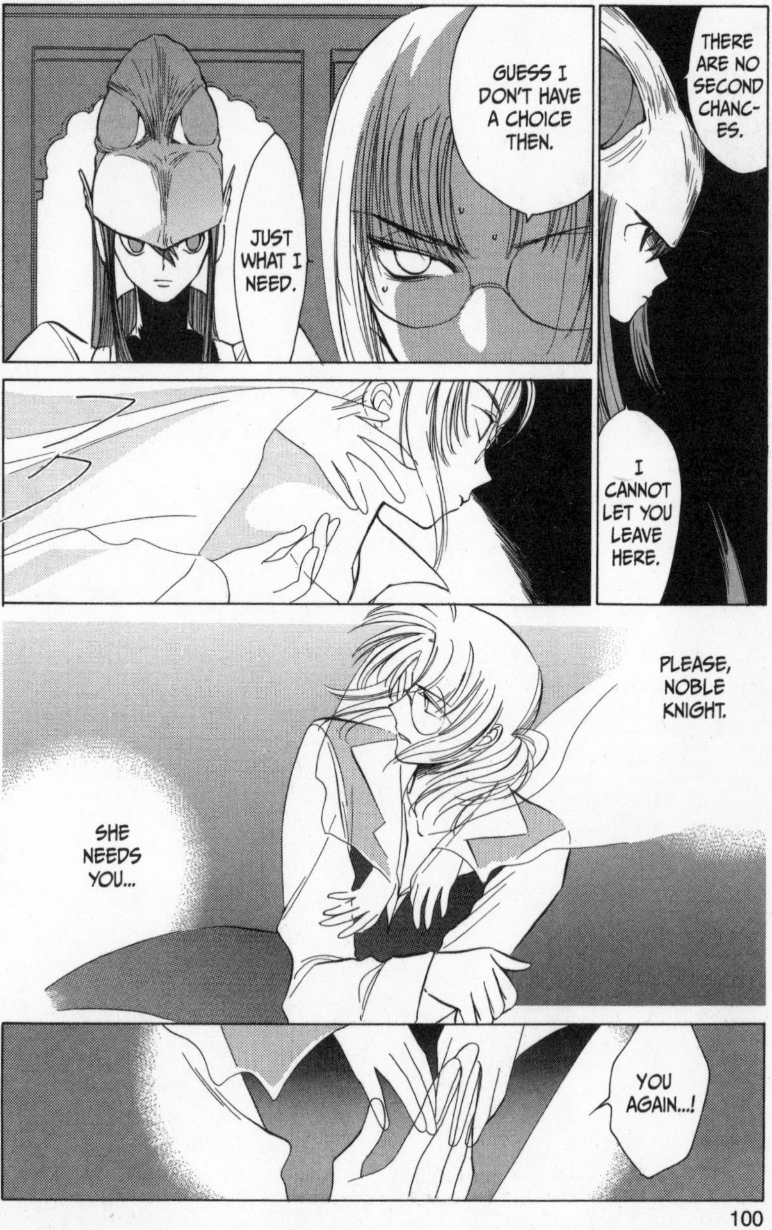
THERE ARE NO SECOND CHANCES.
I CANNOT LET YOU LEAVE HERE.
GUESS I DON'T HAVE A CHOICE THEN.
JUST WHAT I NEED.
PLEASE, NOBLE KNIGHT.
SHE NEEDS YOU...
YOU AGAIN...!

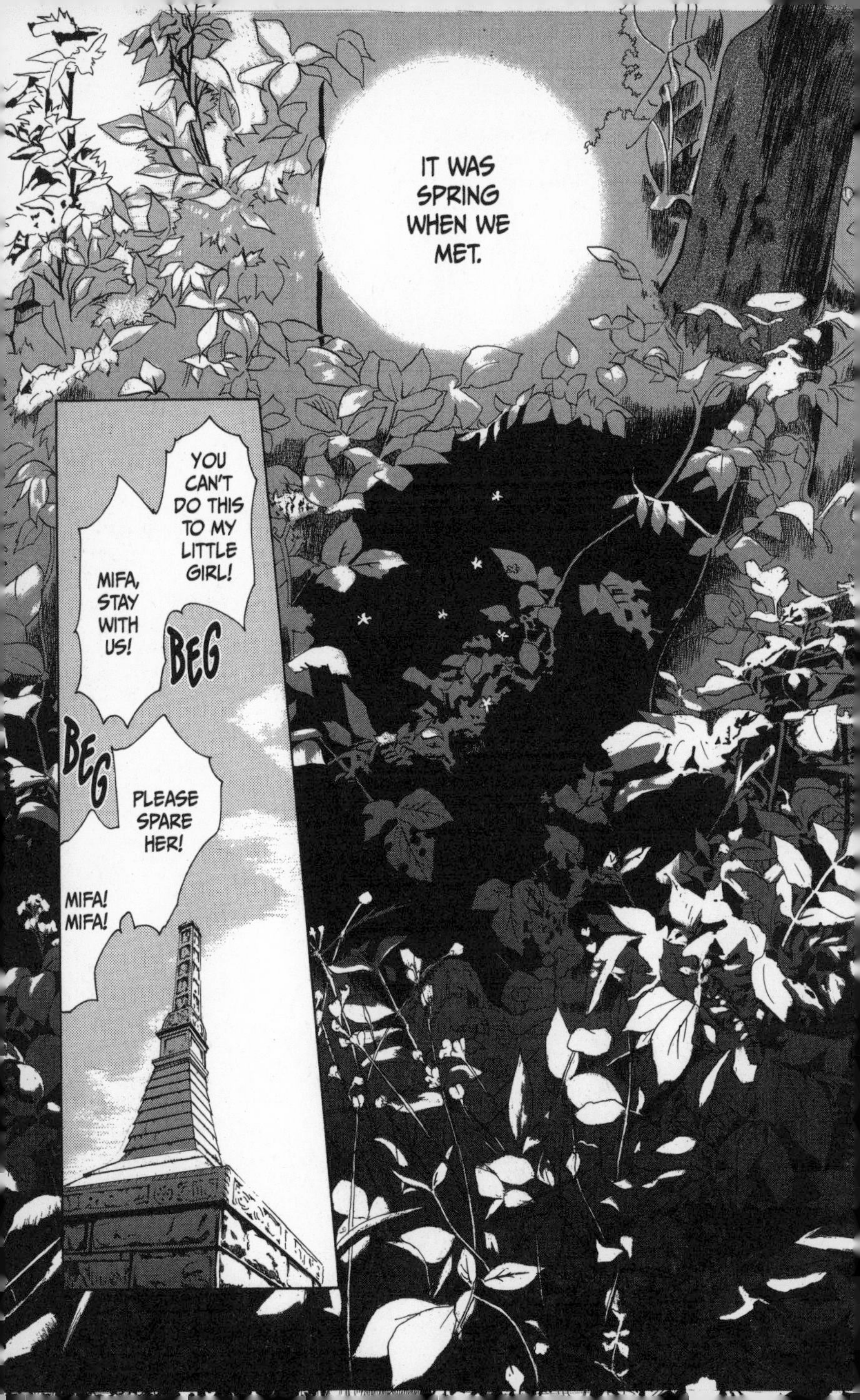
IT WAS SPRING WHEN WE MET.
YOU CAN'T DO THIS TO MY LITTLE GIRL!
MIFA, STAY WITH US!
BEG
BEG
PLEASE SPARE HER!
MIFA! MIFA!

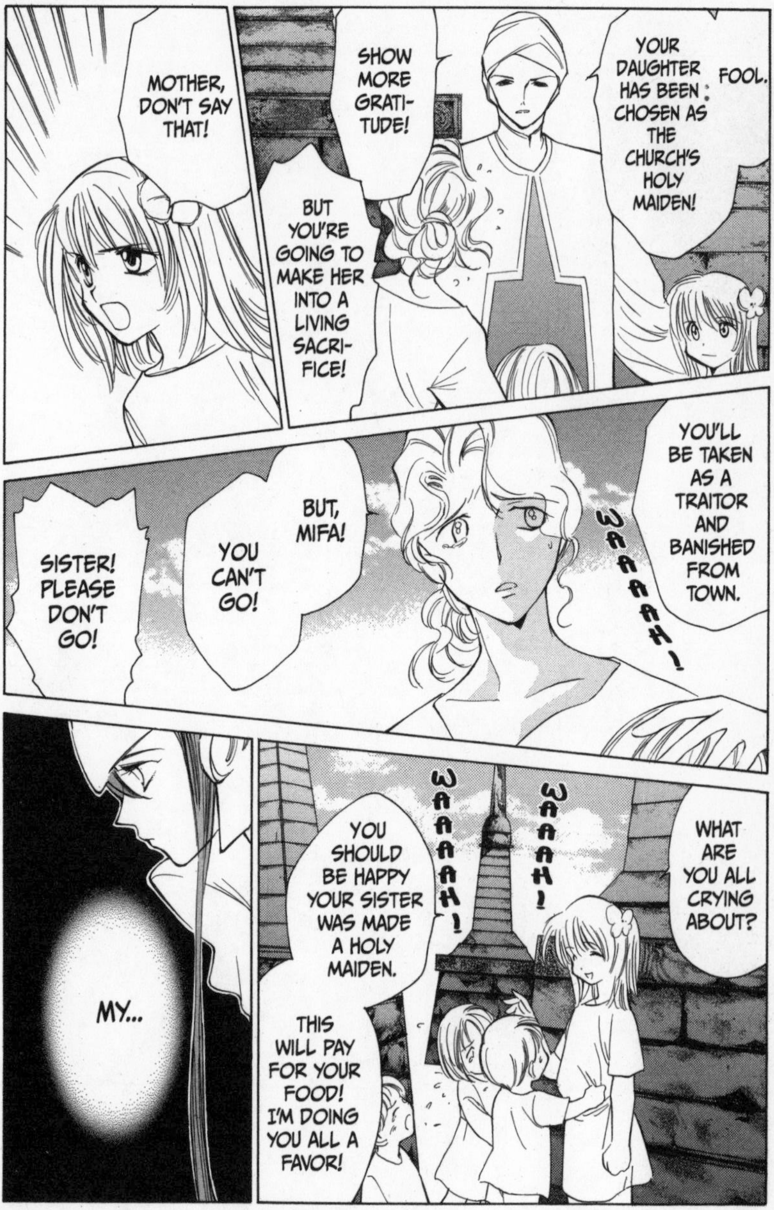
FOOL.
YOUR DAUGHTER HAS BEEN CHOSEN AS THE CHURCH'S HOLY MAIDEN!
SHOW MORE GRATITUDE!
BUT YOU'RE GOING TO MAKE HER INTO A LIVING SACRI-FICE!
MOTHER, DON'T SAY THAT!
YOU'LL BE TAKEN AS A TRAITOR AND BANISHED FROM TOWN.
WAAAAH!
BUT, MIFA!
YOU CAN'T GO!
SISTER! PLEASE DON'T GO!
WHAT ARE YOU ALL CRYING ABOUT?
WAAAAH!
WAAAAAH!
YOU SHOULD BE HAPPY YOUR SISTER WAS MADE A HOLY MAIDEN.
THIS WILL PAY FOR YOUR FOOD! I'M DOING YOU ALL A FAVOR!
MY...

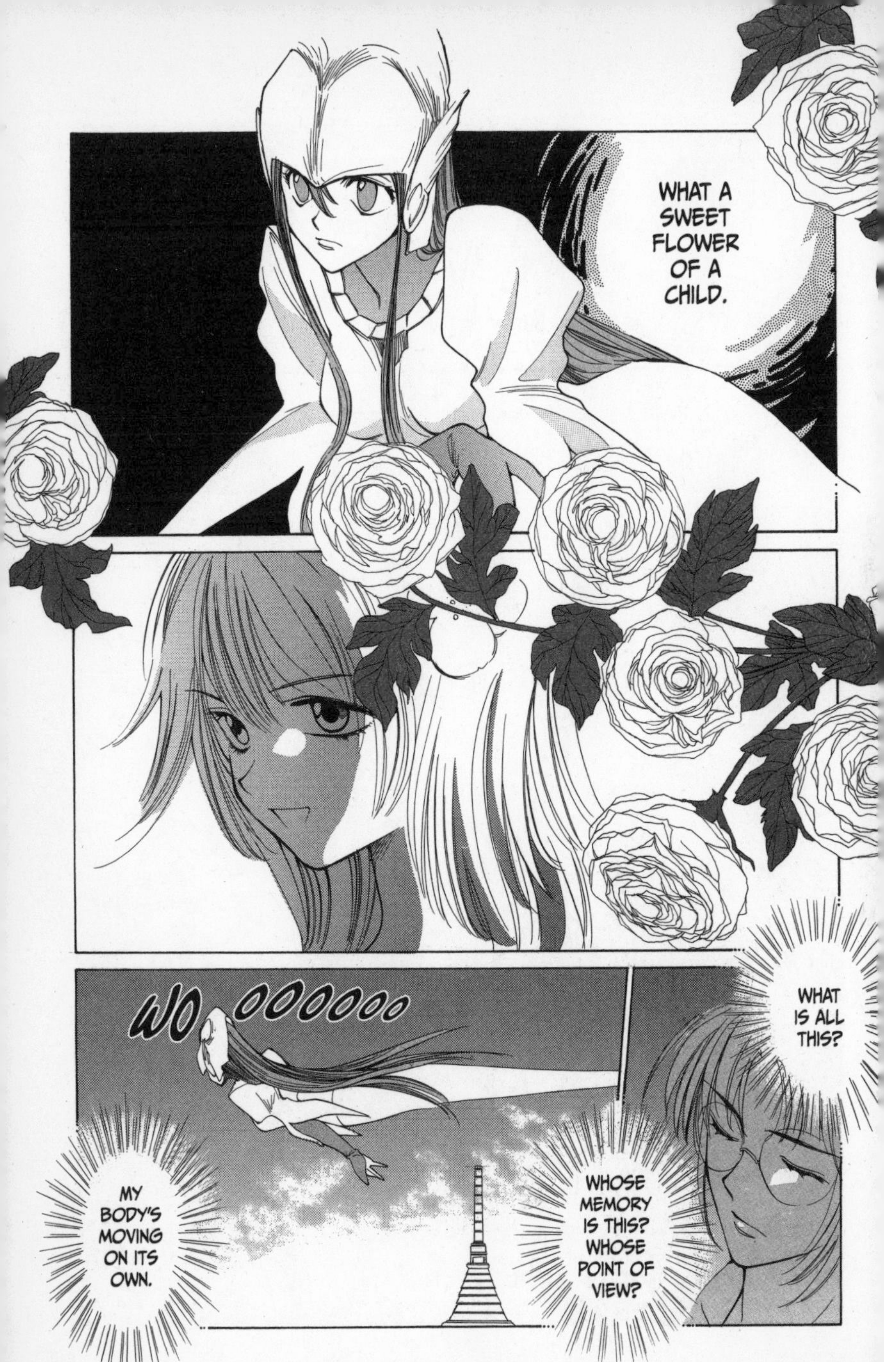
WHAT A SWEET FLOWER OF A CHILD.
WHAT IS ALL THIS?
WO OOOOOO
WHOSE MEMORY IS THIS? WHOSE POINT OF VIEW?
MY BODY'S MOVING ON ITS OWN.

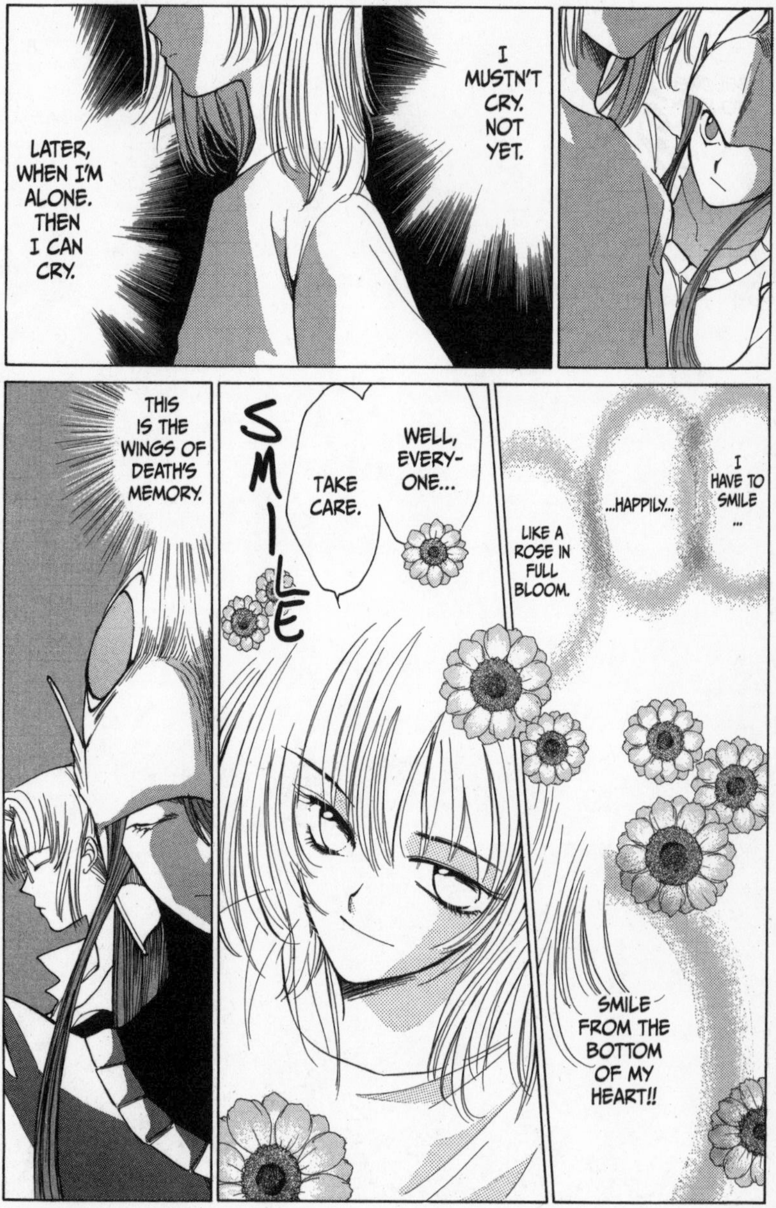
I MUSTN'T CRY. NOT YET.
LATER, WHEN I'M ALONE. THEN I CAN CRY.
I HAVE TO SMILE ...
...HAPPILY...
LIKE A ROSE IN FULL BLOOM.
SMILE FROM THE BOTTOM OF MY HEART!!
WELL, EVERY-ONE...
TAKE CARE.
SMILE
THIS IS THE WINGS OF DEATH'S MEMORY.

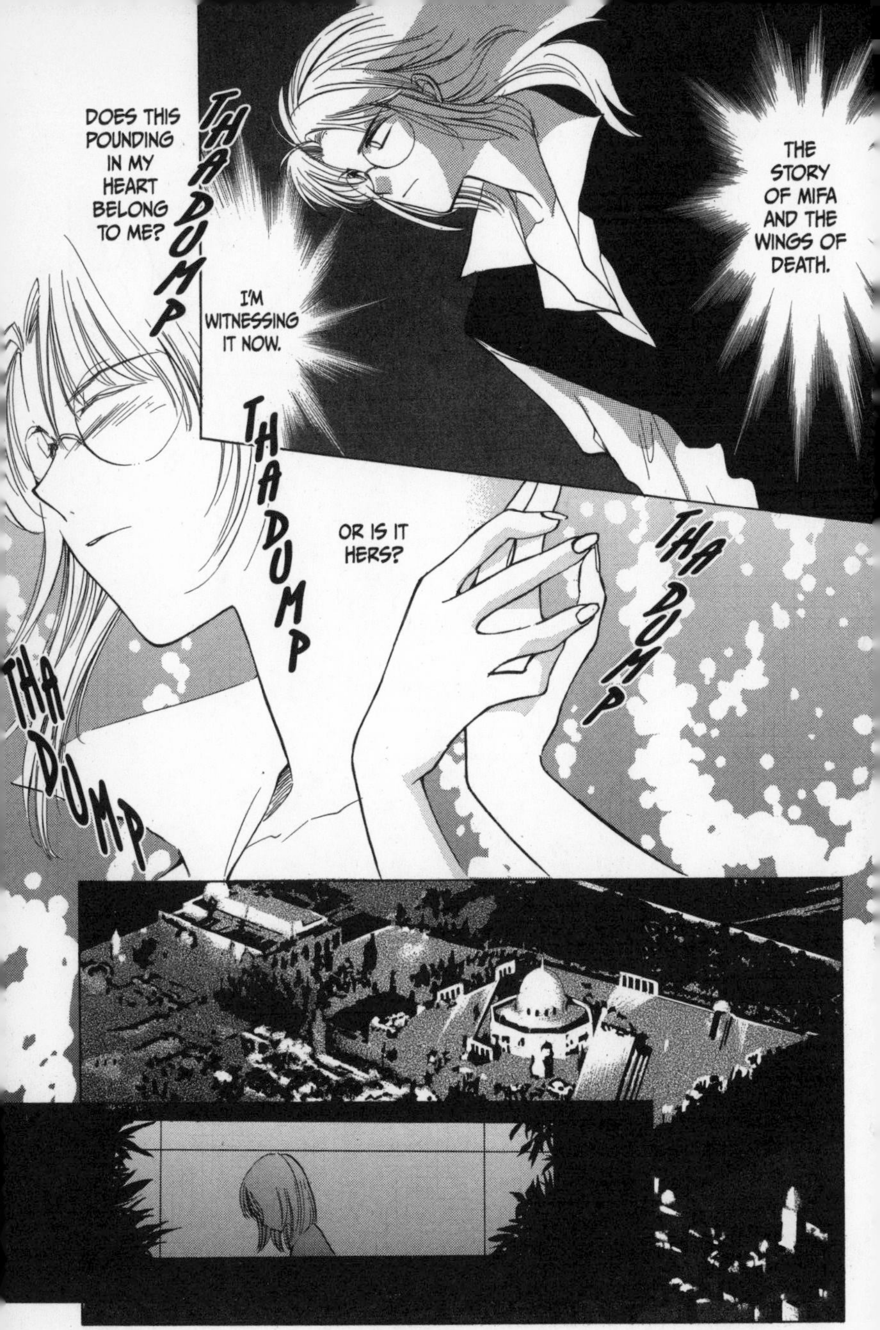
THE STORY OF MIFA AND THE WINGS OF DEATH.
I'M WITNESSING IT NOW.
THADUMP
DOES THIS POUNDING IN MY HEART BELONG TO ME?
THADUMP
OR IS IT HERS?
THADUMP
THADUMP

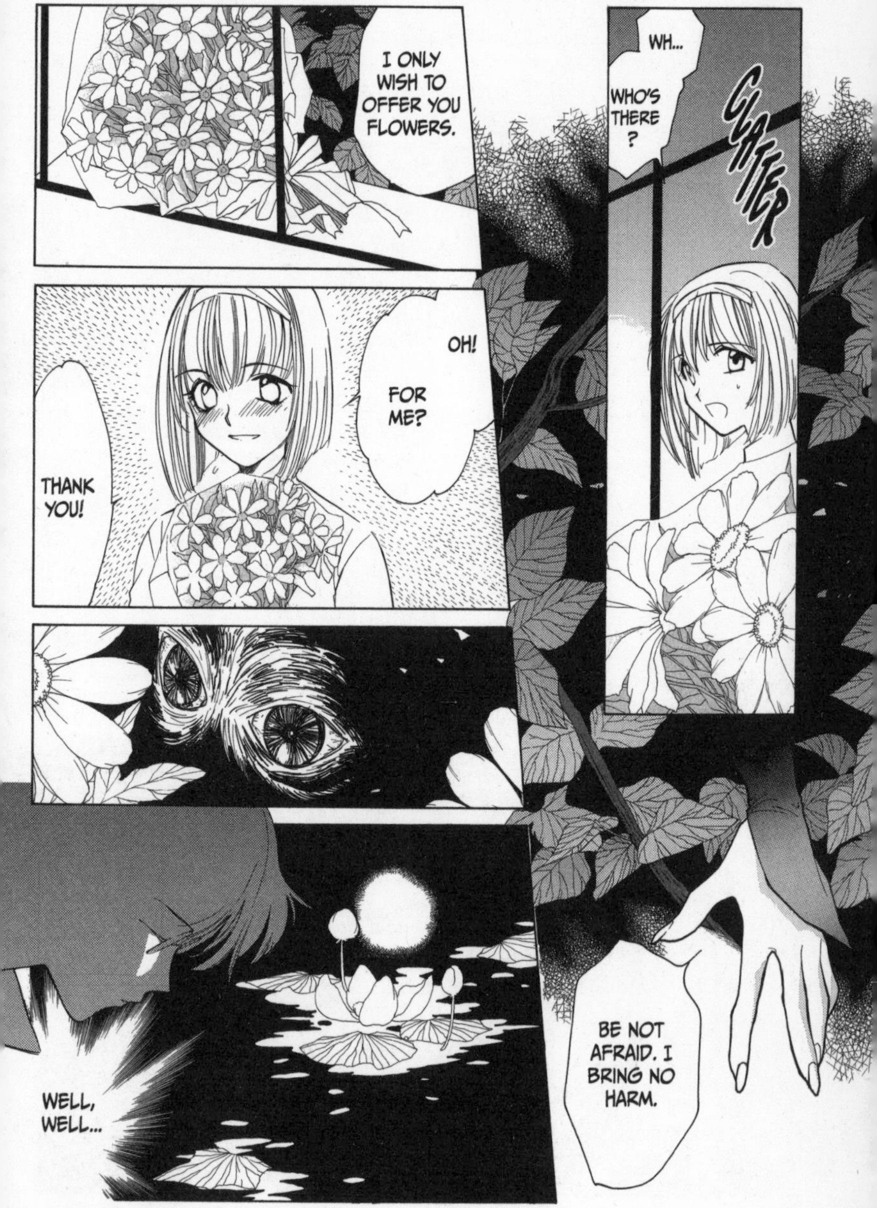
WH...
WHO'S THERE?
CLATTER
BE NOT AFRAID. I BRING NO HARM.
I ONLY WISH TO OFFER YOU FLOWERS.
OH!
FOR ME?
THANK YOU!
WELL, WELL...

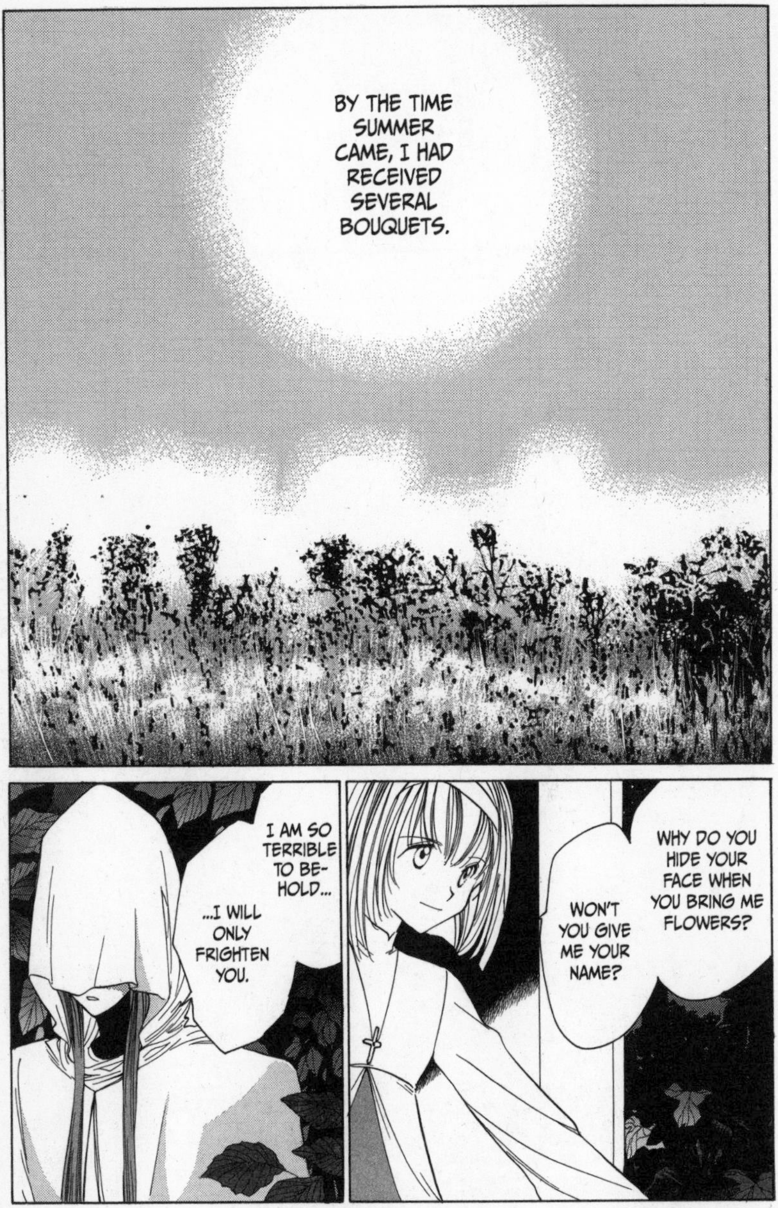
BY THE TIME SUMMER CAME, I HAD RECEIVED SEVERAL BOUQUETS.
WHY DO YOU HIDE YOUR FACE WHEN YOU BRING ME FLOWERS?
WON'T YOU GIVE ME YOUR NAME?
I AM SO TERRIBLE TO BE-HOLD...
...I WILL ONLY FRIGHTEN YOU.

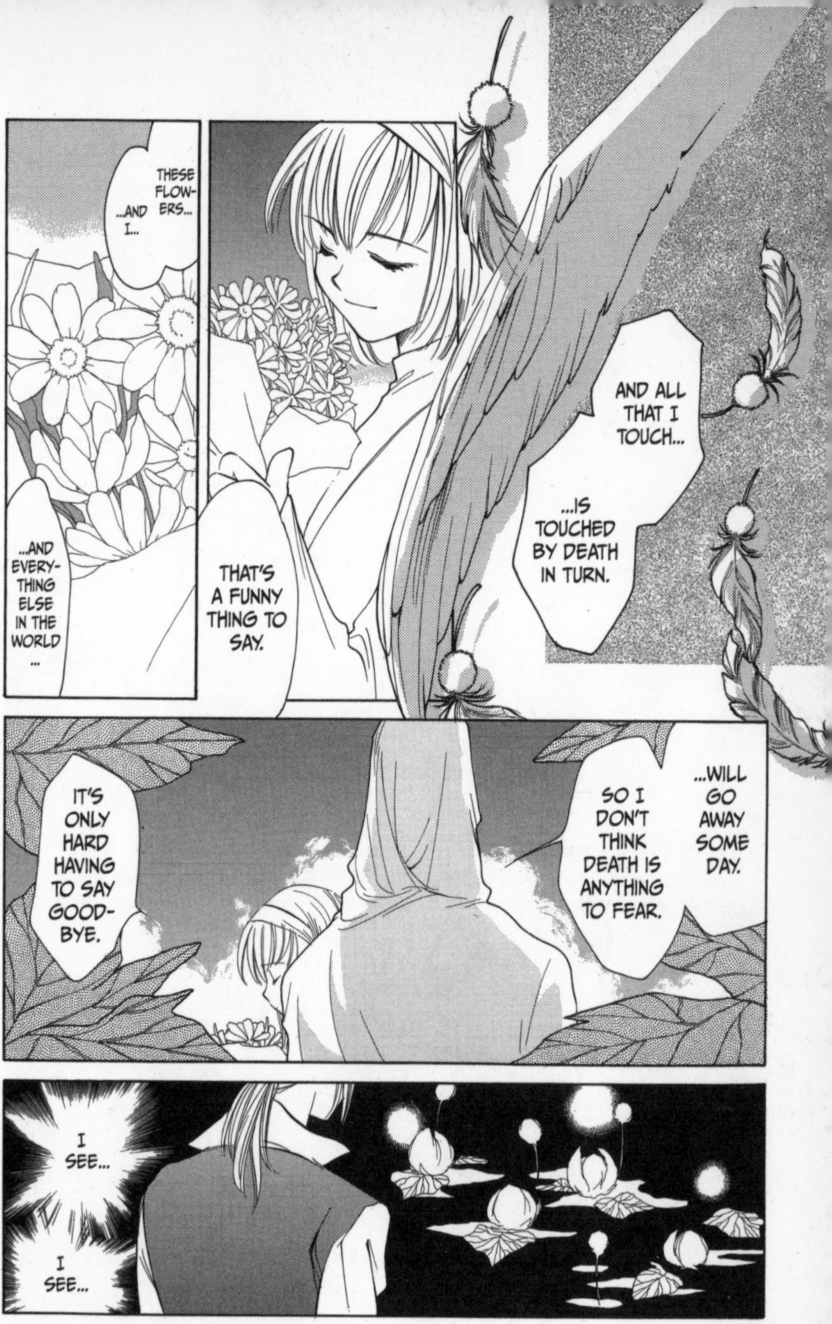
AND ALL THAT I TOUCH...
...IS TOUCHED BY DEATH IN TURN.
THAT'S A FUNNY THING TO SAY.
THESE FLOWERS...
...AND I...
...AND EVERYTHING ELSE IN THE WORLD ...
...WILL GO AWAY SOME DAY.
SO I DON'T THINK DEATH IS ANYTHING TO FEAR.
IT'S ONLY HARD HAVING TO SAY GOODBYE.
I SEE...
I SEE...

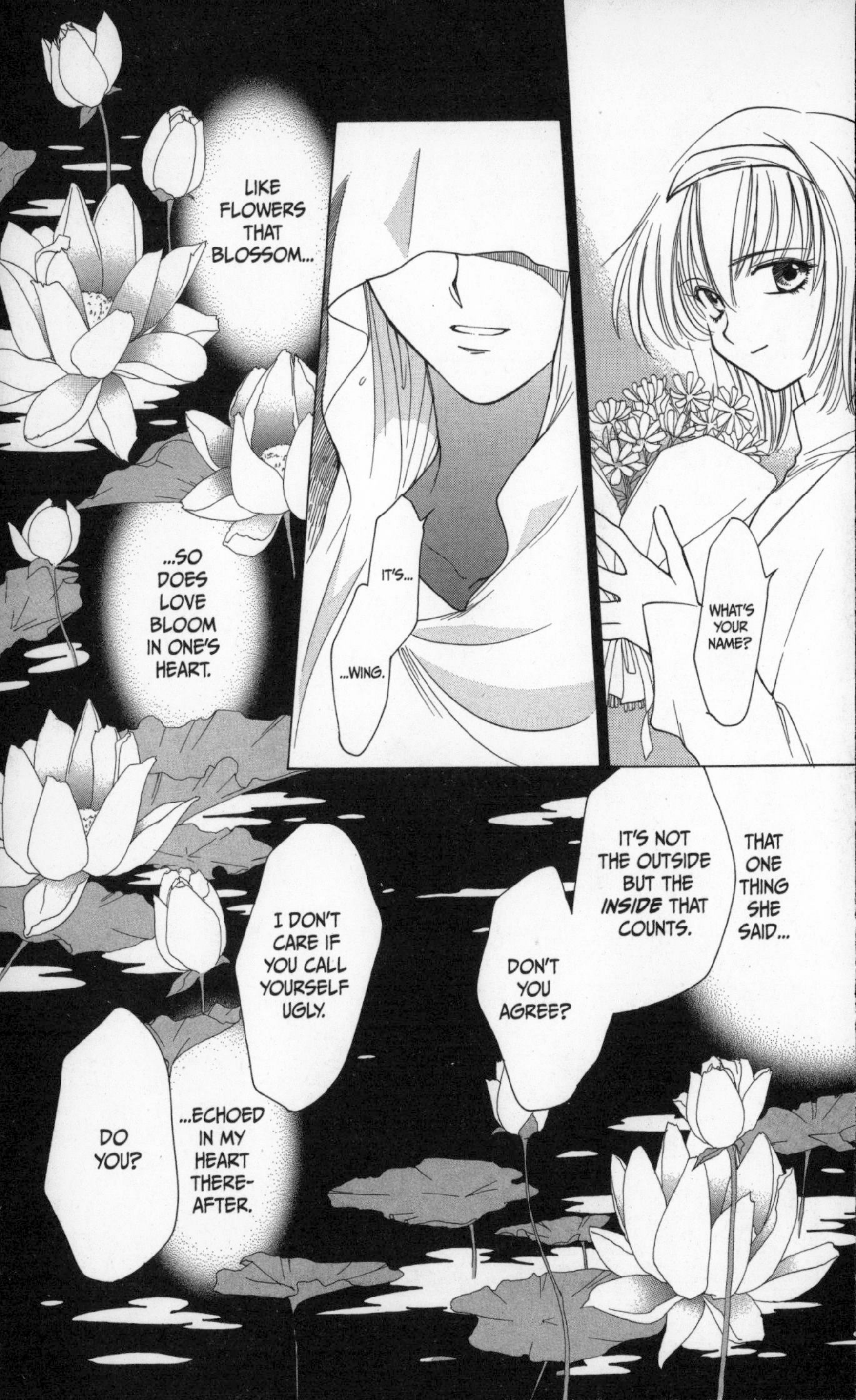
WHAT'S YOUR NAME?
IT'S...
...WING.
LIKE FLOWERS THAT BLOSSOM...
...SO DOES LOVE BLOOM IN ONE'S HEART.
THAT ONE THING SHE SAID...
IT'S NOT THE OUTSIDE BUT THE *INSIDE* THAT COUNTS.
DON'T YOU AGREE?
I DON'T CARE IF YOU CALL YOURSELF UGLY.
DO YOU?
...ECHOED IN MY HEART THEREAFTER.

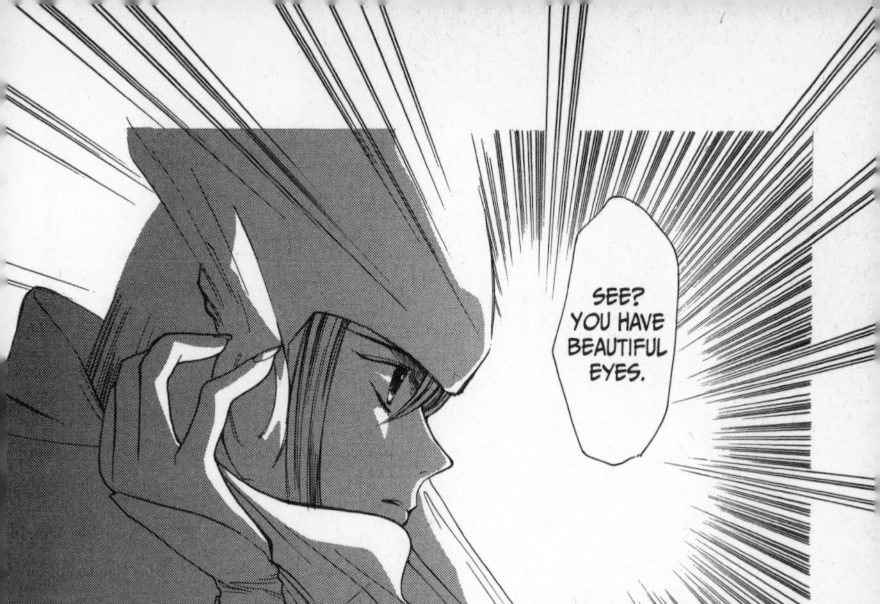
SEE? YOU HAVE BEAUTIFUL EYES.

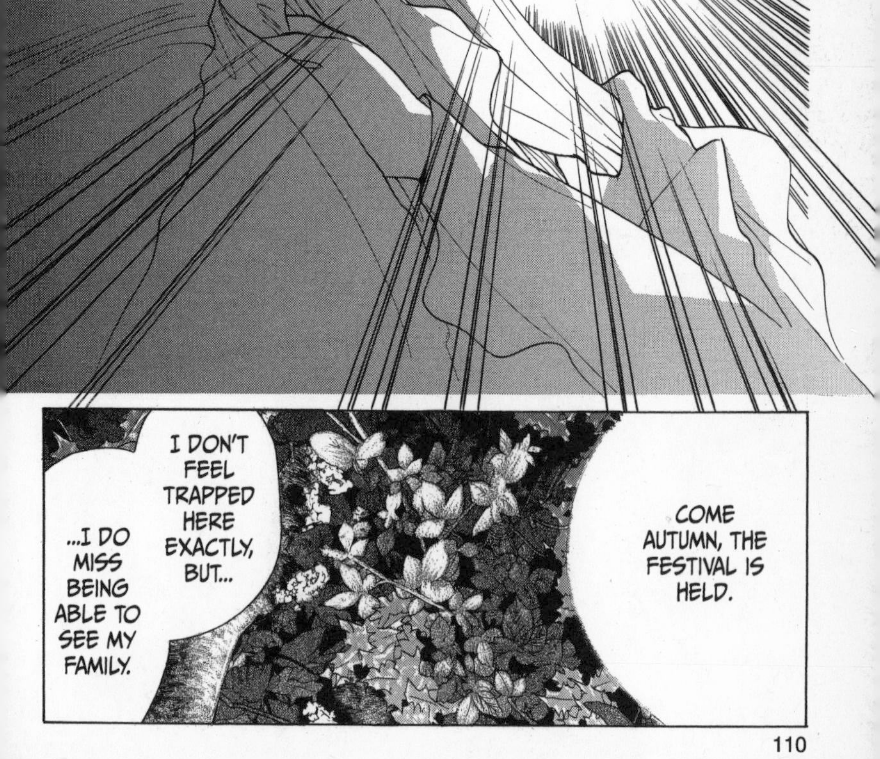
COME AUTUMN, THE FESTIVAL IS HELD.
I DON'T FEEL TRAPPED HERE EXACTLY, BUT...
...I DO MISS BEING ABLE TO SEE MY FAMILY.

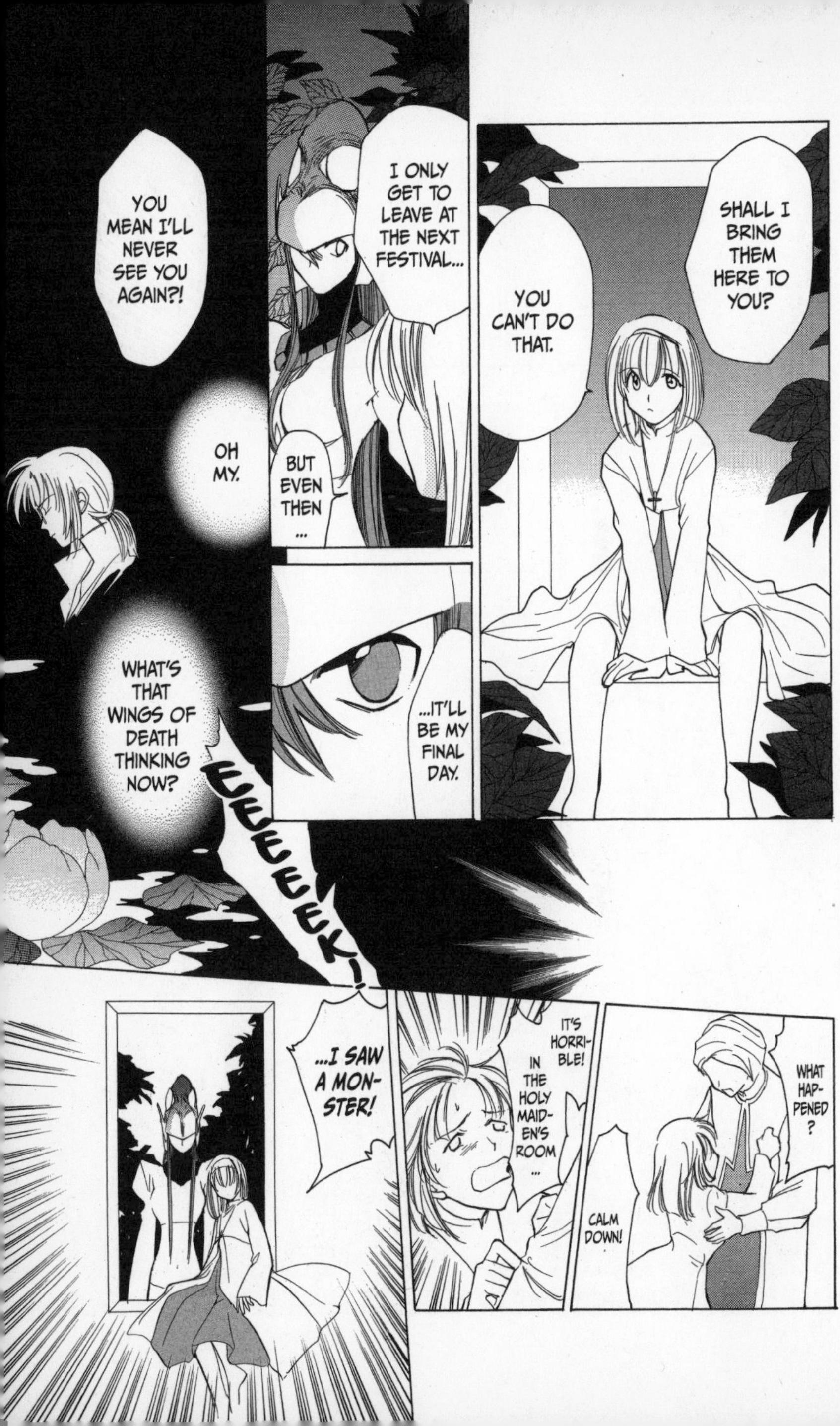
SHALL I BRING THEM HERE TO YOU?
YOU CAN'T DO THAT.
I ONLY GET TO LEAVE AT THE NEXT FESTIVAL...
BUT EVEN THEN ...
...IT'LL BE MY FINAL DAY.
YOU MEAN I'LL NEVER SEE YOU AGAIN?!
OH MY.
WHAT'S THAT WINGS OF DEATH THINKING NOW?
EEEEEEK!
WHAT HAP-PENED ?
CALM DOWN!
IT'S HORRI-BLE!
IN THE HOLY MAID-EN'S ROOM ...
...I SAW A MON-STER!

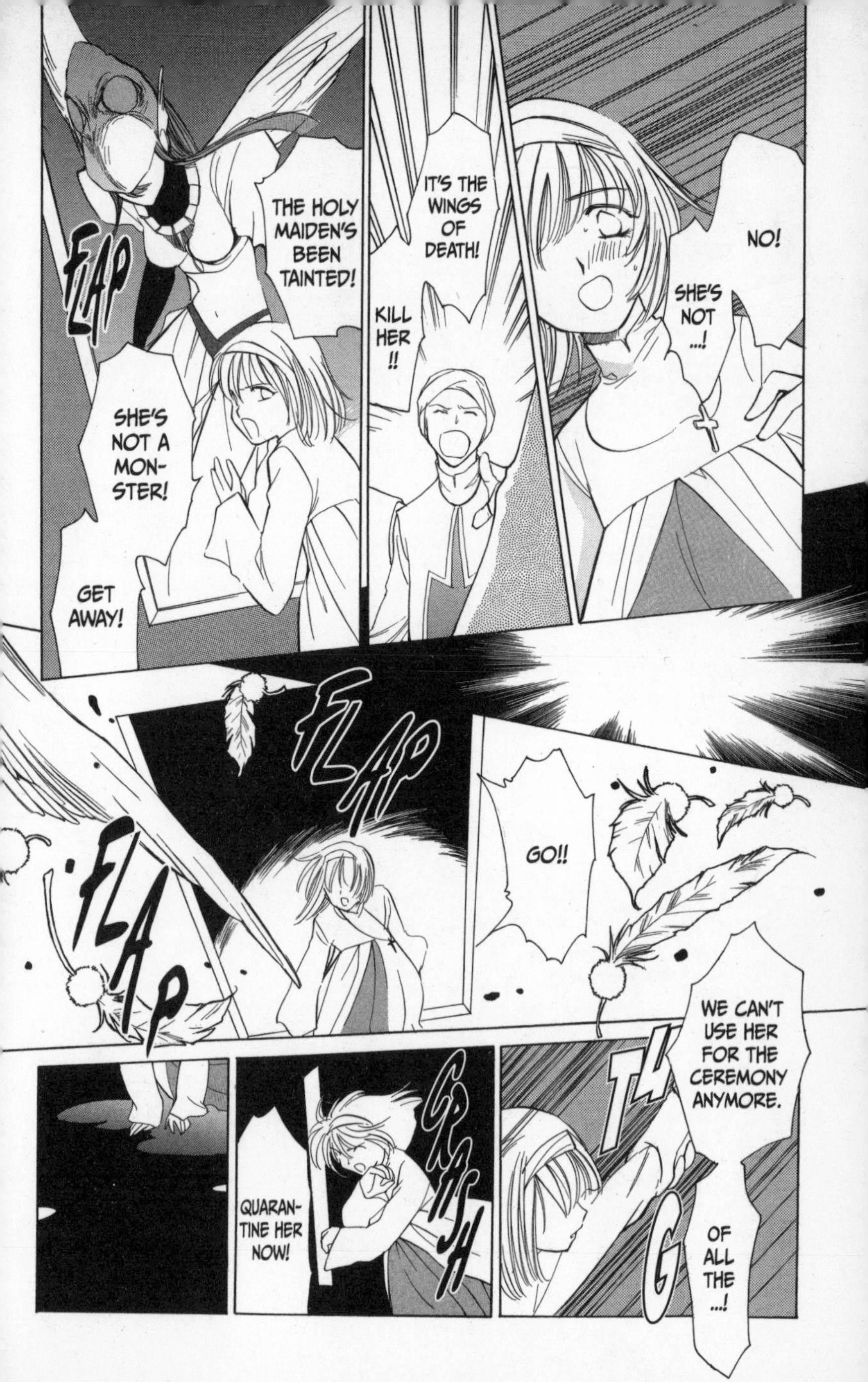
NO!
SHE'S NOT ...!
IT'S THE WINGS OF DEATH!
KILL HER !!
THE HOLY MAIDEN'S BEEN TAINTED!
FLAP
SHE'S NOT A MONSTER!
GET AWAY!
GO!!
FLAP
FLAP
WE CAN'T USE HER FOR THE CEREMONY ANYMORE.
OF ALL THE ...!
CRASH
QUARANTINE HER NOW!

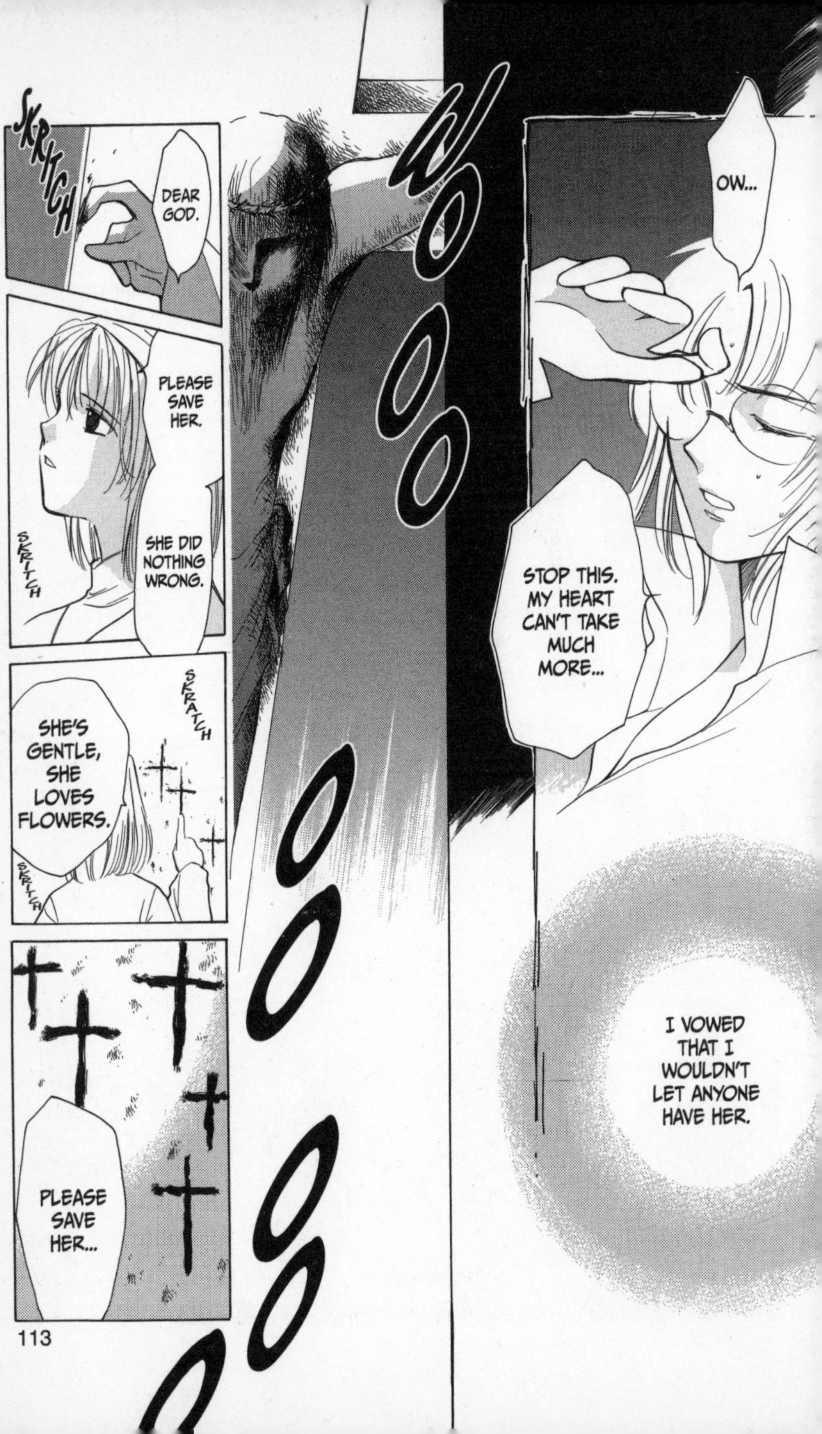
OW...
STOP THIS. MY HEART CAN'T TAKE MUCH MORE...
I VOWED THAT I WOULDN'T LET ANYONE HAVE HER.
SKRITCH
DEAR GOD.
PLEASE SAVE HER.
SHE DID NOTHING WRONG.
SKRITCH
SKRATCH
SHE'S GENTLE, SHE LOVES FLOWERS.
SKRITCH
PLEASE SAVE HER...

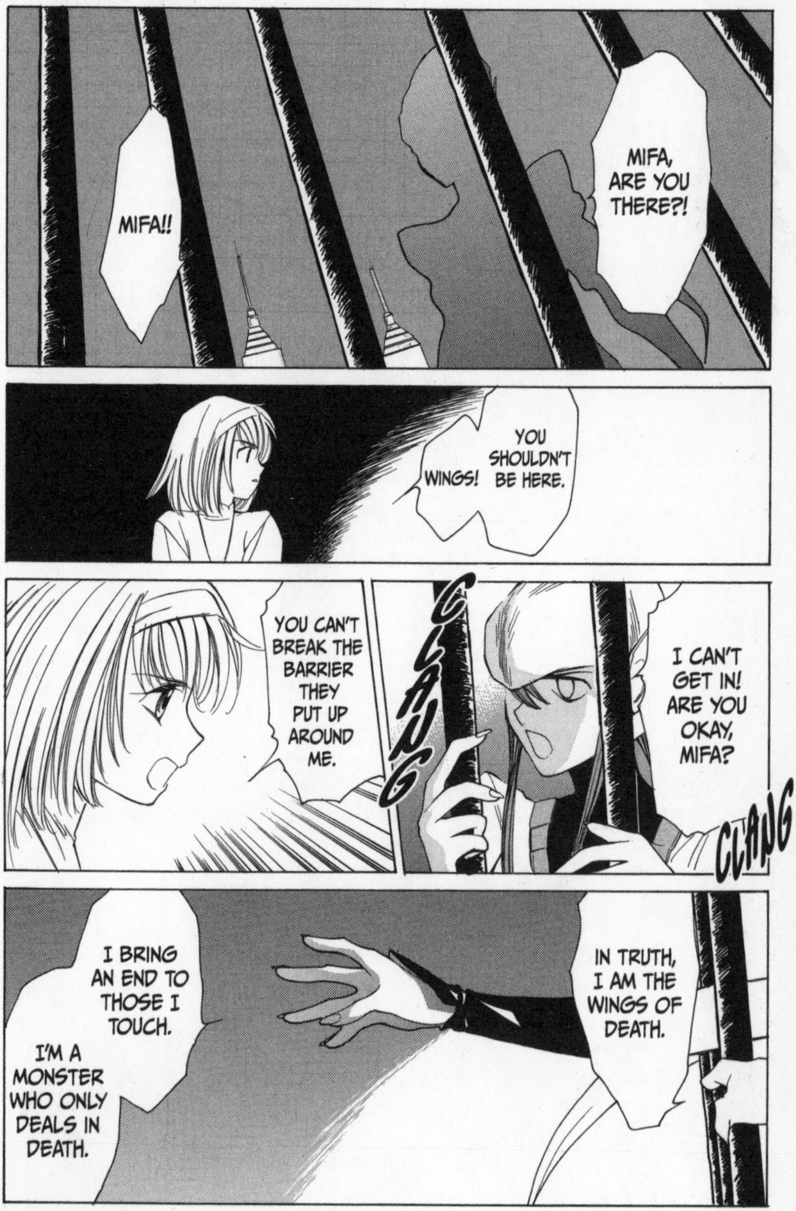
MIFA, ARE YOU THERE?!
MIFA!!
YOU SHOULDN'T BE HERE.
WINGS!
I CAN'T GET IN! ARE YOU OKAY, MIFA?
CLANG
CLANG
YOU CAN'T BREAK THE BARRIER THEY PUT UP AROUND ME.
IN TRUTH, I AM THE WINGS OF DEATH.
I BRING AN END TO THOSE I TOUCH.
I'M A MONSTER WHO ONLY DEALS IN DEATH.

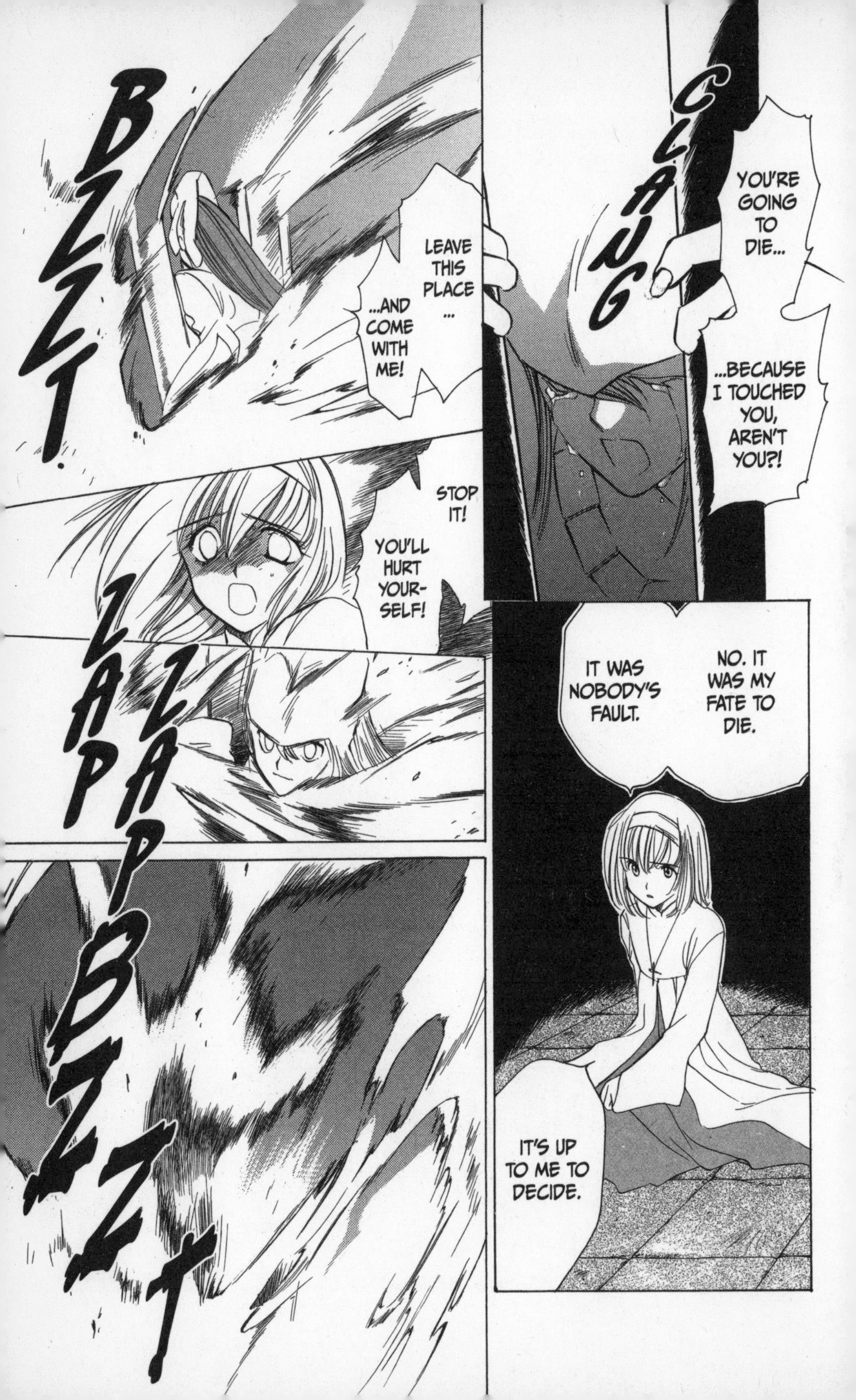
CLANG
YOU'RE GOING TO DIE...
...BECAUSE I TOUCHED YOU, AREN'T YOU?!
BZZZT
LEAVE THIS PLACE...
...AND COME WITH ME!
STOP IT!
YOU'LL HURT YOURSELF!
ZAP ZAP
NO. IT WAS MY FATE TO DIE.
IT WAS NOBODY'S FAULT.
IT'S UP TO ME TO DECIDE.
BZZZT

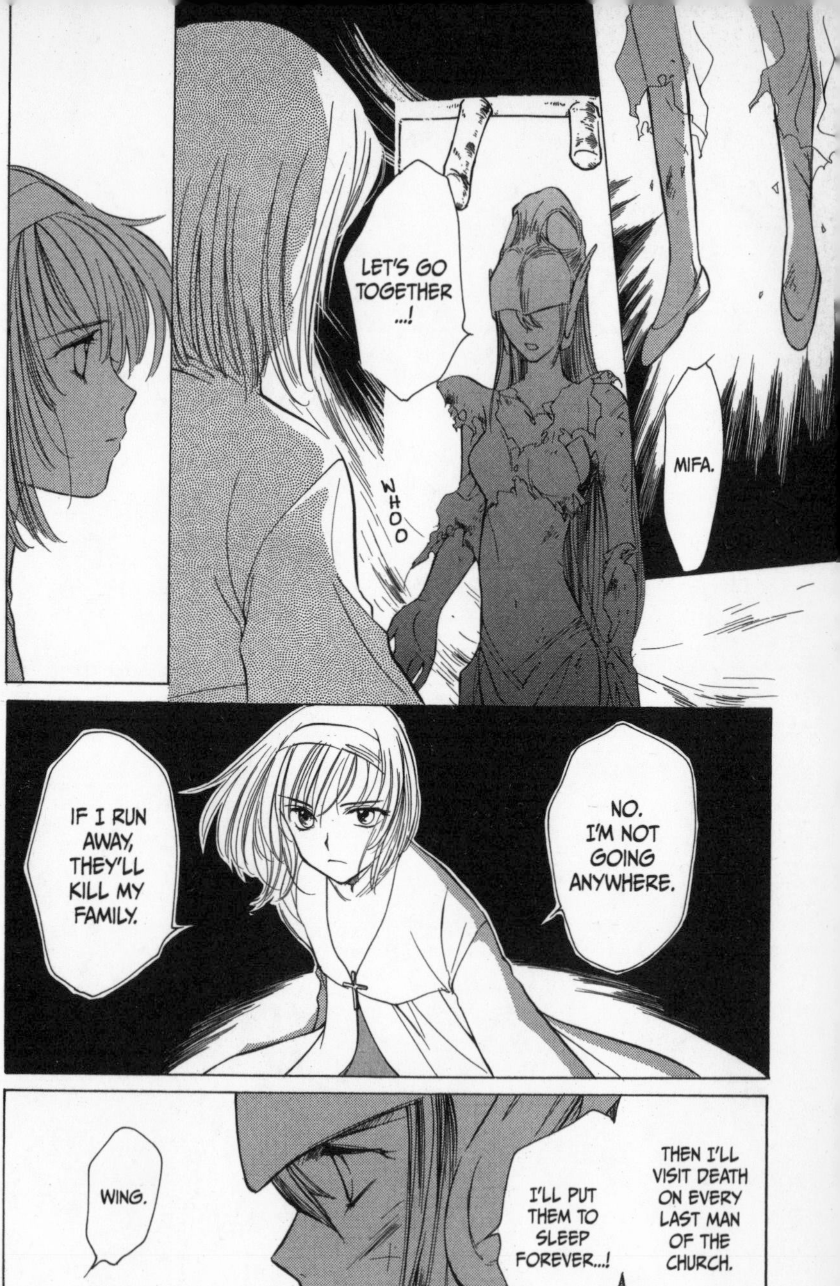
MIFA.
LET'S GO TOGETHER ...!
WHOO
NO. I'M NOT GOING ANYWHERE.
IF I RUN AWAY, THEY'LL KILL MY FAMILY.
THEN I'LL VISIT DEATH ON EVERY LAST MAN OF THE CHURCH.
I'LL PUT THEM TO SLEEP FOREVER...!
WING.

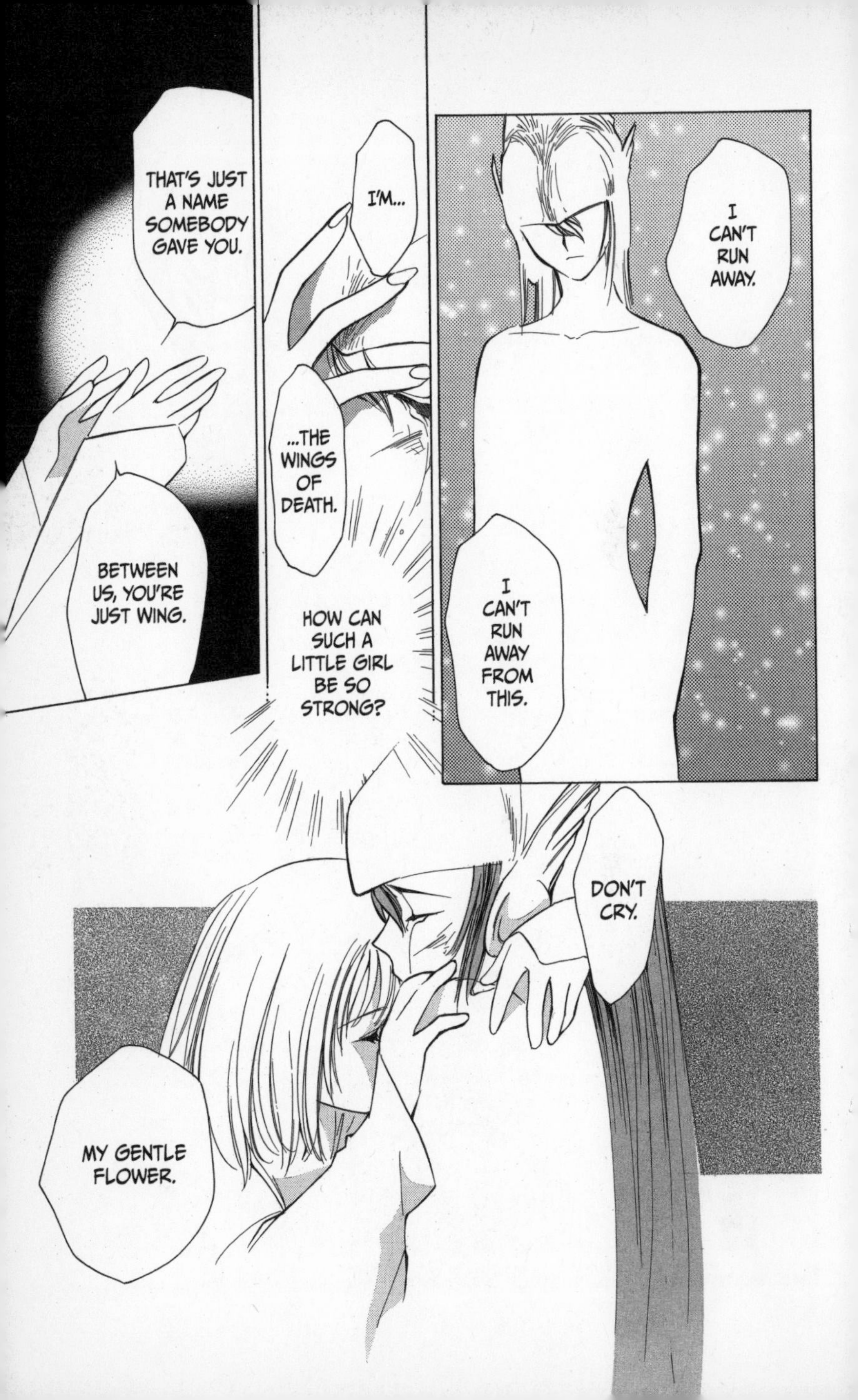
I CAN'T RUN AWAY.
I CAN'T RUN AWAY FROM THIS.
I'M...
...THE WINGS OF DEATH.
HOW CAN SUCH A LITTLE GIRL BE SO STRONG?
THAT'S JUST A NAME SOMEBODY GAVE YOU.
BETWEEN US, YOU'RE JUST WING.
DON'T CRY.
MY GENTLE FLOWER.

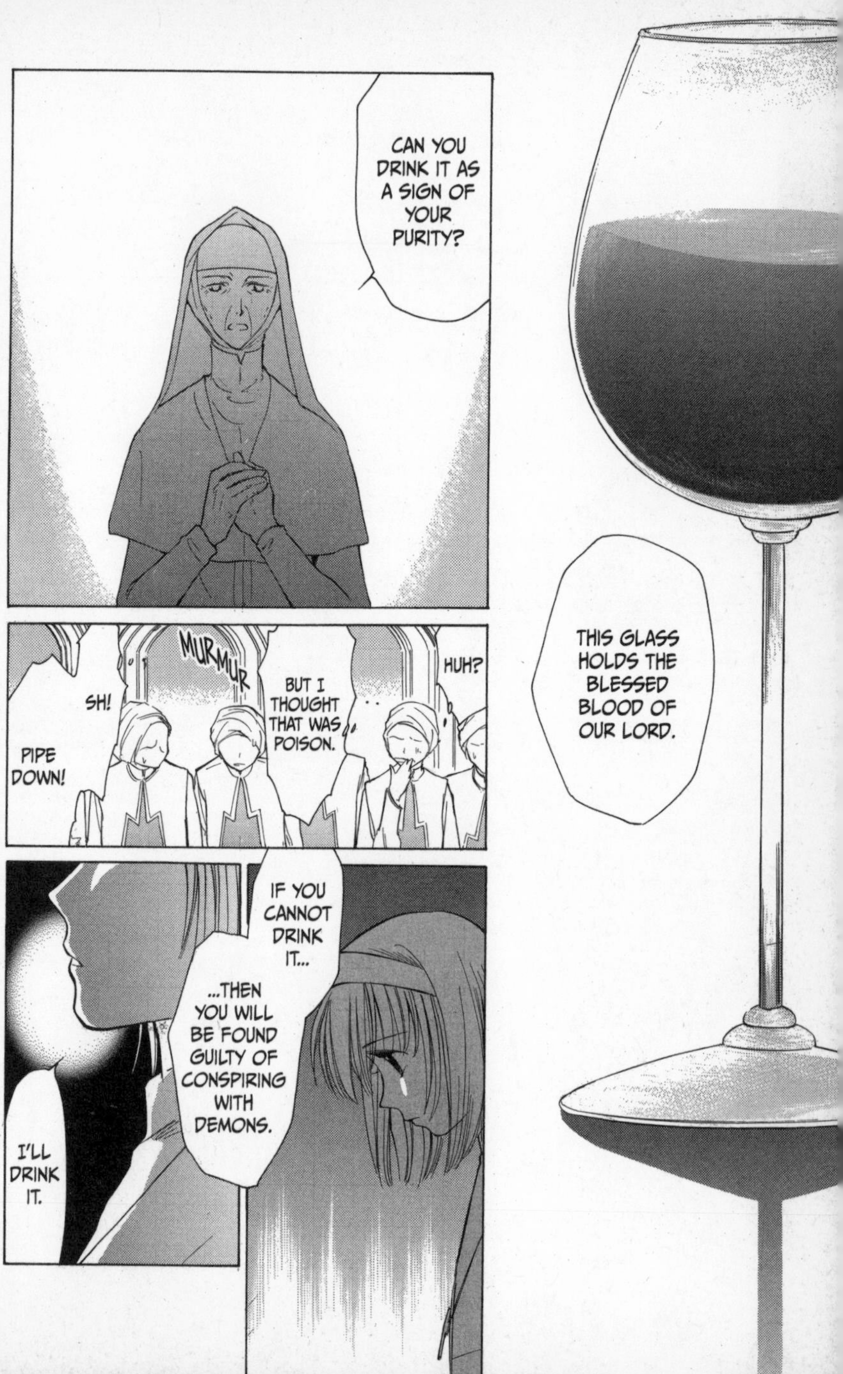
THIS GLASS HOLDS THE BLESSED BLOOD OF OUR LORD.
CAN YOU DRINK IT AS A SIGN OF YOUR PURITY?
HUH?
BUT I THOUGHT THAT WAS POISON.
MURMUR MURMUR
SH!
PIPE DOWN!
IF YOU CANNOT DRINK IT...
...THEN YOU WILL BE FOUND GUILTY OF CONSPIRING WITH DEMONS.
I'LL DRINK IT.

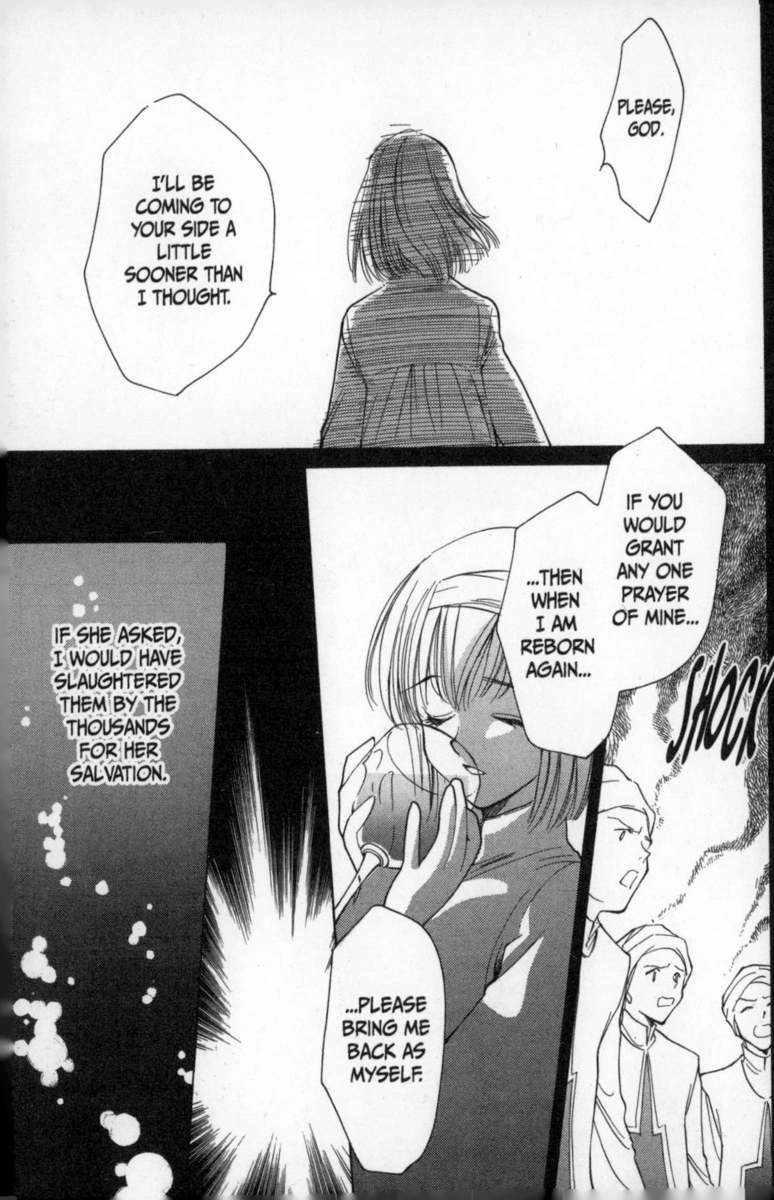
PLEASE, GOD.
I'LL BE COMING TO YOUR SIDE A LITTLE SOONER THAN I THOUGHT.
IF YOU WOULD GRANT ANY ONE PRAYER OF MINE...
...THEN WHEN I AM REBORN AGAIN...
SHOCK
...PLEASE BRING ME BACK AS MYSELF.
IF SHE ASKED, I WOULD HAVE SLAUGHTERED THEM BY THE THOUSANDS FOR HER SALVATION.

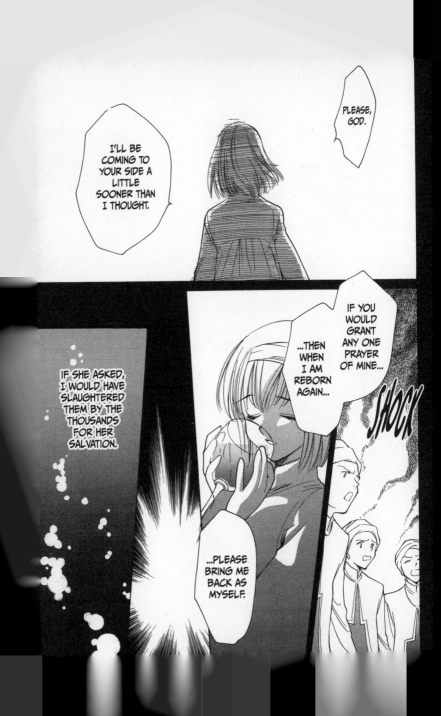

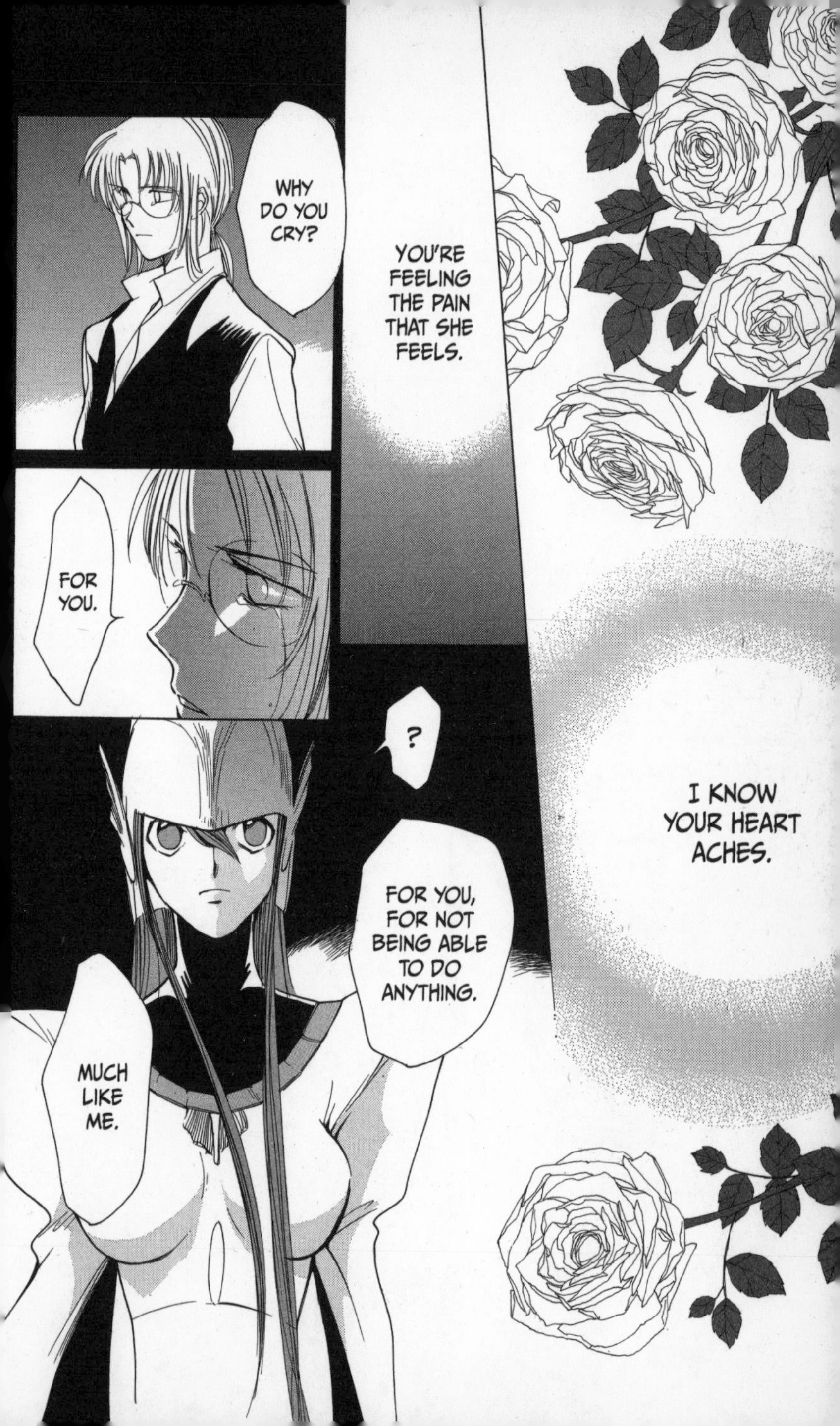
I KNOW YOUR HEART ACHES.
YOU'RE FEELING THE PAIN THAT SHE FEELS.
WHY DO YOU CRY?
FOR YOU.
?
FOR YOU, FOR NOT BEING ABLE TO DO ANYTHING.
MUCH LIKE ME.

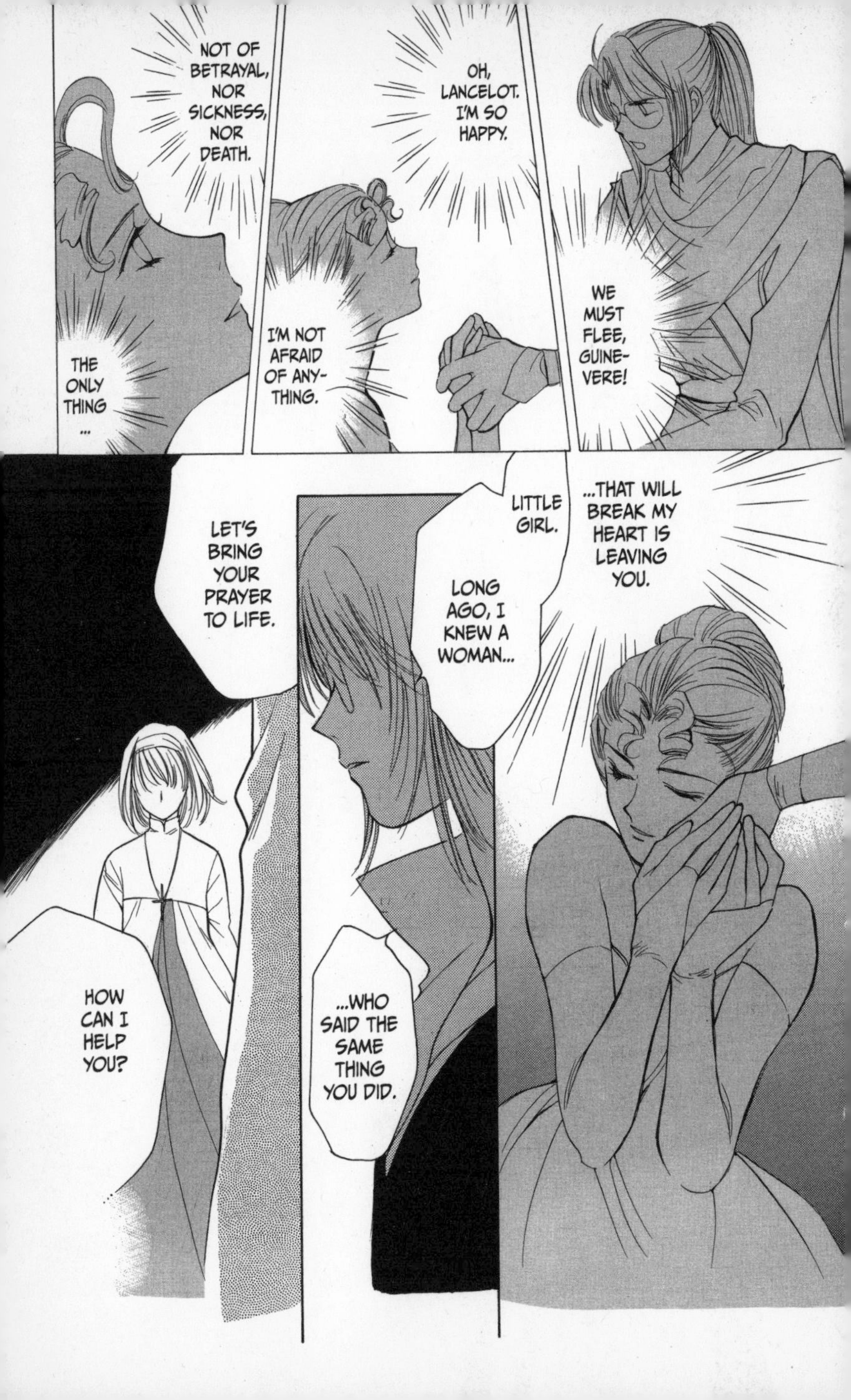
WE MUST FLEE, GUINEVERE!
OH, LANCELOT. I'M SO HAPPY.
I'M NOT AFRAID OF ANYTHING.
NOT OF BETRAYAL, NOR SICKNESS, NOR DEATH.
THE ONLY THING ...
...THAT WILL BREAK MY HEART IS LEAVING YOU.
LITTLE GIRL.
LONG AGO, I KNEW A WOMAN...
...WHO SAID THE SAME THING YOU DID.
LET'S BRING YOUR PRAYER TO LIFE.
HOW CAN I HELP YOU?

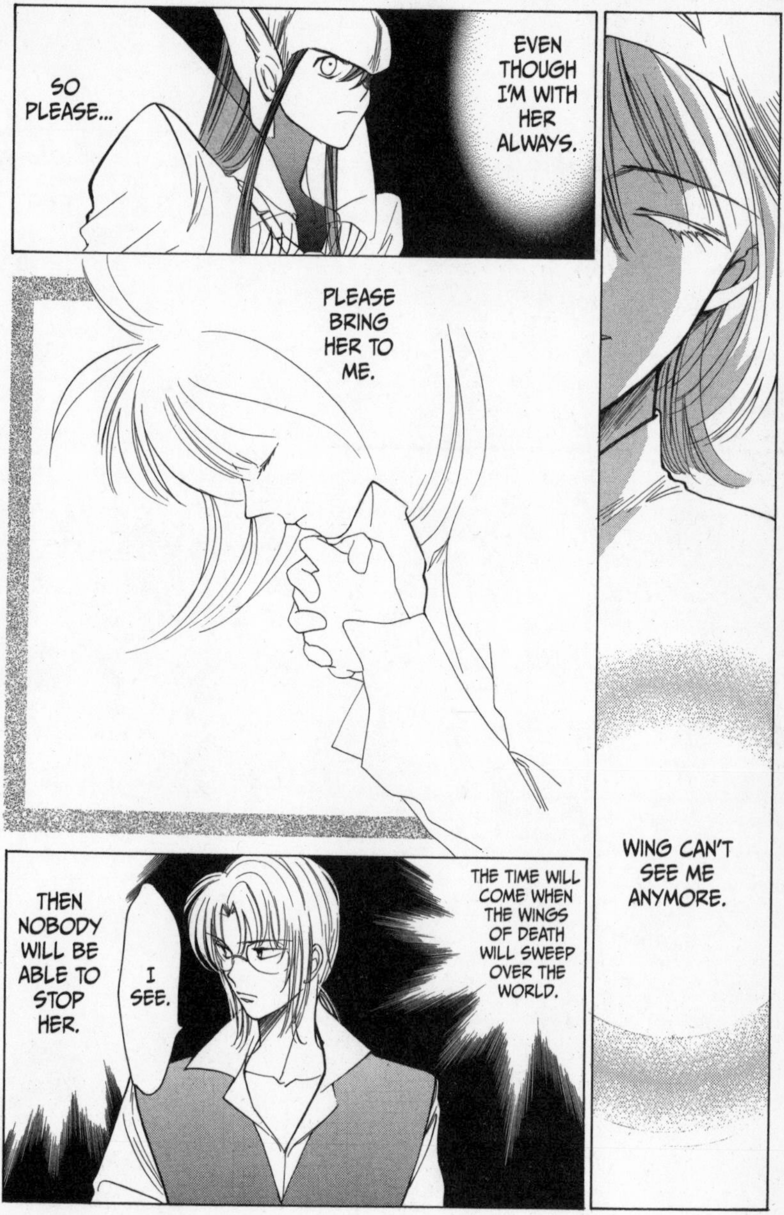
WING CAN'T SEE ME ANYMORE.
EVEN THOUGH I'M WITH HER ALWAYS.
SO PLEASE...
PLEASE BRING HER TO ME.
THE TIME WILL COME WHEN THE WINGS OF DEATH WILL SWEEP OVER THE WORLD.
I SEE.
THEN NOBODY WILL BE ABLE TO STOP HER.

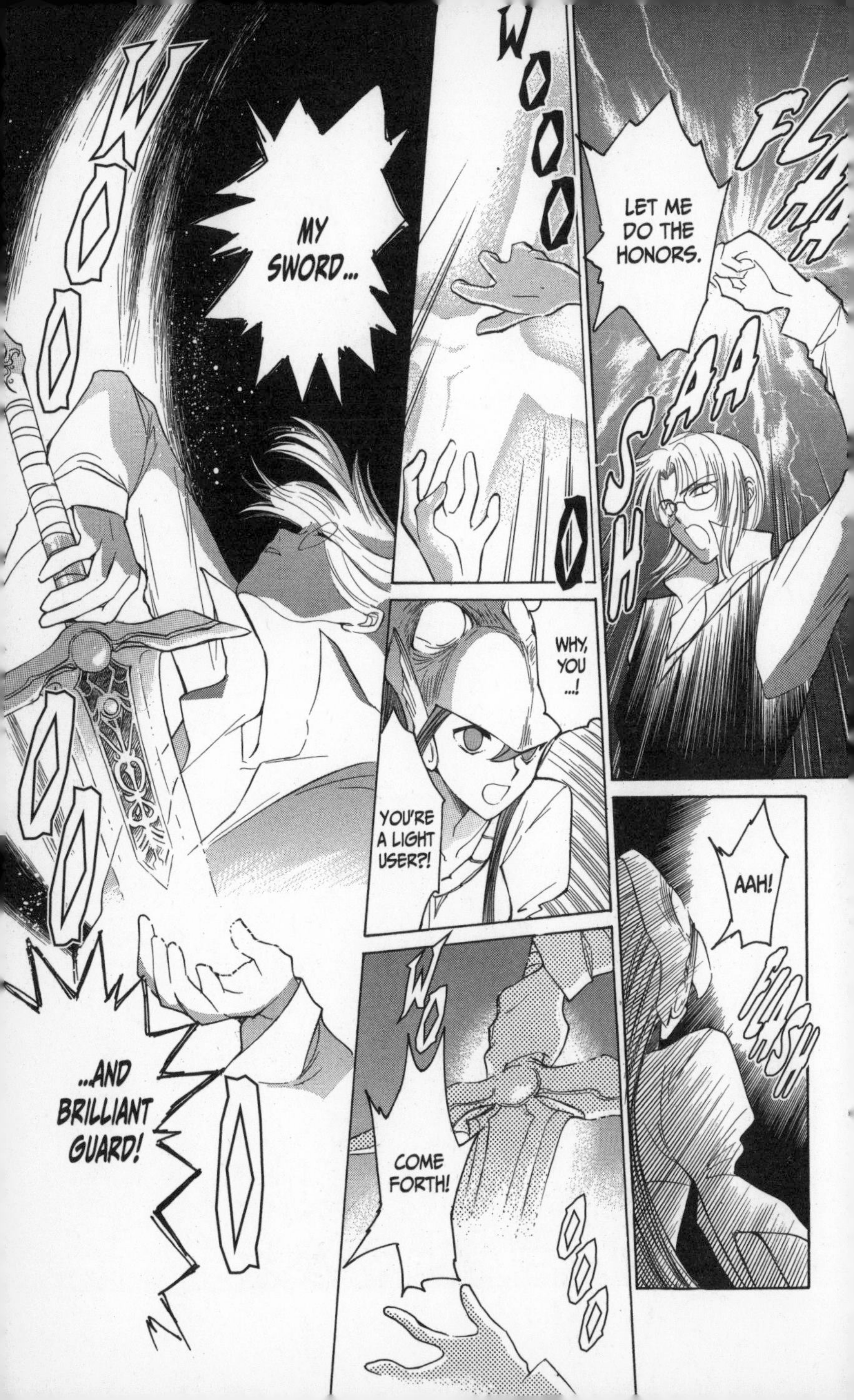
FLA
LET ME DO THE HONORS.
SHAA
WOOOOOO
WHY, YOU ...!
YOU'RE A LIGHT USER?!
AAH!
FLASH
WO
COME FORTH!
OOO
WOOOOOOO
MY SWORD...
...AND BRILLIANT GUARD!

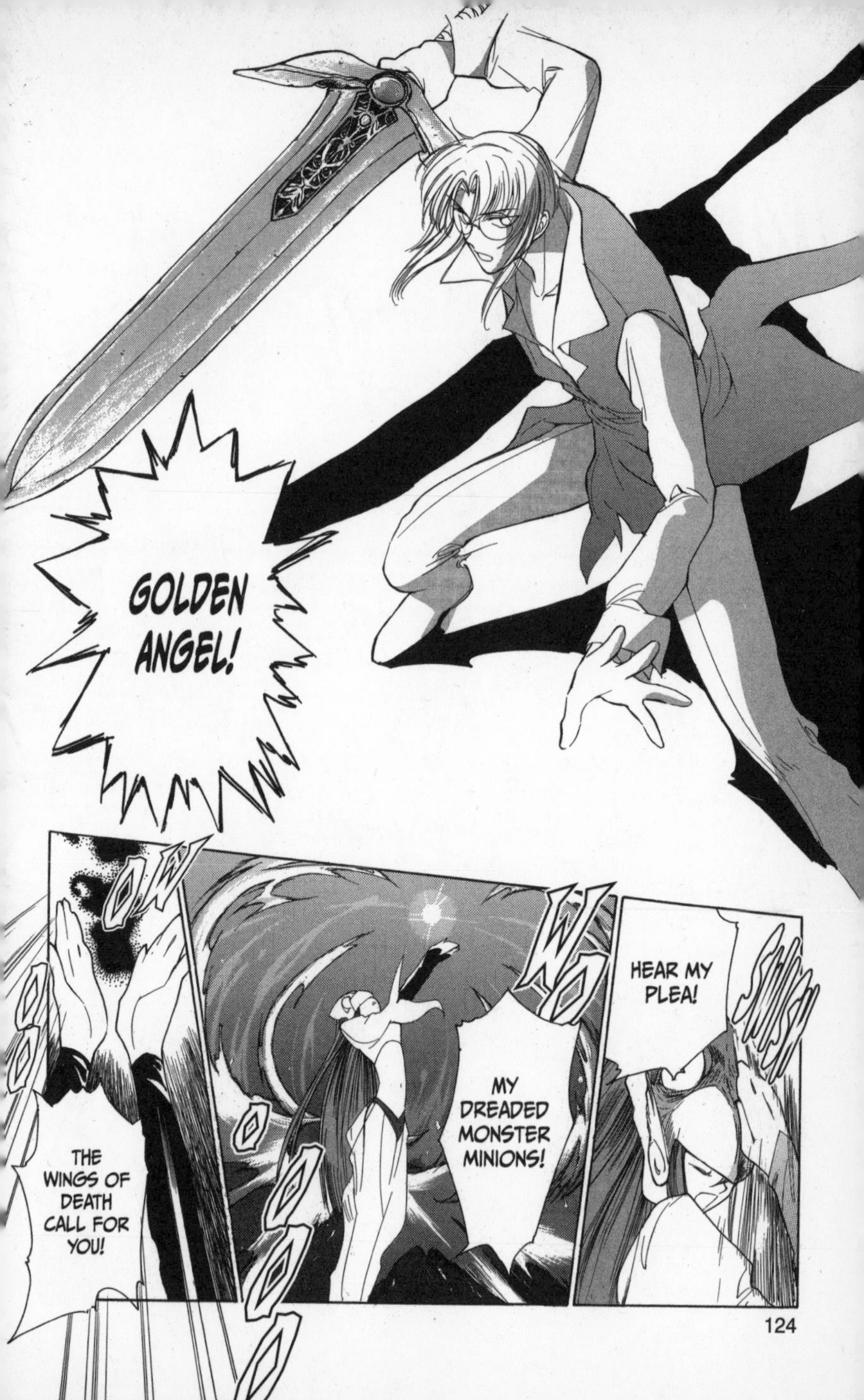
GOLDEN ANGEL!
HEAR MY PLEA!
MY DREADED MONSTER MINIONS!
THE WINGS OF DEATH CALL FOR YOU!

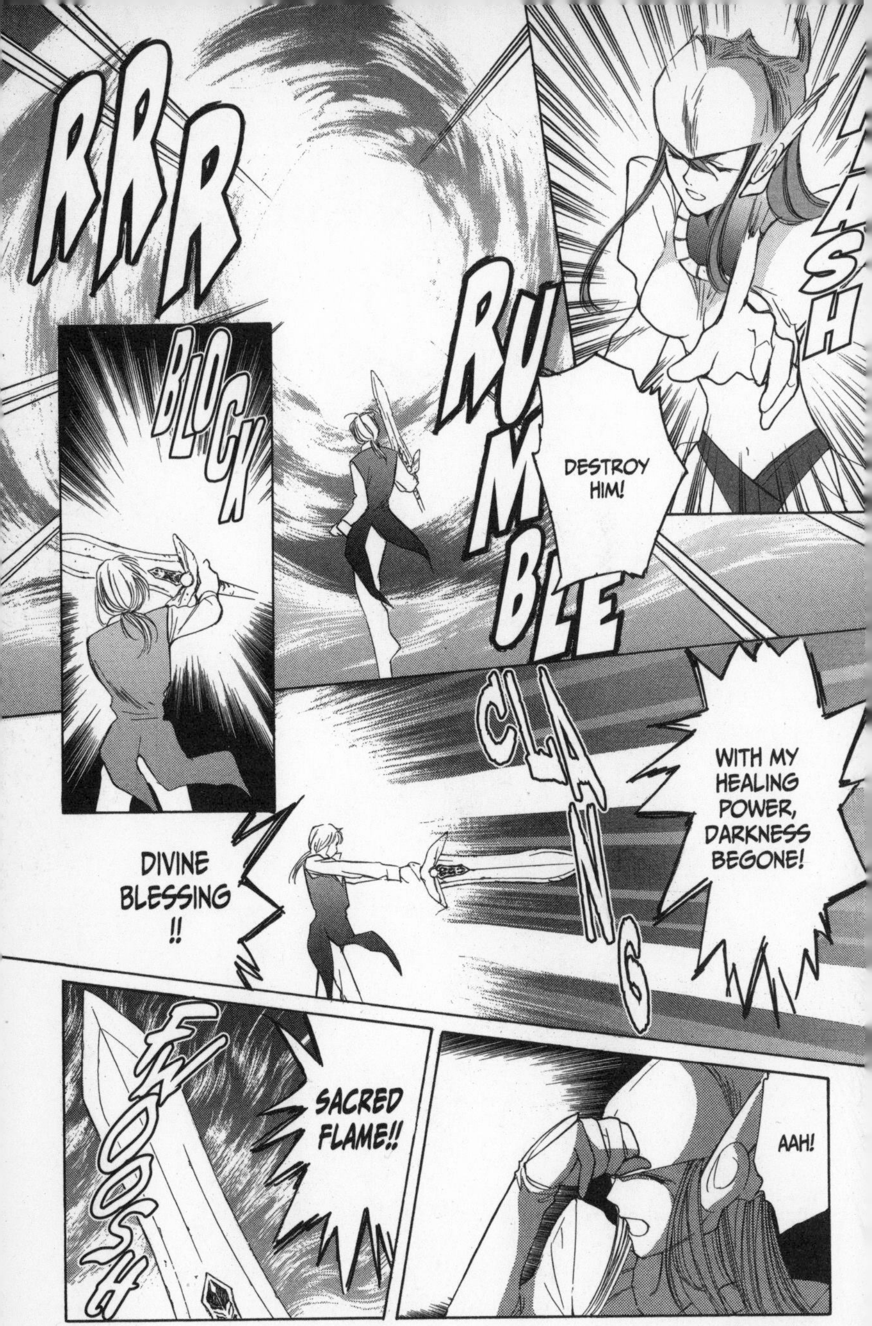
LASH
DESTROY HIM!
RUMBLE
RRR
BLOCK
WITH MY HEALING POWER, DARKNESS BEGONE!
CLANG
DIVINE BLESSING !!
AAH!
SACRED FLAME!!
FWOOSH

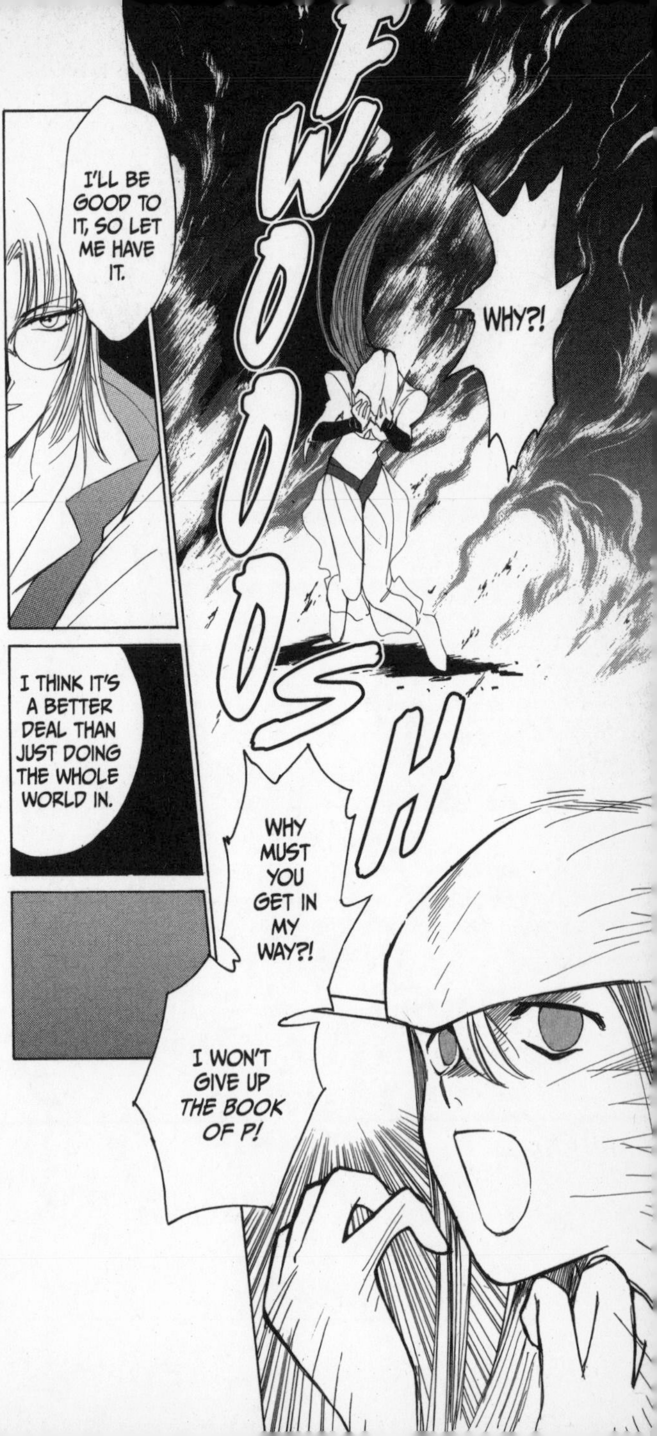
FWOOOOSH
WHY?!
WHY MUST YOU GET IN MY WAY?!
I WON'T GIVE UP THE BOOK OF P!
I'LL BE GOOD TO IT, SO LET ME HAVE IT.
I THINK IT'S A BETTER DEAL THAN JUST DOING THE WHOLE WORLD IN.

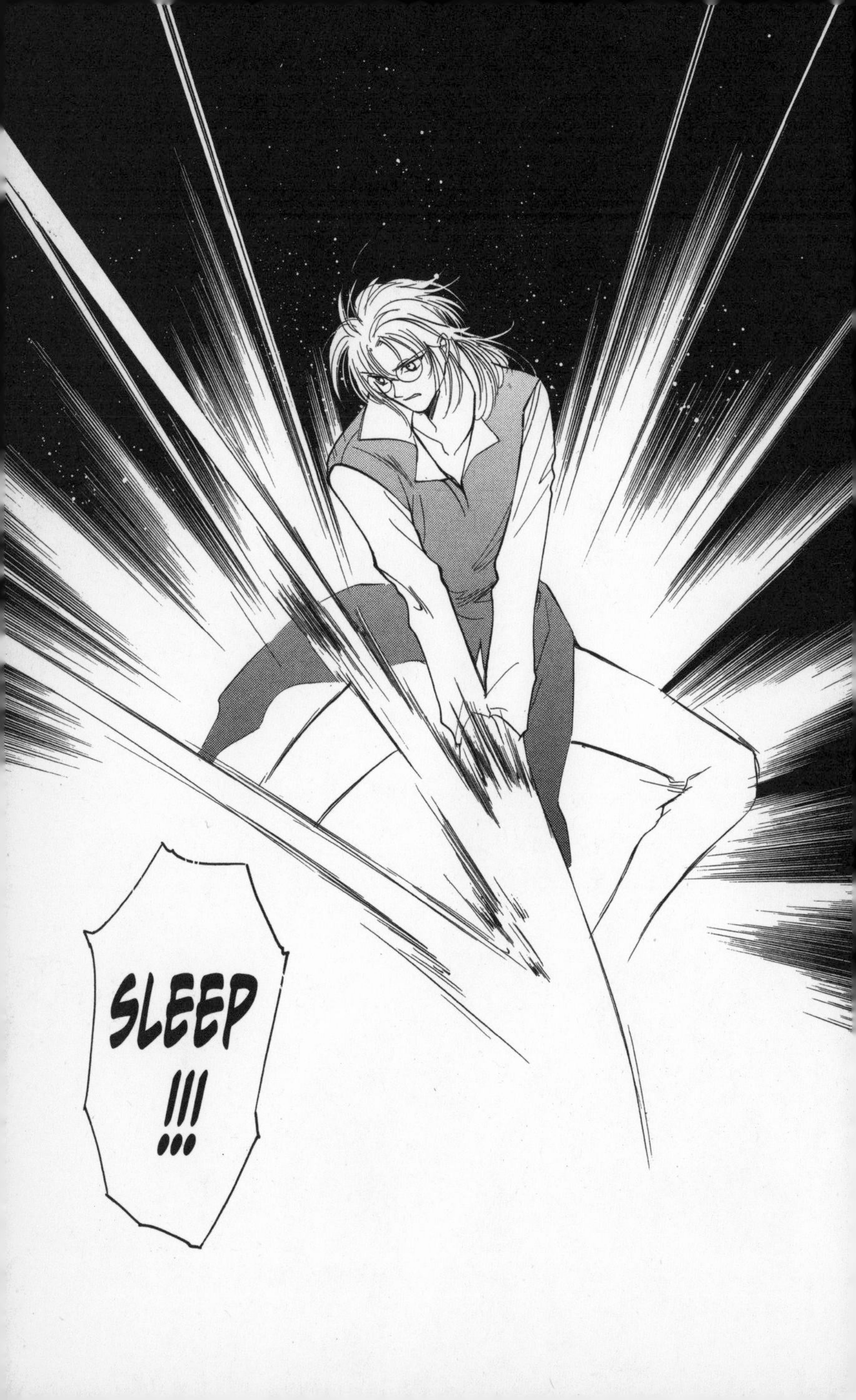
SLEEP !!!

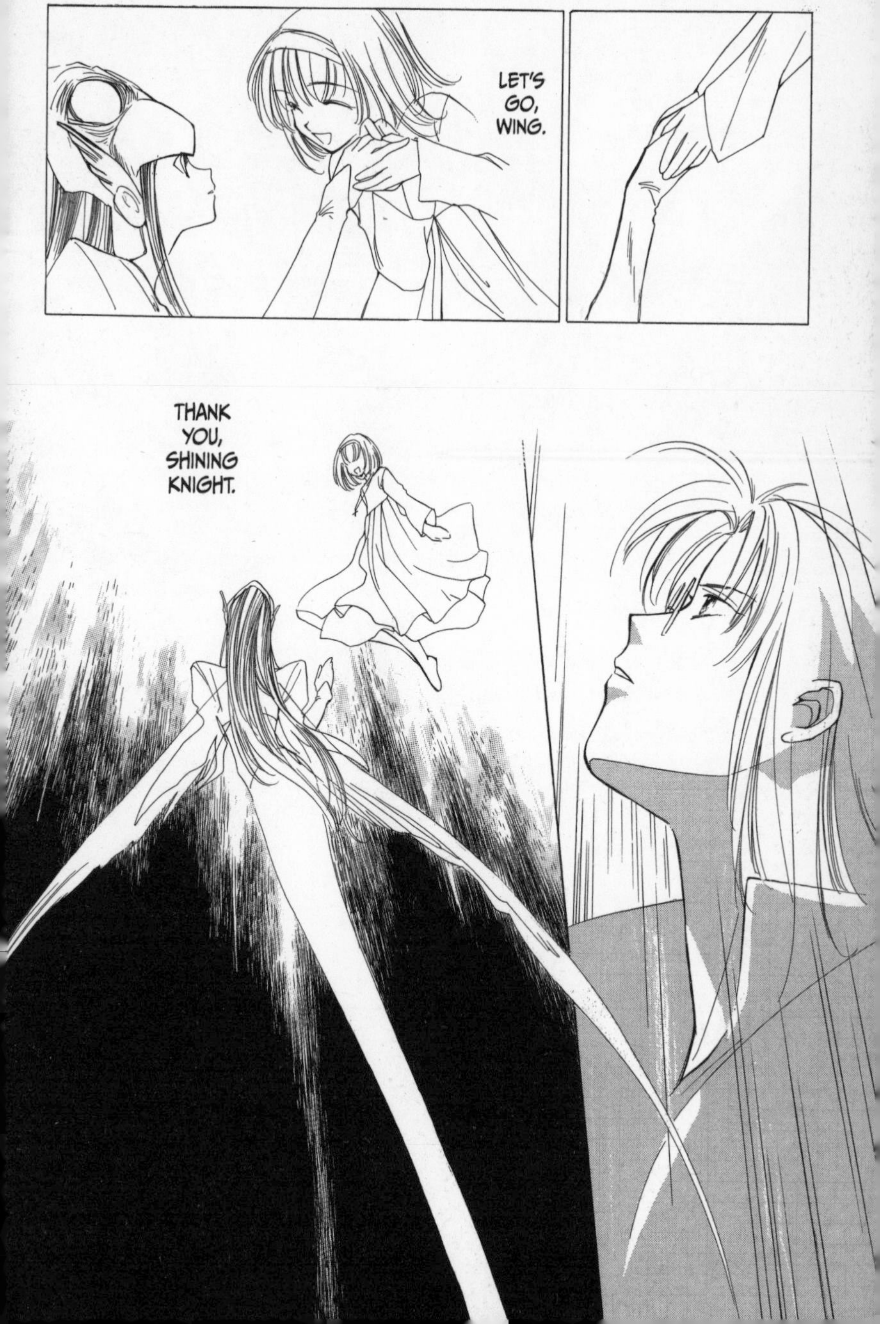
LET'S GO, WING.
THANK YOU, SHINING KNIGHT.

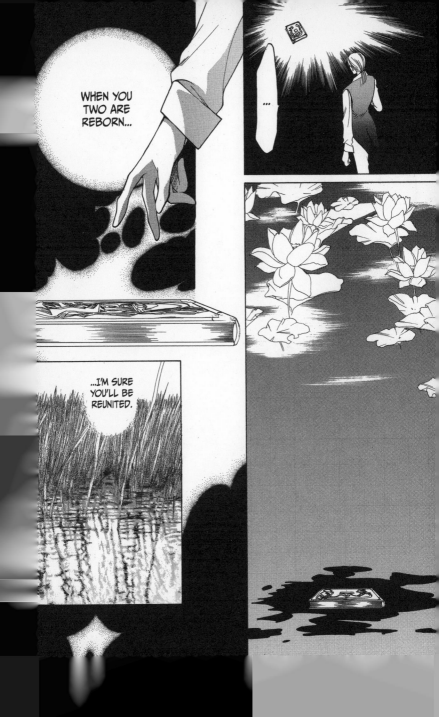

WHEN YOU TWO ARE REBORN...

...

...I'M SURE YOU'LL BE REUNITED.

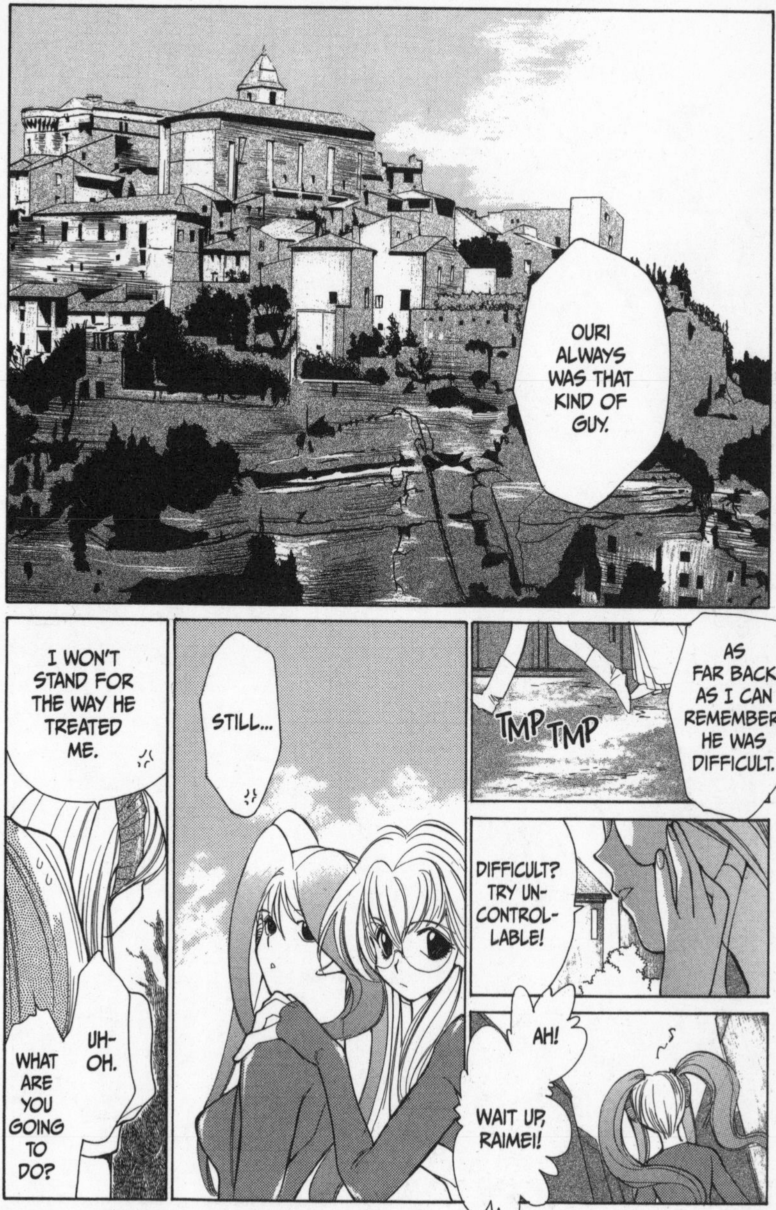
OURI ALWAYS WAS THAT KIND OF GUY.
AS FAR BACK AS I CAN REMEMBER, HE WAS DIFFICULT.
TMP TMP
DIFFICULT? TRY UN-CONTROL-LABLE!
AH!
WAIT UP, RAIMEI!
STILL...
I WON'T STAND FOR THE WAY HE TREATED ME.
UH-OH.
WHAT ARE YOU GOING TO DO?

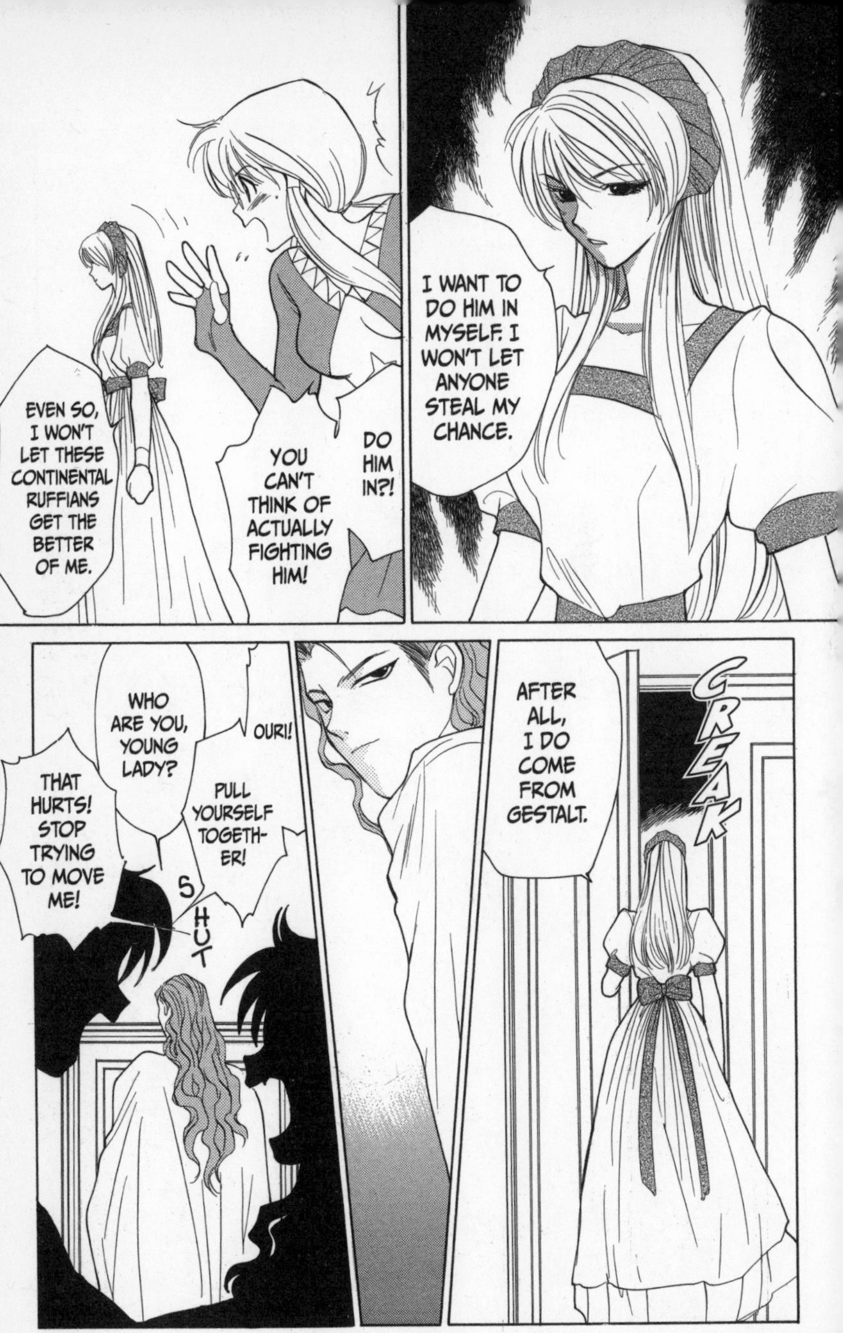
I WANT TO DO HIM IN MYSELF. I WON'T LET ANYONE STEAL MY CHANCE.
DO HIM IN?!
YOU CAN'T THINK OF ACTUALLY FIGHTING HIM!
EVEN SO, I WON'T LET THESE CONTINENTAL RUFFIANS GET THE BETTER OF ME.
CREAK
AFTER ALL, I DO COME FROM GESTALT.
WHO ARE YOU, YOUNG LADY?
OURI!
PULL YOURSELF TOGETH-ER!
THAT HURTS! STOP TRYING TO MOVE ME!
SHUT

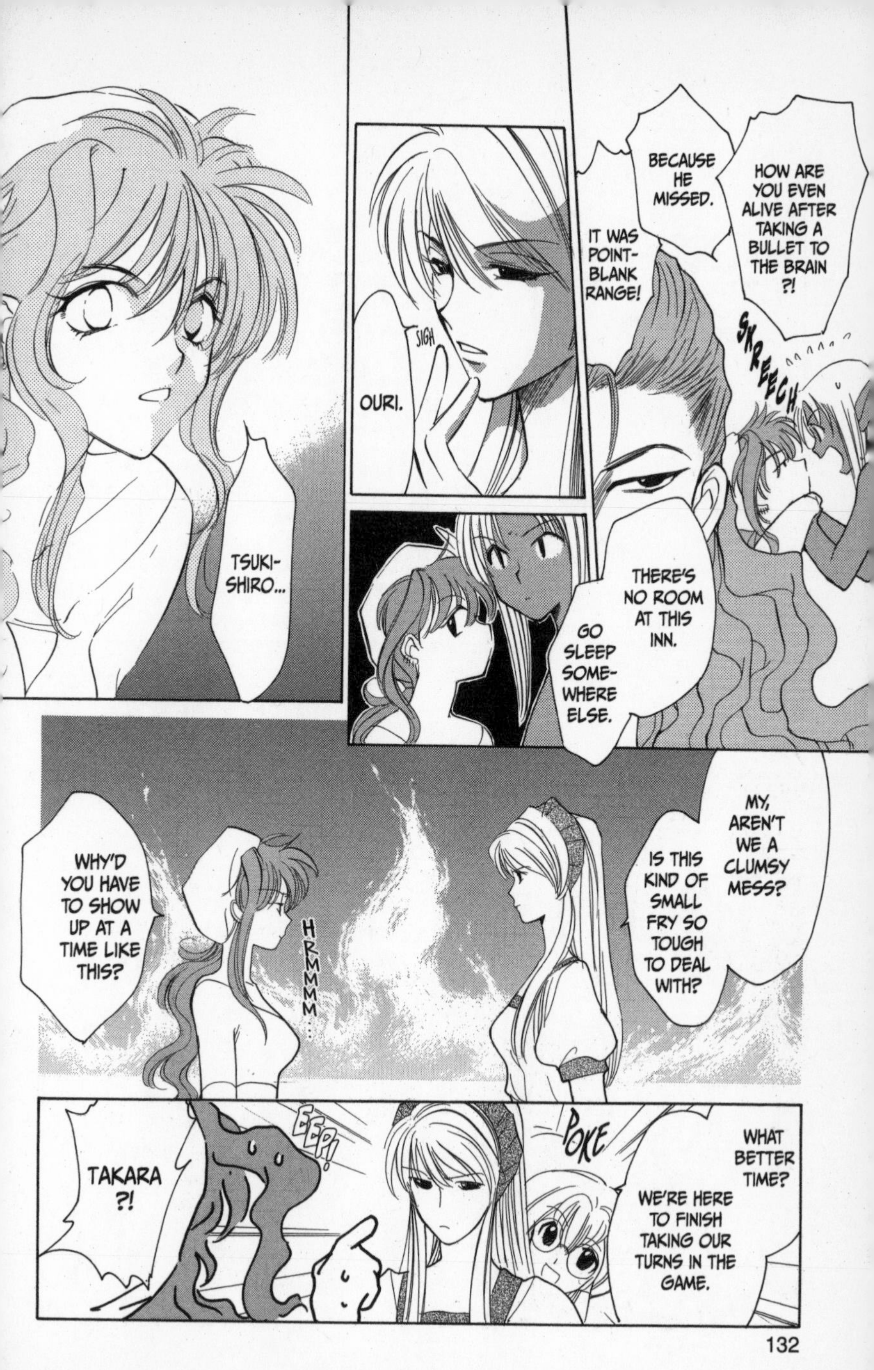
HOW ARE YOU EVEN ALIVE AFTER TAKING A BULLET TO THE BRAIN ?!
BECAUSE HE MISSED.
IT WAS POINT-BLANK RANGE!
SKREECH
THERE'S NO ROOM AT THIS INN.
GO SLEEP SOME-WHERE ELSE.
SIGH
OURI.
TSUKI-SHIRO...
MY, AREN'T WE A CLUMSY MESS?
IS THIS KIND OF SMALL FRY SO TOUGH TO DEAL WITH?
HRMMMM...
WHY'D YOU HAVE TO SHOW UP AT A TIME LIKE THIS?
WHAT BETTER TIME?
WE'RE HERE TO FINISH TAKING OUR TURNS IN THE GAME.
POKE
EEP!
TAKARA ?!

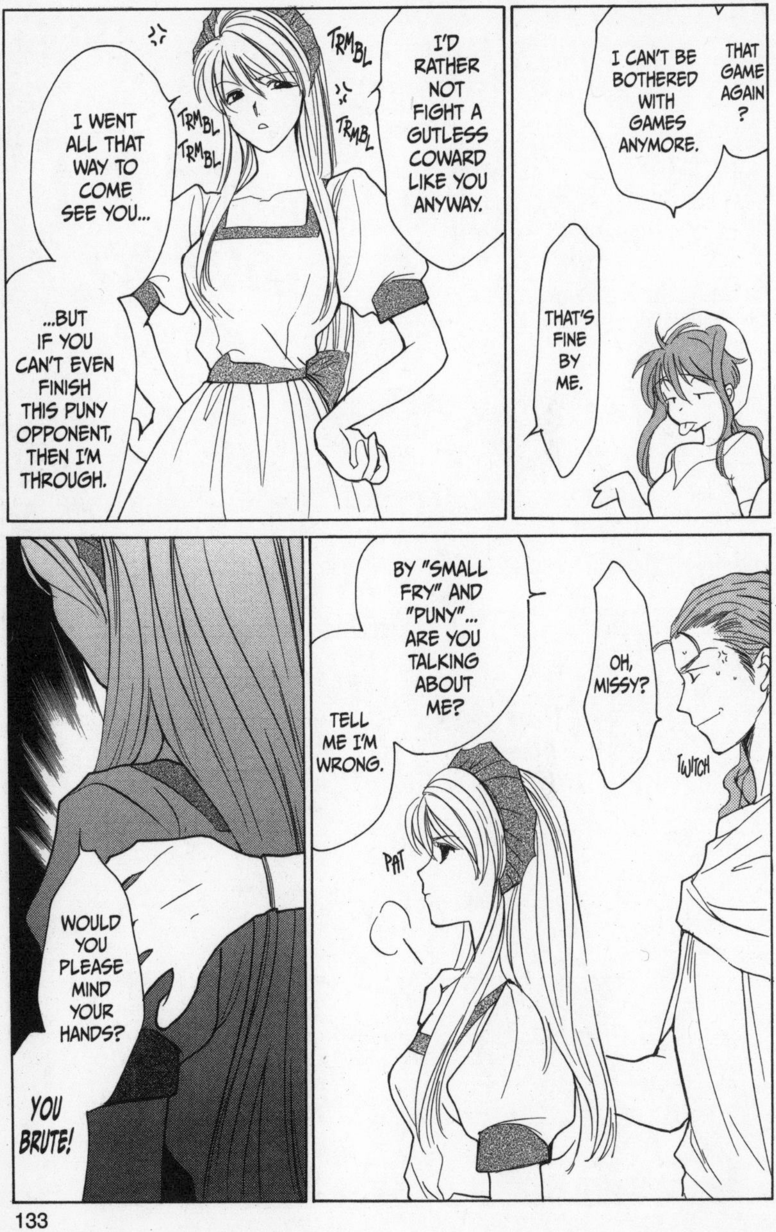
THAT GAME AGAIN?
I CAN'T BE BOTHERED WITH GAMES ANYMORE.
THAT'S FINE BY ME.
I'D RATHER NOT FIGHT A GUTLESS COWARD LIKE YOU ANYWAY.
TRMBL
TRMBL
TRMBL
TRMBL
I WENT ALL THAT WAY TO COME SEE YOU...
...BUT IF YOU CAN'T EVEN FINISH THIS PUNY OPPONENT, THEN I'M THROUGH.
OH, MISSY?
BY "SMALL FRY" AND "PUNY"... ARE YOU TALKING ABOUT ME?
TWITCH
TELL ME I'M WRONG.
PAT
WOULD YOU PLEASE MIND YOUR HANDS?
YOU BRUTE!

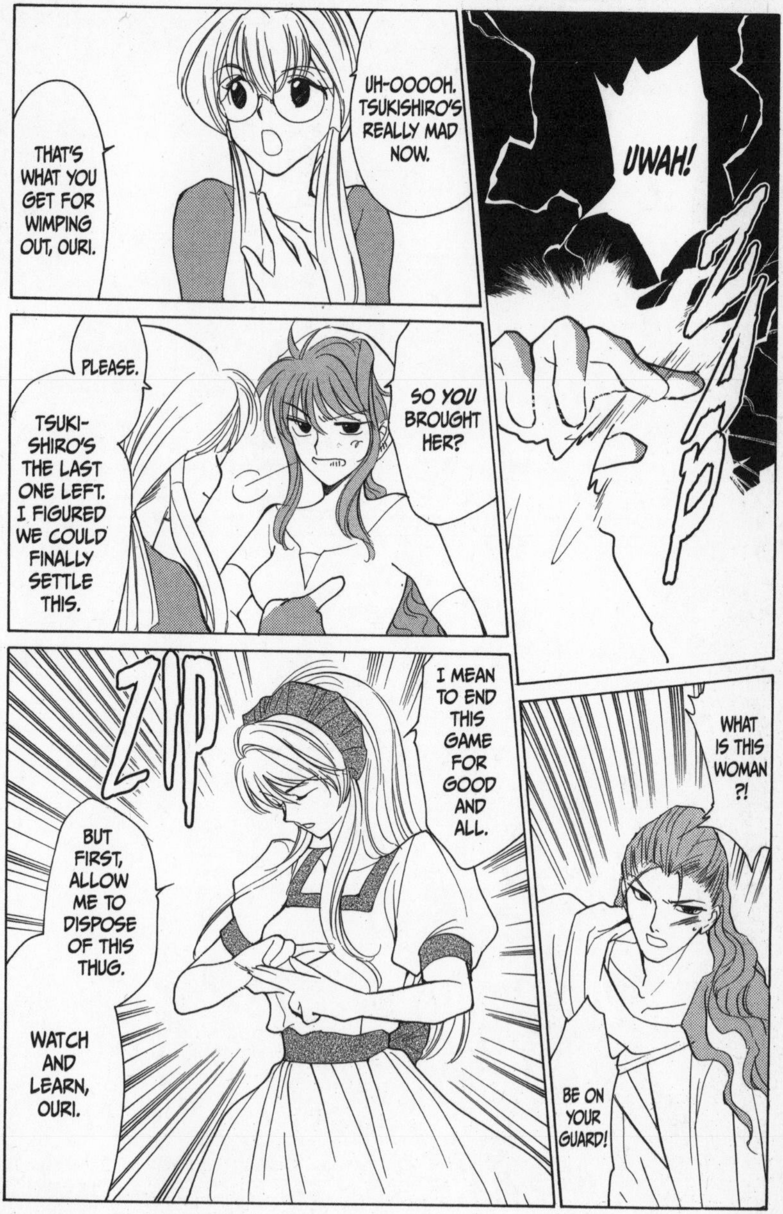
UWAH!
ZAP
UH-OOOOH. TSUKISHIRO'S REALLY MAD NOW.
THAT'S WHAT YOU GET FOR WIMPING OUT, OURI.
SO YOU BROUGHT HER?
PLEASE.
TSUKI-SHIRO'S THE LAST ONE LEFT. I FIGURED WE COULD FINALLY SETTLE THIS.
WHAT IS THIS WOMAN ?!
BE ON YOUR GUARD!
I MEAN TO END THIS GAME FOR GOOD AND ALL.
ZIP
BUT FIRST, ALLOW ME TO DISPOSE OF THIS THUG.
WATCH AND LEARN, OURI.

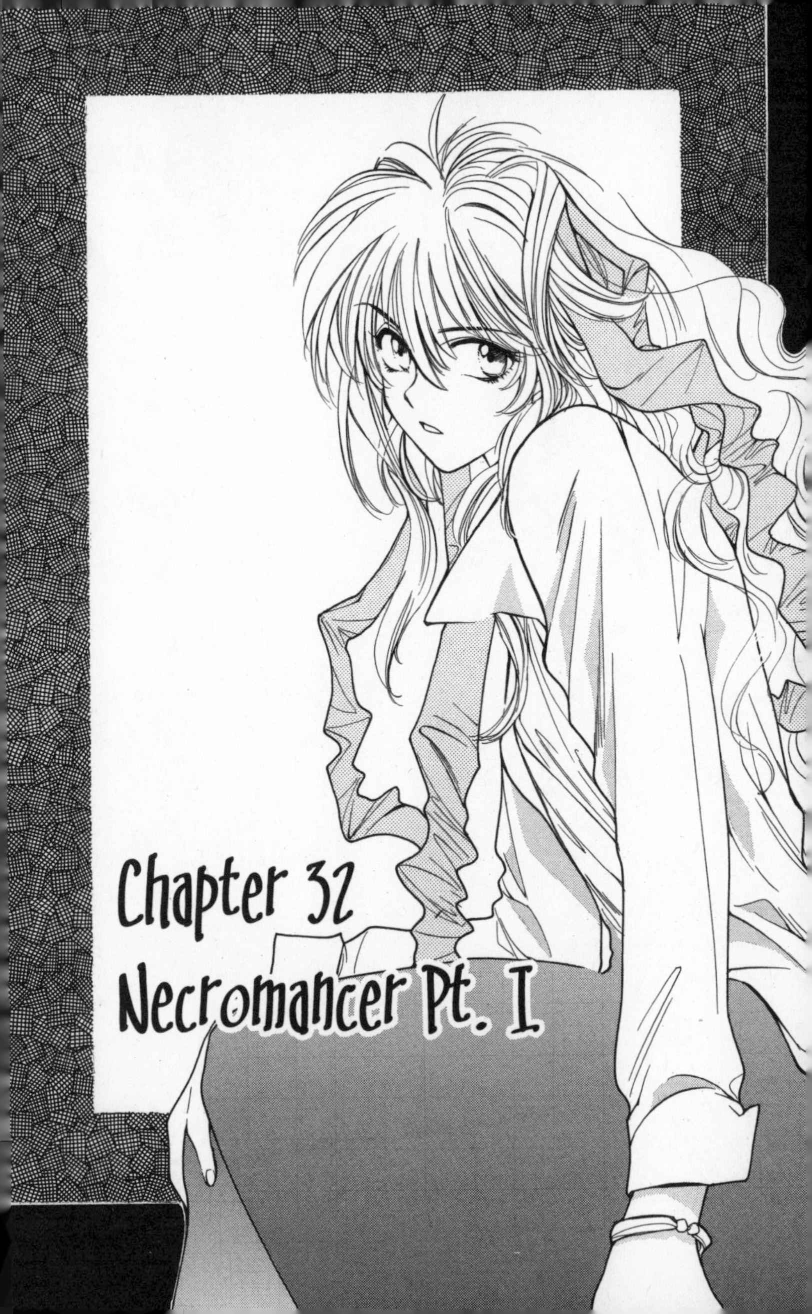
Chapter 32
Necromancer Pt. I

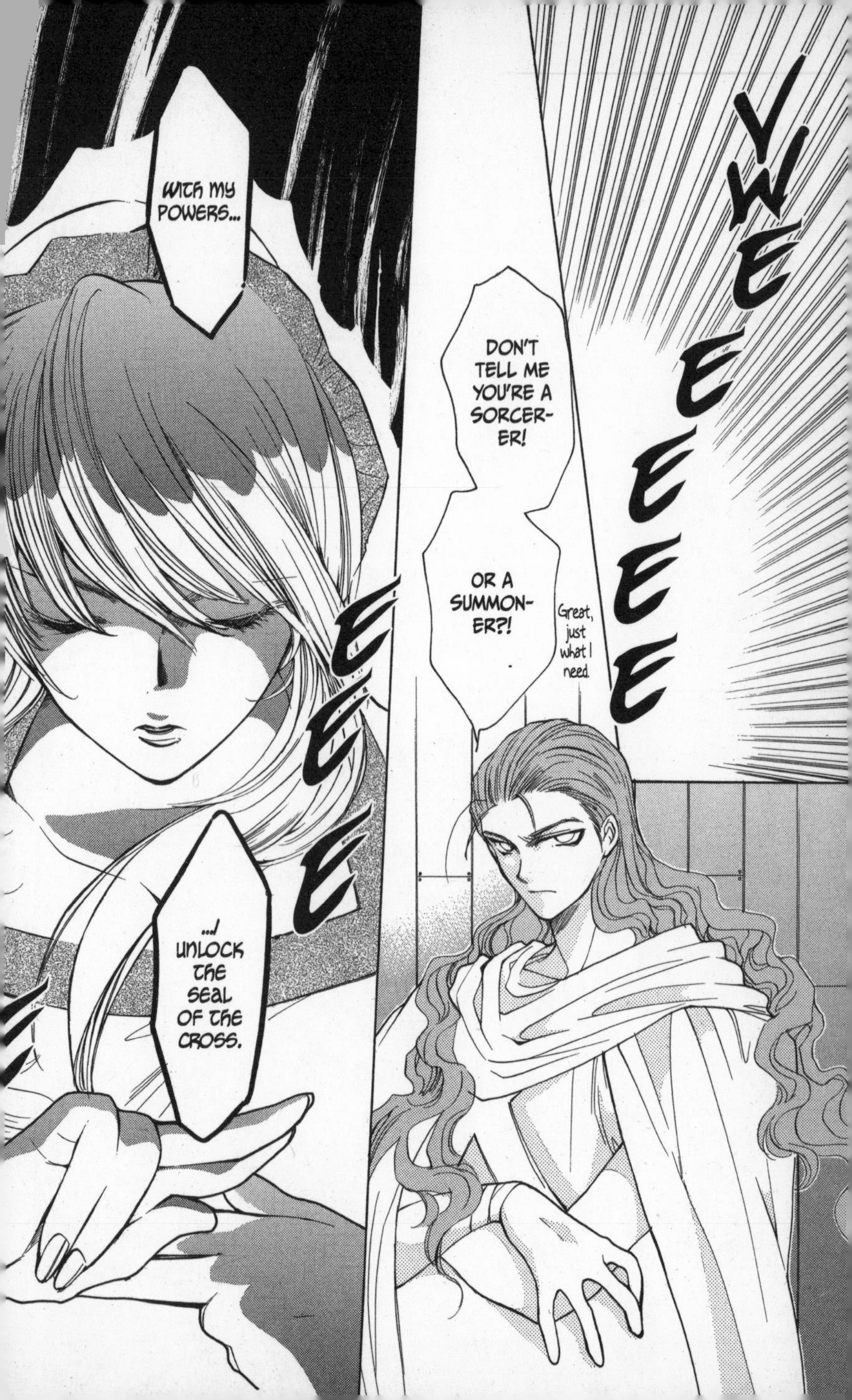
VWEEEEE
DON'T TELL ME YOU'RE A SORCERER-ER!
OR A SUMMON-ER?!
Great, just what I need.
WITH MY POWERS...
EEEE
...I UNLOCK THE SEAL OF THE CROSS.

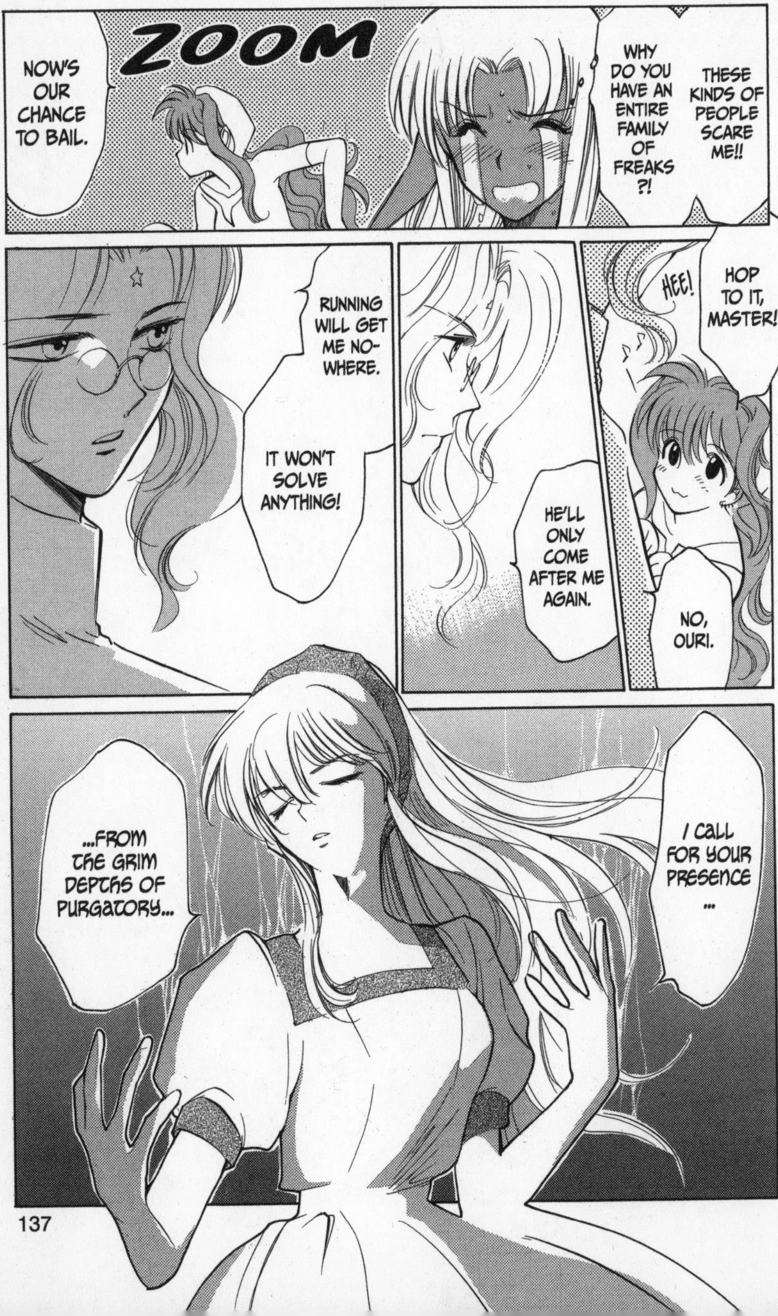
THESE KINDS OF PEOPLE SCARE ME!!
WHY DO YOU HAVE AN ENTIRE FAMILY OF FREAKS ?!
ZOOM
NOW'S OUR CHANCE TO BAIL.
HOP TO IT, MASTER!
HEE!
NO, OURI.
HE'LL ONLY COME AFTER ME AGAIN.
RUNNING WILL GET ME NO-WHERE.
IT WON'T SOLVE ANYTHING!
I CALL FOR YOUR PRESENCE ...
...FROM THE GRIM DEPTHS OF PURGATORY...

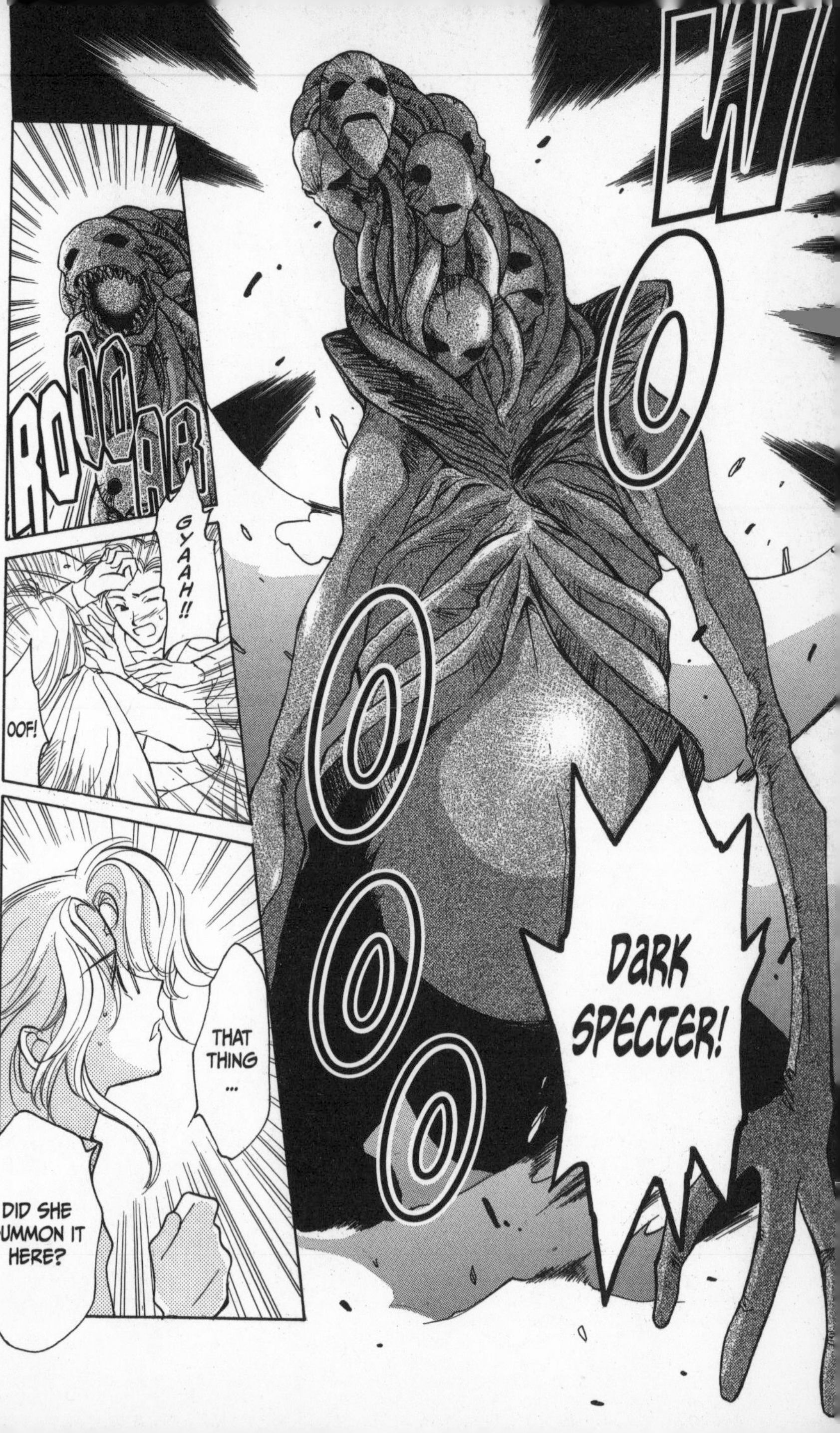
DARK SPECTER!
ROOOAR
GYAAAH!!
OOF!
THAT THING ...
DID SHE SUMMON IT HERE?

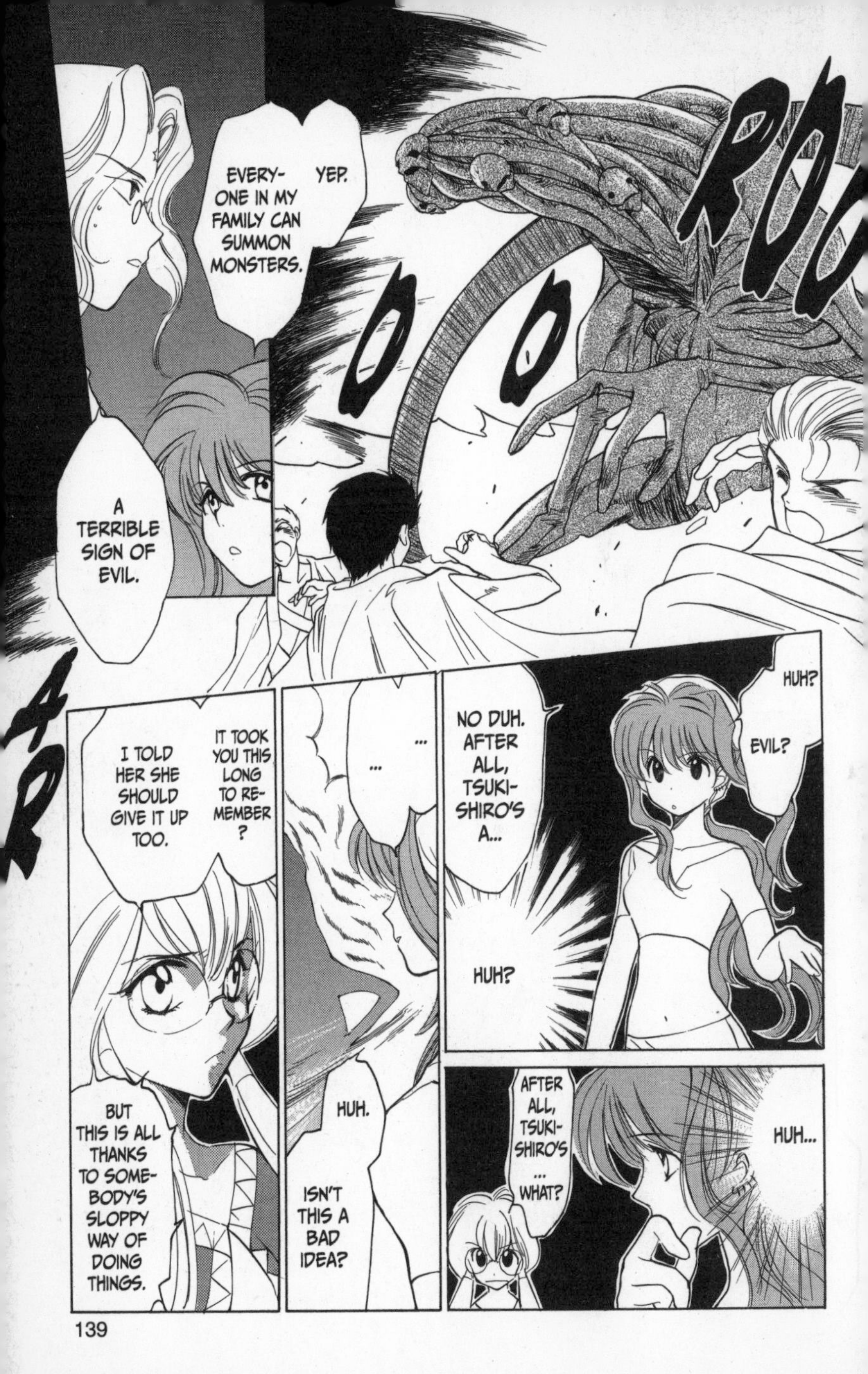
ROOOOAR
YEP.
EVERYONE IN MY FAMILY CAN SUMMON MONSTERS.
A TERRIBLE SIGN OF EVIL.
HUH?
EVIL?
NO DUH. AFTER ALL, TSUKISHIRO'S A...
HUH?
HUH...
AFTER ALL, TSUKISHIRO'S ... WHAT?
...
...
HUH.
ISN'T THIS A BAD IDEA?
IT TOOK YOU THIS LONG TO REMEMBER?
I TOLD HER SHE SHOULD GIVE IT UP TOO.
BUT THIS IS ALL THANKS TO SOMEBODY'S SLOPPY WAY OF DOING THINGS.

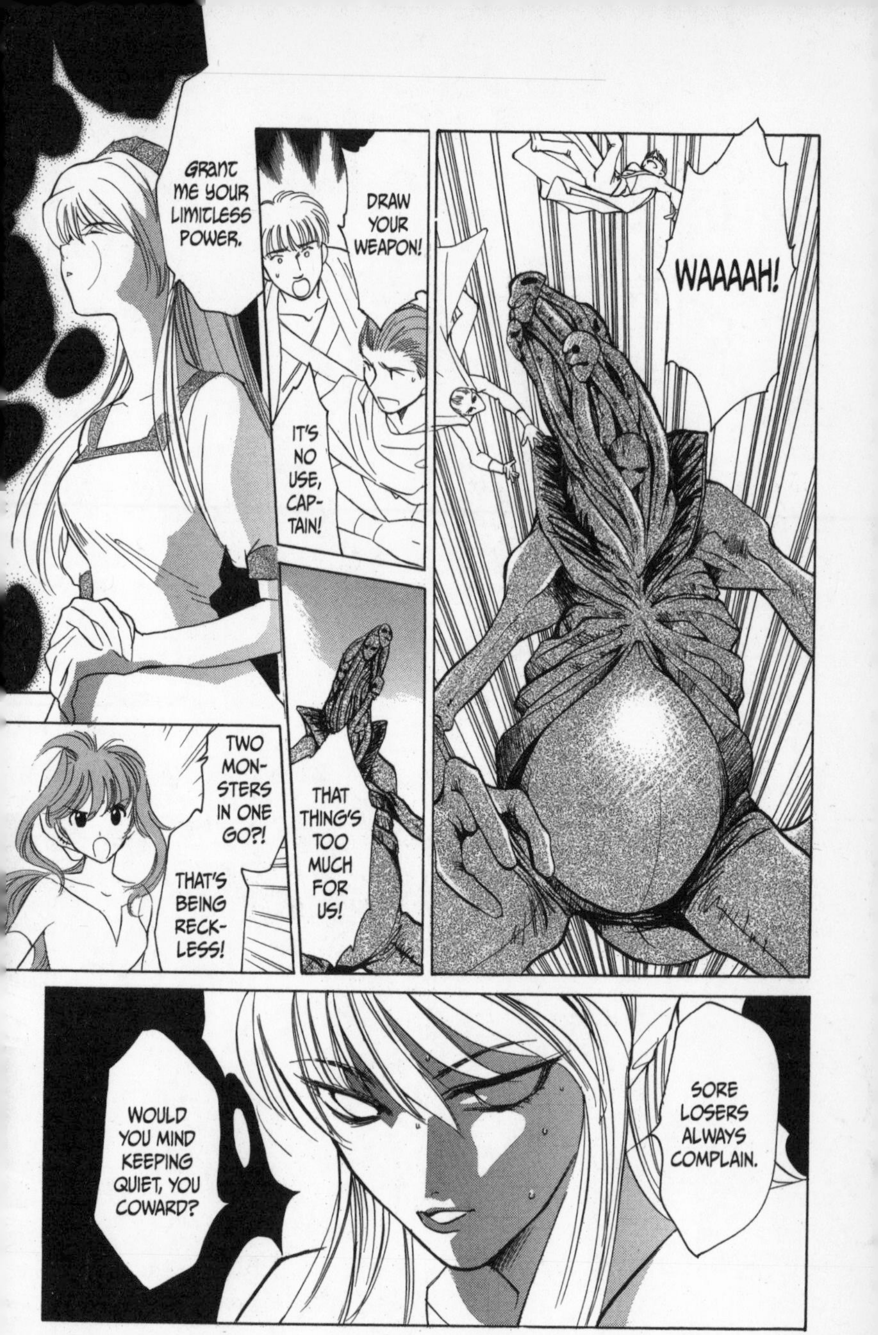
WAAAAH!
DRAW YOUR WEAPON!
IT'S NO USE, CAPTAIN!
THAT THING'S TOO MUCH FOR US!
GRANT ME YOUR LIMITLESS POWER.
TWO MONSTERS IN ONE GO?!
THAT'S BEING RECKLESS!
SORE LOSERS ALWAYS COMPLAIN.
WOULD YOU MIND KEEPING QUIET, YOU COWARD?

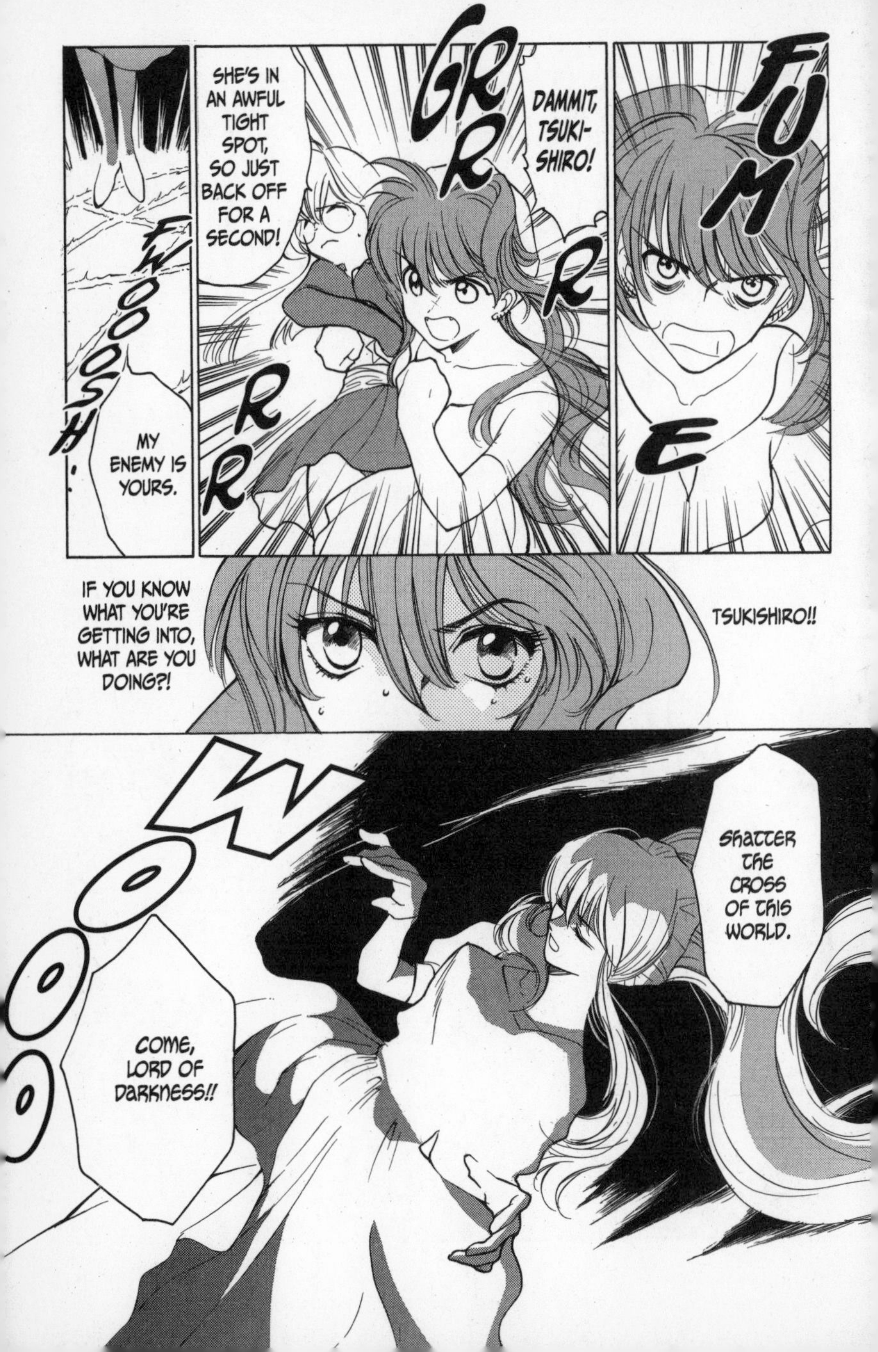
FUME
DAMMIT, TSUKI-SHIRO!
SHE'S IN AN AWFUL TIGHT SPOT, SO JUST BACK OFF FOR A SECOND!
GRRRRR
FWOOOOSH..
MY ENEMY IS YOURS.
TSUKISHIRO!!
IF YOU KNOW WHAT YOU'RE GETTING INTO, WHAT ARE YOU DOING?!
WOOOOO
Shatter the cross of this world.
Come, Lord of Darkness!!

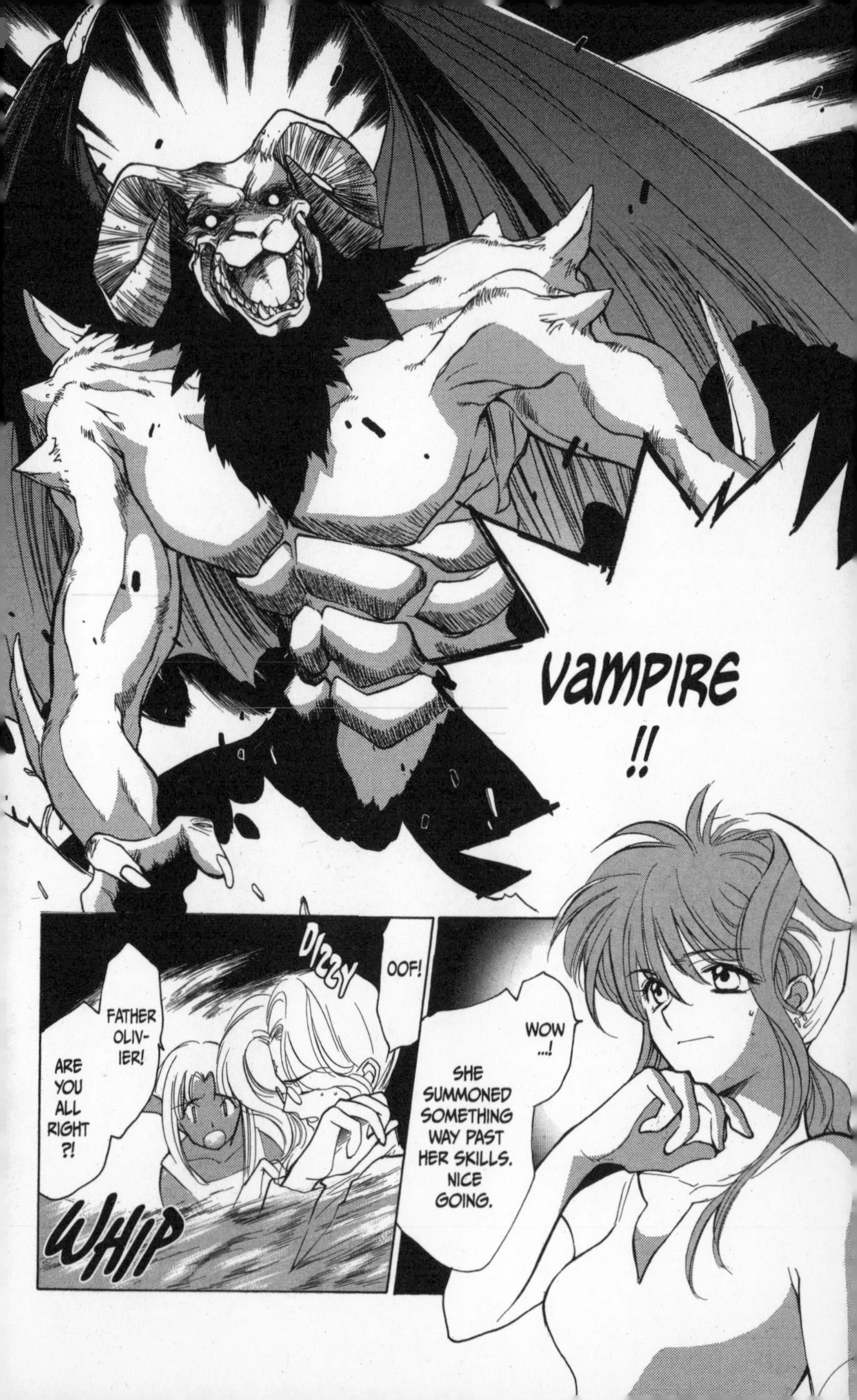
VAMPIRE !!
WOW ...!
SHE SUMMONED SOMETHING WAY PAST HER SKILLS. NICE GOING.
DIZZY
OOF!
FATHER OLIV-IER!
ARE YOU ALL RIGHT ?!
WHIP

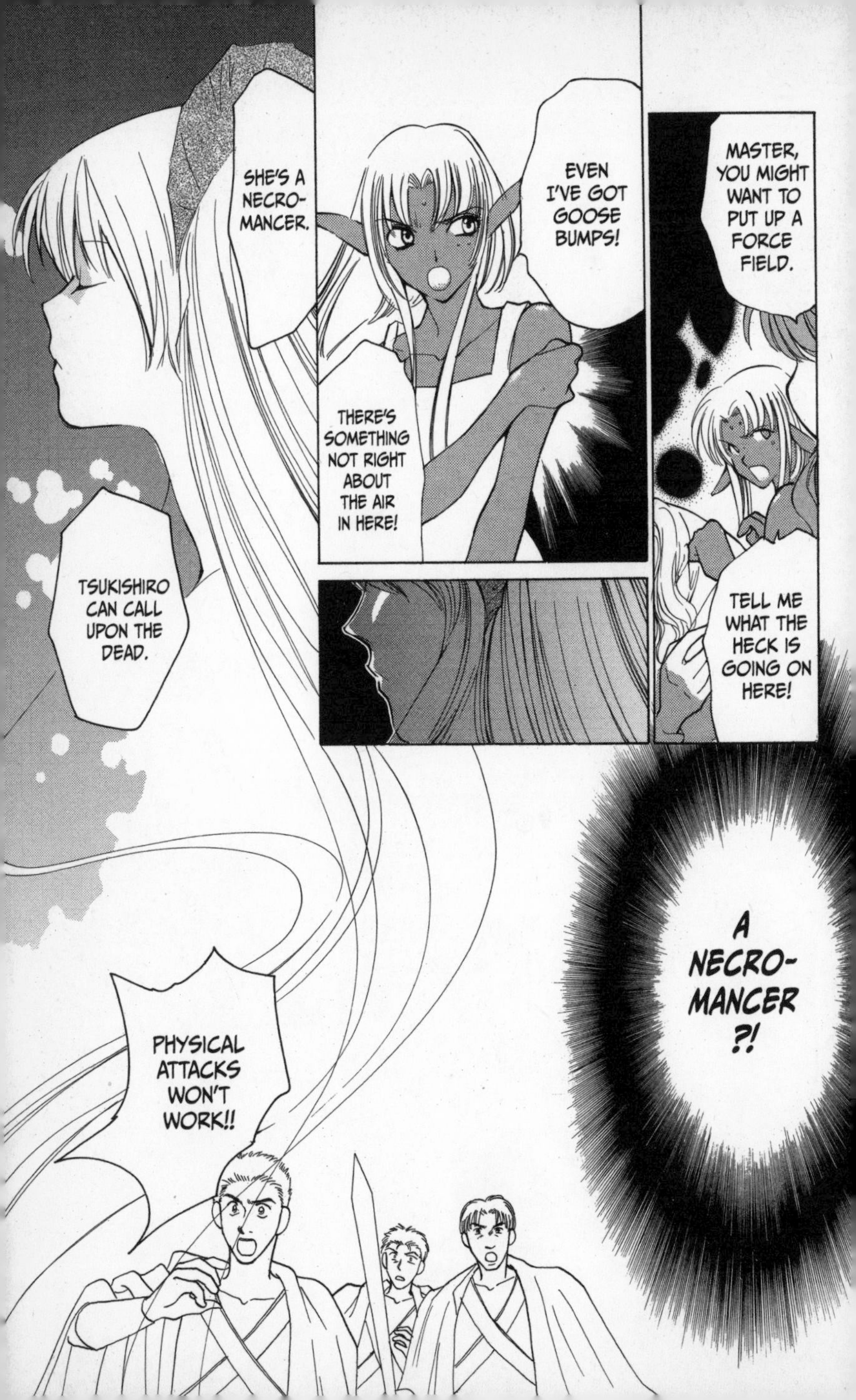
MASTER, YOU MIGHT WANT TO PUT UP A FORCE FIELD.
TELL ME WHAT THE HECK IS GOING ON HERE!
EVEN I'VE GOT GOOSE BUMPS!
THERE'S SOMETHING NOT RIGHT ABOUT THE AIR IN HERE!
SHE'S A NECRO-MANCER.
TSUKISHIRO CAN CALL UPON THE DEAD.
A NECRO-MANCER?!
PHYSICAL ATTACKS WON'T WORK!!

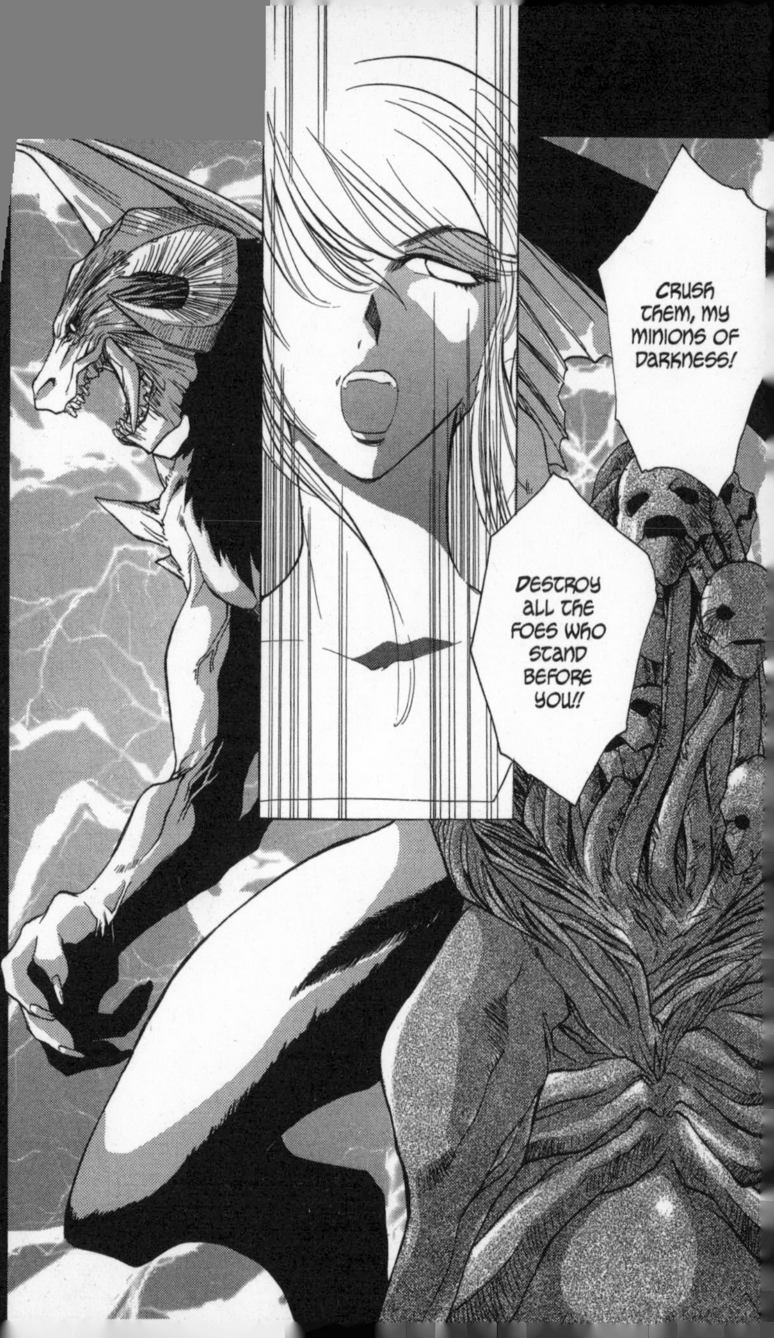
CRUSH THEM, MY MINIONS OF DARKNESS!
DESTROY ALL THE FOES WHO STAND BEFORE YOU!!

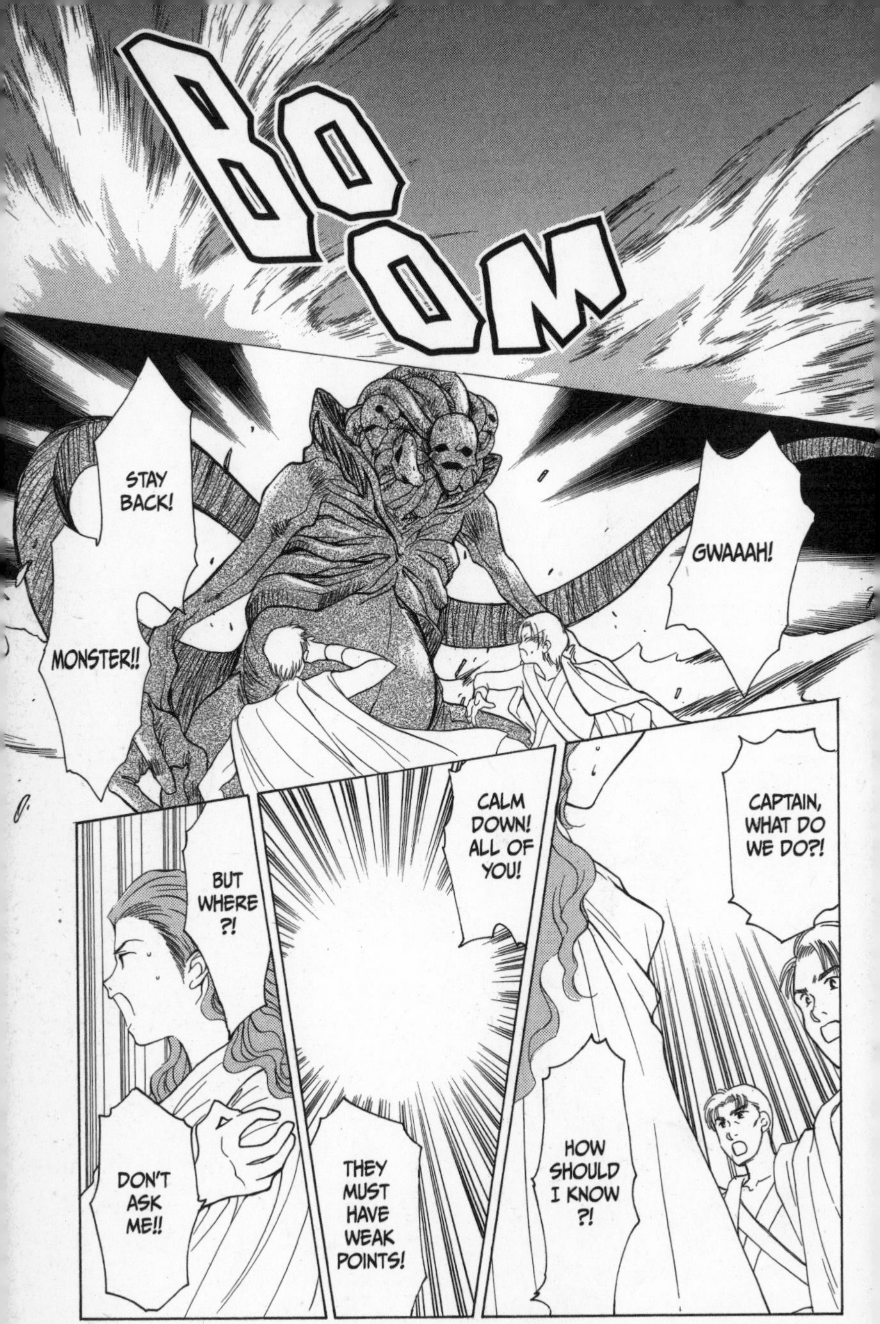
BOOM
GWAAAH!
STAY BACK!
MONSTER!!
CAPTAIN, WHAT DO WE DO?!
HOW SHOULD I KNOW?!
CALM DOWN! ALL OF YOU!
THEY MUST HAVE WEAK POINTS!
BUT WHERE?!
DON'T ASK ME!!

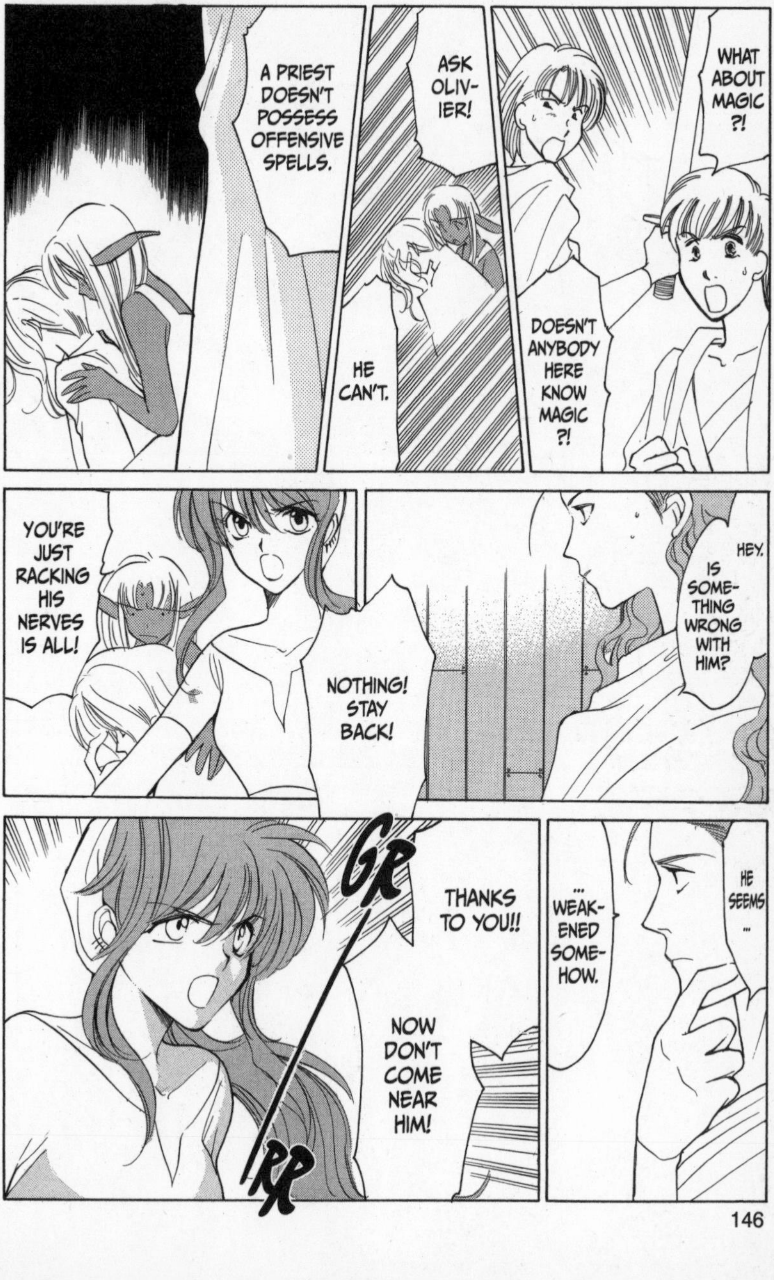
WHAT ABOUT MAGIC?!
DOESN'T ANYBODY HERE KNOW MAGIC?!
ASK OLIVIER!
HE CAN'T.
A PRIEST DOESN'T POSSESS OFFENSIVE SPELLS.
HEY. IS SOMETHING WRONG WITH HIM?
NOTHING! STAY BACK!
YOU'RE JUST RACKING HIS NERVES IS ALL!
HE SEEMS...
...WEAKENED SOMEHOW.
THANKS TO YOU!!
GRRR
NOW DON'T COME NEAR HIM!

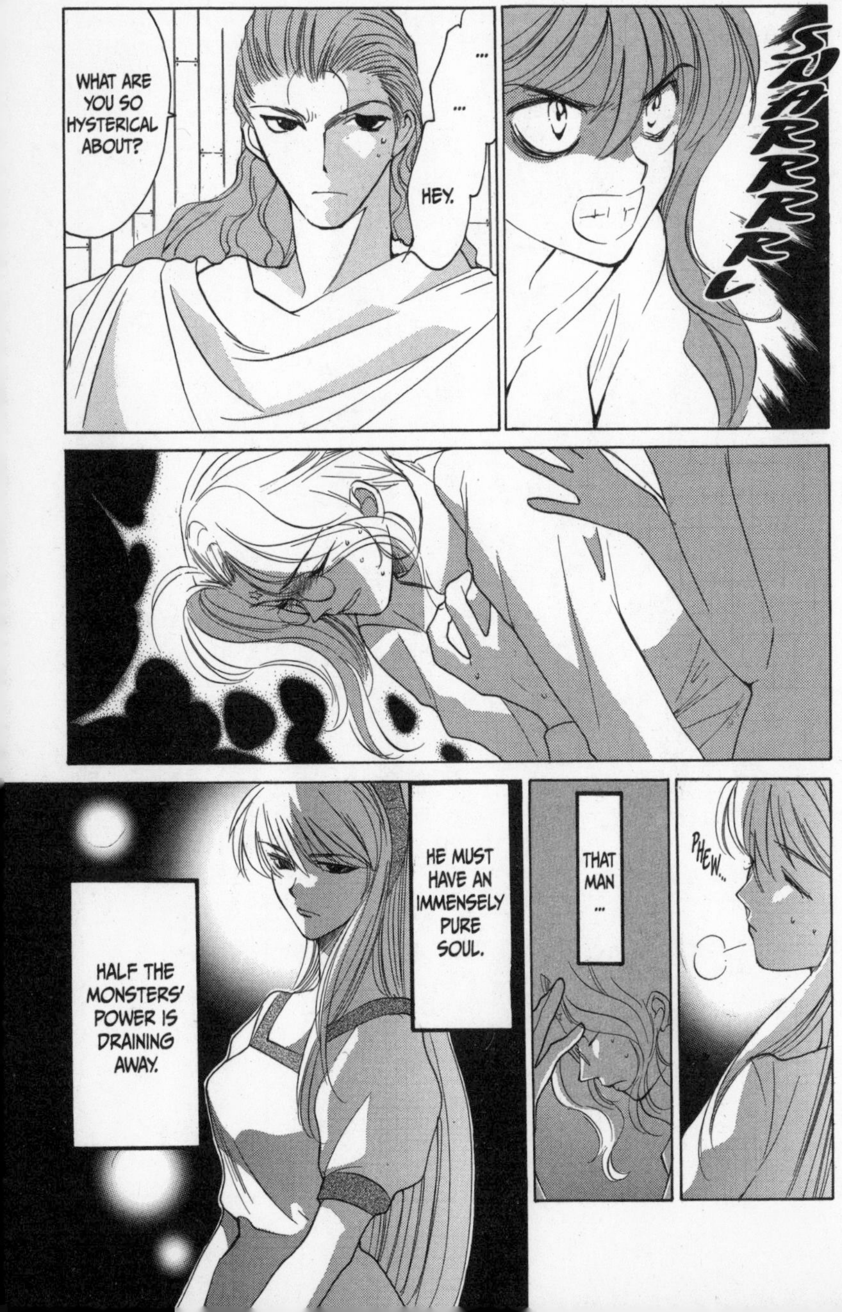
SHARRRRL
...
...
HEY.
WHAT ARE YOU SO HYSTERICAL ABOUT?
PHEW...
THAT MAN ...
HE MUST HAVE AN IMMENSELY PURE SOUL.
HALF THE MONSTERS' POWER IS DRAINING AWAY.

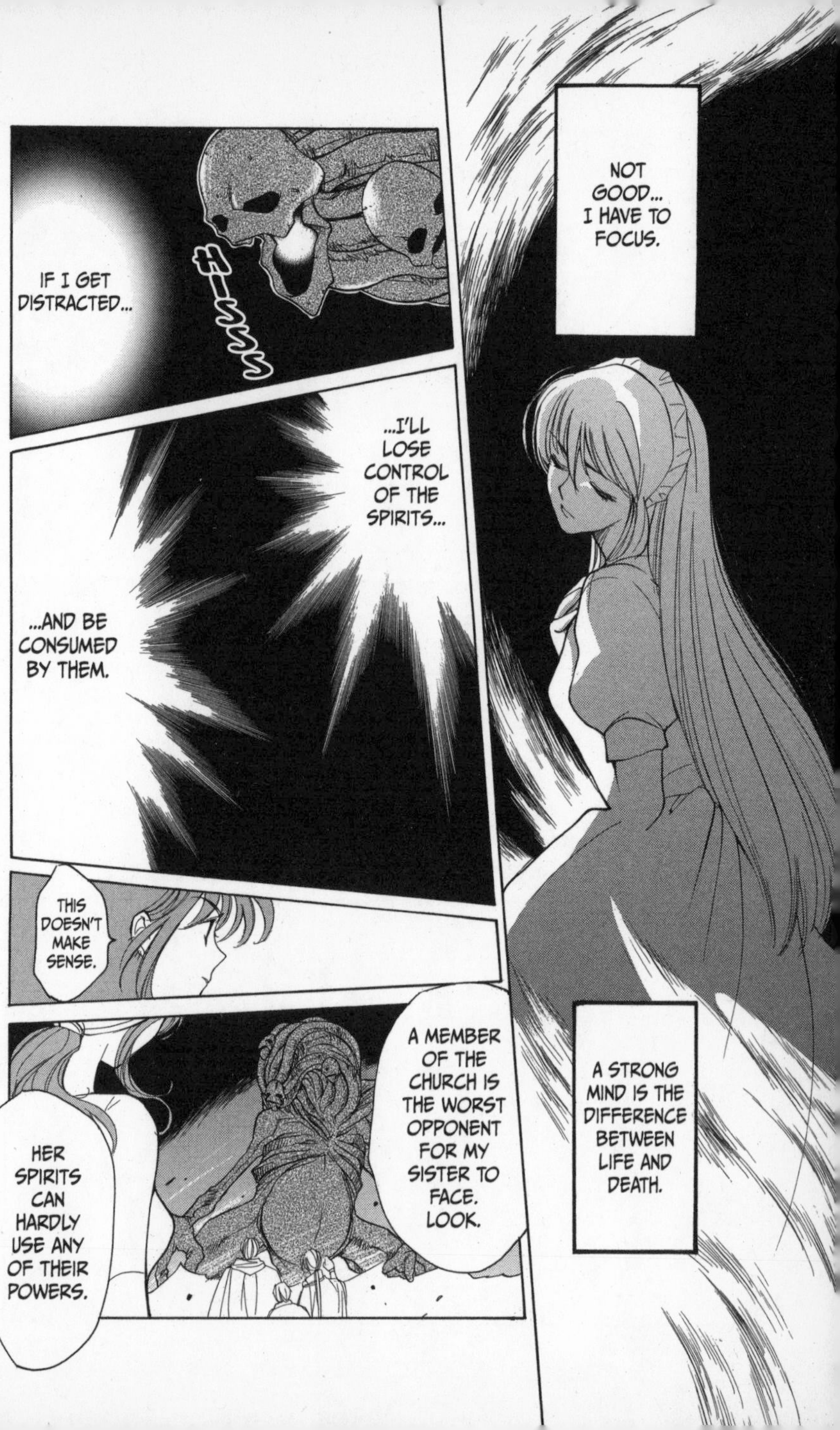
NOT GOOD... I HAVE TO FOCUS.
A STRONG MIND IS THE DIFFERENCE BETWEEN LIFE AND DEATH.
IF I GET DISTRACTED...
HISSS
...I'LL LOSE CONTROL OF THE SPIRITS...
...AND BE CONSUMED BY THEM.
THIS DOESN'T MAKE SENSE.
A MEMBER OF THE CHURCH IS THE WORST OPPONENT FOR MY SISTER TO FACE. LOOK.
HER SPIRITS CAN HARDLY USE ANY OF THEIR POWERS.

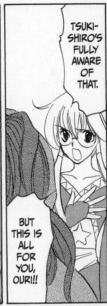

ROOOOAR
SO WHAT?
TSUKI-SHIRO'S FULLY AWARE OF THAT.
BUT THIS IS ALL FOR YOU, OURI!!
THIS HAS NOTHING TO DO WITH ME.
I NEVER KNEW...
A-HA!
POOMF
I THINK I GOT IT!
COME HERE A SEC.
AAAAAAH!
WHAT'RE YOU DOING?!
TURN

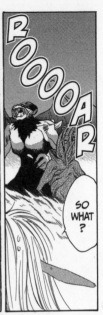

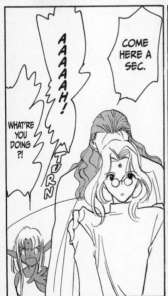

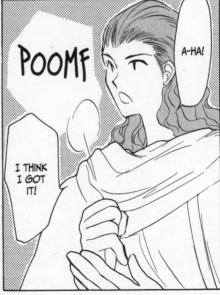

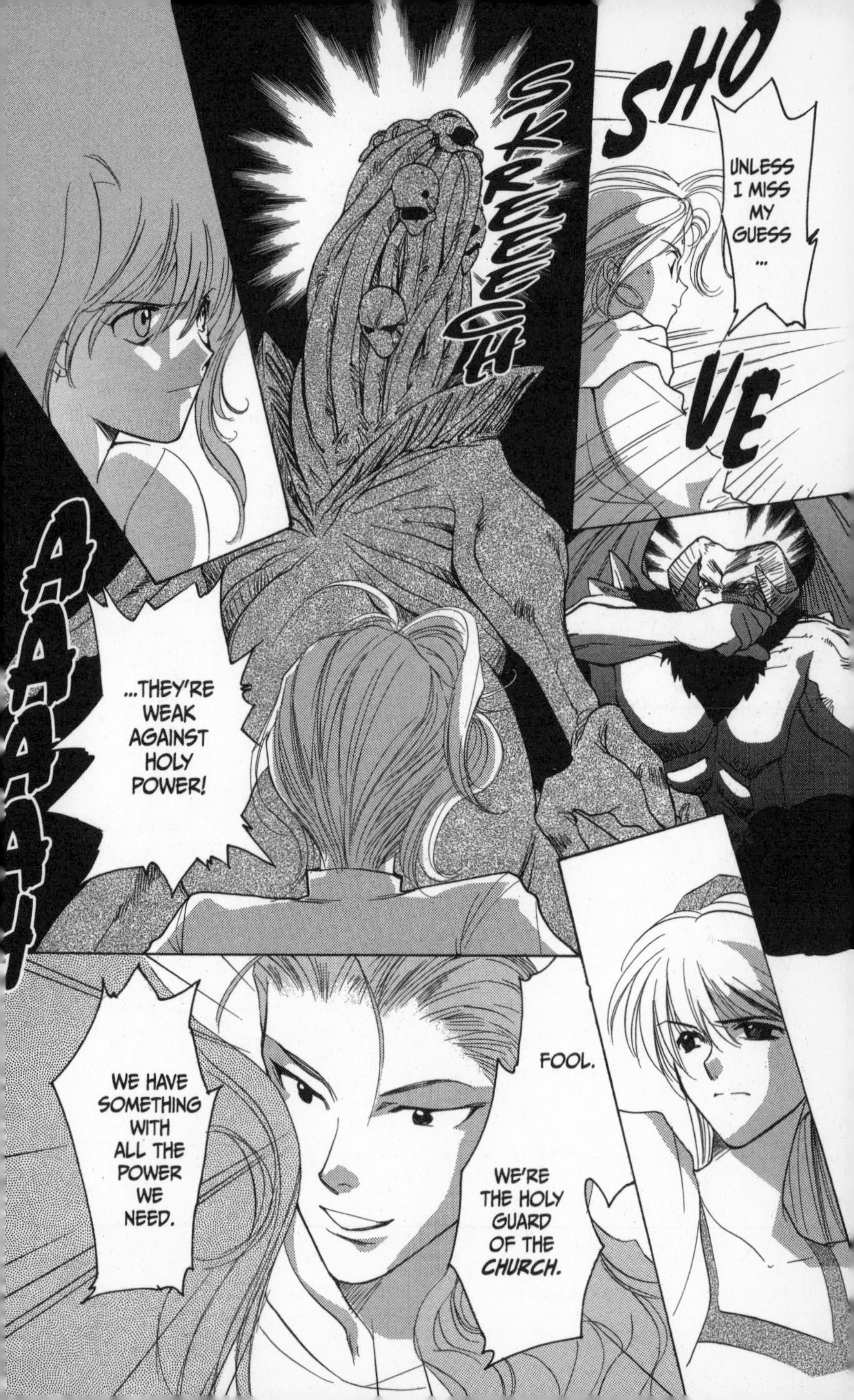
SHOVE
UNLESS I MISS MY GUESS ...
SKREEECH
...THEY'RE WEAK AGAINST HOLY POWER!
AAAAAH
FOOL.
WE'RE THE HOLY GUARD OF THE *CHURCH*.
WE HAVE SOMETHING WITH ALL THE POWER WE NEED.

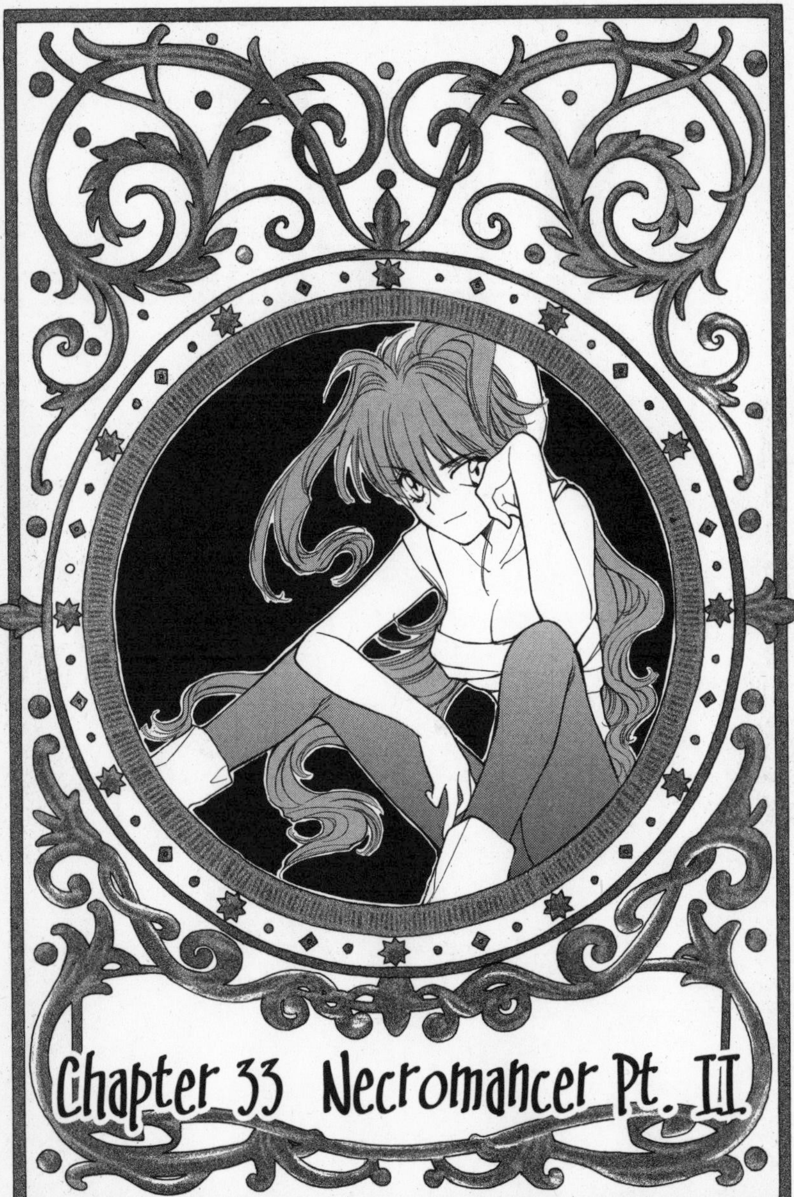

Chapter 33 Necromancer Pt. II

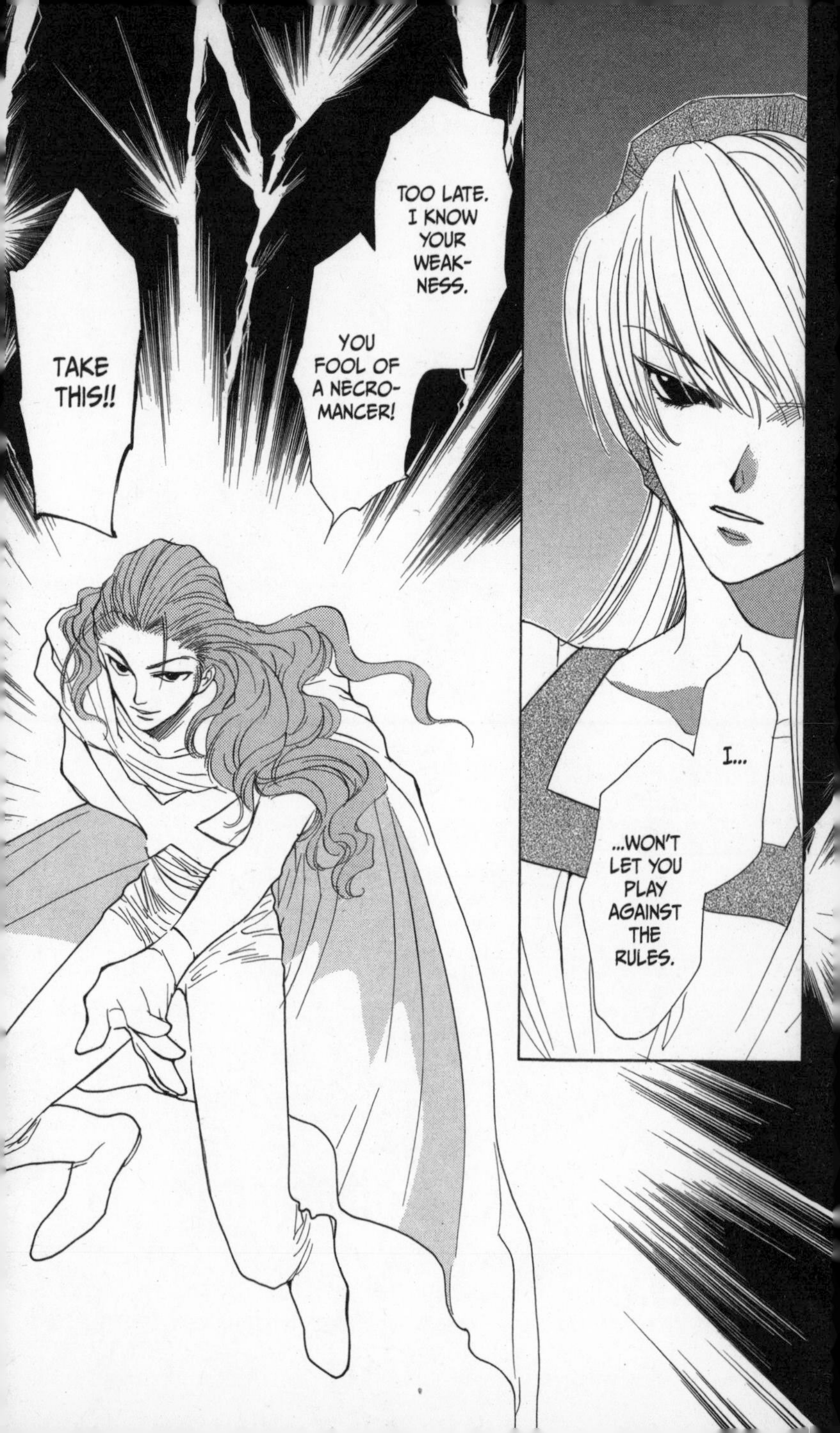
I...
...WON'T LET YOU PLAY AGAINST THE RULES.
TOO LATE. I KNOW YOUR WEAK-NESS.
YOU FOOL OF A NECRO-MANCER!
TAKE THIS!!

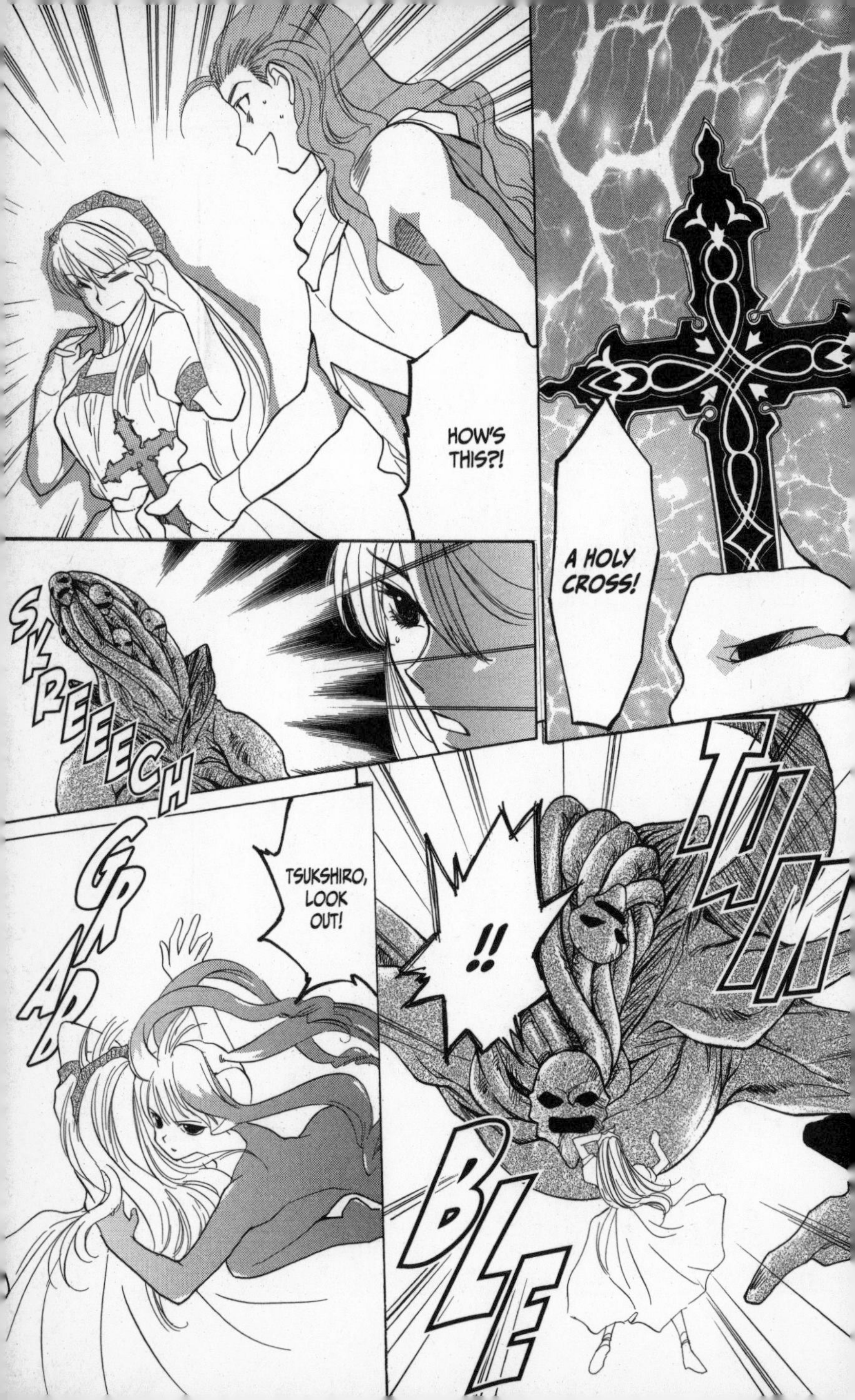
A HOLY CROSS!
HOW'S THIS?!
SKREEECH
TUM
!!
BLE
TSUKSHIRO, LOOK OUT!
GRAB

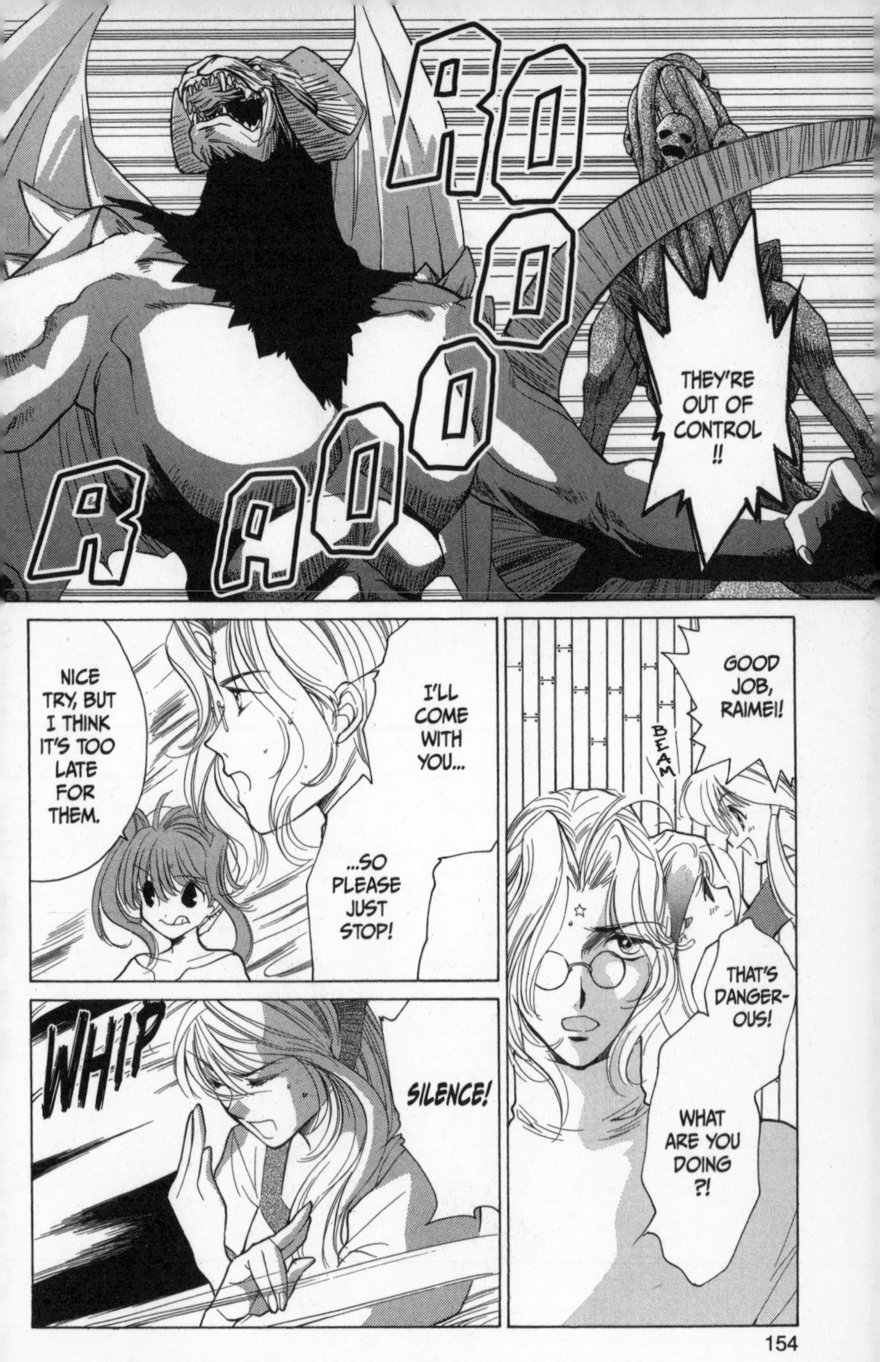
ROOOOAR
THEY'RE OUT OF CONTROL!!
GOOD JOB, RAIMEI!
BEAM
THAT'S DANGER-OUS!
WHAT ARE YOU DOING?!
I'LL COME WITH YOU...
...SO PLEASE JUST STOP!
NICE TRY, BUT I THINK IT'S TOO LATE FOR THEM.
SILENCE!
WHIP

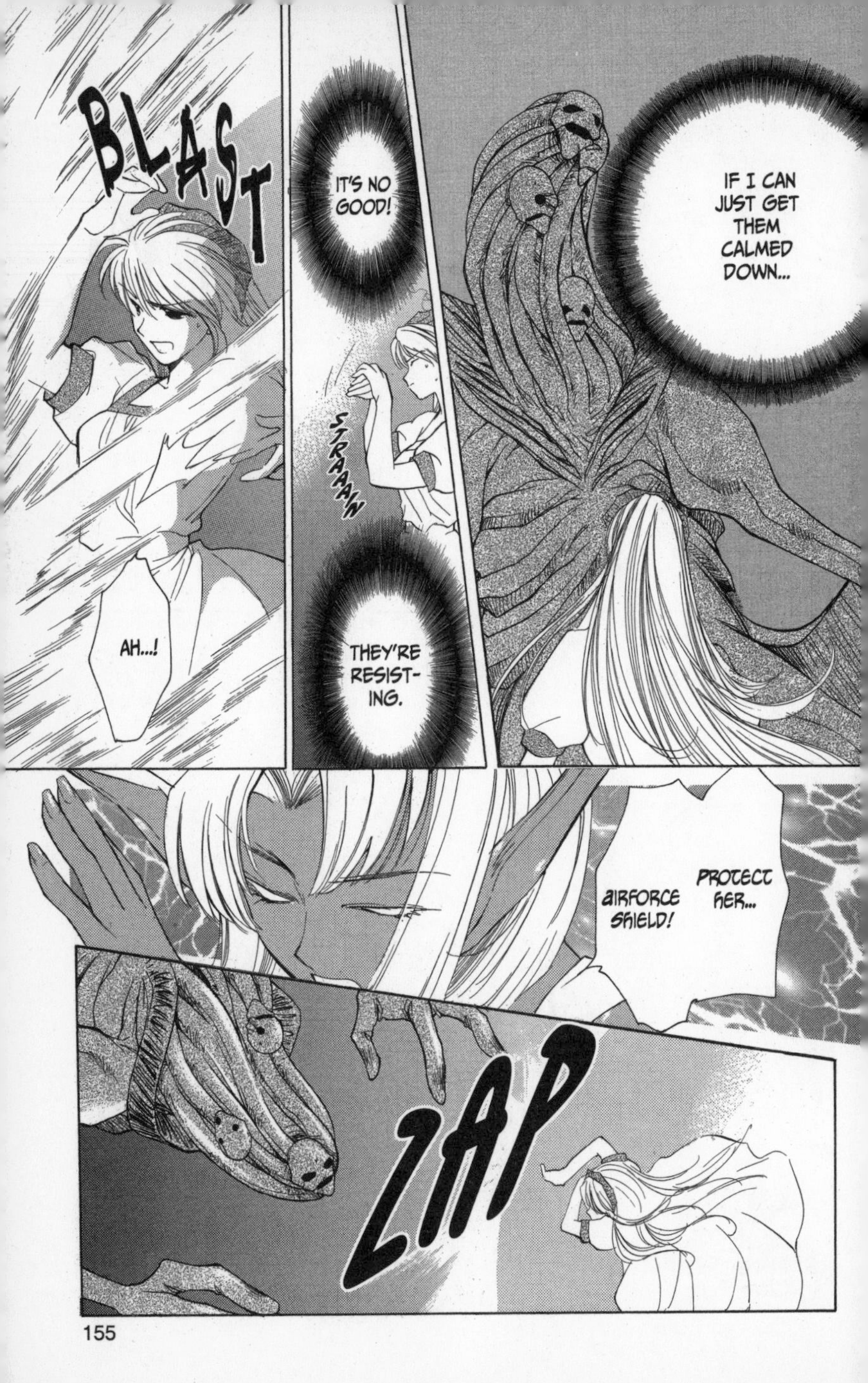
IF I CAN JUST GET THEM CALMED DOWN...
IT'S NO GOOD!
STRAAAIN
THEY'RE RESIST-ING.
BLAST
AH...!
PROTECT HER...
AIRFORCE SHIELD!
ZAP

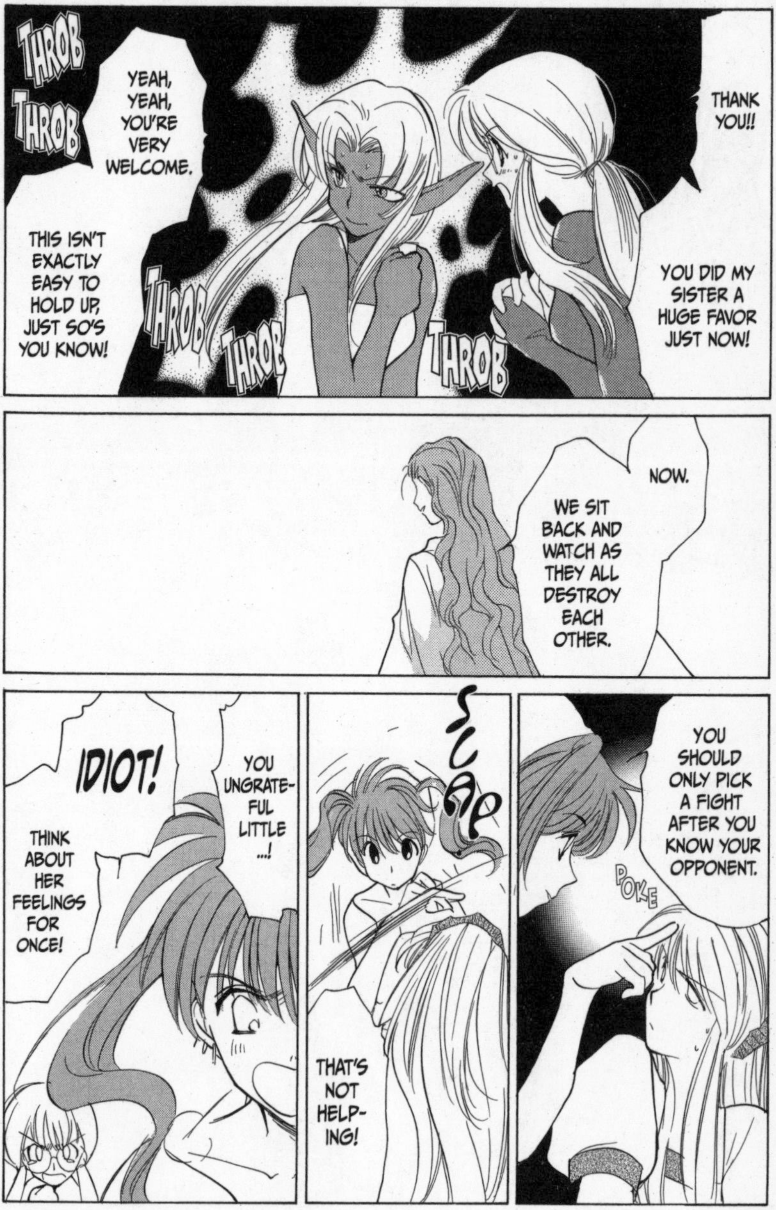
THANK YOU!!
YOU DID MY SISTER A HUGE FAVOR JUST NOW!
THROB THROB
YEAH, YEAH, YOU'RE VERY WELCOME.
THIS ISN'T EXACTLY EASY TO HOLD UP, JUST SO'S YOU KNOW!
THROB
THROB
THROB
NOW.
WE SIT BACK AND WATCH AS THEY ALL DESTROY EACH OTHER.
YOU SHOULD ONLY PICK A FIGHT AFTER YOU KNOW YOUR OPPONENT.
POKE
THAT'S NOT HELP-ING!
YOU UNGRATE-FUL LITTLE ...!
IDIOT!
THINK ABOUT HER FEELINGS FOR ONCE!

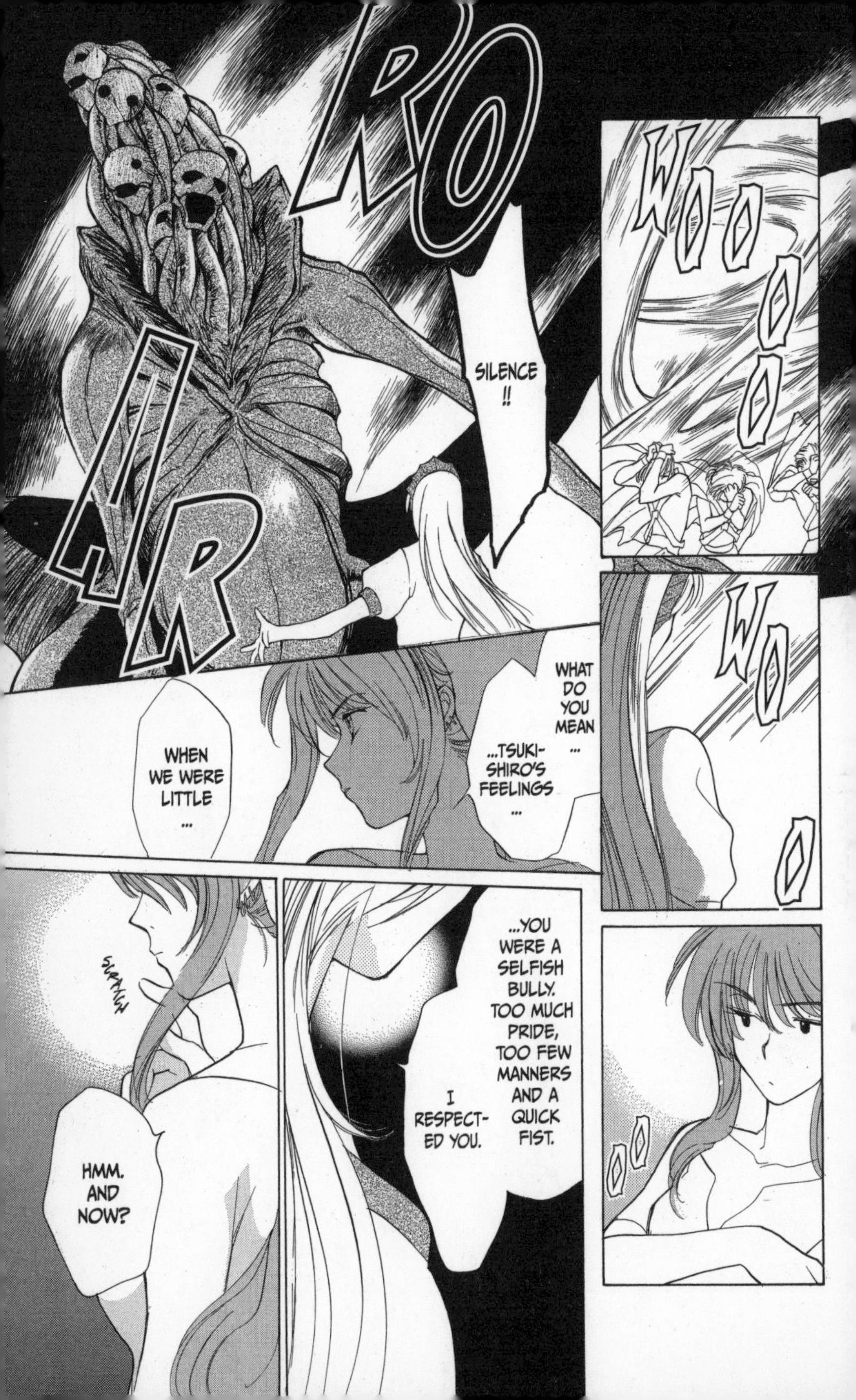
WOOOOOO
ROAR
SILENCE !!
WOOO
WHAT DO YOU MEAN ...
...TSUKI-SHIRO'S FEELINGS ...
WHEN WE WERE LITTLE ...
OO
...YOU WERE A SELFISH BULLY. TOO MUCH PRIDE, TOO FEW MANNERS AND A QUICK FIST.
I RESPECT-ED YOU.
SCRATCH
HMM. AND NOW?

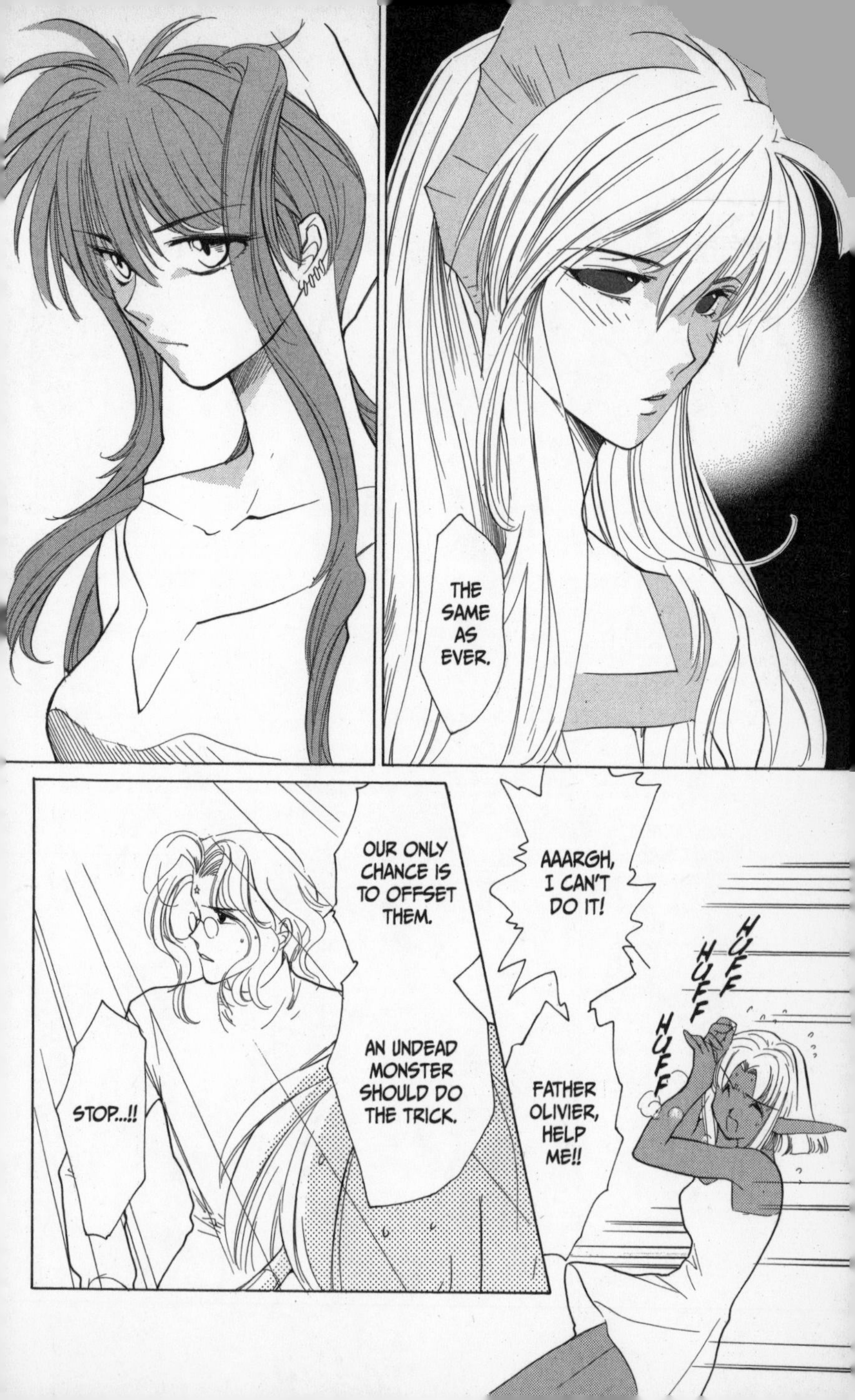
THE SAME AS EVER.
HUFF HUFF HUFF
AAARGH, I CAN'T DO IT!
FATHER OLIVIER, HELP ME!!
OUR ONLY CHANCE IS TO OFFSET THEM.
AN UNDEAD MONSTER SHOULD DO THE TRICK.
STOP...!!

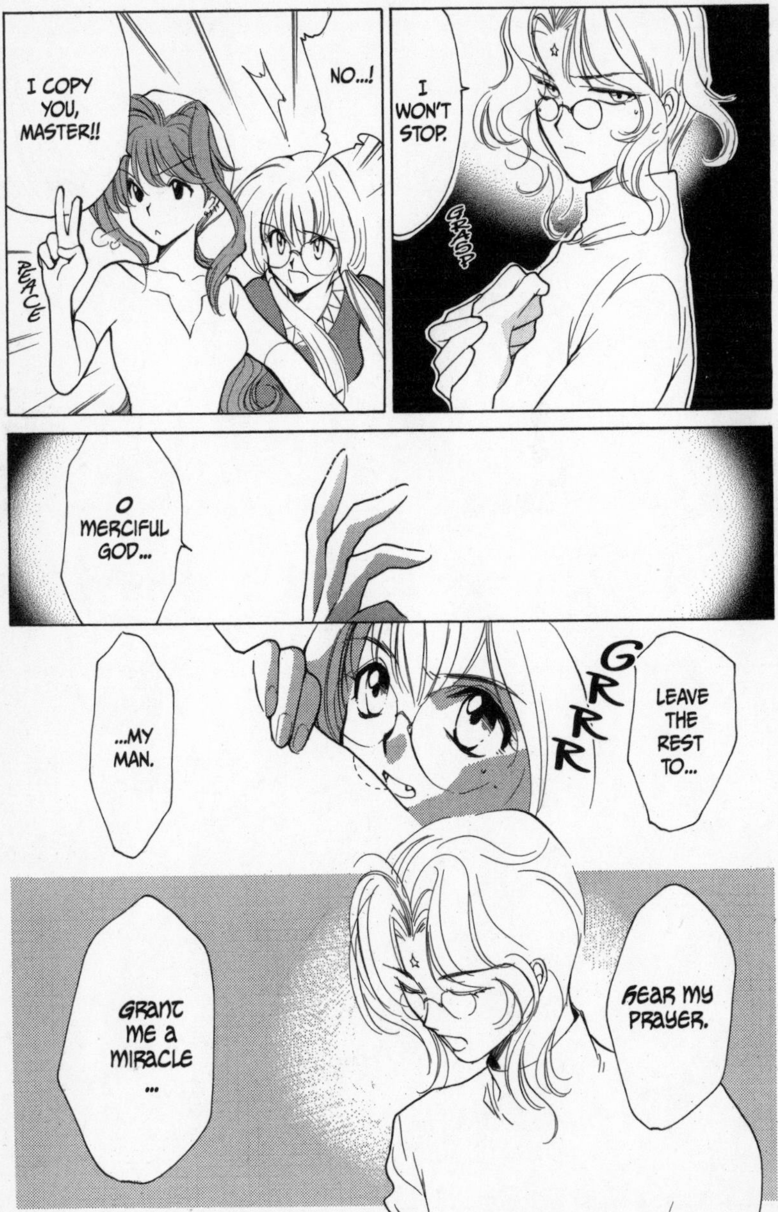
I WON'T STOP.
GRASP
NO...!
I COPY YOU, MASTER!!
PEACE
O MERCIFUL GOD...
LEAVE THE REST TO...
GRRR
...MY MAN.
HEAR MY PRAYER.
GRANT ME A MIRACLE ...

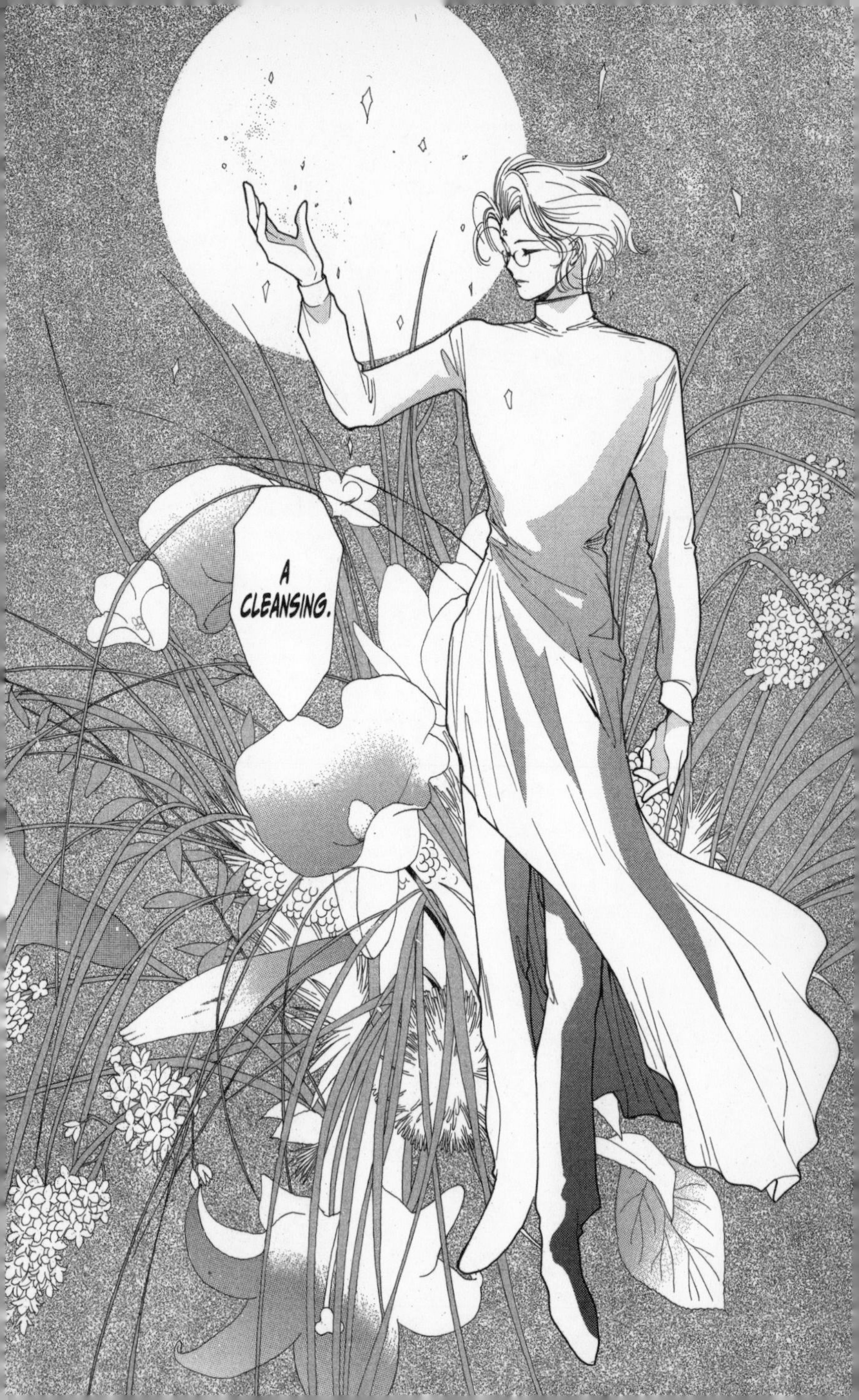
A CLEANSING.

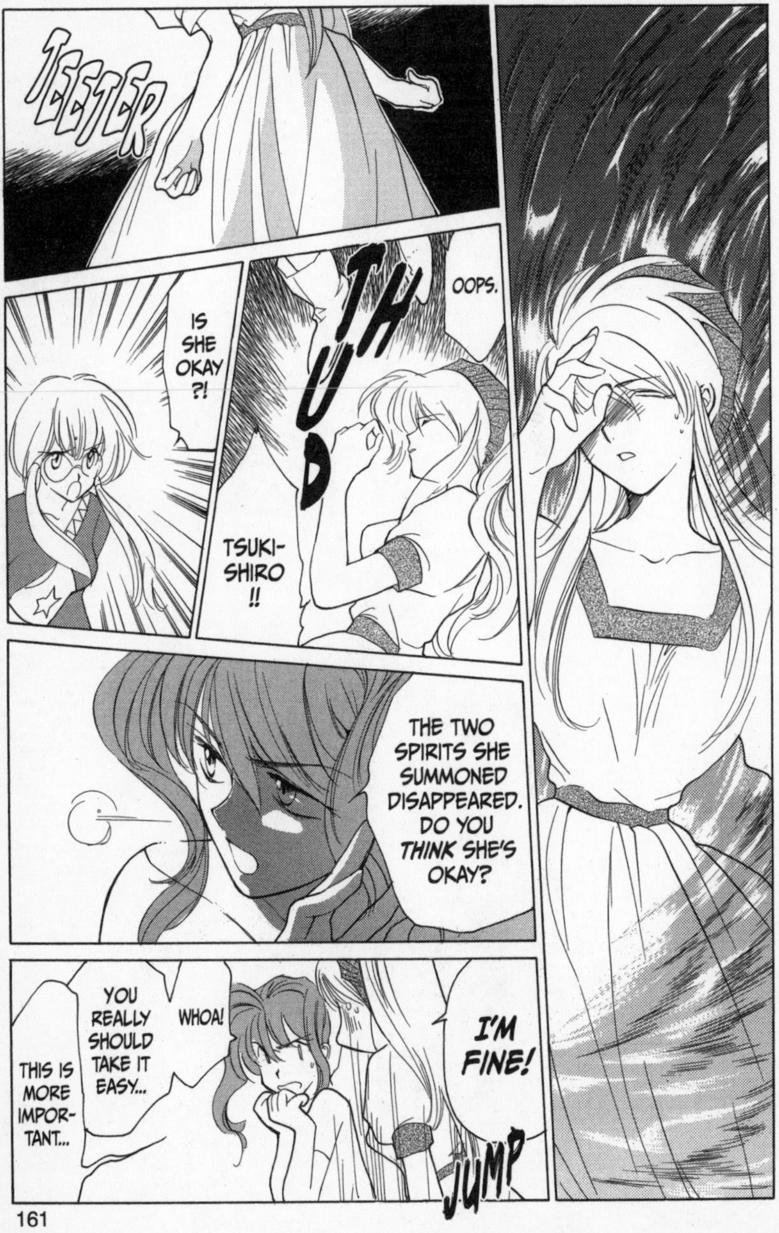
TEETER
OOPS.
THUD
TSUKI-SHIRO!!
IS SHE OKAY?!
THE TWO SPIRITS SHE SUMMONED DISAPPEARED. DO YOU *THINK* SHE'S OKAY?
I'M FINE!
JUMP
WHOA!
YOU REALLY SHOULD TAKE IT EASY...
THIS IS MORE IMPOR-TANT...

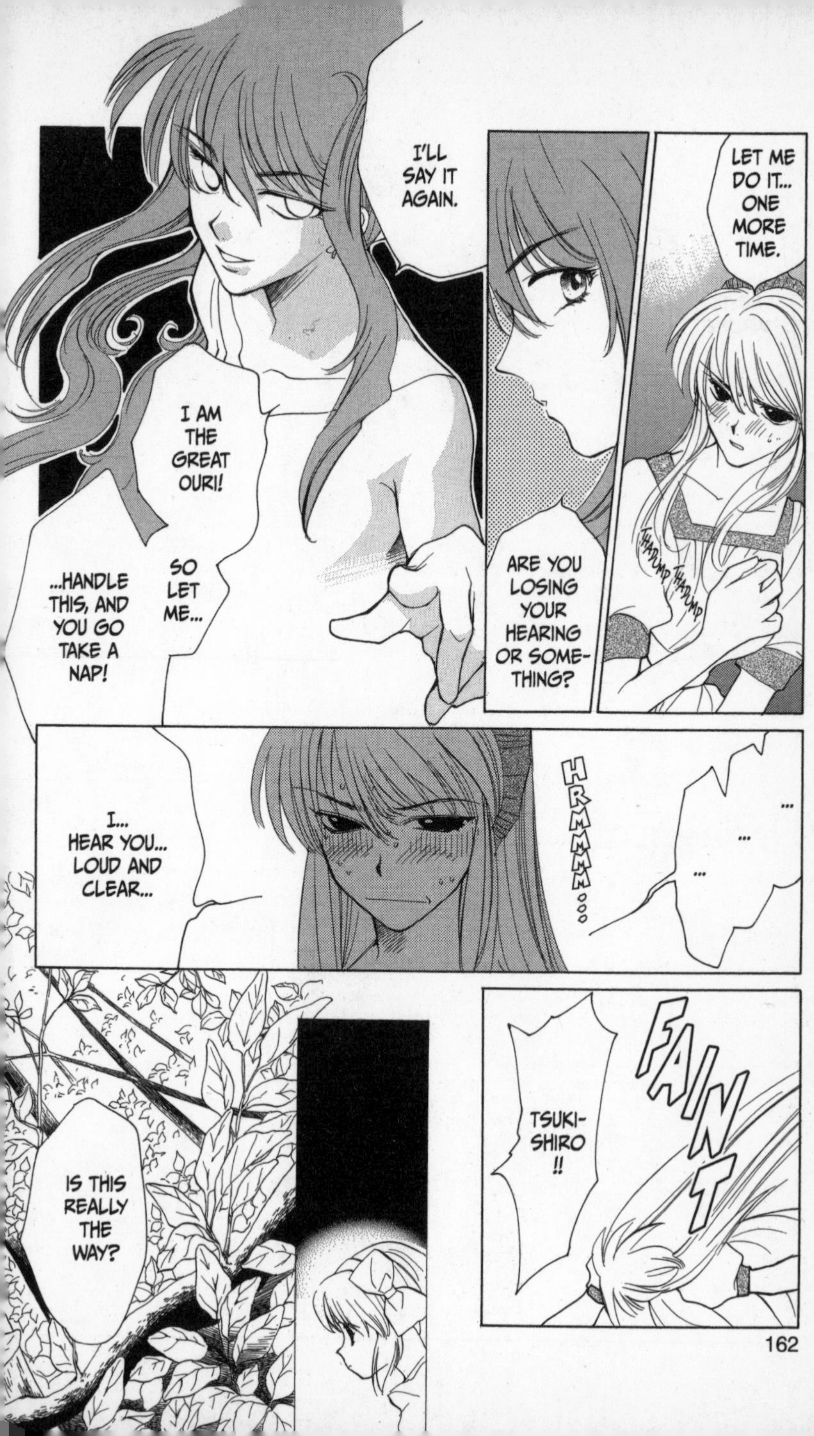

LET ME DO IT... ONE MORE TIME.
THADUMP THADUMP
ARE YOU LOSING YOUR HEARING OR SOME-THING?
I'LL SAY IT AGAIN.
I AM THE GREAT OURI!
SO LET ME...
...HANDLE THIS, AND YOU GO TAKE A NAP!
...
...
...
HRMMMM...
I... HEAR YOU... LOUD AND CLEAR...
FAINT
TSUKI-SHIRO !!
IS THIS REALLY THE WAY?

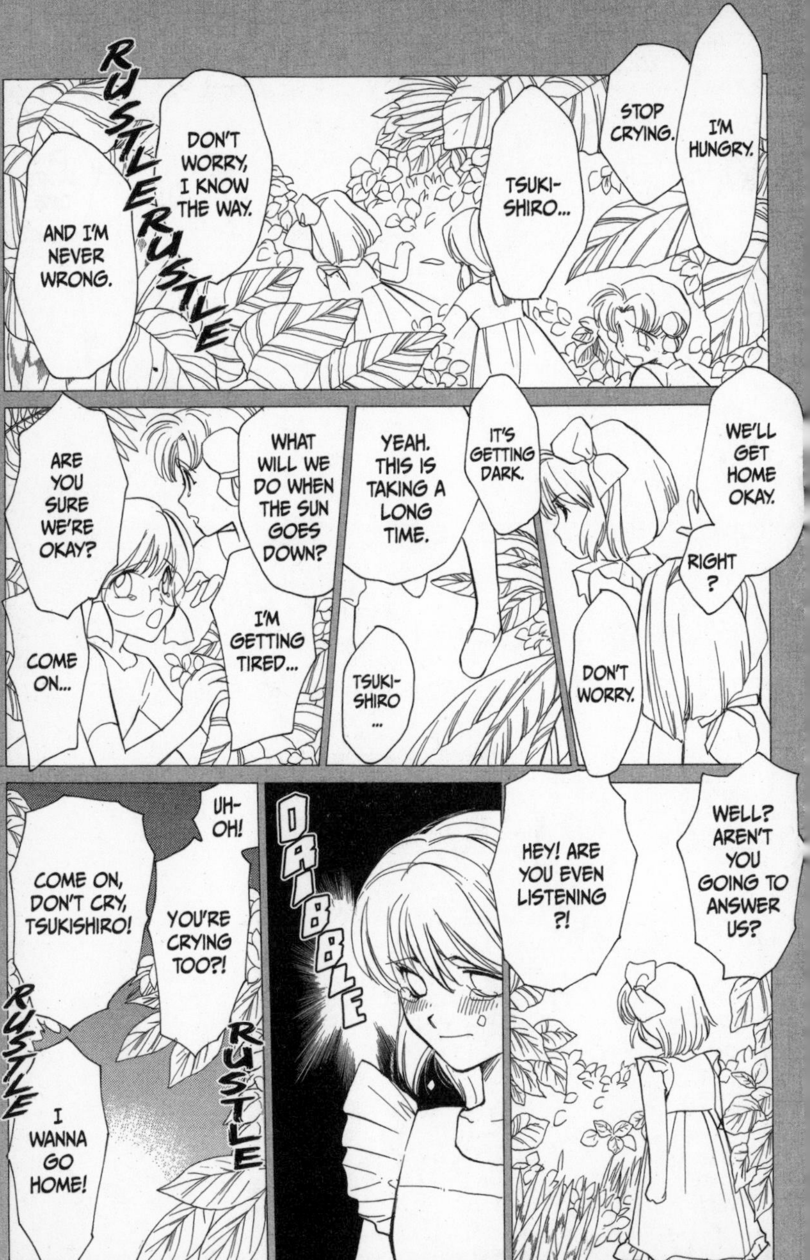
I'M HUNGRY.
STOP CRYING.
TSUKI-SHIRO...
DON'T WORRY, I KNOW THE WAY.
RUSTLE RUSTLE
AND I'M NEVER WRONG.
WE'LL GET HOME OKAY.
RIGHT?
DON'T WORRY.
IT'S GETTING DARK.
YEAH. THIS IS TAKING A LONG TIME.
TSUKI-SHIRO...
WHAT WILL WE DO WHEN THE SUN GOES DOWN?
ARE YOU SURE WE'RE OKAY?
I'M GETTING TIRED...
COME ON...
WELL? AREN'T YOU GOING TO ANSWER US?
HEY! ARE YOU EVEN LISTENING?!
DRIBBLE
UH-OH!
COME ON, DON'T CRY, TSUKISHIRO!
YOU'RE CRYING TOO?!
RUSTLE
RUSTLE
I WANNA GO HOME!

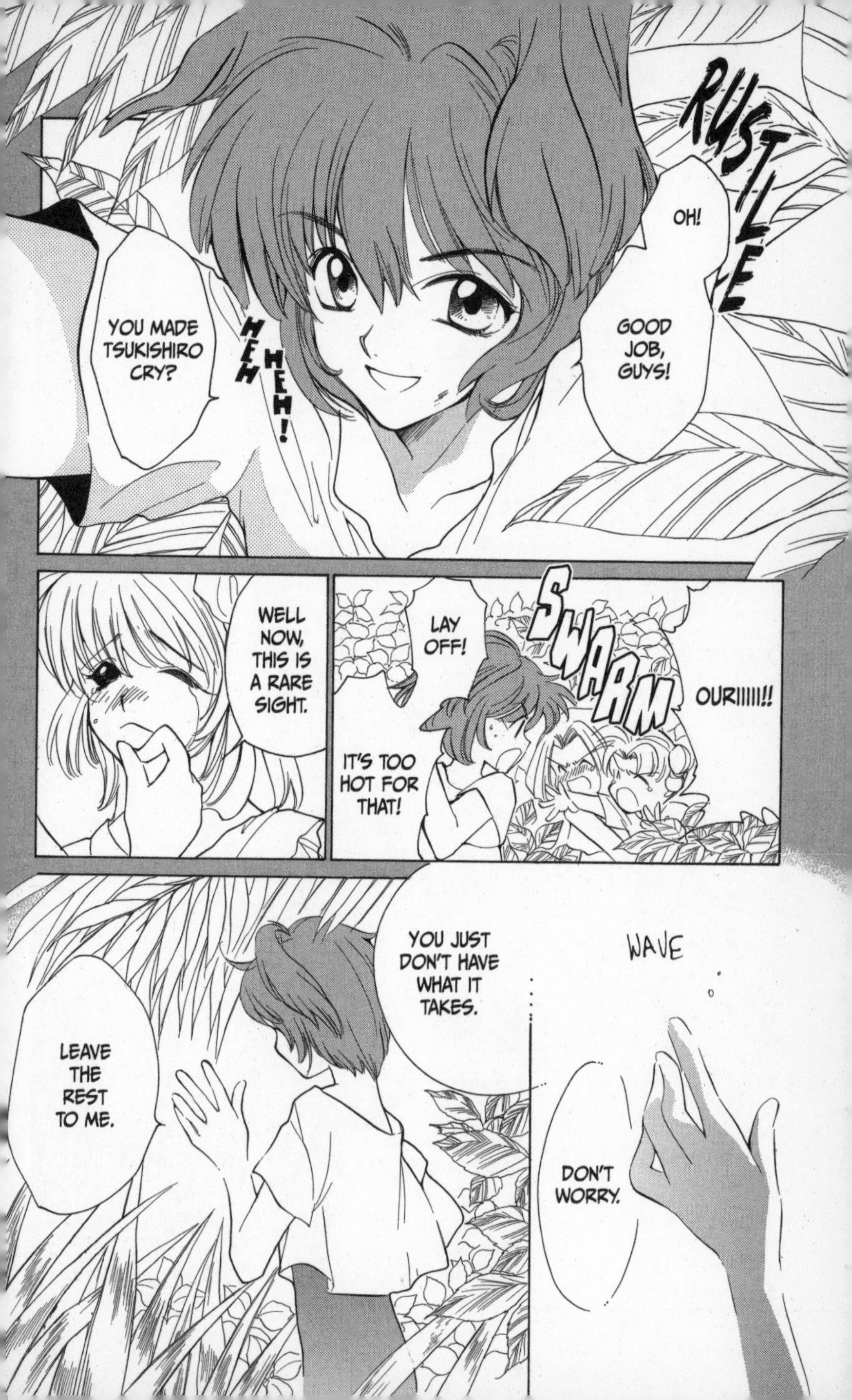
RUSTLE
OH!
GOOD JOB, GUYS!
HEH HEH!
YOU MADE TSUKISHIRO CRY?
SWARM
OURIIIIII!!
LAY OFF!
IT'S TOO HOT FOR THAT!
WELL NOW, THIS IS A RARE SIGHT.
WAVE
DON'T WORRY.
YOU JUST DON'T HAVE WHAT IT TAKES.
LEAVE THE REST TO ME.

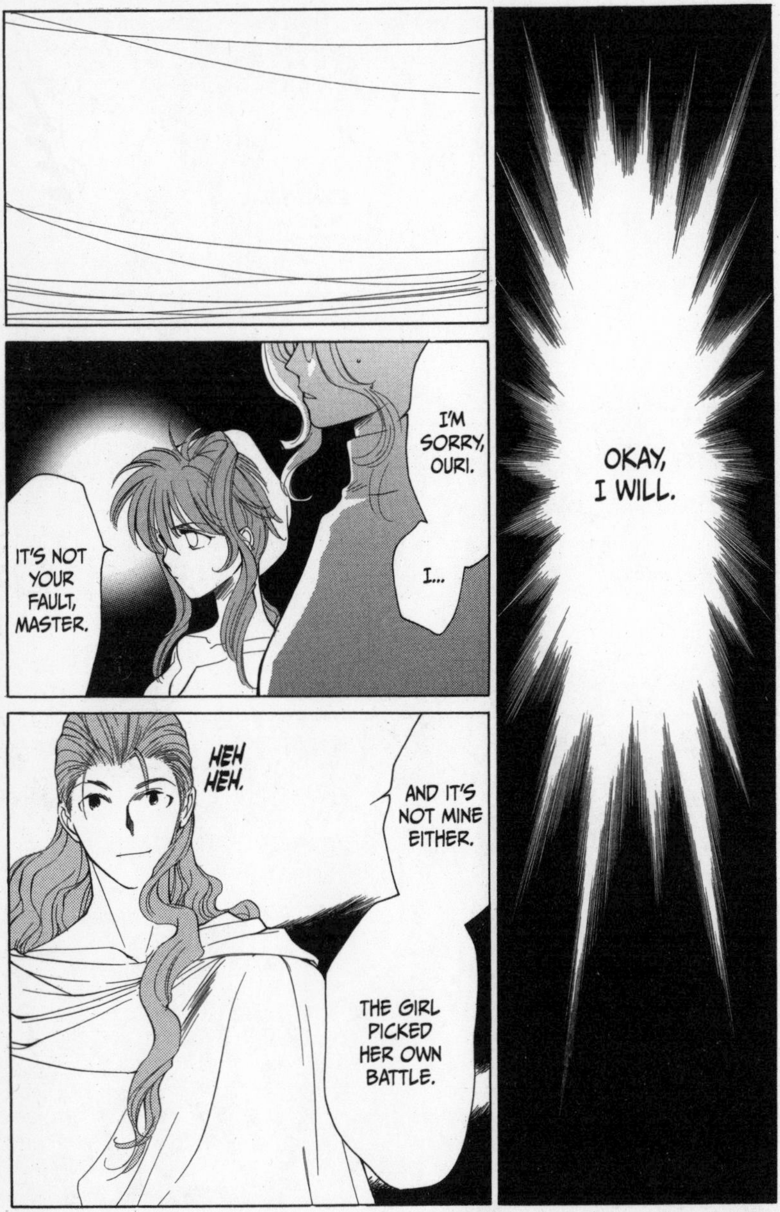
OKAY, I WILL.
I'M SORRY, OURI.
I...
IT'S NOT YOUR FAULT, MASTER.
AND IT'S NOT MINE EITHER.
HEH HEH.
THE GIRL PICKED HER OWN BATTLE.

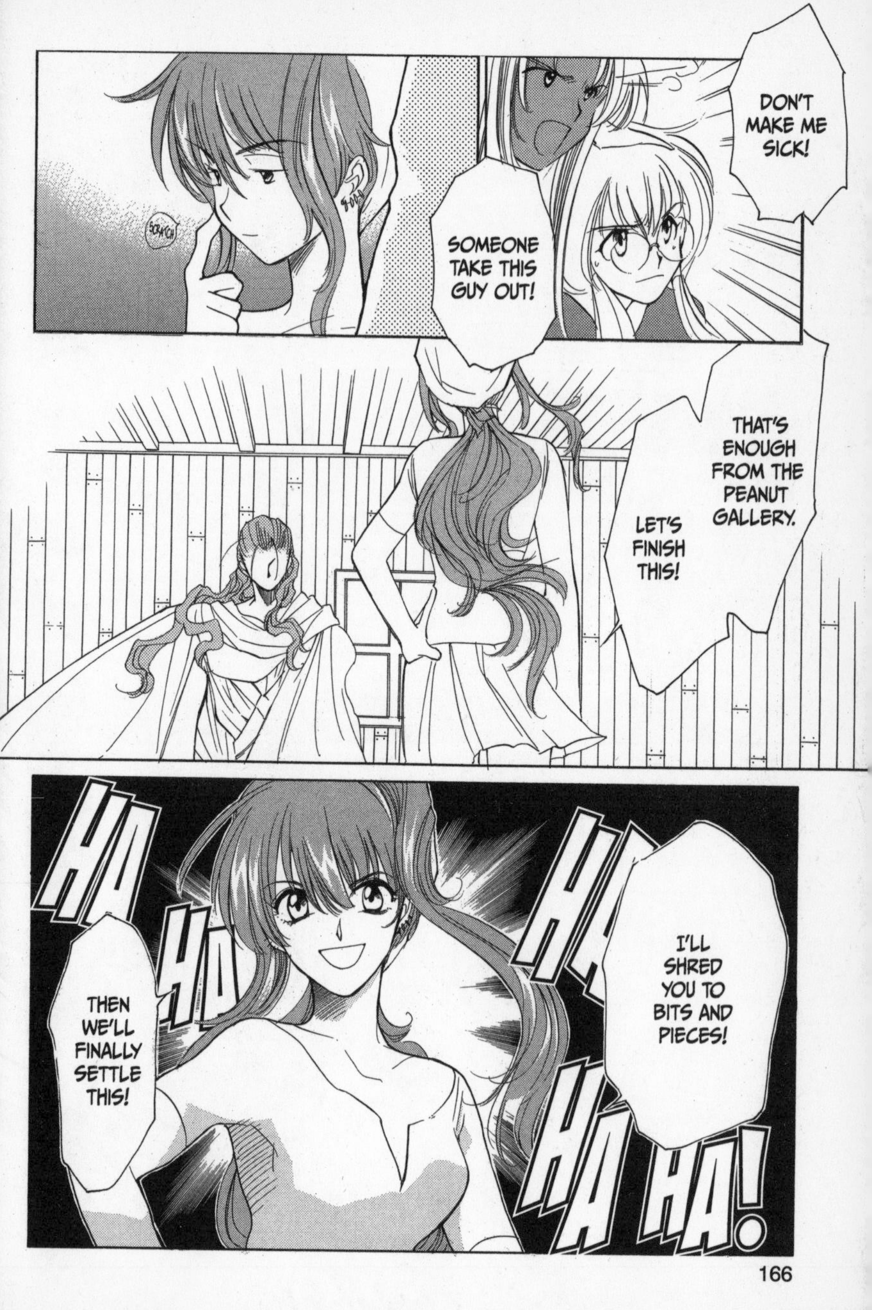
DON'T MAKE ME SICK!
SOMEONE TAKE THIS GUY OUT!
SCRATCH
THAT'S ENOUGH FROM THE PEANUT GALLERY.
LET'S FINISH THIS!
I'LL SHRED YOU TO BITS AND PIECES!
HA HA HA HA!
HA HA
THEN WE'LL FINALLY SETTLE THIS!

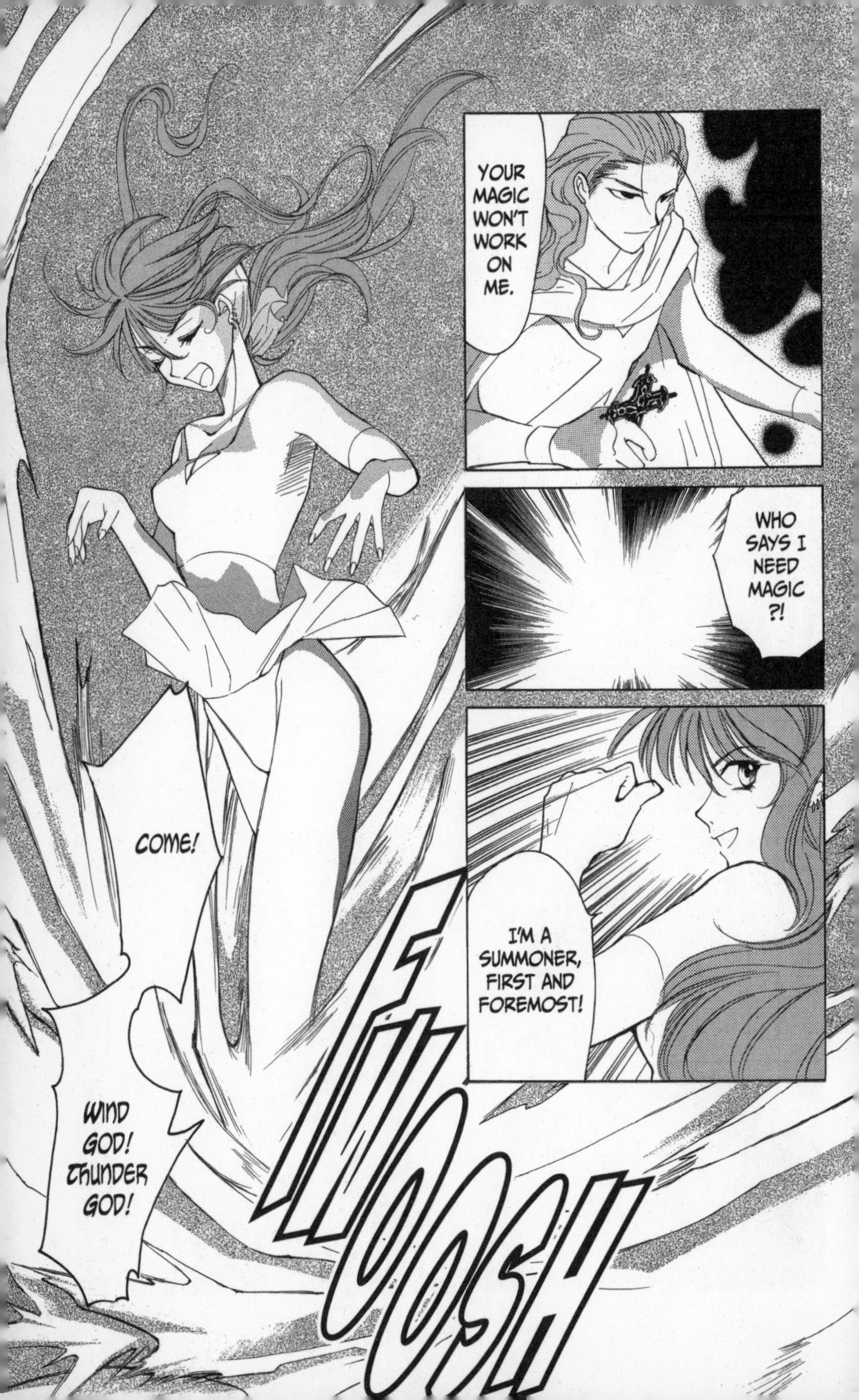
YOUR MAGIC WON'T WORK ON ME.
WHO SAYS I NEED MAGIC ?!
I'M A SUMMONER, FIRST AND FOREMOST!
COME!
WIND GOD! THUNDER GOD!
FWOOSH

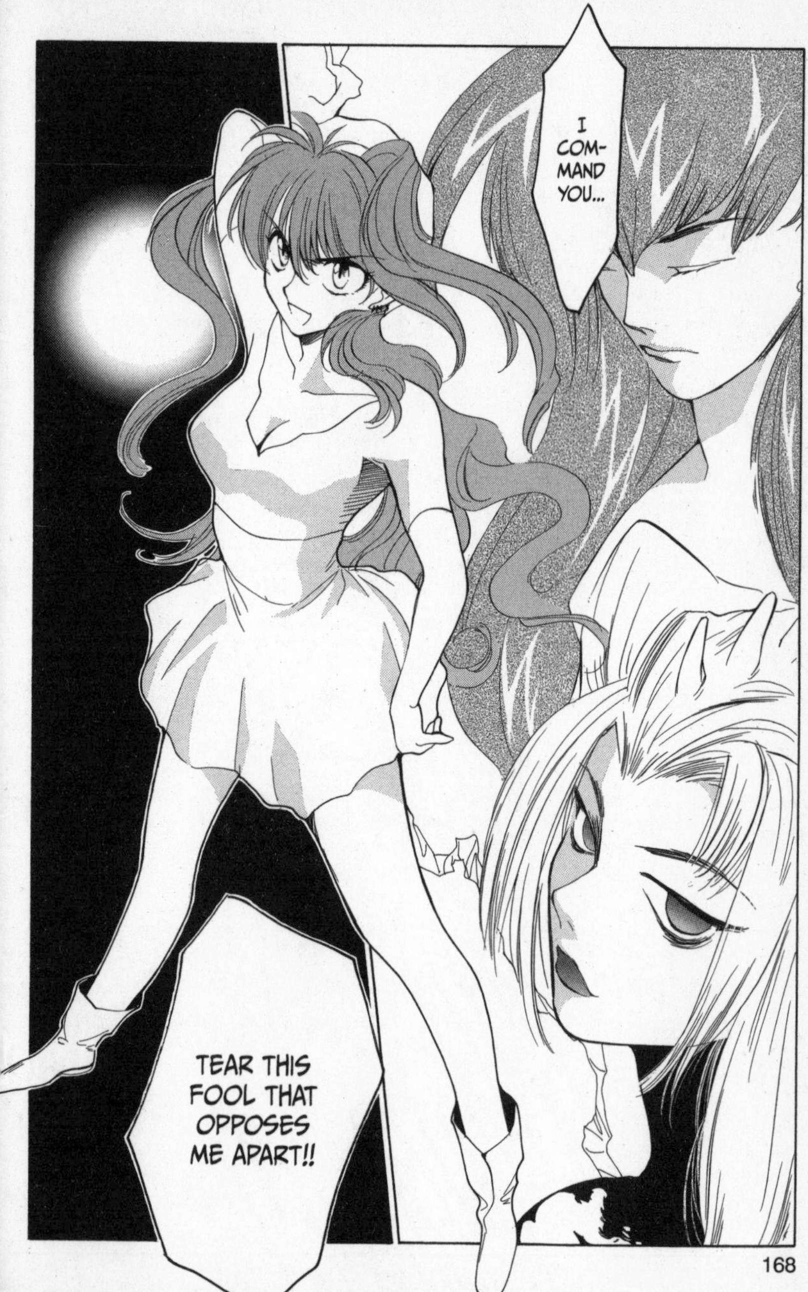
I COM- MAND YOU...
TEAR THIS FOOL THAT OPPOSES ME APART!!

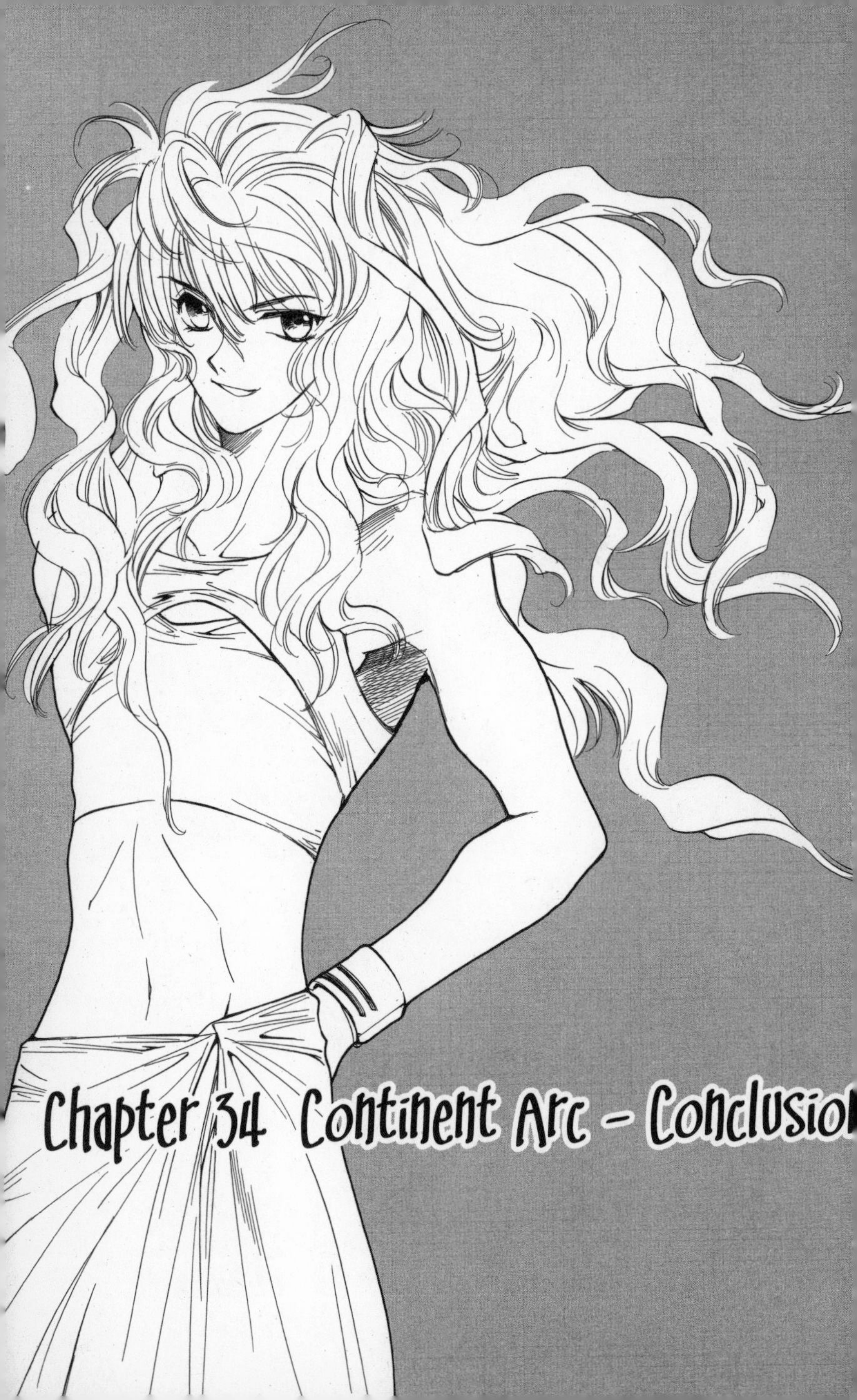

Chapter 34 Continent Arc - Conclusion

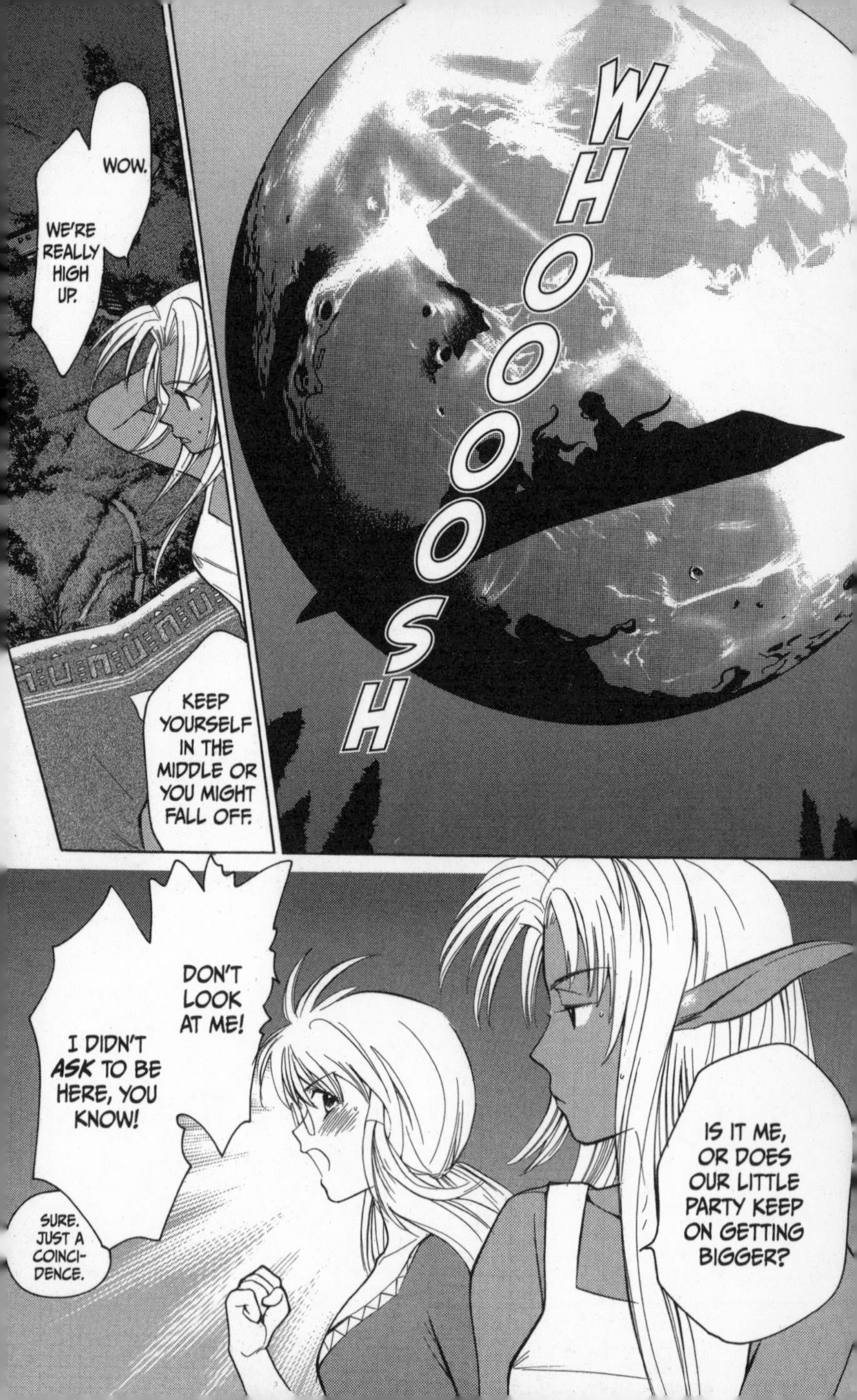
WHOOOOSH
WOW.
WE'RE REALLY HIGH UP.
KEEP YOURSELF IN THE MIDDLE OR YOU MIGHT FALL OFF.
IS IT ME, OR DOES OUR LITTLE PARTY KEEP ON GETTING BIGGER?
DON'T LOOK AT ME!
I DIDN'T **ASK** TO BE HERE, YOU KNOW!
SURE. JUST A COINCI-DENCE.

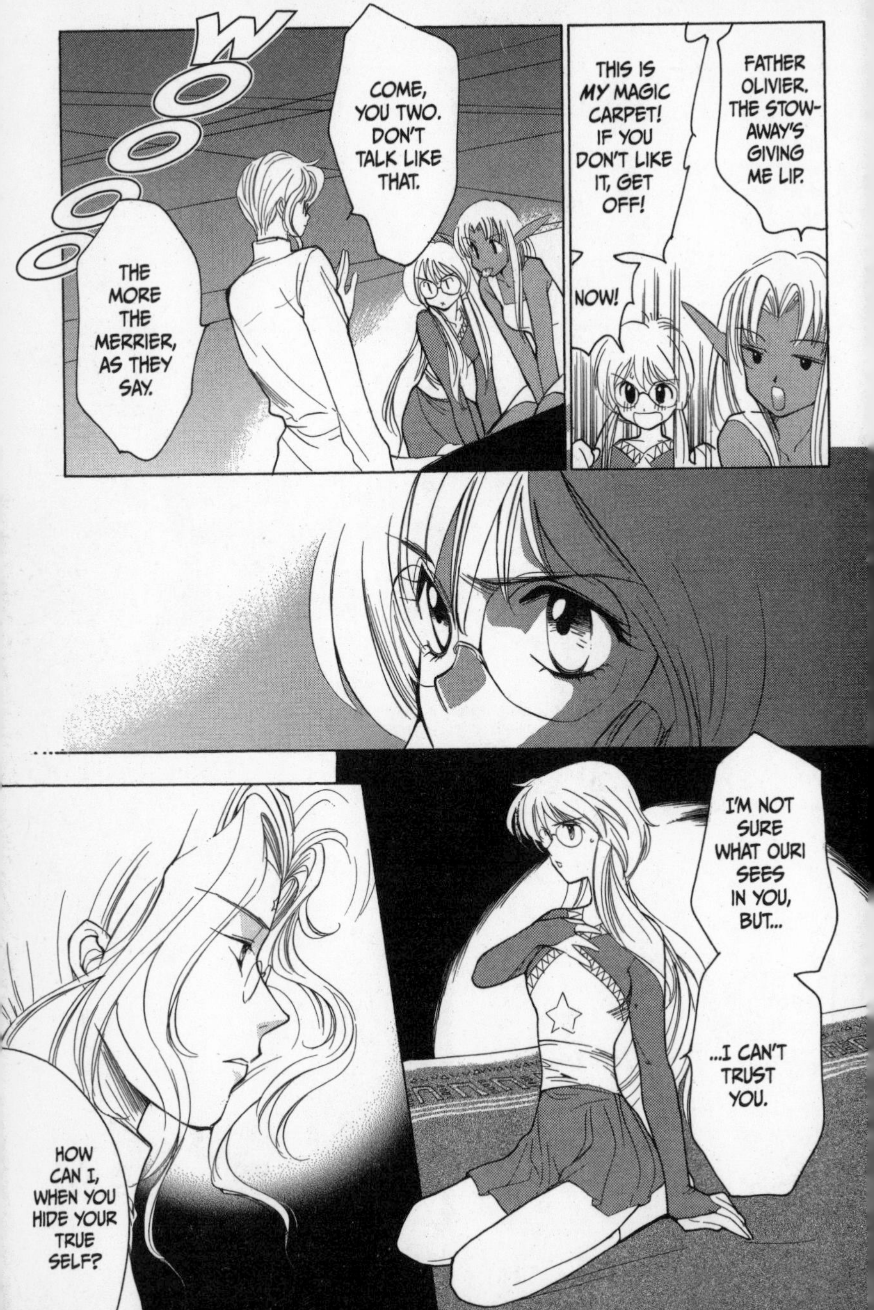
FATHER OLIVIER. THE STOWAWAY'S GIVING ME LIP.
THIS IS MY MAGIC CARPET! IF YOU DON'T LIKE IT, GET OFF!
NOW!
COME, YOU TWO. DON'T TALK LIKE THAT.
WOOOOO
THE MORE THE MERRIER, AS THEY SAY.
I'M NOT SURE WHAT OURI SEES IN YOU, BUT...
...I CAN'T TRUST YOU.
HOW CAN I, WHEN YOU HIDE YOUR TRUE SELF?

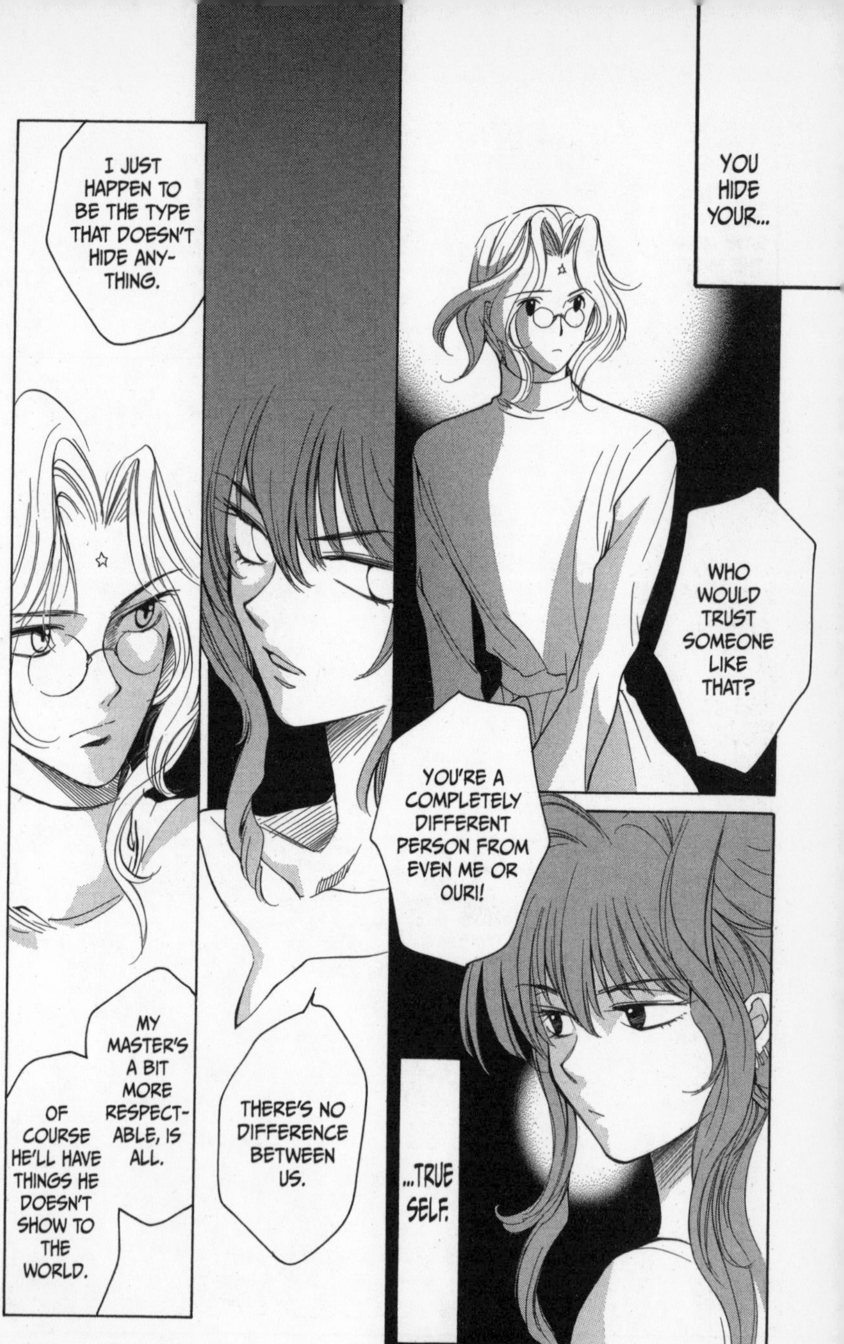
YOU HIDE YOUR...
WHO WOULD TRUST SOMEONE LIKE THAT?
YOU'RE A COMPLETELY DIFFERENT PERSON FROM EVEN ME OR OURI!
...TRUE SELF.
THERE'S NO DIFFERENCE BETWEEN US.
I JUST HAPPEN TO BE THE TYPE THAT DOESN'T HIDE ANY-THING.
MY MASTER'S A BIT MORE RESPECT-ABLE, IS ALL.
OF COURSE HE'LL HAVE THINGS HE DOESN'T SHOW TO THE WORLD.

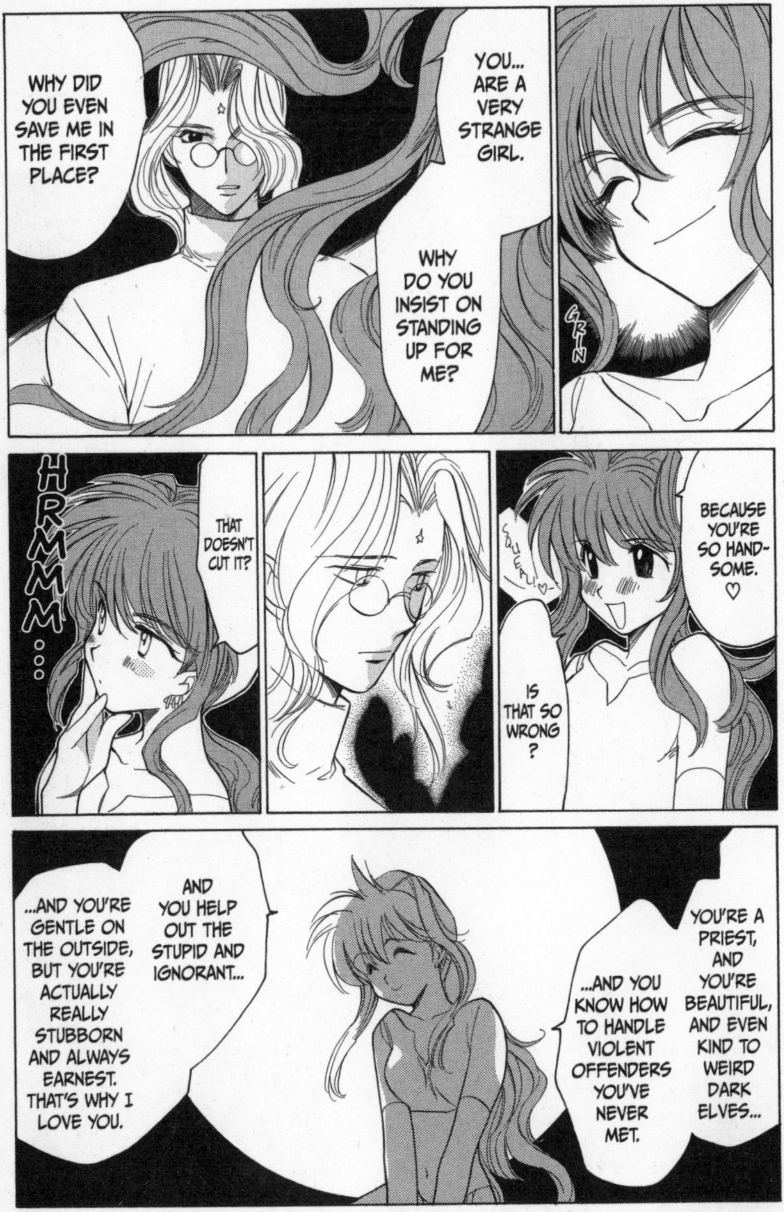
GRIN
YOU... ARE A VERY STRANGE GIRL.
WHY DID YOU EVEN SAVE ME IN THE FIRST PLACE?
WHY DO YOU INSIST ON STANDING UP FOR ME?
BECAUSE YOU'RE SO HAND-SOME. ♡
SQUEAL!♡
IS THAT SO WRONG?
THAT DOESN'T CUT IT?
HRMMM...
YOU'RE A PRIEST, AND YOU'RE BEAUTIFUL, AND EVEN KIND TO WEIRD DARK ELVES...
...AND YOU KNOW HOW TO HANDLE VIOLENT OFFENDERS YOU'VE NEVER MET.
AND YOU HELP OUT THE STUPID AND IGNORANT...
...AND YOU'RE GENTLE ON THE OUTSIDE, BUT YOU'RE ACTUALLY REALLY STUBBORN AND ALWAYS EARNEST. THAT'S WHY I LOVE YOU.

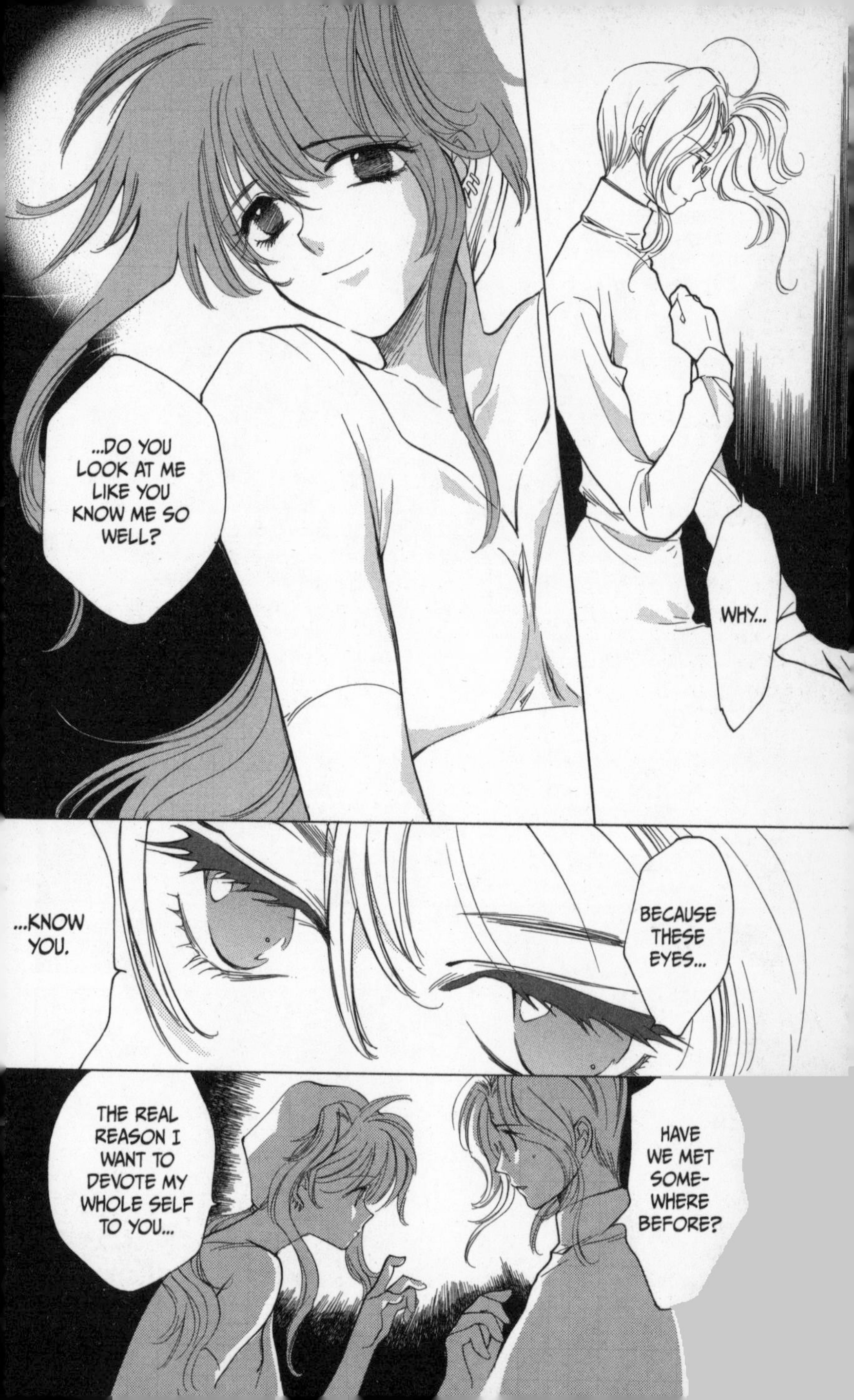
WHY...
...DO YOU LOOK AT ME LIKE YOU KNOW ME SO WELL?
BECAUSE THESE EYES...
...KNOW YOU.
HAVE WE MET SOME-WHERE BEFORE?
THE REAL REASON I WANT TO DEVOTE MY WHOLE SELF TO YOU...

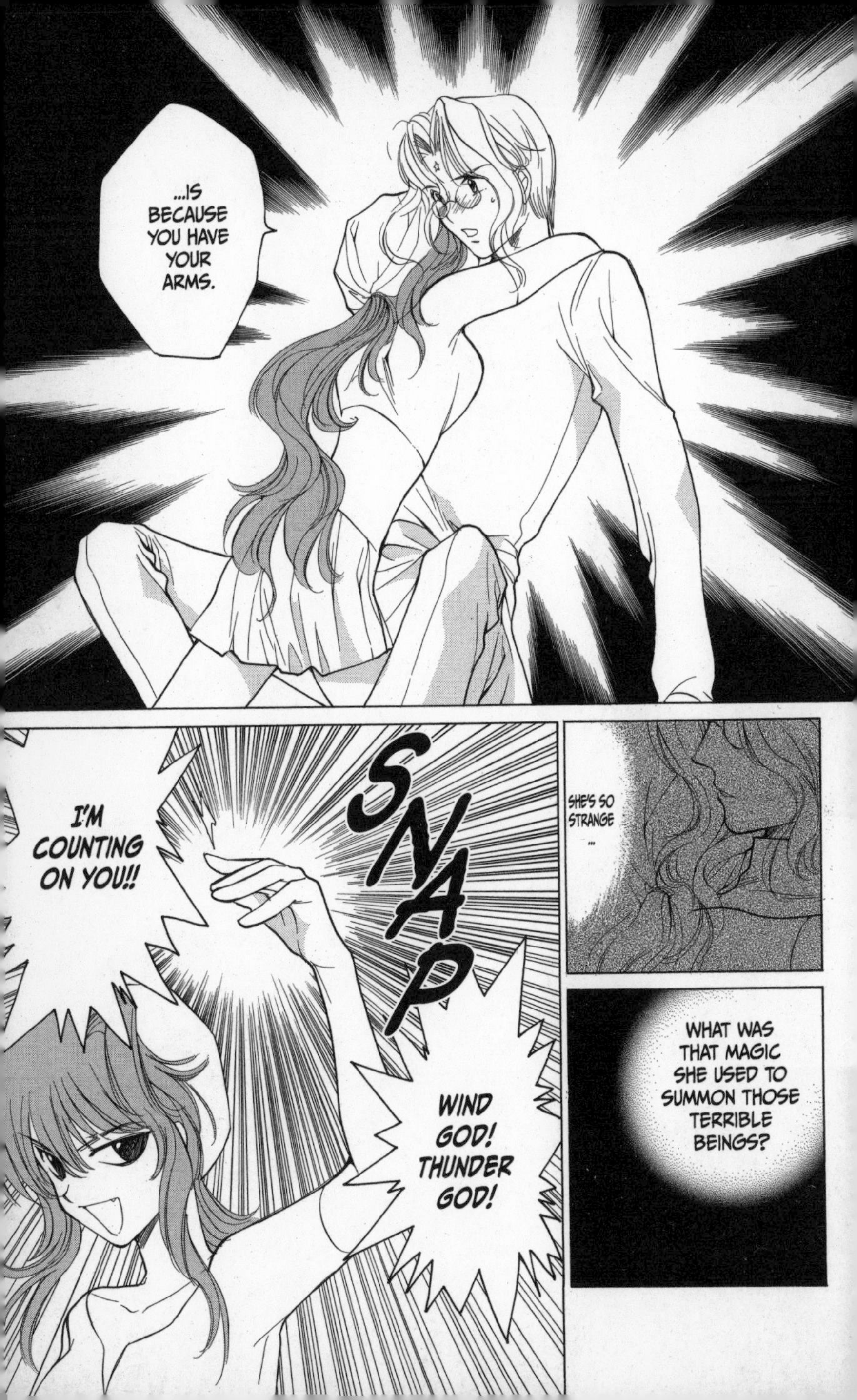
...IS BECAUSE YOU HAVE YOUR ARMS.
SHE'S SO STRANGE...
WHAT WAS THAT MAGIC SHE USED TO SUMMON THOSE TERRIBLE BEINGS?
SNAP
I'M COUNTING ON YOU!!
WIND GOD! THUNDER GOD!

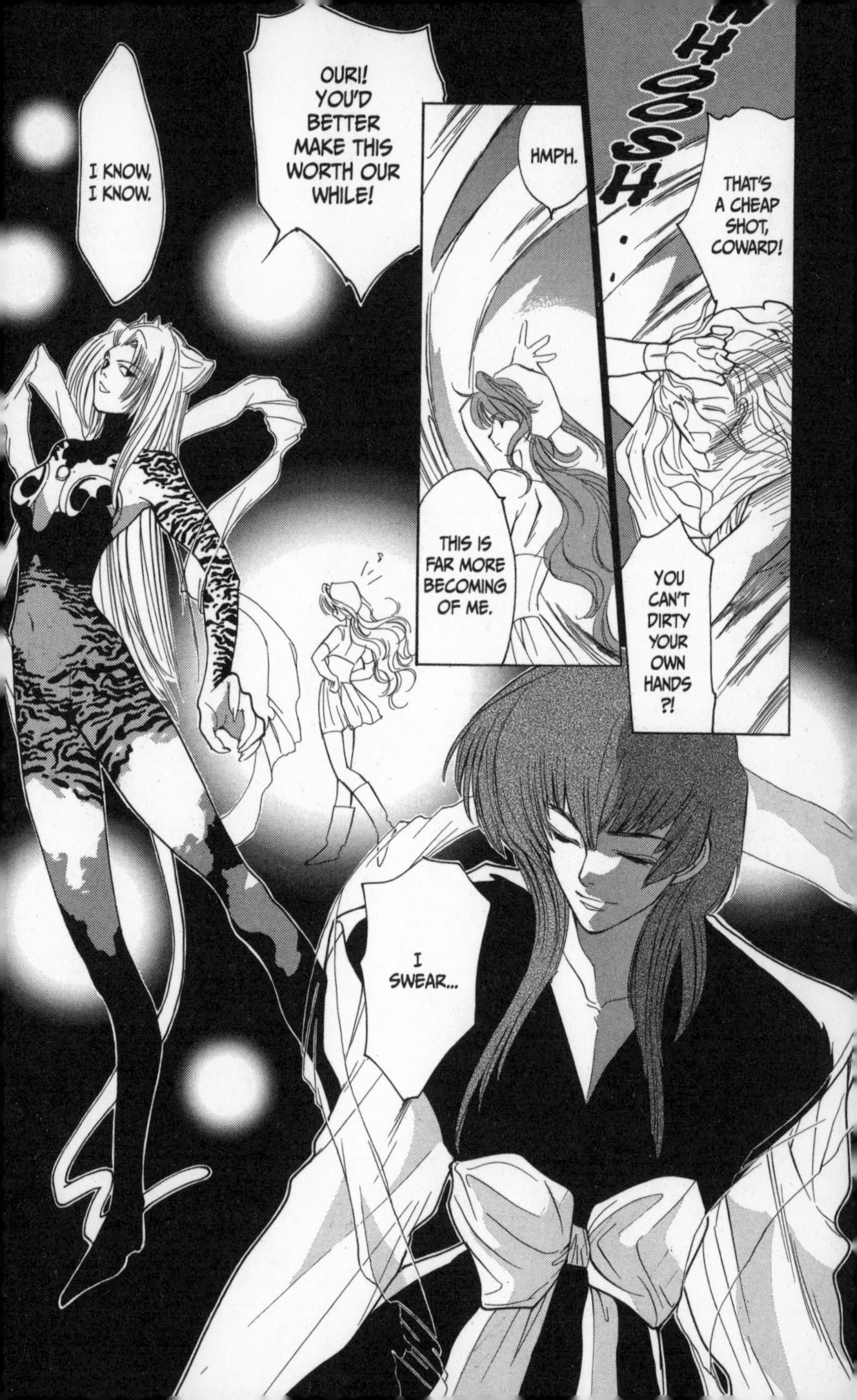
WHOOSH
THAT'S A CHEAP SHOT, COWARD!
YOU CAN'T DIRTY YOUR OWN HANDS?!
HMPH.
THIS IS FAR MORE BECOMING OF ME.
OURI! YOU'D BETTER MAKE THIS WORTH OUR WHILE!
I KNOW, I KNOW.
I SWEAR...

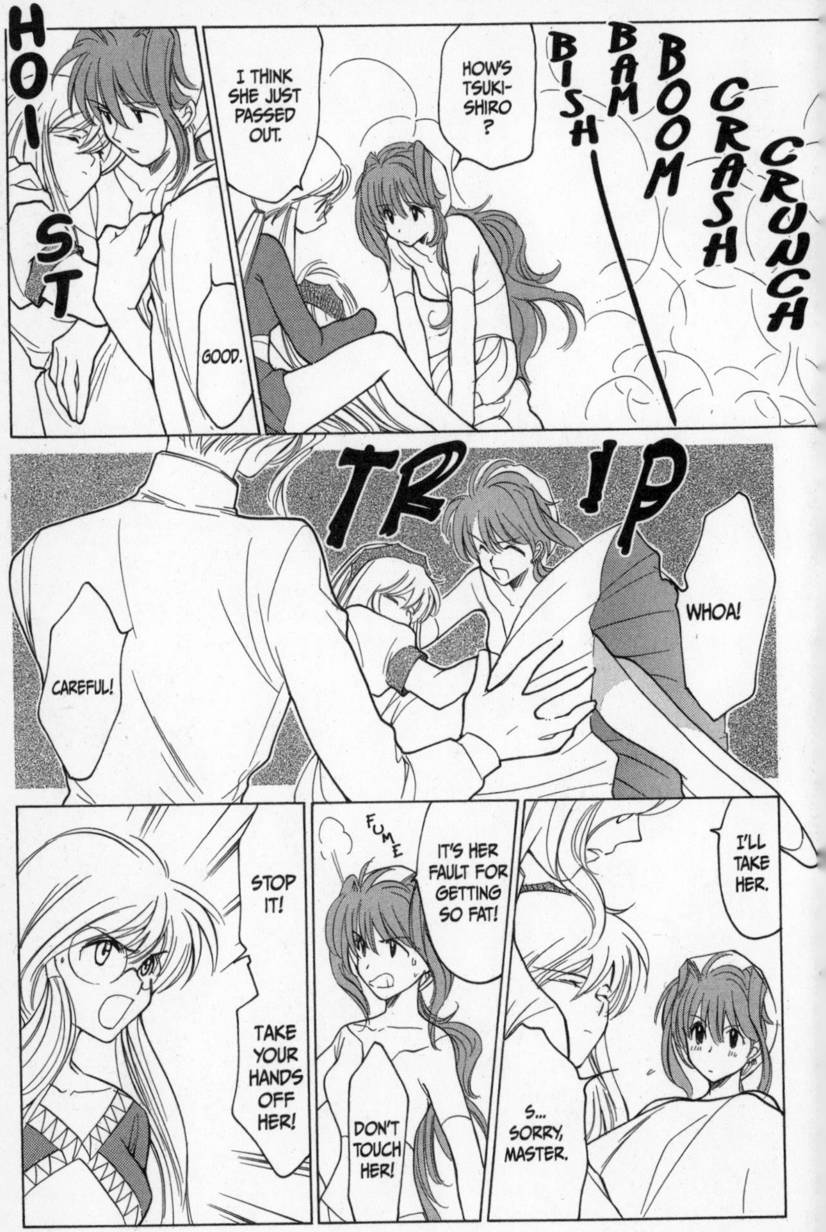
BISH
BAM
BOOM
CRASH
CRUNCH
HOW'S TSUKI-SHIRO?
I THINK SHE JUST PASSED OUT.
HOIST
GOOD.
TRIP
WHOA!
CAREFUL!
I'LL TAKE HER.
S... SORRY, MASTER.
FUME
IT'S HER FAULT FOR GETTING SO FAT!
DON'T TOUCH HER!
STOP IT!
TAKE YOUR HANDS OFF HER!

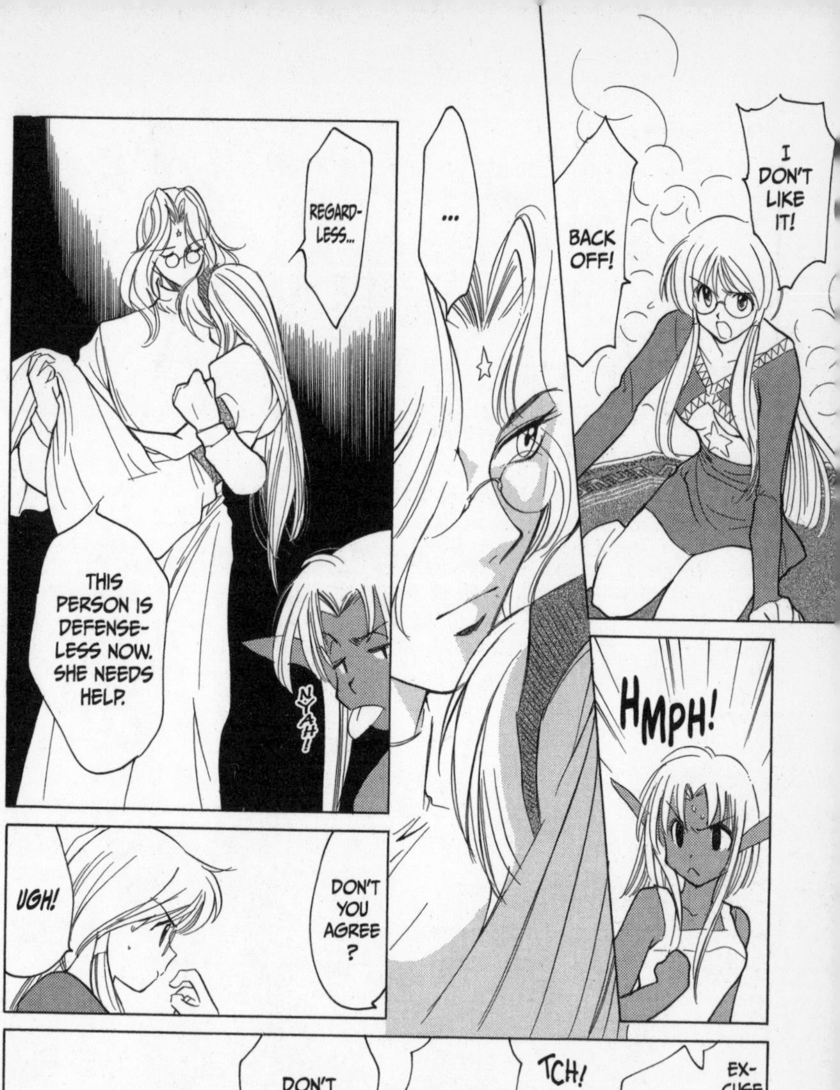
I DON'T LIKE IT!
BACK OFF!
HMPH!
...
REGARDLESS...
THIS PERSON IS DEFENSELESS NOW. SHE NEEDS HELP.
NYAH!
DON'T YOU AGREE?
UGH!
EXCUSE ME?!
DON'T BE SO STUBBORN! JUST LET US HELP HER!
TCH!
PLEASE!
DON'T GET YOUR PANTIES IN A KNOT.
HMPH!

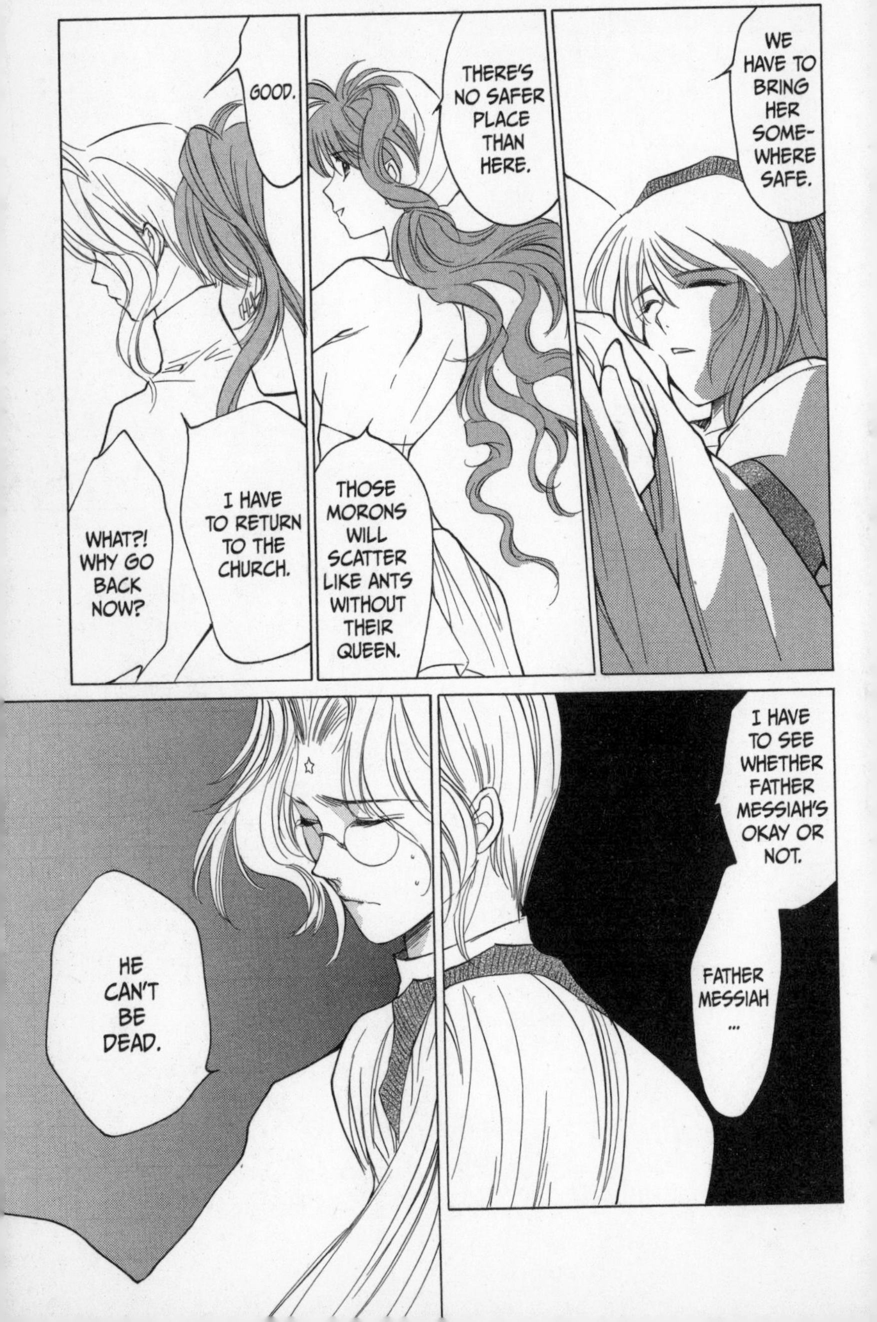
WE HAVE TO BRING HER SOME-WHERE SAFE.
THERE'S NO SAFER PLACE THAN HERE.
THOSE MORONS WILL SCATTER LIKE ANTS WITHOUT THEIR QUEEN.
GOOD.
I HAVE TO RETURN TO THE CHURCH.
WHAT?! WHY GO BACK NOW?
I HAVE TO SEE WHETHER FATHER MESSIAH'S OKAY OR NOT.
FATHER MESSIAH ...
HE CAN'T BE DEAD.

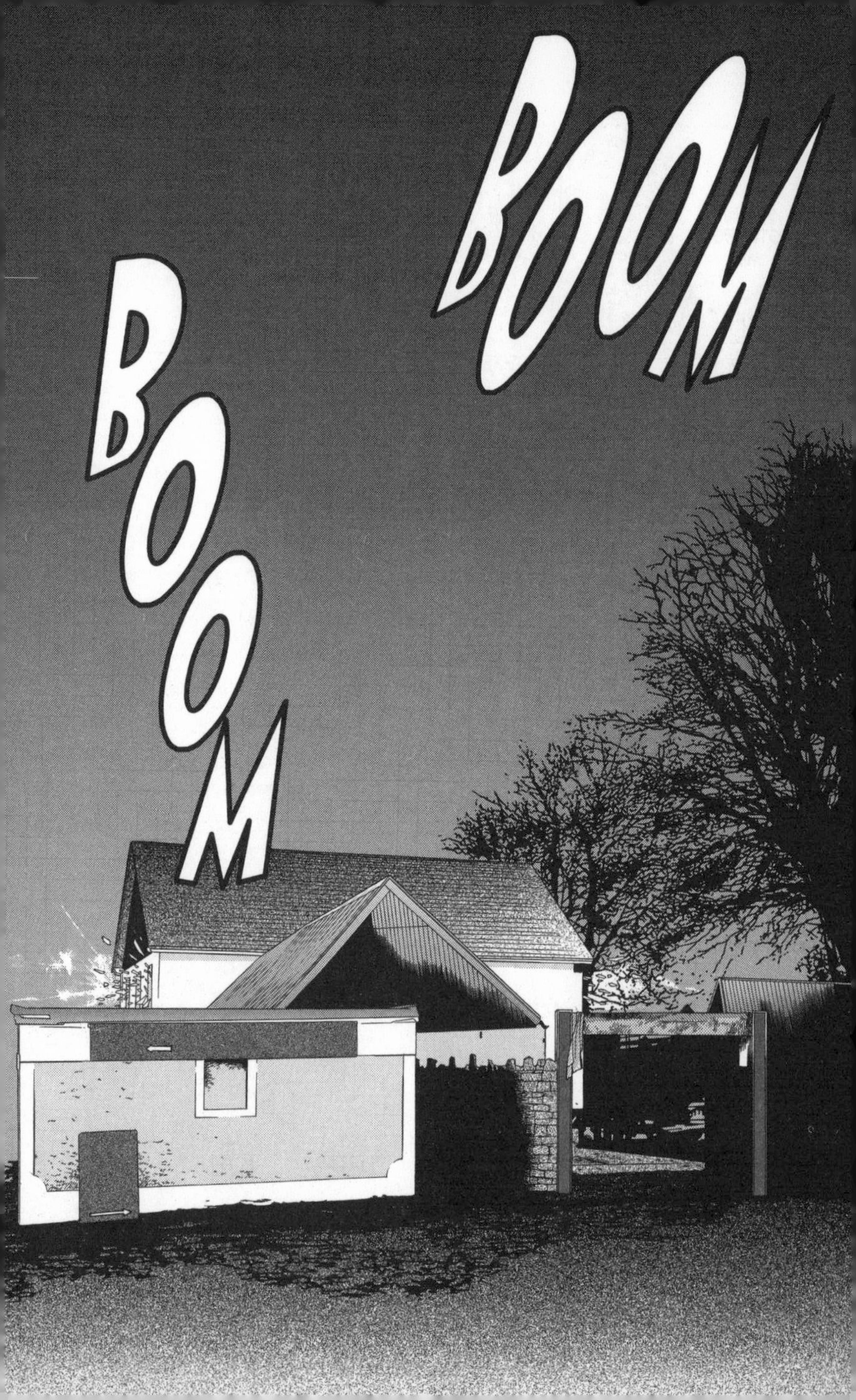
BOOM
BOOM

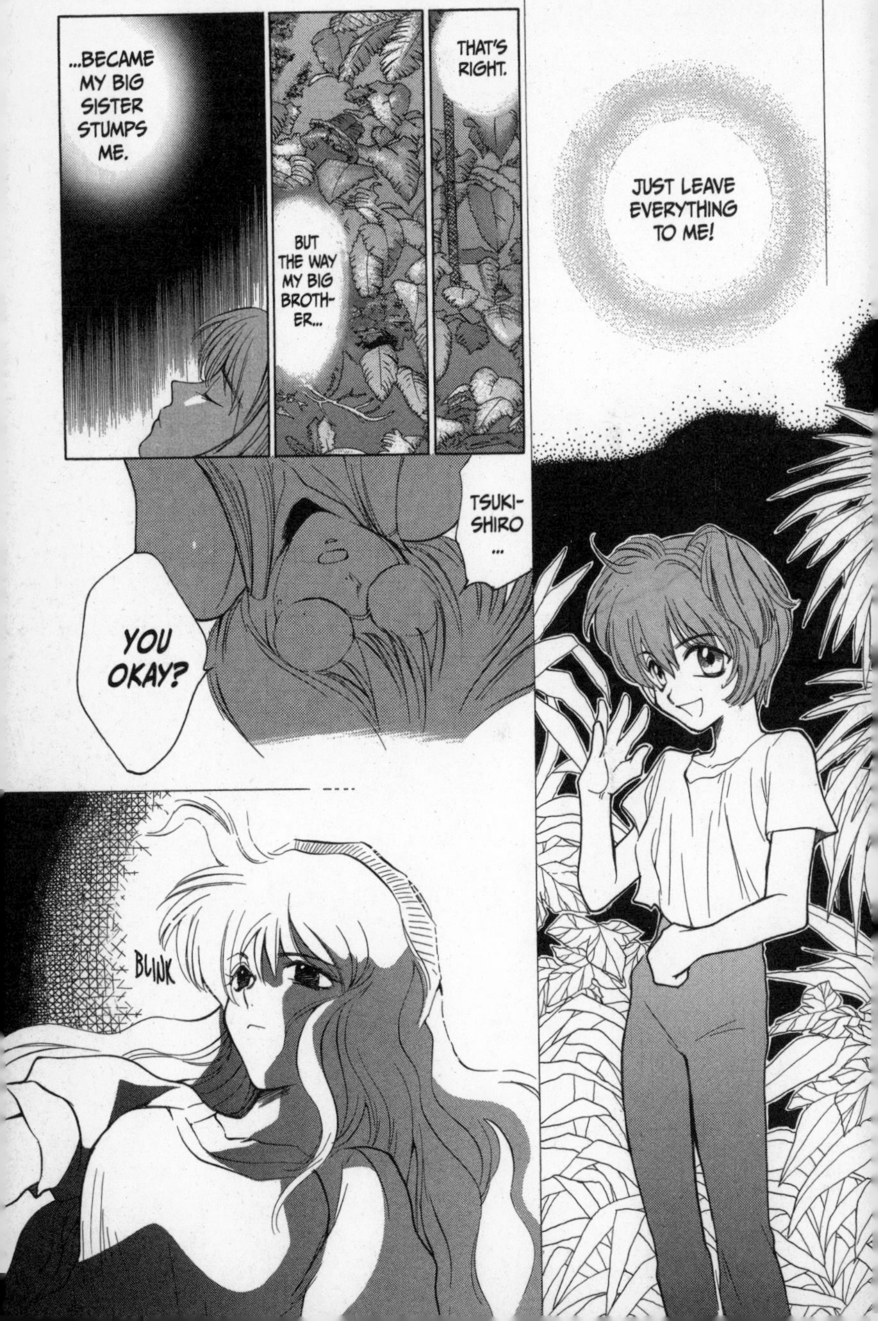
JUST LEAVE EVERYTHING TO ME!
THAT'S RIGHT.
BUT THE WAY MY BIG BROTH-ER...
...BECAME MY BIG SISTER STUMPS ME.
TSUKI-SHIRO ...
YOU OKAY?
BLINK

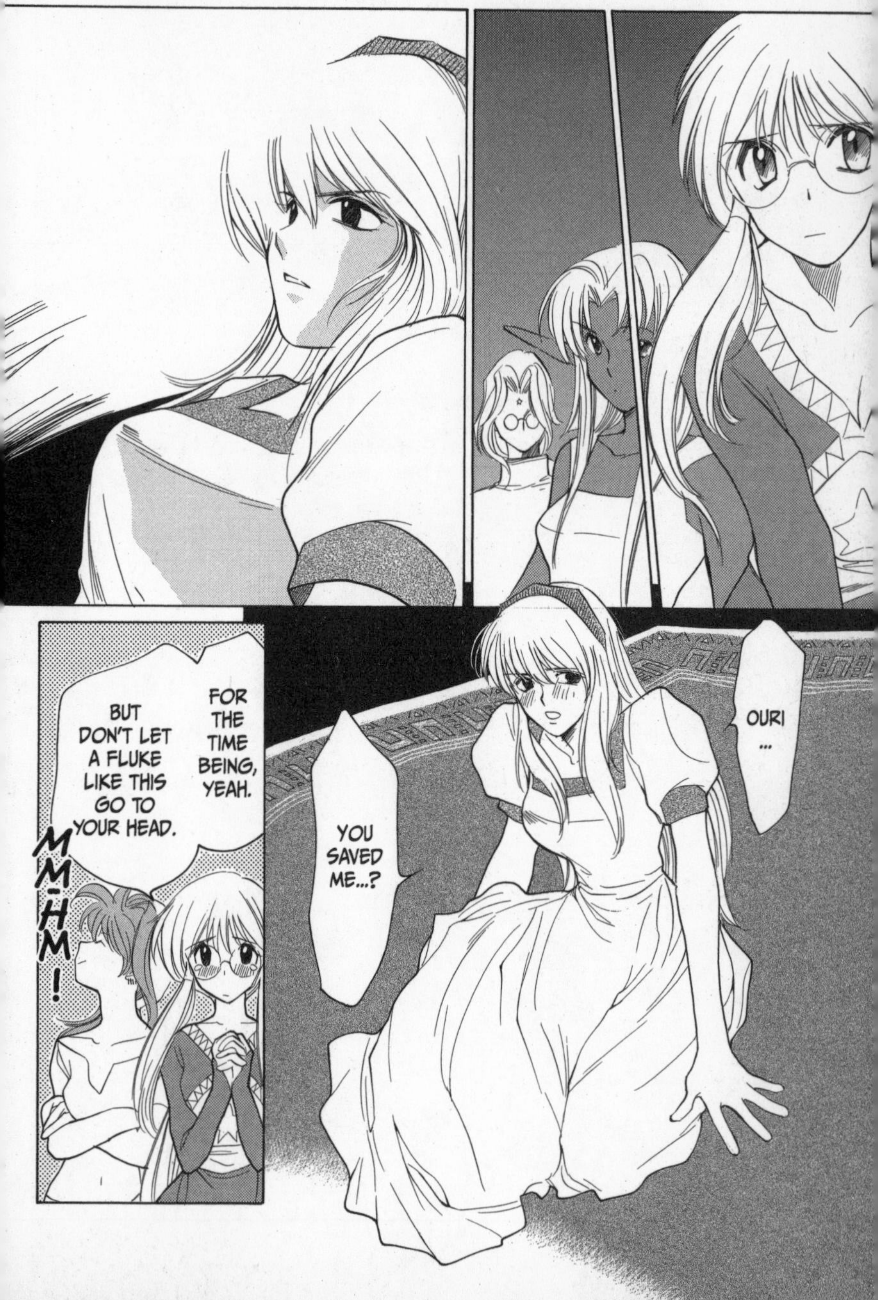
OURI ...
YOU SAVED ME...?
FOR THE TIME BEING, YEAH.
BUT DON'T LET A FLUKE LIKE THIS GO TO YOUR HEAD.
M-HM!

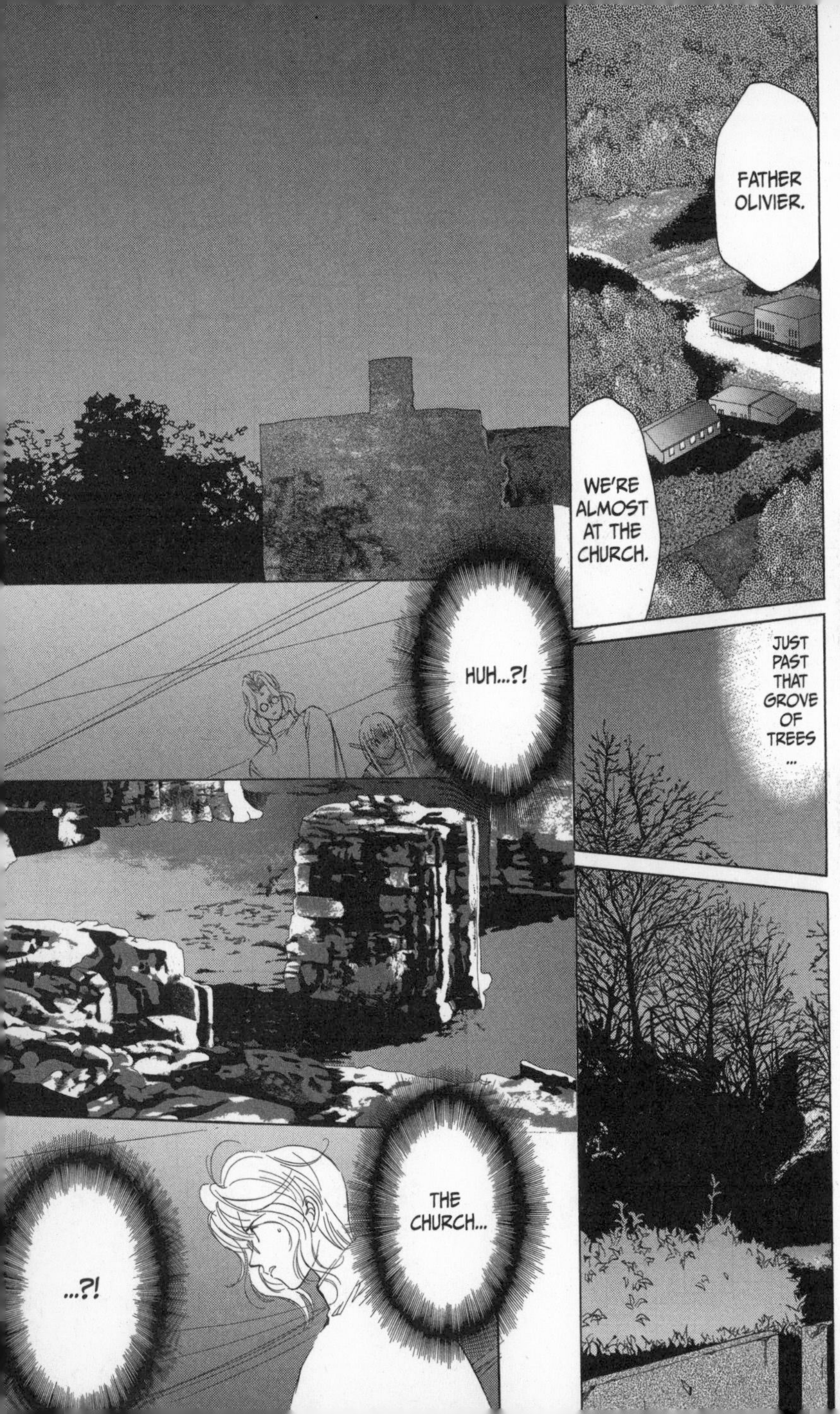
FATHER OLIVIER.
WE'RE ALMOST AT THE CHURCH.
JUST PAST THAT GROVE OF TREES ...
HUH...?!
THE CHURCH...
...?!

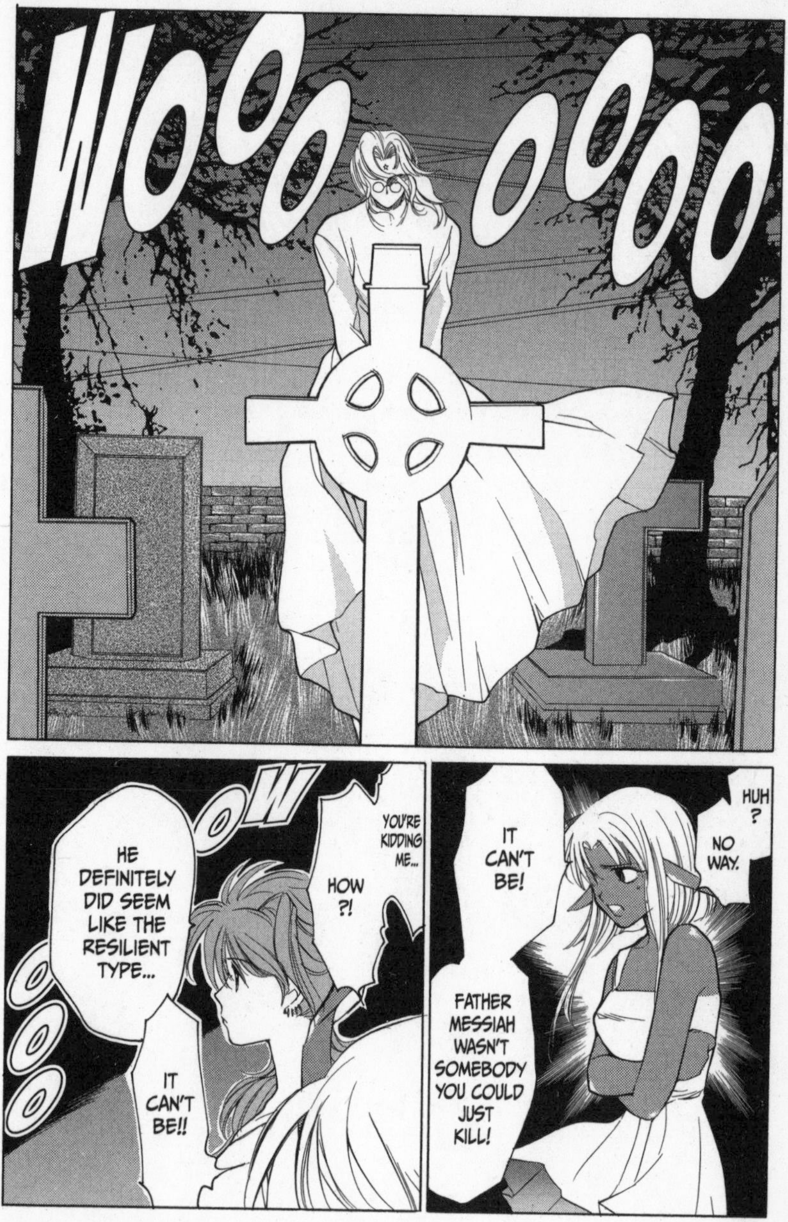
WOOO OOOOO
HUH?
NO WAY.
IT CAN'T BE!
FATHER MESSIAH WASN'T SOMEBODY YOU COULD JUST KILL!
YOU'RE KIDDING ME...
HOW?!
OOW
HE DEFINITELY DID SEEM LIKE THE RESILIENT TYPE...
OOOO
IT CAN'T BE!!

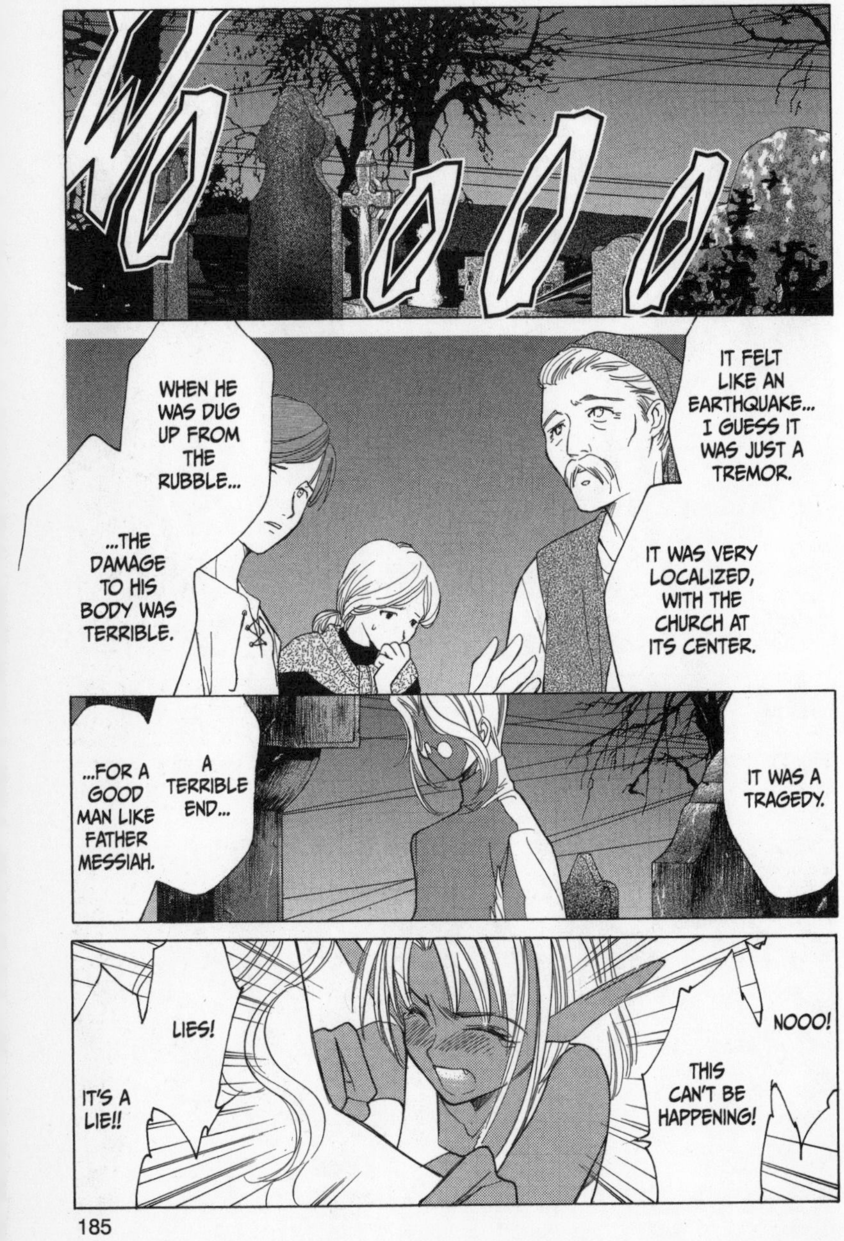
WOOOO
IT FELT LIKE AN EARTHQUAKE... I GUESS IT WAS JUST A TREMOR.
IT WAS VERY LOCALIZED, WITH THE CHURCH AT ITS CENTER.
WHEN HE WAS DUG UP FROM THE RUBBLE...
...THE DAMAGE TO HIS BODY WAS TERRIBLE.
IT WAS A TRAGEDY.
A TERRIBLE END...
...FOR A GOOD MAN LIKE FATHER MESSIAH.
NOOO!
THIS CAN'T BE HAPPENING!
LIES!
IT'S A LIE!!

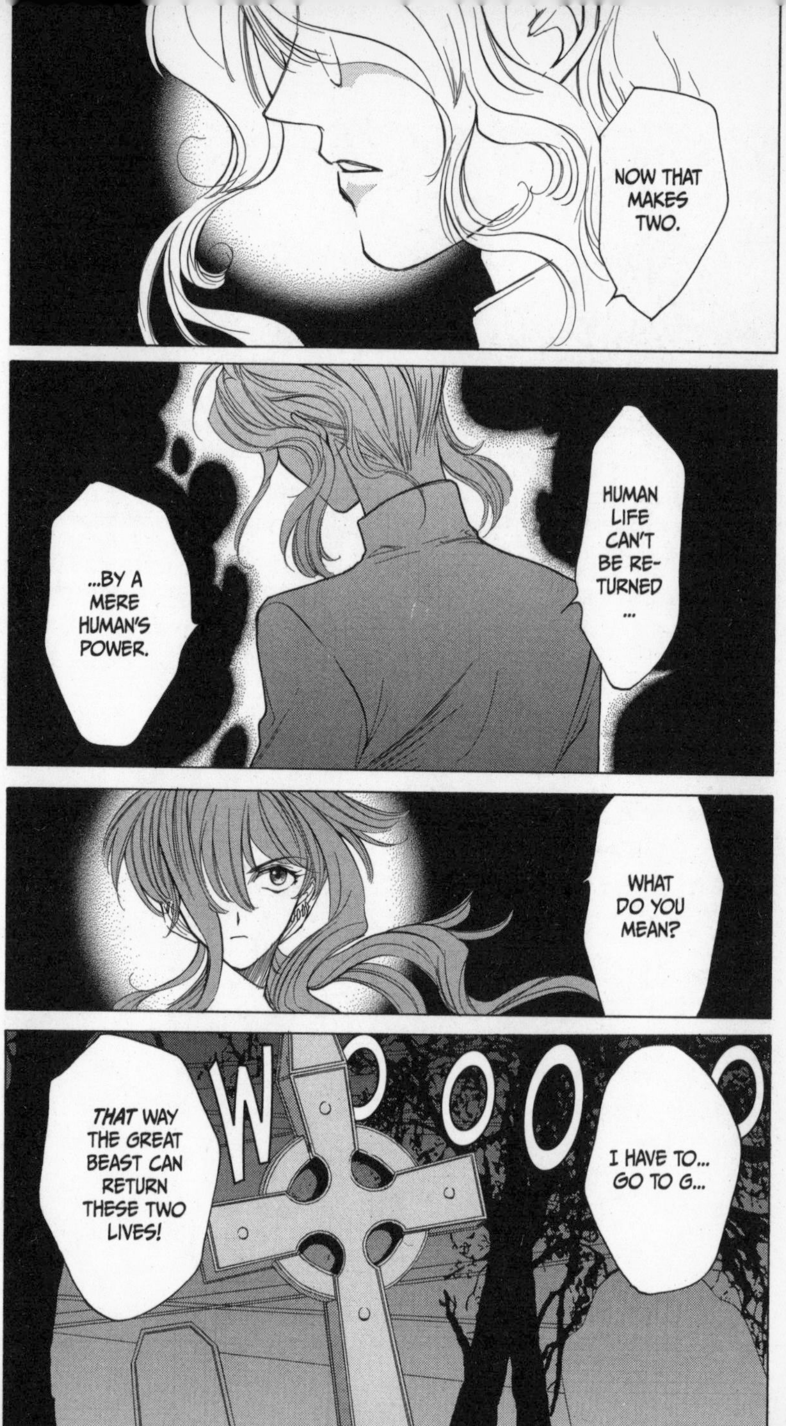
NOW THAT MAKES TWO.
HUMAN LIFE CAN'T BE RE-TURNED...
...BY A MERE HUMAN'S POWER.
WHAT DO YOU MEAN?
WOOOOO
I HAVE TO... GO TO G...
THAT WAY THE GREAT BEAST CAN RETURN THESE TWO LIVES!

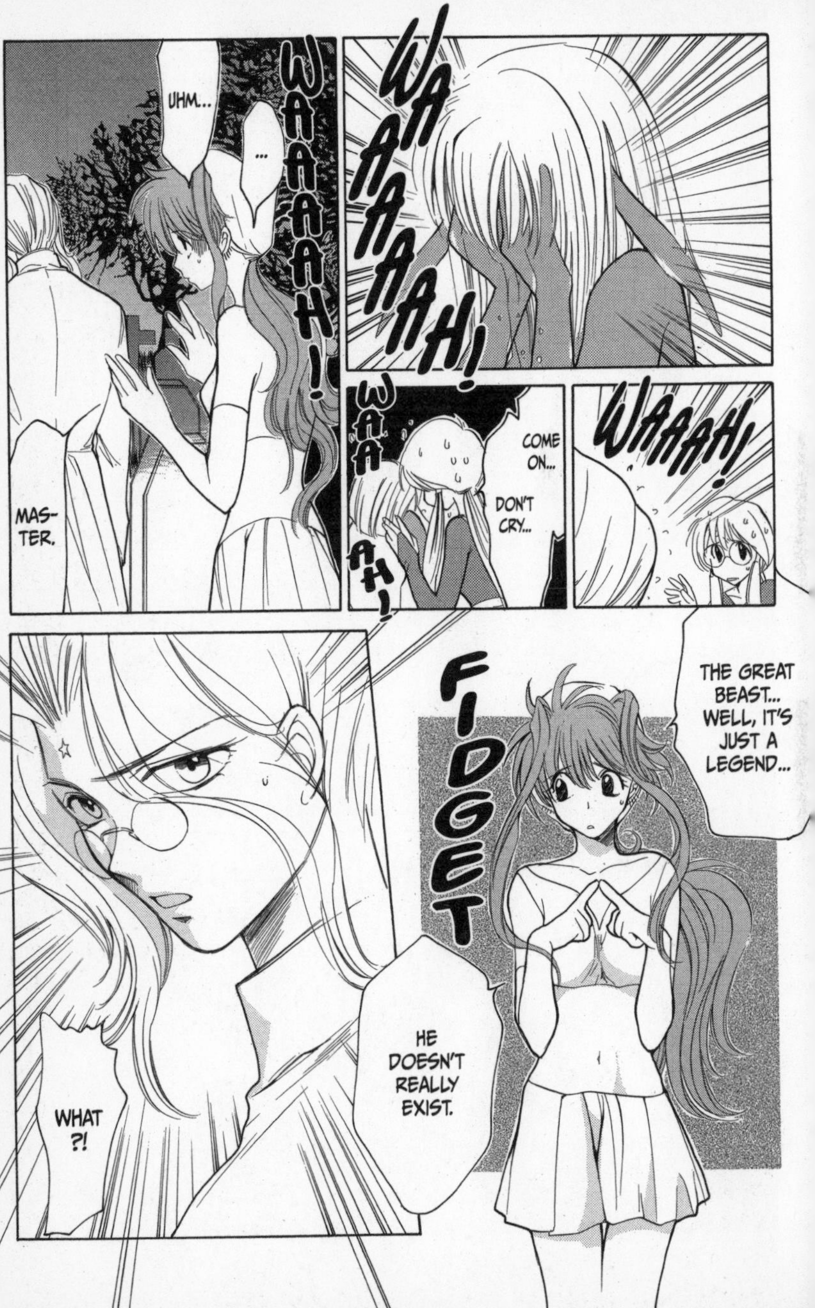
WAAAAAAH!
WAAAH!
WAAAH!
COME ON...
DON'T CRY...
UHM...
...
WAAAAAAH!
MASTER.
THE GREAT BEAST... WELL, IT'S JUST A LEGEND...
FIDGET
HE DOESN'T REALLY EXIST.
WHAT ?!

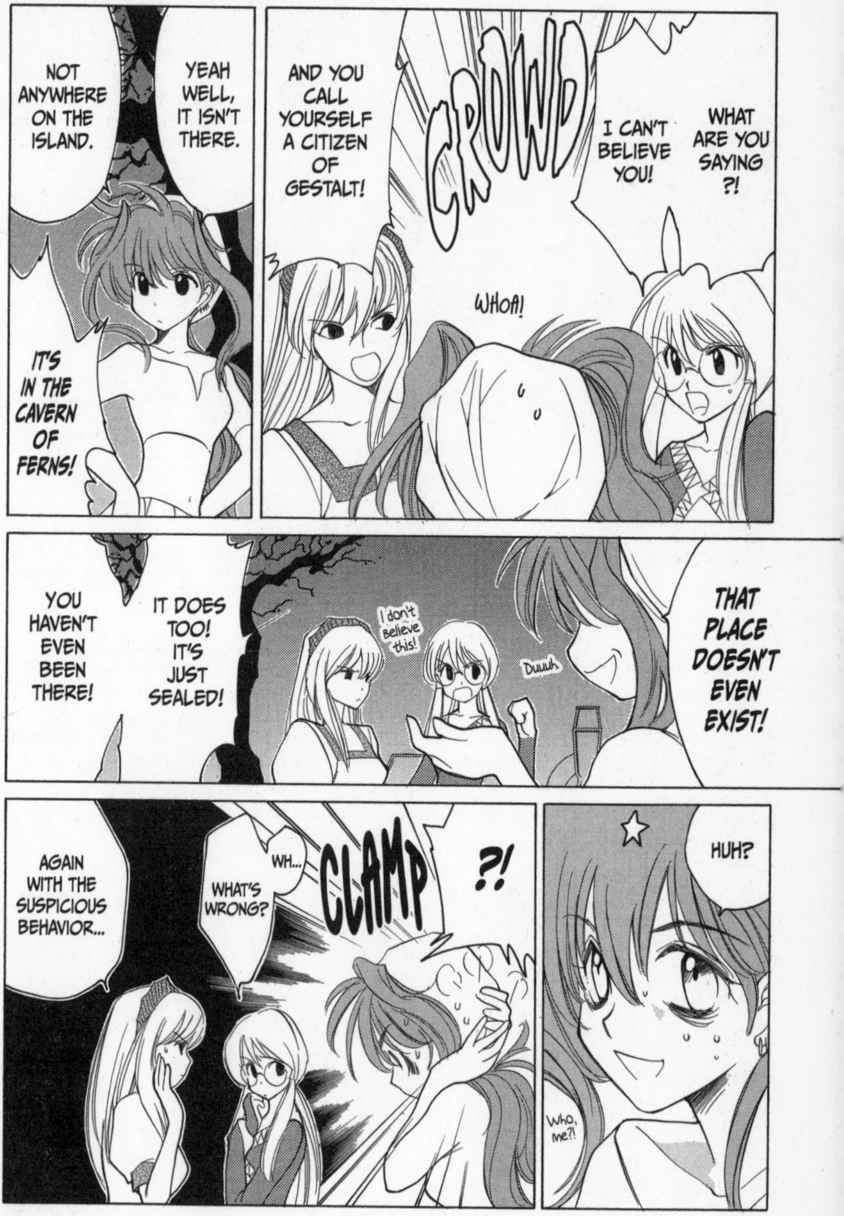
WHAT ARE YOU SAYING ?!
I CAN'T BELIEVE YOU!
CROWD
AND YOU CALL YOURSELF A CITIZEN OF GESTALT!
WHOA!
YEAH WELL, IT ISN'T THERE.
NOT ANYWHERE ON THE ISLAND.
IT'S IN THE CAVERN OF FERNS!
THAT PLACE DOESN'T EVEN EXIST!
Duuuh
I don't believe this!
IT DOES TOO! IT'S JUST SEALED!
YOU HAVEN'T EVEN BEEN THERE!
HUH?
Who, me?!
?!
CLAMP
WH...
WHAT'S WRONG?
AGAIN WITH THE SUSPICIOUS BEHAVIOR...

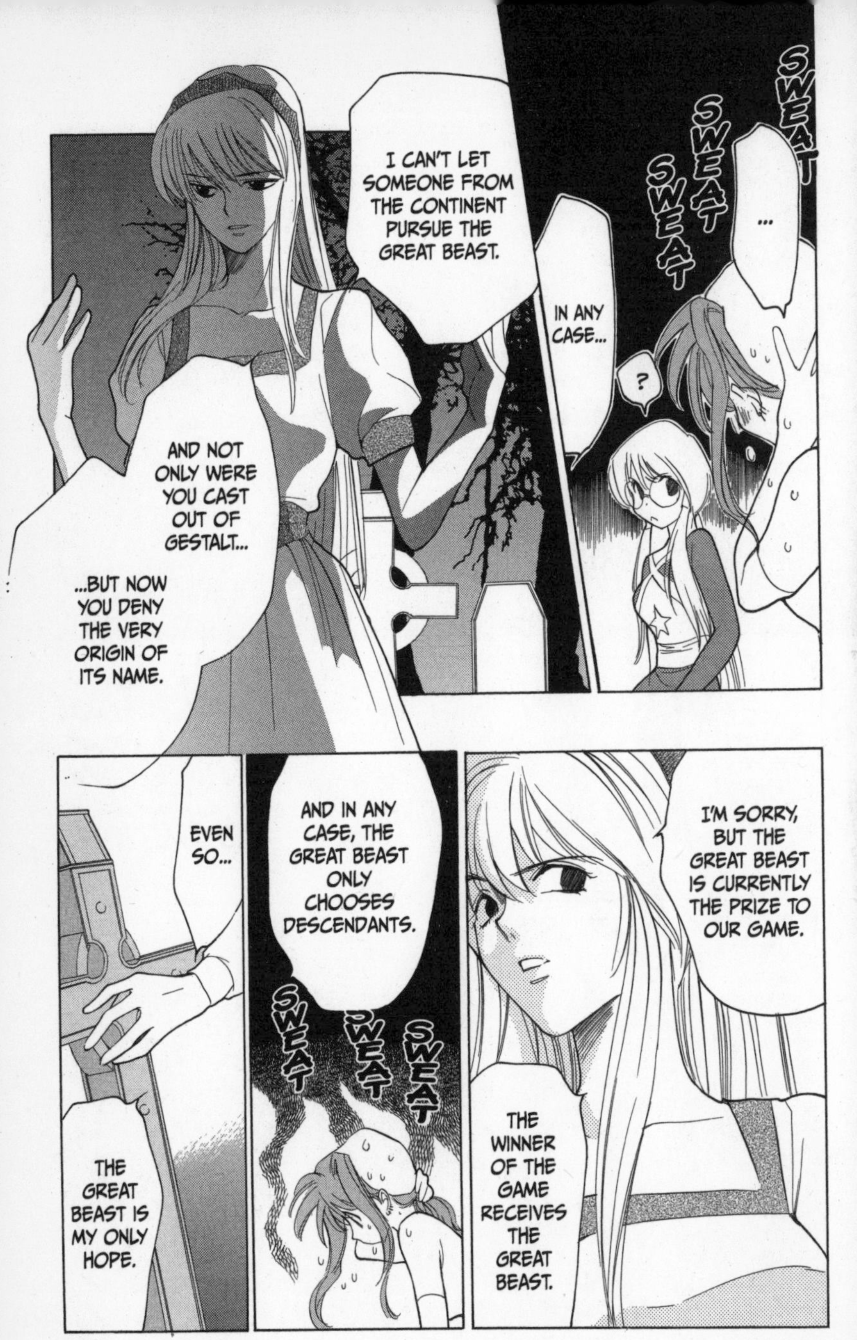
SWEAT
SWEAT
SWEAT
...
IN ANY CASE...
?
I CAN'T LET SOMEONE FROM THE CONTINENT PURSUE THE GREAT BEAST.
AND NOT ONLY WERE YOU CAST OUT OF GESTALT...
...BUT NOW YOU DENY THE VERY ORIGIN OF ITS NAME.
I'M SORRY, BUT THE GREAT BEAST IS CURRENTLY THE PRIZE TO OUR GAME.
THE WINNER OF THE GAME RECEIVES THE GREAT BEAST.
AND IN ANY CASE, THE GREAT BEAST ONLY CHOOSES DESCENDANTS.
SWEAT
SWEAT
SWEAT
EVEN SO...
THE GREAT BEAST IS MY ONLY HOPE.

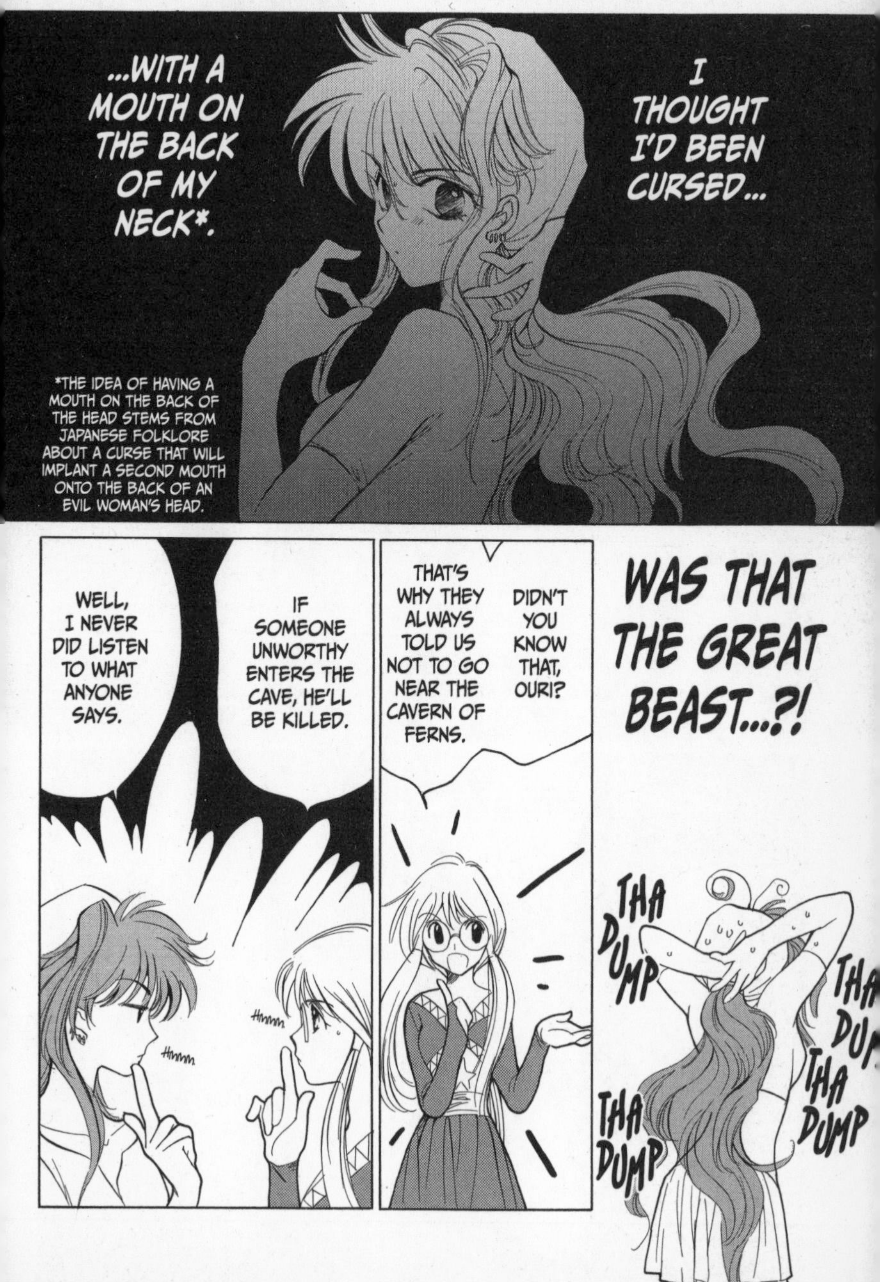
I THOUGHT I'D BEEN CURSED...
...WITH A MOUTH ON THE BACK OF MY NECK*.
*THE IDEA OF HAVING A MOUTH ON THE BACK OF THE HEAD STEMS FROM JAPANESE FOLKLORE ABOUT A CURSE THAT WILL IMPLANT A SECOND MOUTH ONTO THE BACK OF AN EVIL WOMAN'S HEAD.
WAS THAT THE GREAT BEAST...?!
THA DUMP
THA DUMP
THA DUMP
THA DUMP
DIDN'T YOU KNOW THAT, OURI?
THAT'S WHY THEY ALWAYS TOLD US NOT TO GO NEAR THE CAVERN OF FERNS.
IF SOMEONE UNWORTHY ENTERS THE CAVE, HE'LL BE KILLED.
WELL, I NEVER DID LISTEN TO WHAT ANYONE SAYS.
Hmmm.
Hmmm.

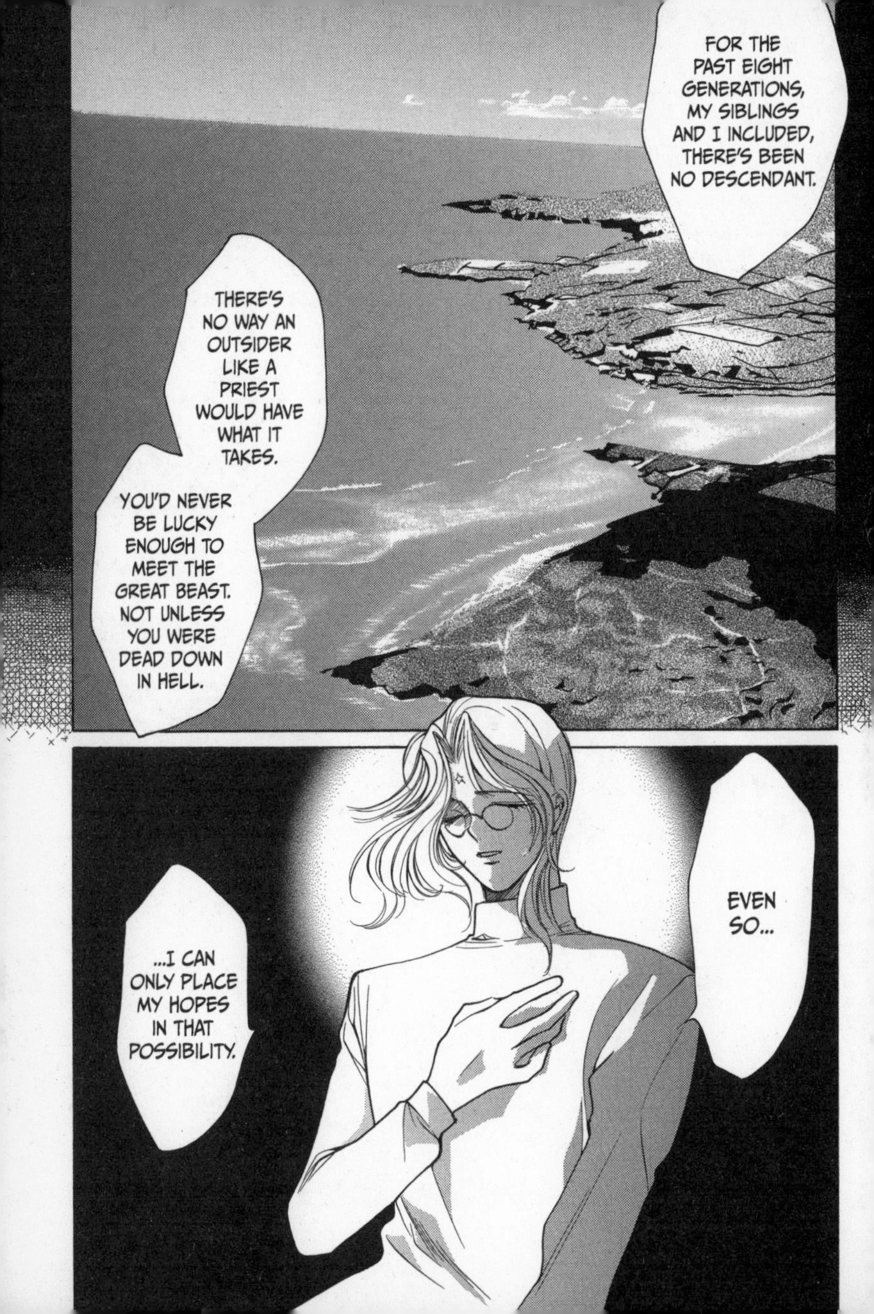
FOR THE PAST EIGHT GENERATIONS, MY SIBLINGS AND I INCLUDED, THERE'S BEEN NO DESCENDANT.
THERE'S NO WAY AN OUTSIDER LIKE A PRIEST WOULD HAVE WHAT IT TAKES.
YOU'D NEVER BE LUCKY ENOUGH TO MEET THE GREAT BEAST. NOT UNLESS YOU WERE DEAD DOWN IN HELL.
EVEN SO...
...I CAN ONLY PLACE MY HOPES IN THAT POSSIBILITY.

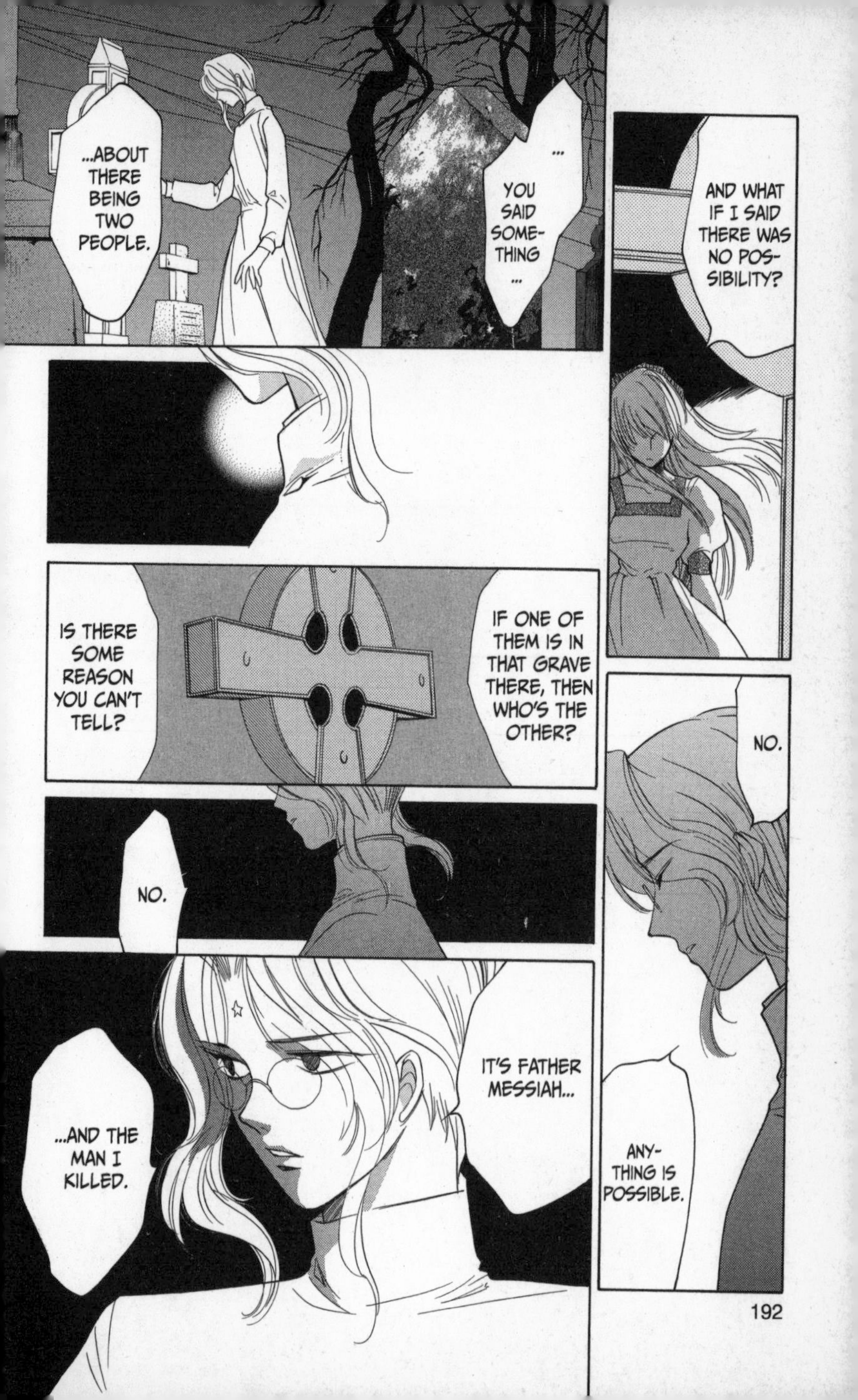

... YOU SAID SOME-THING ...
...ABOUT THERE BEING TWO PEOPLE.
AND WHAT IF I SAID THERE WAS NO POS-SIBILITY?
NO.
ANY-THING IS POSSIBLE.
IF ONE OF THEM IS IN THAT GRAVE THERE, THEN WHO'S THE OTHER?
IS THERE SOME REASON YOU CAN'T TELL?
NO.
IT'S FATHER MESSIAH...
...AND THE MAN I KILLED.

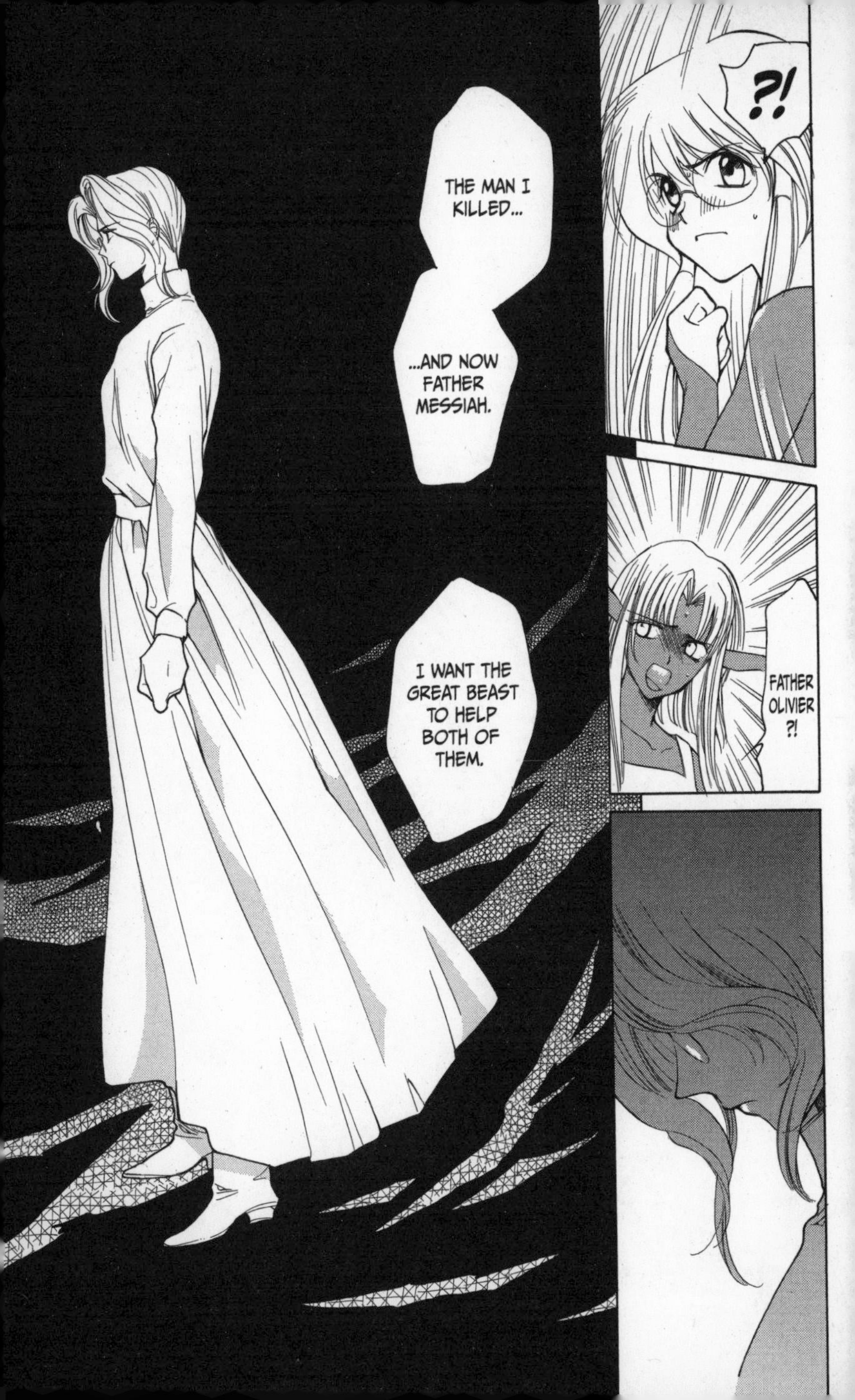
?!
FATHER OLIVIER ?!
THE MAN I KILLED...
...AND NOW FATHER MESSIAH.
I WANT THE GREAT BEAST TO HELP BOTH OF THEM.

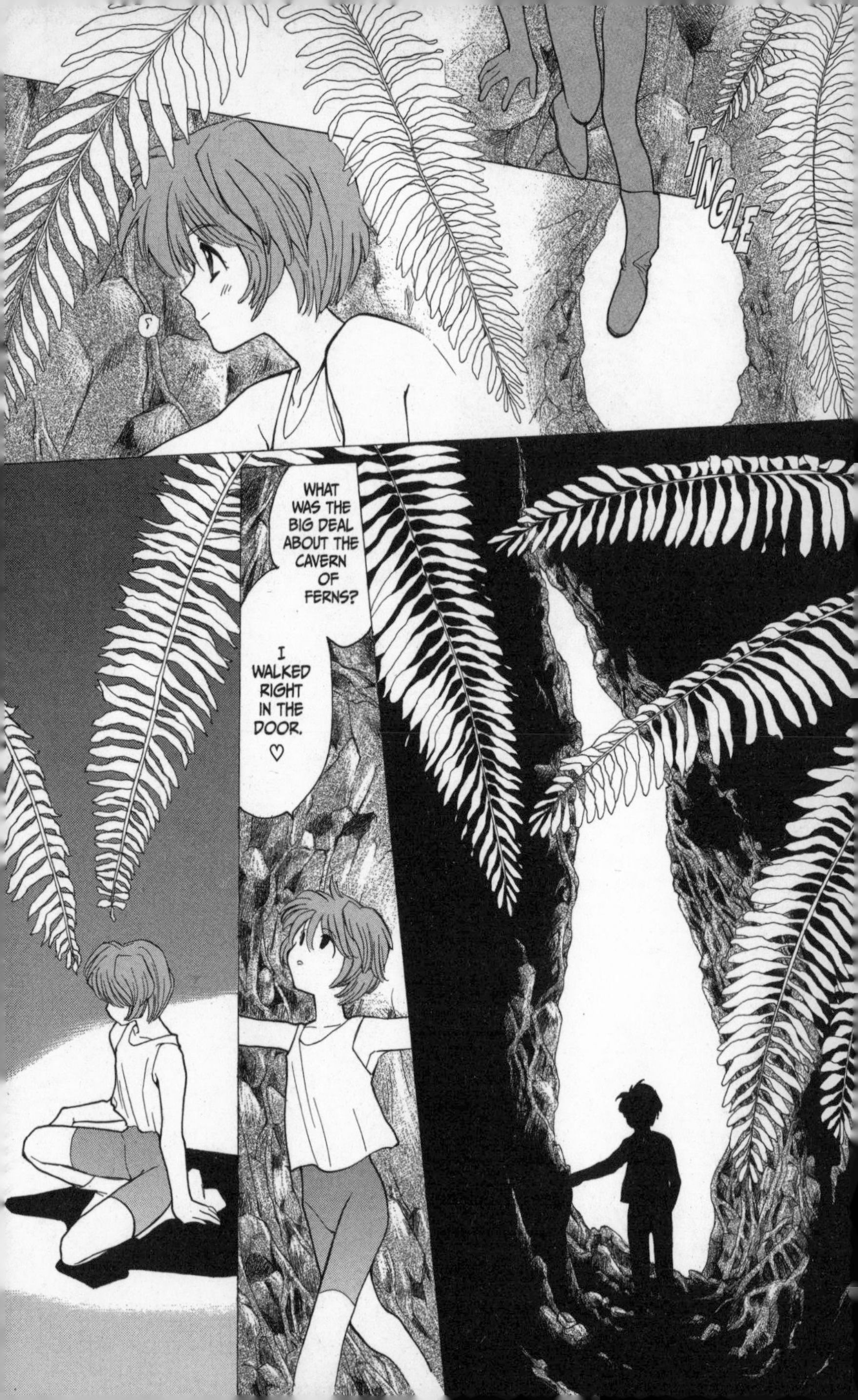
TINGLE
WHAT WAS THE BIG DEAL ABOUT THE CAVERN OF FERNS?
I WALKED RIGHT IN THE DOOR. ♡

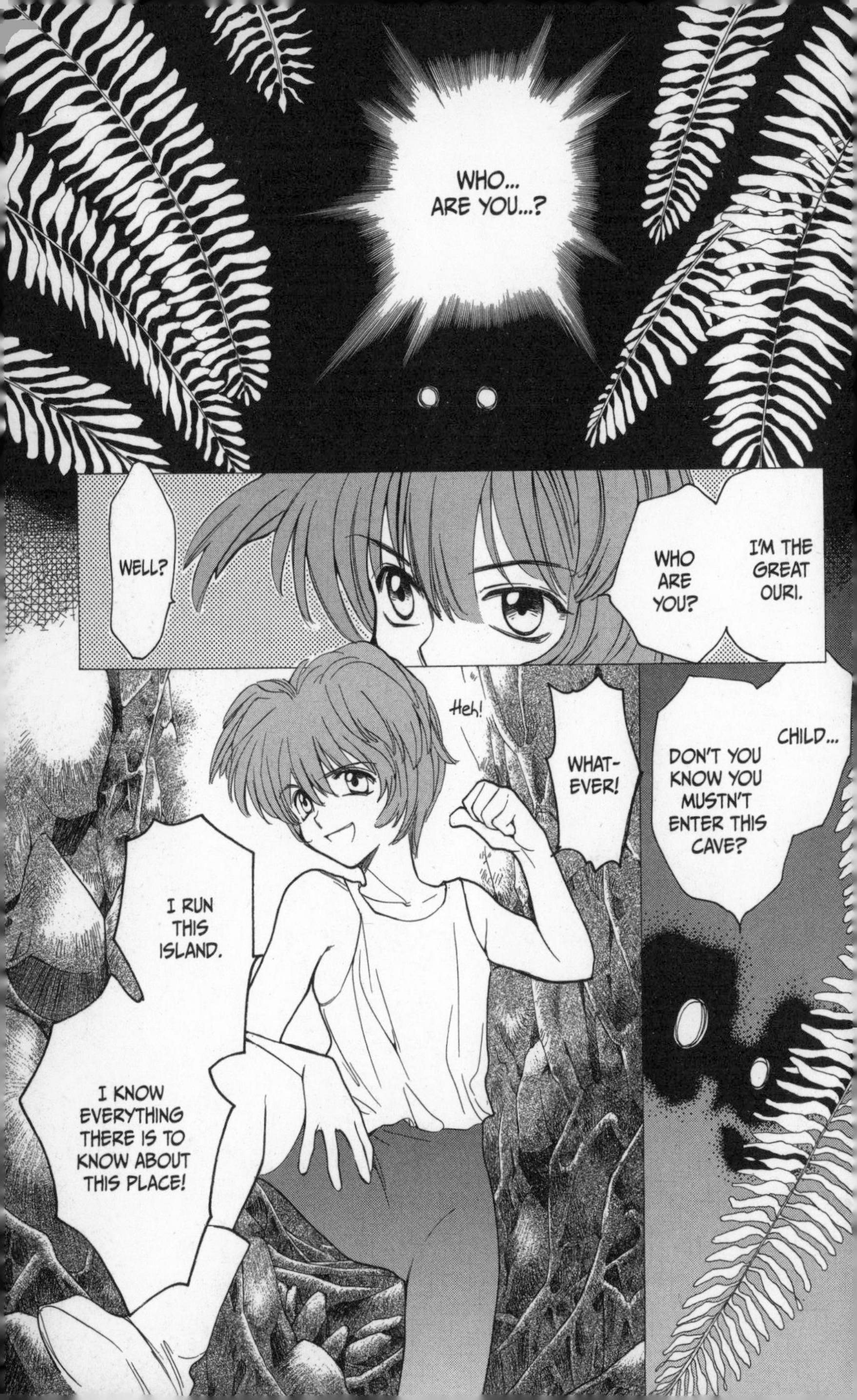
WHO... ARE YOU...?
I'M THE GREAT OURI.
WHO ARE YOU?
WELL?
CHILD...
DON'T YOU KNOW YOU MUSTN'T ENTER THIS CAVE?
Heh!
WHAT-EVER!
I RUN THIS ISLAND.
I KNOW EVERYTHING THERE IS TO KNOW ABOUT THIS PLACE!

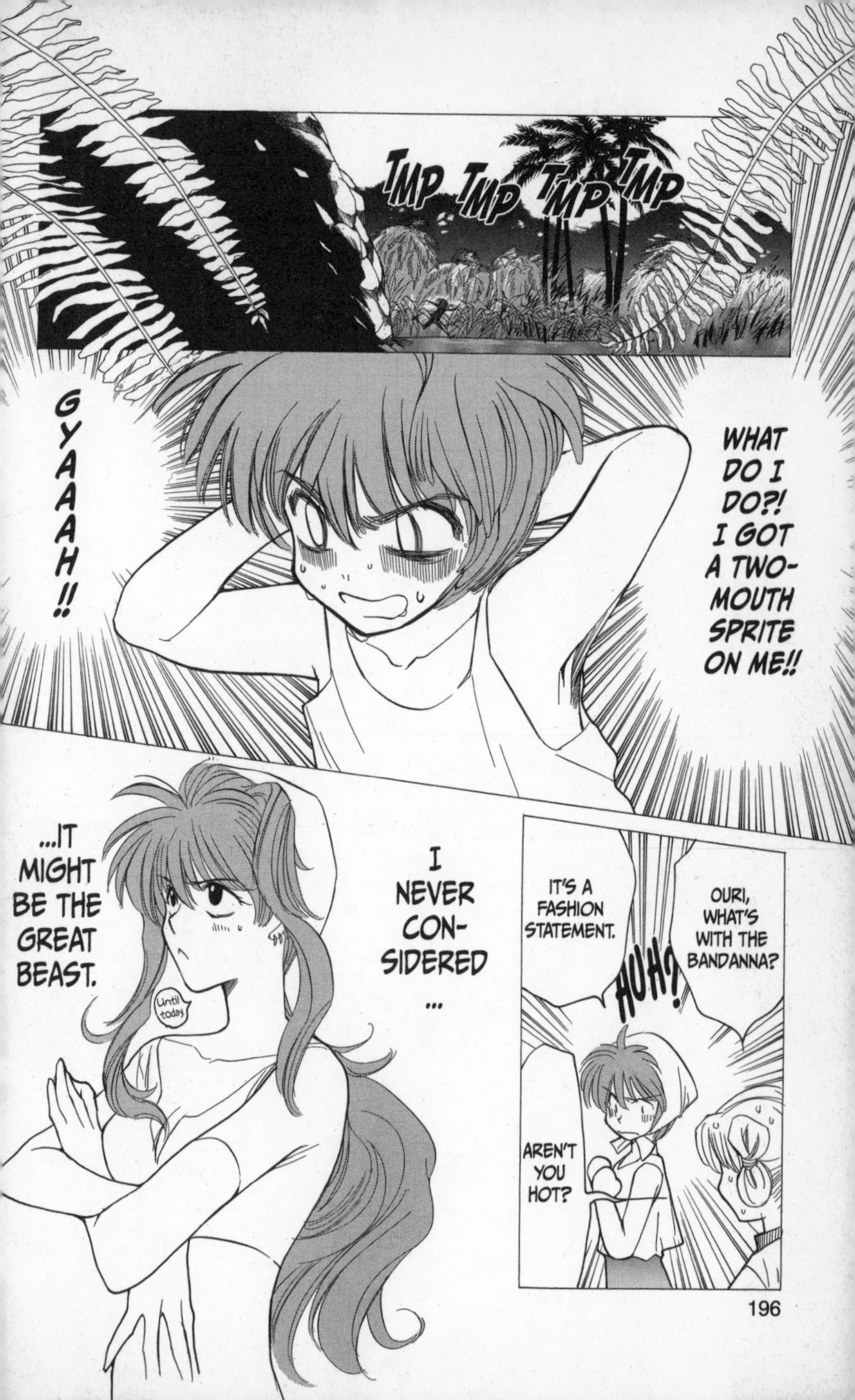
TMP TMP TMP TMP
WHAT DO I DO?! I GOT A TWO-MOUTH SPRITE ON ME!!
GYAAAAH!!
OURI, WHAT'S WITH THE BANDANNA?
HUH?
IT'S A FASHION STATEMENT.
AREN'T YOU HOT?
I NEVER CON-SIDERED...
...IT MIGHT BE THE GREAT BEAST.
Until today.

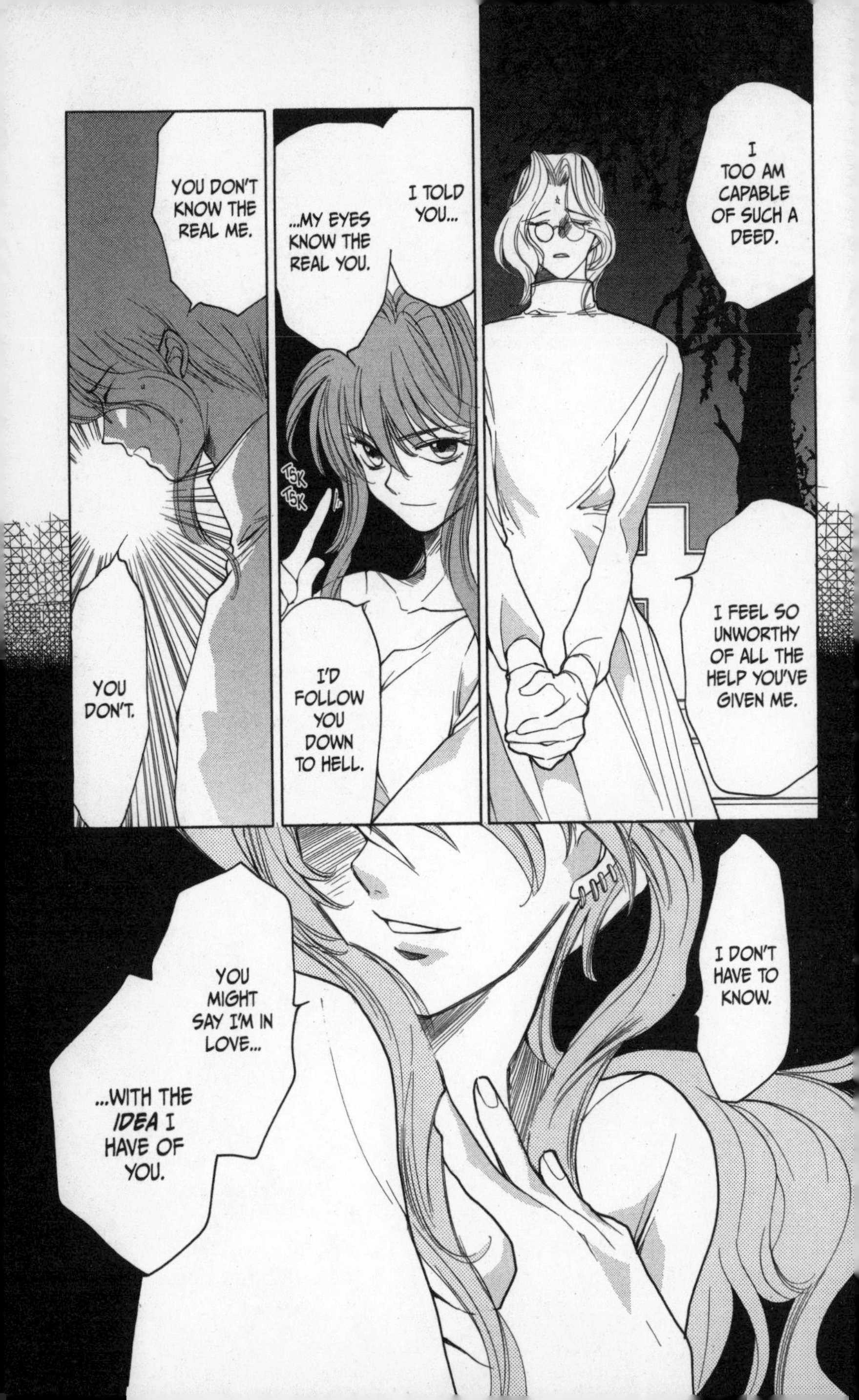
I TOO AM CAPABLE OF SUCH A DEED.
I FEEL SO UNWORTHY OF ALL THE HELP YOU'VE GIVEN ME.
I TOLD YOU...
...MY EYES KNOW THE REAL YOU.
TSK TSK
I'D FOLLOW YOU DOWN TO HELL.
YOU DON'T KNOW THE REAL ME.
YOU DON'T.
I DON'T HAVE TO KNOW.
YOU MIGHT SAY I'M IN LOVE...
...WITH THE *IDEA* I HAVE OF YOU.

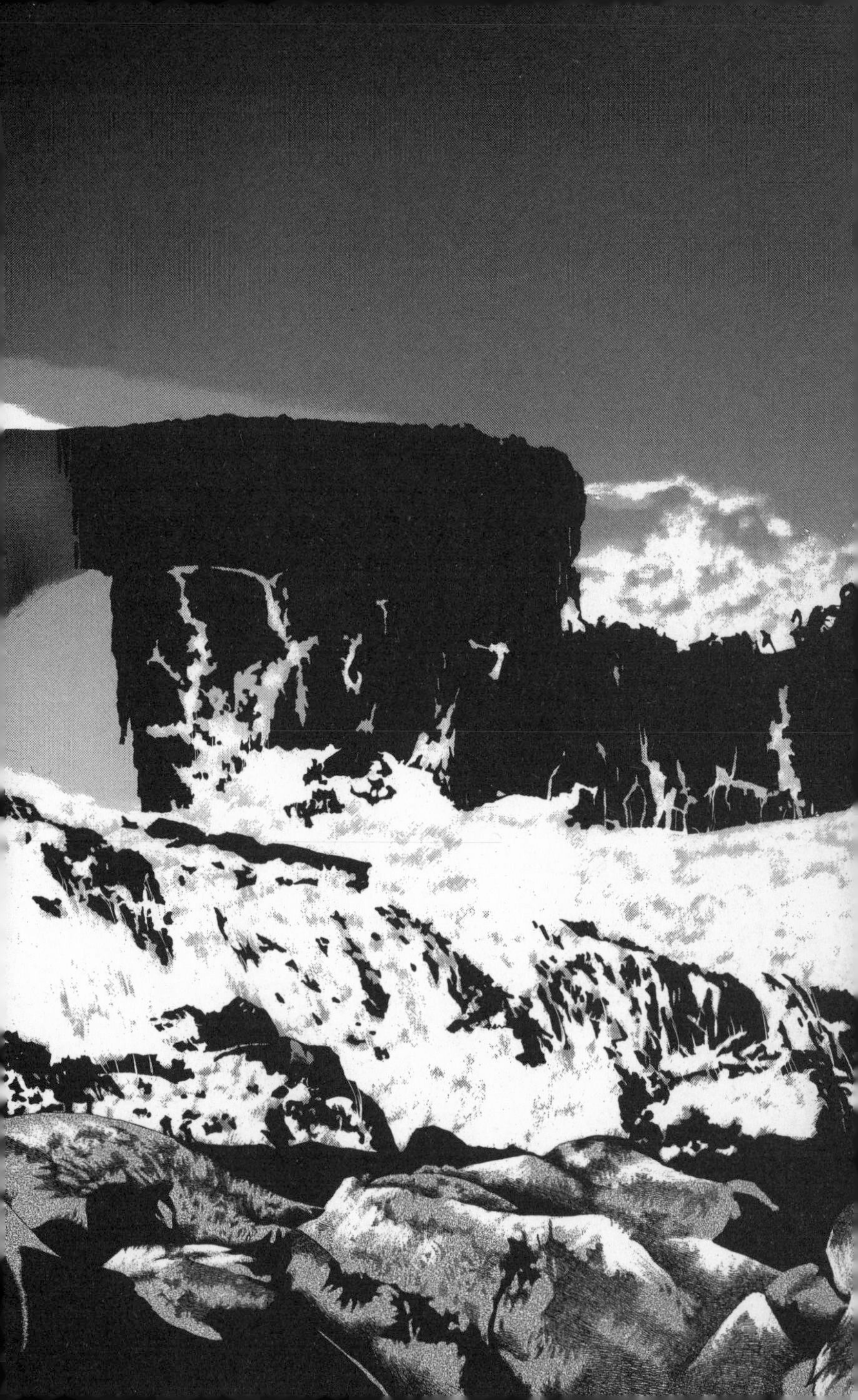

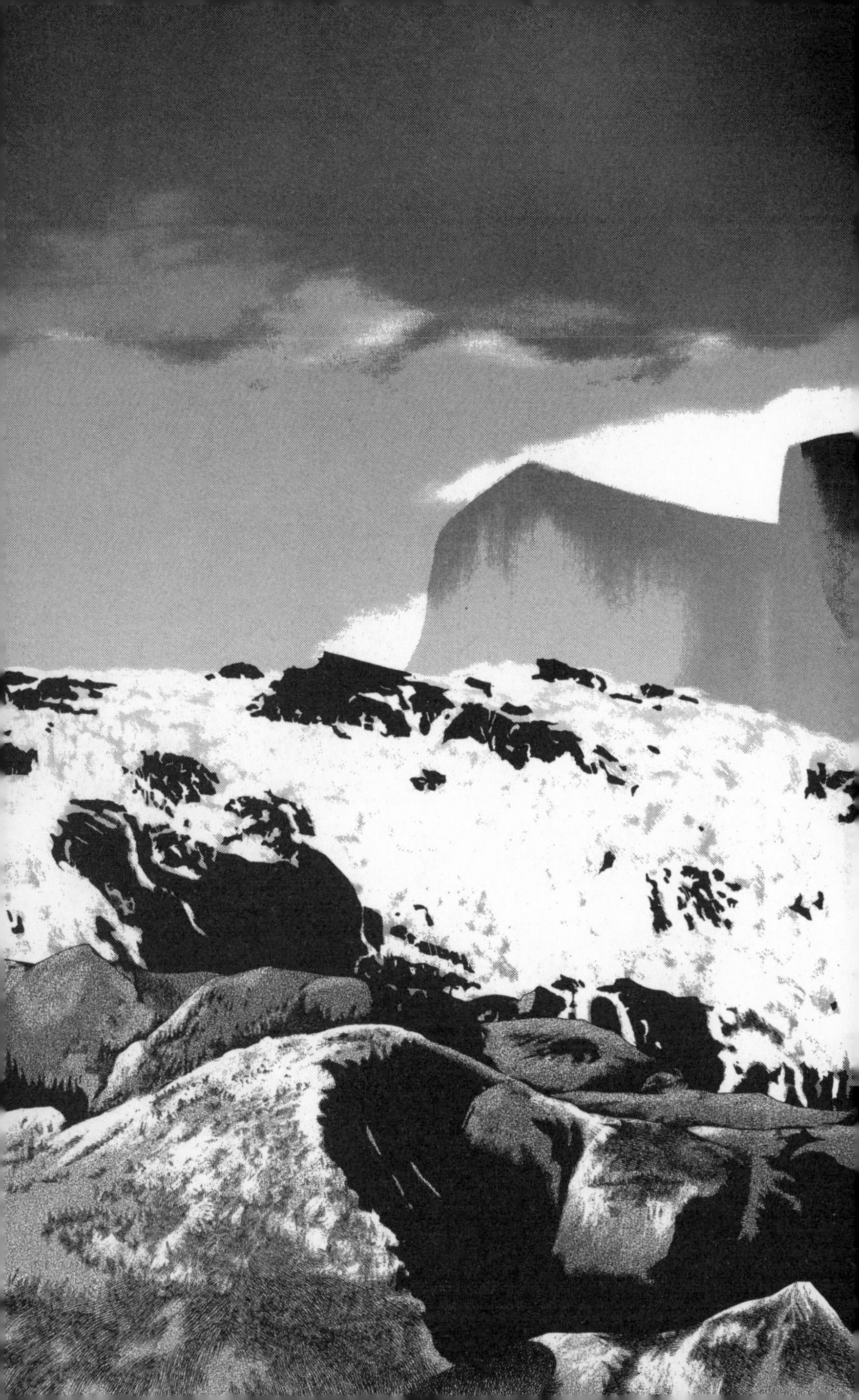

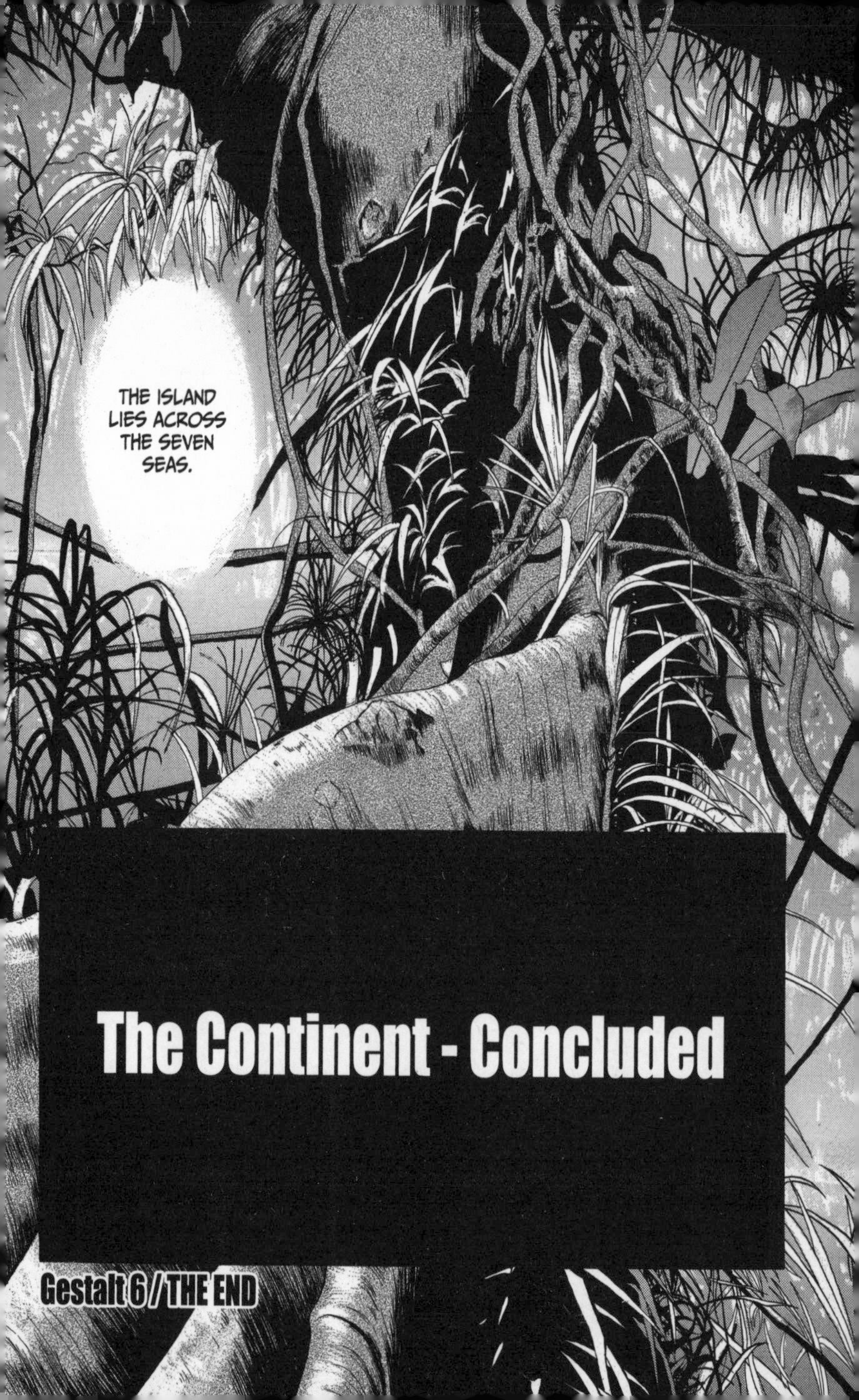
THE ISLAND LIES ACROSS THE SEVEN SEAS.
The Continent - Concluded
Gestalt 6 // THE END

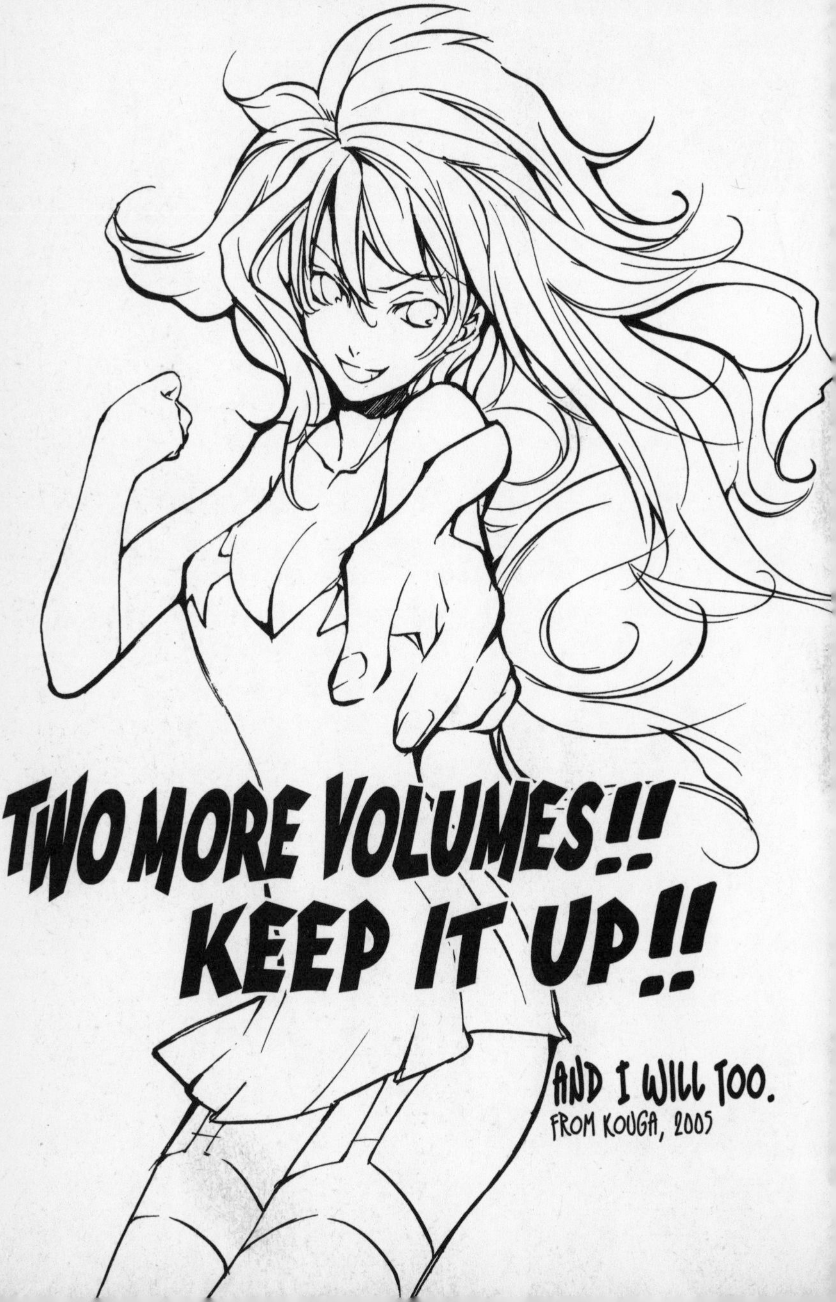
TWO MORE VOLUMES!!
KEEP IT UP!!
AND I WILL TOO.
FROM KOUGA, 2005

HERE

I feel like dropping into the depths of the ocean until my feet reach the very bottom. I imagine that would be pretty relaxing!

Sigh... I wish I could go to Hawaii.

Yun Kouga began her career as a doujinshi and debuted in 1986 with the original manga *Metal Heart*, serialized in *Comic VAL*. She is the creator of the popular series *Loveless* and *Earthian*, along with many manga and anime projects, including character design for *Gundam 00*.

Gestalt
Vol. 6
VIZ Media Edition

Story and Art by Yun Kouga

Translation & English Adaptation/Christine Schilling
Touch-up Art & Lettering/Mark McMurray
Design/Sean Lee
Editor/Chris Mackenzie

VP, Production/Alvin Lu
VP, Sales & Product Marketing/Gonzalo Ferreyra
VP, Creative/Linda Espinosa
Publisher/Hyoe Narita

CHOUJUU DENSETSU GESTALT
© Yun Kouga / ICHIJINSHA

Printed in Canada

Published by VIZ Media, LLC
P.O. Box 77010
San Francisco, CA 94107

10 9 8 7 6 5 4 3 2 1
First printing, April 2010

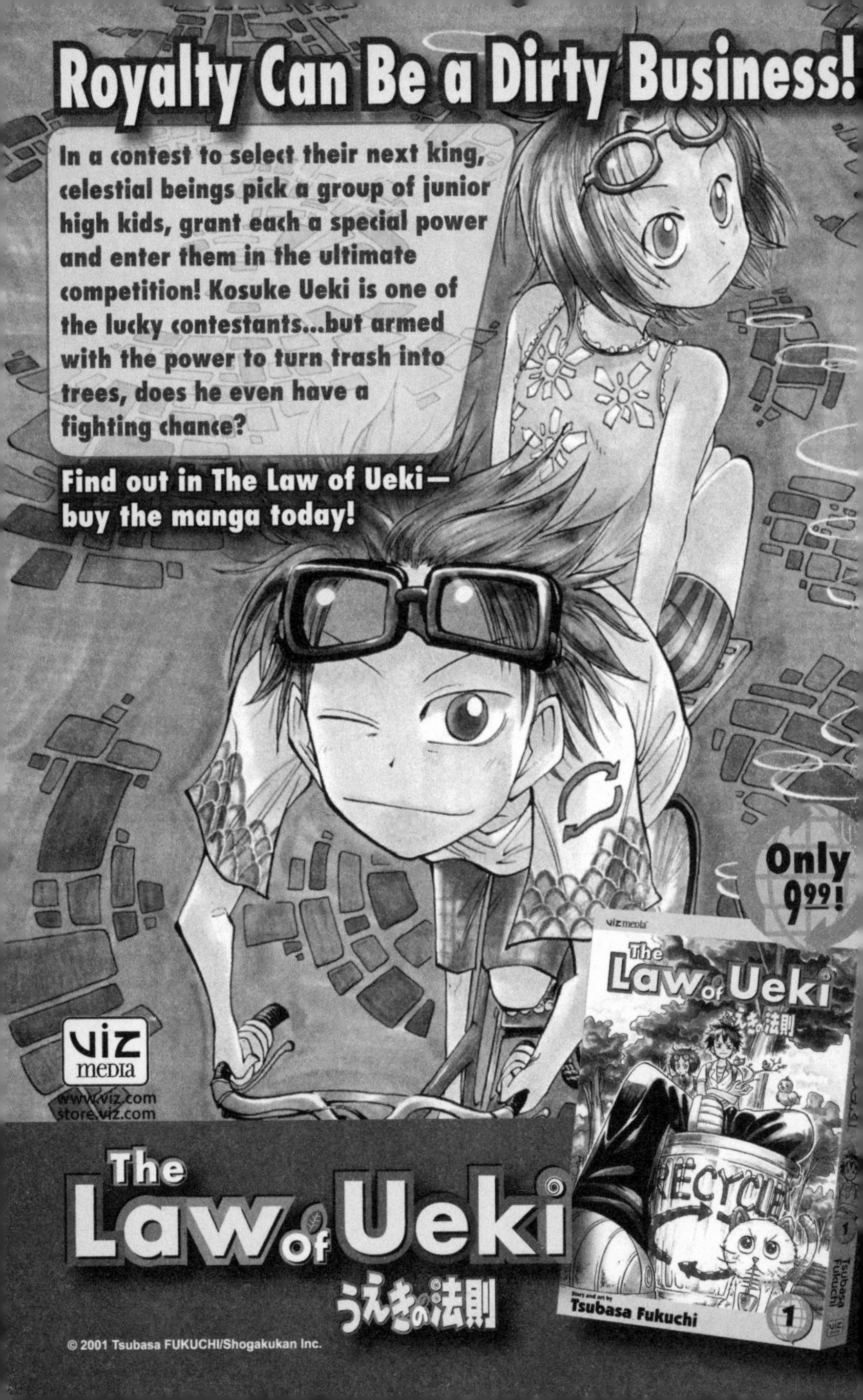
Royalty Can Be a Dirty Business!
In a contest to select their next king, celestial beings pick a group of junior high kids, grant each a special power and enter them in the ultimate competition! Kosuke Ueki is one of the lucky contestants...but armed with the power to turn trash into trees, does he even have a fighting chance?
Find out in The Law of Ueki— buy the manga today!
Only 9.99!
viz media
www.viz.com
store.viz.com
The Law of Ueki
うえきの法則
viz media
The Law of Ueki
うえきの法則
RECYCLE
Story and art by
Tsubasa Fukuchi
1
Tsubasa Fukuchi
© 2001 Tsubasa FUKUCHI/Shogakukan Inc.

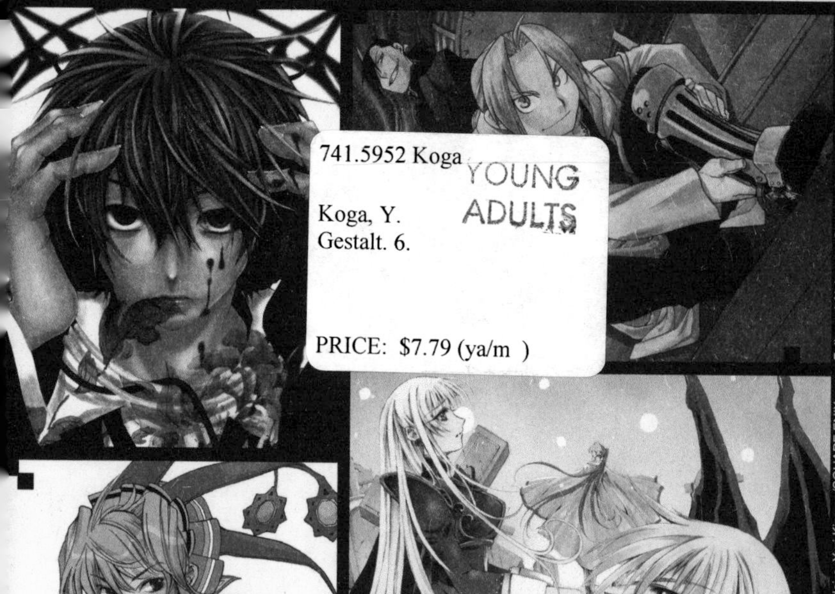

Fullmetal Alchemist © Hiromu Arakawa/SQUARE ENIX.

The Record of a Fallen Vampire © Kyo Shirodaira, Yuri Kimura/SQUARE ENIX.

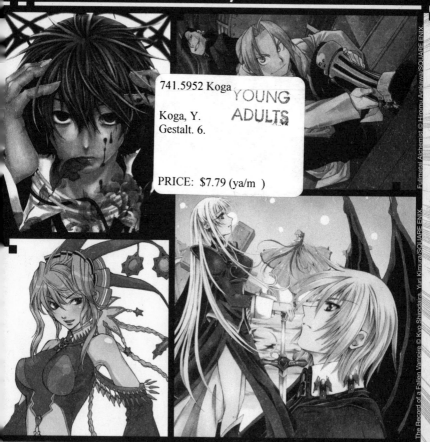